Mishpachah: The Jewish Family in Tradition and in Transition

Studies in Jewish Civilization
Volume 27

Proceedings of the Twenty-Seventh Annual Symposium of the Klutznick Chair in Jewish Civilization, the Harris Center for Judaic Studies, and the Schwalb Center for Israel and Jewish Studies

October 26–27, 2014

Other volumes in the
Studies in Jewish Civilization Series
Distributed by the Purdue University Press

2010 – Rites of Passage:
How Today's Jews Celebrate, Commemorate, and Commiserate

2011 – Jews and Humor

2012 – Jews in the Gym:
Judaism, Sports, and Athletics

2013 – Fashioning Jews:
Clothing, Culture, and Commerce

2014 – Who Is a Jew?
Reflections on History, Religion, and Culture

2015 – Wealth and Poverty in Jewish Tradition

Mishpachah: The Jewish Family in Tradition and in Transition

Studies in Jewish Civilization
Volume 27

Editor:
Leonard J. Greenspoon

The Klutznick Chair in Jewish Civilization

Purdue University Press
West Lafayette, Indiana

Published by Purdue University Press

Manufactured in the United States of America

Library of Congress Cataloging-in-Publication Data

Names: Greenspoon, Leonard J. (Leonard Jay) editor.
Title: Mishpachah : the Jewish family in tradition and in transition / edited by Leonard J. Greenspoon.
Description: West Lafayette, Indiana : Purdue University Press, [2016] | Series: Studies in Jewish civilization ; 27 | Contains papers presented at the 27th Annual Klutznick-Harris-Schwalb Symposium, October 26-27, 2014, in Omaha, Nebraska. | Includes bibliographical references.
Identifiers: LCCN 2016016885| ISBN 9781557537577 (pbk. : alk. paper) | ISBN 9781612494685 (epdf) | ISBN 9781612494692 (epub)
Subjects: LCSH: Jewish families—Congresses. | Domestic relations—Religious aspects—Judaism—Congresses. | Jews—Cultural assimilation—United States—Congresses.
Classification: LCC HQ525.J4 M56 2016 | DDC 306.85/089924—dc23 LC record available at https://lccn.loc.gov/2016016885

Table of Contents

III. THE FUTURE

Acknowledgments

The 27th Annual Klutznick-Harris-Schwalb Symposium took place on October 26 and October 27, 2014, in Omaha, Nebraska. The title of the symposium, from which this volume also takes its name, is "*Mishpachah:* The Jewish Family in Tradition and in Transition."

Anyone who reads carefully and has a phenomenal memory (that sounds a lot like most of my colleagues!) will observe that the sponsors of the 2014 symposium expanded to include as a full partner the Natan and Hannah Schwalb Center for Israel and Jewish Studies. Founded in 2009 at the University of Nebraska at Omaha (UNO), the Schwalb Center and its faculty have had a notable presence at several of our symposia prior to 2014. The new title formalizes this close, productive relationship.

As in past years, the success of this symposium owed much to the unflagging support of two of my colleagues: Dr. Ronald Simkins, Director of the Kripke Center for the Study of Religion and Society at Creighton University, and Dr. Jean Cahan, Director of the Harris Center for Judaic Studies at the University of Nebraska–Lincoln (UNL). To this number, I gratefully add Dr. Sidnie White Crawford of UNL and Drs. Moshe Gershovitz and Curtis Hutt of UNO.

Colleen Hastings, Administrative Assistant for the Klutznick Chair and the Kripke Center, continues her invaluable contributions at all stages in the planning and implementation of the symposium and in preparing this volume for publication. Equally efficient and dependable is Mary Sue Grossman, who is affiliated with the Center for Jewish Life, part of the Jewish Federation of Omaha. In this connection, I offer additional thanks to Kasey Davis, office assistant for the Schwalb Center. Among the innovations for this symposium was a Sunday morning session at UNO that would have been impossible without her active involvement.

With this volume, we are completing seven years in our ongoing relationship with the Purdue University Press. Its staff, under the previous director Charles Watkinson and his successor Peter Froehlich, makes us feel welcome in every possible way. We look forward to many more years of collaboration with the Press.

In addition to the Harris Center, the Kripke Center, the Schwalb Center, and the Jewish Federation of Omaha, this symposium is supported by the generosity of the following:

Creighton University Lectures, Films and Concerts
The Creighton College of Arts and Sciences

The Ike and Roz Friedman Foundation
The Riekes Family
The Center for Jewish Life
The Henry Monsky Lodge of B'nai B'rith
Gary and Karen Javitch
The Drs. Bernard H. and Bruce S. Bloom Memorial Endowment
And others

Leonard J. Greenspoon
Omaha, Nebraska
March 2016
ljgrn@creighton.edu

Editor's Introduction

Dictionary definitions of the term *mishpachah* are quite similar: a Jewish family or social unit including close and distant relatives—sometimes also close friends. Although such definitions—or better, descriptions—are justifiably inclusive, even they fail to capture the diversity and vitality of real flesh-and-blood Jewish families.

The studies collected in this volume, each by a different scholar working in a different context, call attention to features of the Jewish family from a wide variety of perspectives. They explore historical developments, contemporary trends, and future possibilities for Jewish families. In the process, they identify both common and distinctive features in the makeup of, and expectations for, this basic building block of Jewish society and religion.

Jewish families, as messy as they are essential, have been part of Jewish life from the biblical era through the rabbinic period, from the advent of modernity through the threshold of the future. We have not sought to cover every aspect of the Jewish family from all cultural, social, historical, and theological eras. No single volume, however lengthy and weighty, can do that.

Rather, we have given essentially free rein to these scholars and researchers to write about what they know best. Moreover, we have allowed, in fact encouraged, all authors to express themselves in the style in which they are most comfortable and with the emphases they select as most valuable.

We do not apologize that the resultant collection is not comprehensive. We would, however, be disappointed if readers come away with no new insights, questions, or layers of appreciation for an institution that exhibits and embodies so many elements of Judaism's rich and complex experience.

The thirteen papers collected here, all originating as oral presentations at the 27th Annual Klutznick-Harris-Schwalb Symposium, divide chronologically into three groups: six deal primarily with the past, from the biblical period through the nineteenth century; five center on aspects of the Jewish family today; and two look to technological developments that are bound to become increasingly popular for Jews, as for many other groups, in the future. For the reader of this volume, we present each paper under one of these chronological rubrics.

Susan Marks, New College of Florida, is the author of the first essay, "Uncovering the Ongoing Parental Role in Education in the Rabbinic Period." Through it, she examines the family's ongoing impact on the study of the Torah in early rabbinic Judaism, particularly the father-son relationship. In doing so, she pushes back against scholarly discussions emphasizing the significance of the disciple-mentor relationship and the Talmudic replacement of the father with the sage, which thereby creates a new way to trace lineage. While this is important, she argues against essentializing this aspect of rabbinic Judaism at the expense of understanding the continued role played by the disciple's parents. Marks focuses on the Babylonian Talmud tractates *Hullin* and *Berachot,* especially their descriptions of the active role taken by the father in educating his son concerning meal practices, on the one hand, and the topic of sexual relations, on the other, with mixed reception.

Marks's analysis attends to dynamics of ritual practice and lived religion (in light of work by Pierre Bourdieu and others) to suggest that the questions of the son's relationship with the family in which he grew up is more complicated than previous scholarship acknowledges. In examining these fraught encounters, this study reveals the depth of ongoing engagement with family and the need to reexamine the nature of learning as rabbinic Judaism invents itself.

David Brodsky, Brooklyn College, follows with his study, "Mishnah *Gittin:* Family Relations as Metaphor for National Relations." While the rest of Mishnah *Gittin* lays out the laws of the commissioning, writing, and delivery of the bill of divorce in a fairly orderly manner, the beginning, middle, and end of the tractate stand out. Brodsky argues that the three work together to point the reader to the central theme of the tractate, a theme that works simultaneously on the individual and national levels. By opening with the demarcation of the boundaries between that which is in and outside of the land of Israel, the tractate is pointing to divorce as an act that is marking the same boundaries on the individual level.

The middle section of Mishnah *Gittin* explains why these boundaries need to be established: originally [*ba-rishonah*] one ruling was made, but since then things have not turned out the way they were intended, and a corrective must be instated. For the sake of the public welfare, indeed for the sake of peace, things cannot always remain as they were originally established. Sometimes a corrective is necessary. Here, divorce is precisely that corrective for the marriage that is not working. The final mishnah clarifies that while divorce was permitted by the School of Shammai only in cases of adultery (reading the "unchaste matter [*'ervat davar*]" of Deuteronomy 24:1 as truly unchaste [*devar 'ervah*]), the School of Hillel and, later, Rabbi Akiva offered their own correctives, permitting it ultimately any time that the couple were not getting along.

This final mishnah of the tractate (9:10) points us even further to who would seem to be intended here, as it contains one of the only parallels in all of the Mishnah with the New Testament, with the School of Shammai's position directly paralleling Jesus's position in the Sermon on the Mount rather than in opposition to Deuteronomy 24:1. Thus, in this nascent period for both Christianity and rabbinic Judaism, the two may have converged more than they diverged, at least regarding the laws of divorce and their derivation from the Bible. Mishnah *Gittin,* Brodsky proposes, is attempting to declare that there was an earlier period [*ba-rishonah*] before the corrective was needed.

By using the national boundaries as a metaphor for individual boundaries vis-à-vis divorce, the redactor is reversing the prophetic use of divorce as a metaphor for the nation and its ruptured relationship with God (Isa 50:1; Jer 3:1–8; Mal 2:13–16). By linking the two, the redactor opens up the possibility of reading in both directions—of national boundaries as metaphor for individual boundaries and as the marking of these personal boundaries as metaphor for the nation. In this essay, Brodsky explores the implications of that connection.

The first of two essays on the Hebrew Bible is "All in the Family: Ancient Israelite and Judahite Families in Context" by Cynthia Shafer-Elliott, William Jessup University. Historically, she observes, Syro-Palestinian archaeology and biblical studies have focused on monumental places, people, material culture, and the texts that reflect them. Major urban settlements contained palaces, temples, and fortifications. The elite men who oversaw their administration left no shortage of artifacts and texts for analysis.

However, a shift of interest into the daily lives of the average ancient Israelite has occurred. This shift recognizes that in order to understand the daily life of ancient Israel and Judah, the focus needs to change from monumental to minor, from the macro to the micro. In other words, more attention needs to be given to the stage where daily life occurred—the home. This is exactly what Schafer-Elliott accomplishes.

The home was (and indeed still is) the nucleus of the everyday. The home was where the average ancient Israelite *mishpachah* [family] in both urban and rural environments lived out their lives. The purpose of Schafer-Elliott's contribution is to illustrate how the average ancient Israelite family lived within its physical environment, the home, within the Iron Age. Utilizing household archaeology and textual evidence from the Hebrew Bible, Schafer-Elliott's essay examines the typical Israelite household including its dwelling and its members and their activities.

Charles David Isbell, Louisiana State University, has written the second essay that features the Hebrew Bible: "Family Values and Biblical Courtship and Marriage: Spanning the Time Barrier." As he observes, the importance of family within the broader community of Judaism has its roots in some of the most significant narratives in the book of Genesis. From the outset, marriage has stood as the cornerstone of the biblical family. The politically motivated call for a return to biblical marriage in modern America appears to be grounded in non-Jewish ideas of marriage rather than in biblical narratives that actually describe the customs of our ancestors. As is often the case, we are compelled to span the difference between the Bible and the twenty-first century in this matter.

In the attempt to build a bridge from modernity back to the Bible, Isbell raises three questions, each one leading to a clearer understanding of the purpose(s) of family grounded in marriage: (1) When is a house a home? (2) When does "son" or "daughter" mean more than a biological offspring? (3) When are economic considerations important in biblical marriage?

Once these questions have been addressed, we are prepared to discuss the ways in which marriage in the Bible might inform our modern *minhagim* [customs] and values. Isbell's investigation shows that the external customs of biblical marriage and family life are not the crux of the matter, and frantic calls for a return to biblical marriage based on the facile linkage of modern practices to a simplistic interpretation of the Bible merely obscure the real issues. Still, biblical narratives that underscore appropriate partnerships capable of contributing to familial and societal stability can guide us to embrace enduring values that are worth cherishing.

We may, Isbell argues, find it necessary to modernize, redefine, and even reformulate the customs of marriage and the definition of "family," and that is as it should be, for each generation should be granted and must accept the responsibility of such freedom of expression. But we need not abandon the goal of marriages and families that are formed to serve the moral values of the larger human community and built to endure because they consist of partners who share a system of values and ideals that has stood the test of time.

Gail Labovitz, American Jewish University, moves us forward chronologically with her essay, "Presumptuous Halachah: On Determining the Status of Relationships Outside Jewish Marriage." She begins with this observation: according to Jewish law and practice since at least the time of the Mishnah, the legal basis for Jewish marriage is the act of *kiddushin,* in which a man "acquires" a woman. Once this act is performed, the relationship is binding and can be severed only by his giving her a divorce document.

Yet, Labovitz continues, even a cursory study of legal and other sources suggests that Jewish men and women have long engaged in relationships involving sexual relations and/or long-term commitments to one another outside the rubric of *kiddushin.* Examples include cohabitation outside marriage, concubinage, marriage by rites of other religions (where the participants might be forced converts to Christianity or Islam), and, in modernity, civil marriage.

Most recently, there have been some proposals toward new means of marriage beyond the gendered assumptions (and material harm for women) of *kiddushin* and the halachic divorce process. Significantly, halachic decisors have not considered these relationships to be outside the purview of the Jewish legal system. Lebovitz traces this topic through Jewish legal literature with an eye toward when, how, and why decisors have attempted to assimilate these relationships into Jewish marriages or to dismiss them as beyond the bounds of the system.

Haim Sperber, Western Galilee College, looks at the nineteenth century in his essay, "*Agunot,* Immigration, and Modernization, from 1857 to 1896." Through his research and analysis, he presents the *agunot* phenomenon in the second half of the nineteenth century, especially in Eastern Europe.

In the first part of his essay, Sperber analyzes the phenomenon and its main databases. In this part, he discusses the volume of the phenomenon and different variations of *agunot.* Sperber also shows that the main databases—the Jewish media and rabbinical sources—present two different narratives of the phenomenon; he attempts to explain this.

The second half of Sperber's essay analyzes the phenomenon and its effect on the family institution in Jewish Eastern Europe. The discussion also features a section on relations between the *agunot* issue and immigration and changes in the role of rabbis in East European Jewish society.

Broadly speaking, the first six essays speak to the Jewish family as it was. While the implications of such studies are clearly relevant today, their emphasis was on the past. By contrast, the next five essays offer descriptions and analyses of phenomena that characterize large numbers of Jews and their families in the present.

The first essay in this section, "Lost, Hidden, Discovered: Theologies of DNA in North American Judaism and Messianic Judaism," is coauthored by Sarah Imhoff, Indiana University, Bloomington, and Hillary Kaell, Concordia University. They begin with the observation that American Jews have embraced their family trees. With rapid advances in the accessibility of both genetic testing and Internet-enabled ancestry tracking, the potential for "knowing" about oneself and one's family has left the dusty archives and elite laboratories and come into living rooms.

Imhoff and Kaell ask: why and how does family lineage and popular DNA testing matter religiously?

Messianic Jewish congregations—conservative Christian congregations that retain some Jewish practices alongside belief in Jesus as the Messiah—have about twice as many gentile believers as they do believers of Jewish descent. However, only ethnic Jews are considered to be directly descended from the tribes of Israel—and thus part of the lineage of Jesus himself. As Imhoff and Kaell discover, one result of this imbalance is an ongoing discussion among congregants about whether gentile believers do in fact have Jewish lineage. They interpret their own stories of self through secular websites, such as ancestry.com, and through those targeted specifically at non-Jews seeking Jewish roots (e.g., offering lists of Jewish names).

Jews, more traditionally defined, also use ancestry websites and DNA testing to craft narratives for themselves and their families. These narratives, drawing on the cultural importance of *yichus* [family background], often make connections to Jewish peoplehood and even ancient Israelite priestly lineages. Imhoff and Kaell's research uses interviews, media analysis, and history to show the differences and unexpected overlaps in these two groups' theologically freighted stories of family.

The next essay is "Contemporary Modern Orthodox Guidance Books on Marital Sexuality" by Evyatar Marienberg, University of North Carolina at Chapel Hill. In his research, Marienberg discovered that young women and men who are about to be married in *haredi* [Ultra-Orthodox] communities and in some Modern/National Orthodox circles are encouraged to have a few meetings with a specialist on the matter, a person of the same sex whose role is to instruct them about the marital act. In addition, he uncovered a wide range of specialized books and booklets that are available to them. In recent years, manuals were written also for, on the one hand, parents to help them explain sexuality to their young children and, on the other hand, to older adults to help them solve problems in their own sexual life. Schools are also slowly starting to realize that they need to deal with these issues as well, and a growing number of curricula target this market. Marienberg's essay examines several Jewish Orthodox works of these quite various kinds published in Israel and in the United States in the last few decades.

Often written for specific audiences—men, women, couples, Ultra-Orthodox, Modern Orthodox, Chasidim, Sephardim, Ashkenazim, students, parents—these compositions present a broad view of the many ways sex is prescribed in today's Jewish Orthodox world. As part of his analysis, Marienberg found that some of these differences are related to historical and ideological tendencies and some to concepts about the "correct" structure of a good Jewish family. Where relevant, he compares information gathered about oral guidance with the content of these books. He also addresses possible implications of these different prescriptions on the reality in bedrooms.

The next essay is "Challah from Abba: The Modern Jewish Father" by Rabbi Joshua Brown of Omaha's Temple Israel. Since its birth, Judaism has been concerned with the effects of one generation's actions upon another. The rabbis understand not only that every generation is different but also that each generation is dependent upon the ones that came before it and those to come after it.

As Brown sees it, we are currently at a crossroads in gender roles in America. As women increasingly move into being the dominant worker in the American workforce, men are being asked, or at times forced by their family situation, to become the primary parent. This is a role that men have rarely played in the history of parenting but one that Judaism knows well.

In his essay Brown looks at the modern father and the many challenges he faces both at home and in his career as he strives to be an active parent. In particular, Brown focuses on the challenges facing Jewish fathers in the twenty-first century as informed by modern psychology and the potential benefits that Jewish tradition has to offer them should they choose to accept the challenge.

Parenting also forms the subject of the next essay: "'Jewish Education Begins at Home': Training Parents to Raise American Jewish Children after World War II" by Joshua J. Furman, Rice University. During the post–World War II baby boom, Americans increasingly turned to child-rearing authorities such as Benjamin Spock and Arnold Gesell for advice on how to raise happy, healthy sons and daughters. As Furman notes, Jewish parents relied on these same volumes, but they also used and learned from Jewish baby books. These texts offered parents detailed information about the significance and performance of Jewish birth ritual, advised readers on the process of choosing meaningful English and Hebrew names for their newborn, and allowed them to record important milestones in their child's physical and spiritual development.

In Furman's analysis, authors of these texts endeavored to teach mothers and fathers the knowledge and skills they would need to impart a strong sense of Jewish identity to their children. At the same time, the aesthetic and substantive resemblance of these sources to those authored for a broad American audience suggests an interest, on the part of both publishers and purchasers, to render and receive information about Jewish child rearing in a thoroughly contemporary format. This choice, Furman determines, reflects a broader desire on the part of most American Jews to blend seamlessly into American life while simultaneously making some effort to maintain Jewish distinctiveness. This tension between modernity and tradition, between acculturation and preservation, flows through the heart of postwar American Jewish childrearing literature.

The final essay in this section is by Jennifer Sartori, Northeastern University: "Modern Families: Multifaceted Identities in the Jewish Adoptive Family." In discussions of changes in the American Jewish family, attention often focuses on the dramatic increase in the number of interfaith families. Yet American Jewish families, like American families more broadly, are becoming increasingly "multi" in other ways as well: multiracial, multicultural, multiethnic, multinational. In Sartori's analysis, over the past several decades Jewish adoptive families have been at the forefront of these changes. The general trend in adoption toward adopting across boundaries of identity has been even more pronounced in the American Jewish community, with disproportionately high rates of transracial, transnational, and transcultural adoption.

Sartori's analysis explores the ways Jewish adoptive families negotiate their multiple identities. Although adoption experts today emphasize the need for adoptees and their families to engage actively with the adoptees' birth heritage and/or families of origin, the Jewish community, concerned about continuity, often seems to be pulling in the opposite direction, emphasizing the importance of a strong and exclusive Jewish identity for children. Important aspects of Jewish identity—including ideas about race, ancestry, and genetics—may also complicate adoptees' sense of belonging within the Jewish community. Despite these challenges, many Jewish adoptees and their families draw strength from their diverse identities. The experiences of these families, as Sartori shows, can shed valuable light on the growing number of Jews and other Americans whose identities span religious, racial, and ethnic lines.

The first six essays, while set in earlier historical contexts, exhibit discernible links with the present. Likewise, the next five essays, set in the present, find their full significance only through their links with the past. The final two essays, while pointing to the future, cannot be understood apart from issues of technology in the present and questions of ethics that stretch back into the past.

The first of these two essays—"The Jewish Perspective in Creating Human Embryos Using Cloning Technologies"—is by John D. Loike, Columbia University. He begins with a discussion and analysis of recent scientific discoveries that have enhanced the capacity of scientists and clinicians to generate human preimplanted embryos in the laboratory. These embryos can be transferred into a woman's uterus to allow the development of a healthy child.

Beginning in 2013, new technologies in the area of human cloning could also be applied to human reproduction. Loike describes one such biotechnology, known as somatic cell nuclear transfer (SCNT), which involves fusing a blood or skin cell that contains all forty-six chromosomes of DNA into an egg whose nuclear DNA has been removed. This reconstituted egg can now be induced to divide and differentiate in the laboratory to generate a four- to six-day-old human embryo that can be transplanted into a woman's uterus to gestate.

As Loike sees it, one potential clinical advantage of SCNT is the capacity to use nonsperm cells of infertile men to generate a healthy embryo. Yet from a Jewish legal perspective, this technology raises many issues, such as (a) Is human cloning permissible according to Jewish law? (b) What is the status of fatherhood in an embryo generated by "fertilizing" an egg without male sperm? (c) Is it permissible to use SCNT to clone a woman? As part of his essay, Loike addresses these issues from a Jewish legal perspective.

This volume's final essay, by Pamela Laufer-Ukeles, University of Dayton Law School, is titled "Multiplying Motherhood: Gestational Surrogate Motherhood and Jewish Law." As she relates, Jews are some of the most aggressive users of assisted reproductive technologies (ART). Having children is both a halachic [legal] obligation for observant Jews and a cultural tradition for many Jews who do not live halachically observant lives.

According to Laufer-Ukeles, the push to reproduce among Jewish families comes from biblical commandments, a desire to re-create a Jewish population decimated by the Holocaust, cultural traditions that surround family life, and demographic concerns about sustaining Jewish culture and cultural traditions. The use of ART to help couples who struggle to reproduce the Jewish family is therefore a natural integration of tradition and transition in the use of modern technology.

In her research, Laufer-Ukeles has determined that Jewish law largely embraces ART with some reservations, particularly regarding artificial insemination by donor. Jewish families use ART in all its varieties with great and joyous success. But problems do arise for those who engage in the use of ART. In particular, controversies have arisen regarding (1) when conversion is necessary to sustain the Jewishness of children born of ART; (2) when ART should be allowed, given the importance of biologically based legal parenthood in Jewish law as well as Jewish ethics that weigh against exploitation and commodification of surrogates and gametes; and (3) whether children born of ART could potentially have a compromised legal status [*mamzerut*] that could prevent them from marrying within the Jewish religion and thereby creating their own Jewish families. Some potential problems can be solved relatively easily; others cannot. In this essay, Laufer-Ukeles discusses potential problems for those using ART in the context of surrogacy, artificial insemination by donor, and egg donation. She then considers what the Jewish community can and should do to support the use of ART in creating Jewish families while avoiding ethical or legal pitfalls that can hurt ART participants or children born of ART.

Laufer-Ukeles's essay has both theoretical and practical appeal, as many in the Jewish community are faced with these dilemmas or may be unaware of the potential consequences. Discussions of the meaning of the Jewish family and the use of fertility treatments can be beneficial to a wide potential audience of scholars and laypeople alike.

While of necessity not doing full justice to the wealth of insights and nuances that these essays contain, an editor such as myself does have a responsibility to provide some sort of summation. For this volume, I shall do so simply by recalling some of the points that remain fixed in my mind:

1. The family has consistently played a major role in Judaism as experienced over countless generations in innumerable cultural and historical contexts.
2. The makeup of the Jewish family has typically gone beyond the nuclear family to encompass a wide circle of relatives and nonrelatives. In real life, *mishpachah* is almost as likely to exclude some blood relatives as it is to include those with no genetic connections.
3. The role of family members could on many occasions be expressed in terms of a hierarchical flow chart, but even for traditional societies these charts often mask rather than mirrored the way in which real power and influence are wielded.
4. Jewish families have been, are, and almost certainly will continue to be dynamic rather than static. To a considerable extent, this is due to the fact that Jews, even the most traditional Jews, are innovators whose respect for the past is typically balanced by recognition of the realities of the present.

5. And finally (though in no particular order), Jewish families are different from others and are largely the same. For the most part, except when living in forced (or self-imposed) isolation from others, Jews are not immune to larger social and cultural influences, which they can adopt, adept, or even on occasion initiate.

Leonard J. Greenspoon

Contributors

David Brodsky	Judaic Studies James Hall Room 3111 Brooklyn College 2900 Bedford Avenue Brooklyn, NY 11210 davidmbrodsky@gmail.com
Rabbi Joshua Brown	Temple Israel 91 Springside Drive Akron, OH 44333 joshuambrown@gmail.com
Joshua J. Furman	Rice University Program in Jewish Studies 6100 Main St. MS-340 Houston, TX 77005 joshua.furman@rice.edu
Sarah Imhoff	Religious Studies and Borns Jewish Studies Program Sycamore Hall 223 Indiana University Bloomington, IN 47405 seimhoff@indiana.edu
Charles David Isbell	2130 Fairway Drive Baton Rouge, LA 70809 cisbel1@lsu.edu
Hillary Kaell	2236 Rue Plessis Montreal, Quebec H2L 2Y3 Canada hillarykaell@gmail.com
Gail Labovitz	American Jewish University 15600 Mulholland Drive Bel Air, CA 90077 GLabovitz@aju.edu

Pamela Laufer-Ukeles	University of Dayton School of Law 300 College Park Dayton, OH 45469-2760 plauferukeles1@udayton.edu
John D. Loike	179-20 Tudor Road Jamaica Estates, NY 11432 jdl5@cumc.columbia.edu
Evyatar Marienberg	The Department of Religious Studies The University of North Carolina at Chapel Hill 112 Carolina Hall, CB #3225 Chapel Hill, NC 27599-3225 evyatarm@unc.edu
Susan Marks	Division of Humanities New College of Florida 5800 Bay Shore Road Sarasota, FL 34243-2109 smarks@ncf.edu
Jennifer Sartori	Jewish Studies Program Northeastern University 360 Huntington Avenue Boston, MA 02115 j.sartori@neu.edu
Cynthia Shafer-Elliott	Faculty of Theology William Jessup University 2121 University Avenue Rocklin, CA 95765 cshaferelliott@jessup.edu
Haim Sperber	Western Galilee College Akko 24121 Israel haimsperber@gmail.com

I. THE PAST

Uncovering the Ongoing Parental Role in Education in the Rabbinic Period

Susan Marks

Parents today involve themselves in their children's higher education in myriad, often contradictory ways. On the one hand, privacy laws now insist that eighteen-year-olds need not share college transcripts with their parents. On the other hand, many students rely on their parents to pay a portion of tuition, and twenty-first century "helicopter" parenting does not always end at high school graduation. From this perspective, we might wonder why we so often think of rabbinic disciples—many of whom were certainly younger than today's college students—as taught only by rabbis. Certainly, their mothers and fathers could have continued to play formative roles. Identifying those ongoing educational functions of the rabbinic parent is the aim of this essay.

Educating young adults is, almost by definition, a fraught affair. I happened upon a wonderful outside-the-classroom reminder of this at the newly renovated Salvador Dalí Museum in St. Petersburg, Florida. The audio tour first led us through Dalí's early paintings and then narrated the end of his art school career: he declined to take final exams because, he explained, none of his teachers knew as much as he did. Teachers will likely join me in recalling a student or two who felt that we had nothing new to teach them. Perhaps Dalí was correct, albeit not particularly politic, in his self-assessment. (Whether the self-satisfied students we have encountered could claim genius on the level of Dalí's I leave to our own recollections.) There is, of course, also another player in this educational equation: the one paying the bills and looking out for the future of the student and the family. Need I add that Dalí's father blew up at his son when he heard that his son withdrew? This is the relationship that interests me. The analogous dynamic deeply hidden within rabbinic literature—whereby a parent offers guidance, which is then met with the child's acceptance or rejection—is ripe for dissection.

The historic focus on rabbi and disciple obscures the teaching relationship between father and son.[1] Rhetorically, rabbis put their own importance as teachers ahead of fathers, a high valuation that culminates in a prescription requiring that if faced with such a dilemma, a disciple must redeem his teacher from captivity before his father:

> If his father and his teacher were each taken captive, he must first ransom his teacher and afterwards ransom his father; but if his father was also a Sage he must first ransom his father and afterward ransom his teacher.[2]

Research into issues of redeeming captives examines the complexities of these prescriptions;[3] here I want us only to recognize this attempted sleight of hand, which emphasizes that a father's authority should have limits.[4] When we look behind this veil, the importance of the father can be appreciated.

Our sense of the significance of rabbis as educators owes something to the fame of the rabbinic schools of Sura and Pumpaditha. Nevertheless, recent research challenges the power of these so-called academies and the place of formal education in the earliest rabbinic periods as discussed in the Mishnah and talmudic literature.[5] This research argues instead that teachers are taught not in academies but rather in small circles of disciples. Extending this line of interrogation, my research challenges us to consider another overlooked relationship revealed by this new model of more intimate education: the relationship of the father and son, which continued despite rabbi-centric rhetoric.

Concerning the dietary matter of waiting between eating meat and milk, one disciple invokes his father as a standard:

> Said Mar 'Ukba, "In this matter of [waiting between eating meat and milk] I am lax compared with my father's stringency [*chala bar chamra l'gabai abba*]. For if my father were to eat meat now he would not eat cheese until the very hour tomorrow, whereas I do not eat [cheese] in the same meal but I do eat it in my next meal."[6]

Is the son accepting the greater knowledge of the father or challenging its appropriateness? Elsewhere also, these nuances have not been visible until the salient question concerning the pedagogical relationship of father and son was asked. Finding evidence that the son's relationship to his father continues to loom over his education requires a portrait of education capable of including this complexity.

Analyzing education and considering ritual and lived religion, I argue, reveals the ongoing, important, and ambivalent educational relationship between parent and child, refining our understanding of transmission of ideas in the rabbinic period. Our present examination of largely underappreciated dynamics is in line with recent studies that have destabilized the image of rabbinic education as formal, institutional instruction. If we also take into account certain ideas that are well accepted in social theory but have not yet been applied to the study of education in the rabbinic era, we can come to a more nuanced understanding of how the sons in these narratives might perceive their world. These critical advances enable us to see anew the father-son relationships that have until now been hidden in plain sight.

INFORMAL INSTITUTIONS AND GENERATIONAL SHIFTS

When the ninth century Babylonian rabbinic academies of Pumbedita and Sura traced their own histories, they portrayed their institutions as dating back to the third century and perhaps even earlier.[7] That backdated pedigree had been accepted until David Goodblatt spearheaded a recent move toward historical skepticism about these early academies, a skepticism that appears to be coalescing into a new consensus. A consideration of linguistic evidence began the challenge: why should we translate "yeshiva" or *metivta* as "academy" when other possibilities, such as "study session," exist?[8] The terms *beit midrash* and *bei rav,* Hebrew and Aramaic, respectively, for "house of study," appear about five times as often as the terms "yeshiva" and *metivta,* so perhaps this "academy" concept is not as foundational as has been assumed.[9]

The scholars examining early Jewish higher education argue persuasively that by bracketing our own emotional investment in the image of the academy, we come to recognize it as an anachronism. Study circles would have been more fluid—powerful as long as a particular rabbi was teaching, and then at some point students would move elsewhere. The resulting analytical framework has already led to insights about early Jewish and Christian education, since the latter also seems to have not so immediately developed the formality once assumed.[10] This paradigm shift opens a great many questions concerning how teachers related to their students, to one another, and to others—all are matters of communication and of power.[11]

Given this focus on the more informal and direct dynamics between teachers and students, it is not much of a leap to insert the question of how parents figure into this picture. In the area of meal studies, where I have done much of my research, Gil Klein has recently argued for the importance of considering the banquet hall space as an important locus for halachic discussions.[12] He insists that the meal itself functions not only as a setting for communal reflection but also as an interactive space for the making of halachic decisions.[13] Taken together, this suggests that we move our thinking from a model of academies to multiple and porous households as a context for law and, I would add, learning. Spilling over into mealtimes, this instruction was hardly the classroom-bound phenomenon that earlier critics might have retrojected onto rabbinic-era settings.

The model of the removed and ascendant academy is being supplanted with more intimate alternatives. This is one step toward viewing the pedagogical relationship of father and son anew. Social science methodologies that examine community change over time, such as discussions of cohort replacement, provide additional steps, mapping the changing attitudes of new generations.[14] In considering rabbinic literature, we do not have a mass of data, but these mathematically based methodologies do a service nonetheless: they reverse the landscape for us. They suggest that despite appearances to the contrary, rabbinic emphasis on transmission of tradition is only part of the story. They cause us to ask how rabbinic literature, as it conserves earlier wisdom, presents these moments of change. The tensions in rabbinic texts start to surface.

Of more help than simply revealing the underlying tensions, Pierre Bourdieu theorizes the self-reflexive aspect of acting from a differing point of view. Bourdieu expects us to look at change, but he also insists on our examining the structure that precedes this change as a prior moment. This is not, he explains, the Lévi-Straussian "structure" but instead is a continually revised "structuring structure" that will serve as social context for actions that will, in turn, restructure this context and so forth.[15] In our case, these "symbolic struggles over the perceptions of the social world" mean that students understand, act, and develop social capital in a world that never overlaps entirely with that of their parents or teachers.[16] Our challenge becomes recognizing this disjuncture or lack of overlap in the discrete points of view concealed or revealed when fathers and sons contest each other's ability to know and act.

RABBINIC FATHERS AND SONS

In recent years, a *sugya,* or talmudic grouping from the Babylonian Talmud tractate Berachot, has received much attention because of the clues it offers concerning rabbinic ideas about women, asceticism, and the construction of gender.[17] Despite this flurry of study, little attention has been paid to the ongoing appearance of fathers in this set of narratives. As explained above, researchers had expected education and learning to happen within the academy, so there was no need to examine these interactions as peculiar. Contrary to this expectation, each example depicts a different fraught teaching and learning relationship between father and son. I will examine these three cases out of order so as to consider the most successful, the scariest, and, only then, the one with the most ambiguity.

Despite the fact that the father may send his son to a disciple circle, the father is responsible for helping the son find a bride. As becomes apparent below, this is a teachable moment. Or, in other words, the father persists in teaching his son about other aspects of life, including the importance of getting married:

> Later he was engaged in preparations for the marriage of his son into the family of R. Jose b. Zimra. It was agreed that [the son] should spend twelve years at the house of study [*bei rav*]. When the girl was led before him he said to them, "Let it be six years." When they made her pass before him [a second time] he said, "I would rather marry [her first] and then proceed [to the house of study]." He felt abashed before his father, but the latter said to him, "My son, you have the mind of your creator; for in Scripture it is written first, 'You will bring them and plant them,' and later it is written, 'And let them make Me a sanctuary that I may dwell among them.'"[18]

The father arranges for the chosen bride to pass before his hesitant son. When the son chooses marriage, he stands sheepishly before his father. And we do see the power relationship: the father has a hold on his son, and the son has filial obligations. In this particular glimpse, the father teaches his son about this balance of sexual relations and asceticism. His son does not know more than his father; the son comes to recognize a truth that his father has understood. Nevertheless, Bourdieu's insights concerning struggles over perception help us realize that the separate perspective he represents is not altogether absent: had he (or someone like him) not perceived this question of marriage differently and not thought that his need to go study trumped his need to marry, there would be no purpose to telling the story.

The peaceful communication of father and son concerning the balance of Torah and family characterizes the narrative. Toward the end of this *sugya* we learn of a more violent clash. This father also presents his own opinion of how to balance study and sexual activity:

> R. Joseph the son of Raba [was] sent [by] his father to the house of study to study before R. Joseph, and they arranged for him [to stay there for] six years. Having been there three years and the eve of the Day of Atonement approaching, he said, "I would go and see my family." When his father heard [of his premature arrival] he took

> up a weapon and went out to meet him. He said to him, "You have remembered your whore!"
>
> Another version: He said to him, "You have remembered your dove!" They got involved in a quarrel and neither the one nor the other ate of the last meal before the fast.[19]

Things became so tense between this father and son that they began Yom Kippur without a last meal. The weapon in the father's hand certainly represents a contest of power, but the narrative underscores the incomplete success of the father's argument. Aside from his need to resort to violence, the father's language itself seems to be uncomfortable for the talmudic compilers. An additional angle is offered: some accounts read "dove" instead of "whore." Those hearing the story have even wondered whether both father and son miss the meal because they are dead, each killing the other in the culmination of the violence percolating throughout.[20] Ultimately, whatever the outcome there is no question here that the episode involves (a) an argument, (b) different perspectives, and (c) teaching from father to son. Regardless of what learning may occur, the father offers his son another perspective.

One more parental story appears in this *sugya.* In this narrative, the father finds his son's behavior as fantastic as the previous father found his son's opposition:

> R. Hama b. Bisa went away [from home and] spent twelve years at the house of study. When he returned he said, "I will not act as did b. Hakina [surprising and thus scaring his wife to death]." He therefore entered the [local] house of study and sent word to his house. Meanwhile his son, R. Oshaia, entered, sat down before him and addressed to him a question on [one of the] subjects of study. [R. Hama,] seeing how well versed he was in his studies, became very depressed. "Had I been here," he said, "I also could have had such a child." When he entered his house his son came in, whereupon he rose before him, believing that [the other] wished to ask him some [further] legal questions. His wife chuckled. "What father stands up before a son?!"
>
> [As an epilogue to this story, since from Bisa to Hama to Oshaia is the three generations,] Rami b. Hama applied to him [the following scriptural text:] And a threefold cord is not quickly broken is a reference to R. Oshaia, son of R. Hama, son of Bisa.[21]

Here, the father, like the son in our earlier text, balances marriage and study. He does wed first, but then he goes off to study before settling into his marital home. Upon his return, he encounters a model young man: one well educated and respectful. We see him indulge in a private dream that this could be his son, which turns out to be true on one level. But isn't such a compliant son still a fantasy, especially when the father has been absent? He encounters his son twice, and they don't argue! We have the modern language of those who study adoption reminding us that he is only the biological father.

The wife of the absent father guffaws as he mistakenly rises before his son, for this father is turning the expected roles upside down. It would be appropriate to rise before a guest scholar but not before his own son.[22] This erroneous posture becomes a joke, as the text both reveals and calls into question the appropriateness of behavior between this father and this son. The son has inadvertently assumed the father's role of the one who commands honor, thus transforming the relationship into a very different fantasy involving a weak father and a usurping son. The text does not tell us how this pair will move from the fantasy roles of father and son to a real relationship, but it does reveal a disconnect. The epilogue celebrates Oshaia as the third generation, the threefold cord that cannot be broken, but in doing so it may also be answering a concern that the father's absence has endangered this legacy.

The three texts above, situated in this single *sugya,* offer a range of visions: a relationship between father and son that is productive of learning, a relationship based only on biology that can serve as a fantasy for at least a moment or two, and, in the final vignette, a father greeting his son with violence. Despite the backdrop of students going off to study, the learning relationship between father and son still exists, however successful or unsuccessful. In fact, this variety suggests the tenacity of this relationship despite available alternatives. Because all the stories describe the encounters using the third person, however, we don't have the sons' perspective on this learning. That point of view resurfaces when we turn to the text examined briefly at the beginning and its twin:

> Said Mar 'Ukba, "In this matter of [waiting between eating meat and milk] I am lax compared with my father's stringency [*chala bar chamra l'gabai abba*]. For if my father were to eat meat now he would not eat cheese until the very hour tomorrow, whereas I do not eat [cheese] in the same meal but I do eat it in my next meal."
>
> Samuel said, "In this matter I am lax compared with my father's stringency [*chala bar chamra l'gabai abba*]. For my father used to inspect his property twice a day, but I do so only once a day." Samuel here follows his maxim, for Samuel declared,

> "He who inspects his property daily will find a half-zuz coin [or the equivalent as profit]."[23]

In these accounts we see two sons, each in the same position and each offering an account of his personal practice. Each declares that his father is "stricter" than he is about these matters of dining and accounting. Each son describes his father's practice and his own, neither denying what he learned from his father nor following it exactly.

Ironically, despite the first-person presentation, ambiguity remains. What does it mean when a son says that his father is "stricter"? A couple of translations try to decide the issue: "I [the son] cannot hold a candle to my father" or "I am as vinegar is to wine compared with my father," working to make it clear that the son envies the father and would, if he could, aspire to such a pinnacle.[24] But "stricter" does not always convey this nuance; it can also mean mulish and stubborn. For whatever reason, each son has arrived at a practice different from his father's, even though he is aware of his father's position. Does the son know more? Bourdieu would remind us that the social structure in which he operates differs from that of his father and will differ again through the son's acting within and through these structuring structures. In this last case, the son's actions diverge from his father's actions because he, the son, lives in a world that is wholly other.

CONCLUSION: IMPLICATIONS FOR LEARNING

This study is an early exploration of these questions of fathers and sons. It has considered only a handful of examples and makes no claim that these are necessarily representative of other rabbinic presentations of parenting. Nevertheless, all of these encounters between fathers and sons prove both significant and ambiguous. The texts shows fathers who continue to teach their sons and who stand as models for their sons even after the sons have gone to study with other teachers. The texts also reveal sons who may or may not follow the guidance their fathers offer.

This picture complicates a son's obligation to ransom his teacher first. In their array, these fathers together reveal that while the rabbis may have aspirations of replacing fathers with teachers, we must not assume that we know where one role leaves off and the other begins. This understanding urges us to revisit, from a refreshed perspective, texts that advocate an exploration of asceticism. Each young man who lives away from his wife and home also has a natal family with whom to contend. We understand these young men differently when we focus on the parent-child relationship. While some of the fathers explored above certainly count as sages in their own right, they act here as fathers. Further, the above struggles reveal the possibility of generational change, since the son's point of view must be different than that of his father for such a contest to be required.

We would not have been able to observe either the involvement of the fathers or the ambivalent responses of their sons if research into anachronistic assumptions about the academies had not paved the way for conceiving more intimate environments for learning. Similarly, even the vivid distance separating the house of study from the family home in some of these narratives does not sever the household relationships. By following learning back to the family, we witness aspects of family relationships too long overlooked. Just as we can begin to glimpse sons framing their own lives in dialogue with their fathers, attention to ritual and lived religion may have the power to reveal other consequential aspects of household activities and relationships.

ACKNOWLEDGMENTS

With great pleasure and awe, I dedicate this exploration to my wonderful learned daughter, Madeline H. Black.

Thank you to Jonathan Brumberg-Kraus for encouragement at an early stage of this project. And many thanks indeed to all who made the Klutznick-Harris-Schwalb Symposium such a joyful and rewarding event, including the helpful questions and comments from my colleagues and others in the audience.

NOTES

1. The present essay explores only the relationship of fathers and sons. For consideration of the teaching relationship of mother and son, see Susan Marks, "Bayit versus Beit Midrash: Jewish Mother as Teacher," in *A Most Reliable Witness: Essays in Honor of Ross Shepard Kraemer* (ed. S. Harvey et al.; Providence: Brown University Press, 2015).

2. *m. Baba Mezi'a* 2.11. See also *b. Baba Mezi'a* 33a. While the Mishnah aims to draw a firm distinction between the father who can prepare his son only for this life and the teacher who can prepare him for the next, the Gemara appears to complicate this clear distinction in exploring the necessity for multiple teachers. Gail Labovitz, in an unpublished paper, observes the insertion of the teacher in the case of mourning, where it interrupts the possible gender parity of how "father and mother" should be mourned.

3. Youval Rotman, "Captives and Redeeming Captives: The Law and the Community," in *Judaea-Palaestina, Babylon and Rome: Jews in Antiquity* (ed. B. Isaac and Y. Shahar; Leiden: Brill, 2013), 227–47.

4. Gerald J. Blidstein, "Master and Parent: Comparative Aspects of a Dual Loyalty," in *The Mishnah in Contemporary Perspective* (ed. A. J. Avery-Peck and J. Neusner; Leiden: Brill, 2002), 255–66.

5. David Goodblatt, "The History of the Babylonian Academies," in *The Cambridge History of Judaism,* Vol. 4, *The Late Roman-Rabbinic Period* (ed. S. T. Katz; Cambridge: Cambridge University Press, 2006), 821–39; Catherine Hezser, "Private and Public Education," in *The Oxford Handbook of Jewish Daily Life in Roman Palestine* (ed. C. Hezser; Oxford: Oxford University Press, 2010), 465–81; Jeffrey L. Rubenstein, *The Culture of the Babylonian Talmud* (Baltimore: Johns Hopkins University Press, 2003).

6. *b. Hullin* 105a.

7. Goodblatt, "The History of the Babylonian Academies," 822.

8. Ibid., 832.

9. Ibid., 834.

10. Adam H. Becker, "The Comparative Study of 'Scholasticism' in Late Antique Mesopotamia: Rabbis and East Syrians," *Association for Jewish Studies Review* 34:1 (2010): 91–113. Concerning differences between the early and later rabbinic movement, see also Hezser, "Private and Public Education." Concerning differences between Palestinian and Babylonian communities, see Rubenstein, *The Culture of the Babylonian Talmud.*

11. Scholars have also just begun studying rabbinic curricula, and it will be interesting to see what these new approaches yield. See, for instance, Marjorie Lehman and Jane Kanarek, "Talmud: Making a Case for Talmud Pedagogy—the Talmud as an Educational Model," in *International Handbook of Jewish Education* (ed. H. Miller et al.; Dordrecht: Springer, 2011), 581–96.

12. Gil P. Klein, "Torah in Triclinia: The Rabbinic Banquet and the Significance of Architecture," *Jewish Quarterly Review* 102:3 (2012): 325–70.

13. Ibid., 341–70. In the second part of his essay, Klein emphasizes the relationship of banquet hall and street and thus the traffic into and out of this space.

14. Clem Brooks and Catherine Bolzendahl, "The Transformation of US Gender Role Attitudes: Cohort Replacement, Social-Structural Change, and Ideological Learning," *Social Science Research* 33 (2004): 106–33. A popular treatment of the impact of different cohorts considers the differing contributions of the traditionalist, boomer, Gen X, and millennial generations. Lynne C. Lancaster and David Stillman, *When Generations Collide: Who They Are, Why They Clash, How to Solve the Generational Puzzle at Work* (New York: HarperCollins, 2002).

15. Pierre Bourdieu, "Social Space and Symbolic Power," in *In Other Words: Essays towards a Reflexive Sociology* (trans. M. Adamson; Stanford: Stanford University Press, 1990), 123–39, esp. 123–26.

16. Ibid., 134. Bourdieu notes that the properties of objects of the social world "are submitted to variations in time so that their meaning, in so far as they depend on the future, is itself held in suspense and relatively indeterminate" (133). Regarding education, Bourdieu recalls in a parenthetical discussion of his earlier work, "we showed how a social relation of understanding is constructed in and by misunderstanding . . . how teachers and students agree, by a sort of tacit transaction, tacitly guided by the need to minimize costs and risks, to accept a minimal definition of the situation of communication" (124). See also discussions of lived religion in David D. Hall, *Lived Religion in America: Toward a History of Practice* (Princeton: Princeton University Press, 1997).

17. Daniel Boyarin, *Carnal Israel: Reading Sex in Talmudic Culture* (Berkeley: University of California Press, 1993); Aryeh Cohen, *Rereading Talmud: Gender, Law and the Poetics of Sugyot* (Atlanta: Scholars Press, 1998); Rubenstein, *The Culture of the Babylonian Talmud.*

18. *b. Berachot* 62b. Quotations of Exodus 15.17 and 25.8 are from the New Jewish Publication Society *Tanakh.*

19. *b. Berachot* 63a.

20. My students at New College of Florida wondered about this, as did the audience in Omaha. Ari Elon takes a slightly different approach, characterizing it as a tragedy that "ends in a nightmare frozen in nondeath till eternity." Ari Elon, *From Jerusalem to the Edge of Heaven: Mediations on the Soul of Israel* (Philadelphia: JPS, 1996), 88.

21. *b. Berachot* 62b.

22. Elsewhere I discuss the mother's teaching in this moment. See Marks, "Bayit versus Beit Midrash."

23. *b. Hullin* 105a.

24. For these translations, see "Talmud Bavli Hullin 105a–b—Translation by Tzvee Zahavy," A Talmudic View of the World, October 9, 2011, http://tzvee.blogspot.com/2011/10/talmud-bavli-hullin-105a-b-translation.html, and I. Epstein, ed., *The Babylonian Talmud: Seder Kodashim* (trans. E. Cashdan; London: Soncino, 1948), II:582.

Mishnah *Gittin*: Family Relations as Metaphor for National Relations

David Brodsky

DIVORCE IN THE HEBREW BIBLE

The biblical heritage on divorce is brief and enigmatic.[1] In the whole of the Torah, only one passage in Deuteronomy discusses the topic at all, and even that passage addresses a specific case, taking the general category for granted. Deuteronomy 24:1–4 states:

1. When a man takes a woman and has intercourse with her, it shall be that if she does not find favor in his eyes because he found in her some unchaste matter [*'ervat davar*], and he wrote [*ve-khatav*] her a writ of separation and put [*ve-natan*] it in her hand and sent her [*ve-shilleḥah*] from his house,
2. and she went out from his house and was to another man,
3. and the latter man hated her and wrote her a writ of separation and put it in her hand and sent her from his house, or if the latter man who took her as a wife passed away,
4. her first husband who sent her away may not take her again to be his wife after she has been defiled, for it is an abomination before the Lord, and you shall not cause the land which the Lord your God gave you as an inheritance to sin.[2]

Verses 1–3 are a long conditional case (protasis), with verse 4 being the conclusion (apodosis), the ruling regarding the case described in verses 1–3. The case is that of a divorced wife who remarried and then was divorced or widowed by her second husband. The ruling is that she is no longer free to remarry her first husband. Such a union is described as an abomination and leading the land into sin. I would concur with the medieval Jewish commentator Nahmanides that the Deuteronomist is attempting to close a loophole. While the author allows for divorce and remarriage, he (and I do assume a male, patriarchal voice here) is against two men sharing a single wife, and he recognizes that divorce with remarriage could be used to allow two men to share a wife, divorcing her as they pass her back and forth between them. As Nahmanides explains, "The purpose of this negative commandment is so that [men] should not exchange their wives with one another, writing her a divorce document in the evening, and in the morning she returns to him" (Nahmanides on Deut 24:4). Closing this loophole, the Deuteronomist declares that once the divorcée has married another man, she may never return to her first husband.[3]

The problem for those attempting to formulate a more general biblical/rabbinic law of divorce (as the author of tractate *Gittin* of the Mishnah clearly needs to do) is that they lack a biblical source that lays it out, since verses 1–3 are descriptive of this specific case rather than prescriptive of the general law. That is, read this way, verses 1–3 do not define how divorce in general must be conducted; they merely describe a specific case that the author wishes to proscribe. They do not prescribe that a bill of divorce must be written and given by the husband to the wife; they merely indicate that if said bill has been given (which could be but one of many ways for a couple to divorce legally) and if she then goes and marries another man and divorces him, she may not return to her first husband.[4]

When read out of the context of verses 2–4, however, verse 1 can be read prescriptively, with its own protasis and apodosis, simply by reading *vav*-conjunctive as *vav*-consecutive:

A. When a man takes a woman and has intercourse with her, it shall be that if she does not find favor in his eyes because he found in her some unchaste matter,
B. he *shall* write [*ve-khatav*] her a writ of separation and put [*ve-natan*] it in her hand and send her [*ve-shilleḥah*] from his house.

Section A therefore becomes the necessary condition for a generic divorce, with section B the required action to be taken. It is this reading that seems to motivate the rabbinic law of divorce delineated in this tractate. Thus, most of Mishnah *Gittin* (a second to third century rabbinic code on the laws of divorce) focuses on qualifying what constitutes the proper writing [*ve-khatav*] and delivery [*ve-natan be-yadah*] of the divorce document, and Mishnah *Gittin* 9:10 debates what constitutes an "unchaste matter" [*'ervat davar*] now required for a divorce.

DIVORCE AT ELEPHANTINE: A PRE-RABBINIC INTERPRETATION OF DEUTERONOMY?

While the later Rabbinic reading of Deuteronomy 24:1 permitted the man alone to give the bill of divorce, the Jews of fifth century BCE Elephantine, an island outpost along the Nile River in upper Egypt allowed both women and men to divorce the other party. Thus, a Jewish marriage contract found in Elephantine dated to 449 BCE offers the following egalitarian pair of provisos:

> Tomorrow or [the] next day, should Anani stand up in an assembly and say: "I hated Tamet my wife," silver of hatre[d] is on his head. He shall give Tamet silver, 7 shekels [2 q(uarters)][5] and all that she brought in in her hand she shall take out, from straw to string.
>
> Tomorrow or [the] next day, should Tamet stand up and say: "I hated my husband Anani," 2 q[uarters] silver of hatre[d] is on her head. She shall give to Anani silver, 7 shekels and all that she brought in in her hand she shall take out, from straw to string.[6]

This is a world away from the divorce law of the Mishnah some five hundred to seven hundred years later.[7] In Elephantine, divorce is not unilateral and a written document is not required. Rather, either party may simply stand up and say "I hate So-and-So my husband/wife" and pay a relatively small fine (the Mishnah will later institute a much larger fine). Therefore, in fifth century BCE Elephantine it would seem that the Jewish community was either ignoring Deuteronomy or reading Deuteronomy 24:1 as describing a specific case rather than prescribing how to conduct a divorce, leaving the divorce process much more open than it would later become. How mainstream this practice was among Jews is unclear. For example, this is not the only practice of the Elephantine community that seems to conflict with common Jewish readings of Deuteronomy, leading us to question whether the Jews of Elephantine had Deuteronomy or chose to follow its proscriptions. Thus, for example, Deuteronomy repeatedly ordains that various sacrifices shall be made "in the place that the Lord shall choose" (Deut 12:14 and 18; 14:23; 15:20; and 16:2, 7, 11, 15, and 16), which Jews have classically taken to refer to the Temple Mount in Jerusalem, implying that sacrifices shall be offered in Jerusalem (and nowhere else). Yet the Jews of Elephantine built a temple in their enclave in which they offered sacrifices in seemingly flagrant violation of this commandment.[8] Of course, Deuteronomy never specifies where this place is that the Lord shall choose, and indeed, not all descendants of the ancient Israelites have taken it to refer to the Temple Mount in Jerusalem (or to refer to all sacrifices). The Samaritans, descendants of remnants of the inhabitants of the Northern Kingdom, interpret those self-same verses as referring to Mt. Gerizim in Samaria, outside of Shechem, and Onias IV, son of Onias III, the high priest in Jerusalem, built a temple in Leontopolis in Egypt in which sacrifices were offered from 154 BCE until its destruction in 73 CE (Josephus, *Antiquities*

XIII, 62–73). Thus, not all Israelites and not all Jews seem to have interpreted these verses as limiting all sacrifices to Jerusalem, although that is generally how those verses tend to be understood. So, while the Elephantine community may simply be an aberrant community that either barely knew or did not observe the laws of Deuteronomy, they may just as plausibly have been rather mainstream for their time in their practice and simply had different interpretations of the relevant verses in Deuteronomy from those that became prevalent later on.

THE MISHNAH

Returning to our topic of divorce, this leaves us unclear as to what Jewish divorce practice was before the Mishnah.[9] Nevertheless, what is clear is that once the rabbis came to read Deuteronomy 24:1 as prescriptive rather than descriptive, a Jewish divorce would now come with the requirement that the husband (1) write a bill of divorce, which he must then (2) give to his wife. Interestingly, with this stringency in place, the Mishnah spends most of its time exploring the leniency of permitting him to designate others as his agent for both tasks. Thus, most of the tractate is concerned with the details of how the husband can designate agency for others to write the bill of divorce for him and how and when his messenger may deliver the bill to his wife.

While this exegetical history helps explain both the Mishnah's rulings and its focus, it fails to explain the Mishnah's organization. Rather than lead us into or through these laws in a clear and organized fashion—starting with the more general principles and working its way to the more technical details, or beginning with the laws in Deuteronomy 24:1 and walking us through the laws that ensue therefrom—the Mishnah begins by plunging into the highly specific case of a bill of divorce that has been brought to Israel from outside of the land, which immediately requires a detailed delineation of Israel's borders. Thus, the Mishnah opens by stating that "One who brings a divorce document from the province of the sea[10] must say, 'it was written in front of me and signed in front of me'" (Mishnah *Gittin* 1:1), which leads to R. Judah defining "From Reqem to the east, and Reqem is like the east. From Ashkelon to the south, and Ashkelon is like the south. From Akko to the north, and Akko is like the north" (Mishnah *Gittin* 1:2)[11]—marking off the eastern, southern, and northern borders of the land of Israel, with the western border presumably marked off by the Mediterranean Sea.[12] From a logical perspective, starting with this sub-subcategory of the law is a terrible place to begin. It assumes knowledge of the general category of bills of divorce and even assumes knowledge that such bills may be sent by messenger, a caveat that is not intuitively obvious from the Bible. I would argue that this is not the product of sloppiness or disorganization but instead is a concerted effort on the part of the author to signal from the beginning that the purpose of this tractate is much more than simply to delineate the laws of divorce.

THE STRUCTURE OF THE MISHNAH IN LIGHT OF SECOND TEMPLE LITERATURE

Scholars have shown that the Mishnah is a carefully structured text with an organization that is not classically modern but nevertheless is carefully planned.[13] Second Temple and rabbinic period Jewish texts in general (particularly the works of Apocrypha and Pseudepigrapha) often deftly signal the central theme of the work through the framing of the text—that is, through subtle references embedded in the opening and closing sections of the work. Where the modern author will write an overt introductory and concluding thesis statement, the late antique Jewish author may camouflage it. Thus, for example, the Septuagint's version of the book of Esther adds a prophetic dream that Mordechai receives at the beginning of the story and then is referenced again, envelope style, at the end, completely reframing the older Hebrew story, which had conspicuously lacked any mention of God, as now entirely God's plan.

Indeed, often the theme is signaled to the reader in the beginning, middle, and end of each work. Thus, 2 Maccabees opens with a seemingly unrelated wish by the authors for the Jews of Egypt to whom they are writing that God grant them "a heart to worship and do his will with a strong heart and a willing spirit," that he open their hearts "to his law and his commandments, and may he bring peace," and that he hear their prayers and be reconciled to them and not forsake them in time of evil (2 Macc 1:3–5).[14] While this letter is technically just a formal greeting and is ostensibly unrelated to the story that follows, it is the central theme of the text and the way that the author wishes to (re)frame the story of the revolt: it is only through worshipping and keeping God's laws and commandments that God will have mercy on the Jewish people again and restore his Temple. This theme is reiterated in a crucial martyrdom scene centrally located in the middle of the story in which—unlike their predecessors at the beginning of the story who had brought God's wrath upon Israel for abandoning God's ways—the martyrs now stay faithful to

God's commandments even at the cost of their own lives. As the youngest of the seven sons admonishes the Seleucid king in 7:30–33:

> I will not obey the king's command, but I obey the command of the law that was given to our ancestors through Moses. But you, who have contrived all sorts of evil against the Hebrews, will certainly not escape the hands of God. For we are suffering because of our own sins. And if our living Lord is angry for a little while, to rebuke and discipline us, he will again be reconciled with his own servants.

This crucial chapter acts as the turning point in the story, and it is immediately followed by the Maccabees's change in fortune, "for the wrath of the Lord had turned to mercy" (2 Macc 8:5). Finally, in the last battle at the end of the book, Judah Maccabee "stretched out his hands toward heaven and called upon the Lord who works wonders; for he knew that it is not by arms, but as the Lord decides, that he gains the victory for those who deserve it" (2 Macc 15:21). Together, the beginning, middle, and end of 2 Maccabees signal the central theme of the text: God will protect those who obey his law and abandon those who abandon it.[15]

Let me offer one more brief example. The book of Jubilees, which coincidentally is divided into exactly fifty chapters (at least in the Ethiopic version, the only complete extant version), matching the fifty years of the Jubilee, is framed at its beginning and end by chapters that emphasize the importance of the Sabbath. Thus, from its very opening and closing sections (chapters 2 and 50), the book of Jubilees emphasizes the importance of the Sabbath, which is the culmination of the week of days, even as the book as a whole emphasizes the Jubilee, which is the culmination of the week of weeks of years. Indeed, in chapter 50, the author marks the giving of the book of Jubilees as following on the Jubilee of Jubilees since the opening of the book with the days of Adam (and the first Sabbath). The framing of the book of Jubilees, opening and closing with its central theme of the Sabbath and the week (of days/years), seems striking.

What is less clear is whether the book of Jubilees also uses its center to establish its theme. On the one hand, I do not believe that all ancient Jewish texts necessarily use the exact same structure, and therefore, perhaps we should leave Jubilees as using its beginning and end (and not the middle) to establish its central theme. On the other hand, it is possible that the central chapter (25) is being used as well to help establish the core theme of the book. If part of the purpose of keeping the Sabbath is to be holy, to be right with God, and to be allowed to dwell in the land thereby (as Jubilees puts it, "the land will keep its Sabbaths when they dwell upon it" [Jub 50:3]),[16] then Rebecca's exhortation of Jacob in chapter 25 not to marry the daughters of the Canaanites and her subsequent blessing of Jacob—that he may follow in the way of righteousness, multiply and inherit the land, and have "a blessed and holy seed" (25:16–18)—may be no less central to the theme of the book than its opening and closing sections on the Sabbath. It is through the keeping of the Sabbath and through the separation from the ways of the Canaanites that Israel, the seed of Jacob, follow in the path of righteousness and that they merit to multiply and inherit the land and ultimately become a blessed and holy seed. Thus, these three sections seem to be working together to establish the central theme of the book.

Many more examples of this type of structure can be offered from the literature of the Second Temple period, but these three should suffice for the moment. The point is that late Second Temple period texts sometimes (I would argue often) (1) signal their thesis in the beginning, middle, and end of the text, and (2) they sometimes do so covertly through passages that at first blush appear to be ancillary, such as in the greeting in the opening letter of 2 Maccabees.

WHAT MISHNAH *GITTIN*'S STRUCTURE CAN TEACH US ABOUT ITS MESSAGE

I would argue that the Mishnah should be read very much in context of this relatively contemporary Second Temple period genre: at times signaling its intent in the beginning, middle, and end of the tractate.[17] I shall demonstrate that *Gittin* is a prime example of this phenomenon. In Mishnah *Gittin,* the beginning, middle, and end of the tractate are strikingly out of place where they are found, drawing attention to themselves.[18] The opening section, as we have seen, addresses a bill of divorce that is brought from outside of the land of Israel, forcing a discussion of the borders of Israel: what is in and what is out. At the center of the tractate is a lengthy tangent about those rulings that were made for the sake of the public welfare. While they begin with divorce-related rulings, they quickly digress to list the numerous other rulings that were made for these purposes, wandering from there to those rulings that were made for the sake of peace, a related though separate category. The final mishnah of the tractate has little to do with the mishnayot that precede it, though it is central to the topic of divorce, delineating the three main rabbinic interpretations of Deuteronomy 24:1 and the conditions required for divorce. In fact, this mishnah is so central to any delineation of the rabbinic law of divorce that it is difficult to understand why the redactor of the tractate saved it until the very end. It is one of only two places where the Mishnah makes any attempt to connect its law back to this key biblical verse and the only place where the Mishnah explains its ideology behind divorce. Ostensibly, the tractate should have opened with this explanation before moving into the detailed laws rather than the reverse.

While the rest of the tractate lays out the laws of the commissioning, writing, and delivery of the bill of divorce in a fairly orderly manner, the beginning, middle, and end of the tractate stand out. I would argue that the three work together to point the reader to the central theme of the tractate, a theme that is simultaneously on the individual level and the national level. By opening with a marking of the boundaries between that which is inside and outside of the land of Israel, I would suggest that the tractate is pointing to divorce as an act that is marking the same boundaries on the individual level. The middle section explains why these boundaries need to be established: originally [*ba-rishonah*] one ruling was made, but since then circumstances have not turned out the way they were intended, and a corrective must be instituted. For the sake of the public welfare, indeed for the sake of peace, matters cannot always remain as they were originally established. Sometimes a corrective is necessary. Here, divorce is precisely that corrective for the marriage that is not working. The final mishnah clarifies that while divorce was only permitted by the School of Shammai in cases of adultery (reading the "unchaste matter [*'ervat davar*]" of Deuteronomy 24:1 as truly unchaste [*devar 'ervah*]), the School of Hillel and later Rabbi Akiva offered their own correctives, permitting it ultimately any time that the two were not getting along.

By using the national boundaries as a metaphor for individual boundaries vis-à-vis divorce, the redactor is reversing the prophetic use of divorce as a metaphor for the nation and its ruptured relationship with God (Isa 50:1, Jer 3:1–8, and Mal 2:13–16). Yet by linking the two, the redactor opens up the possibility of reading in both directions—of national boundaries as metaphor for individual boundaries and as the marking of these personal boundaries as metaphor for the nation.[19] Indeed, most of the rulings "for the public welfare" and "for the sake of peace" delineated in the epicenter of the tractate (from Mishnah *Gittin* 4:2 to 5:9, one mishnah shy of two full chapters), which have little if anything to do with divorce, point to the welfare of the nation as a whole, culminating in the final mishnah of this central section, which addresses the issue of peace between members of the *ḥavurah* [the rabbinic community] and nonmembers of the *ḥavurah* [the non-rabbinic community] and ultimately between Jews and gentiles (5:9). The importance of this middle section cannot be overemphasized. It comprises more than one-fifth of the tractate. It is placed smack in the middle of the tractate, and except for one or two mishnayot used to segue into it, it has almost nothing ostensibly to do with the topic of divorce. These very facts call attention to this section and force us to ask what its role is here. I would argue that it gives the central theme to the tractate on several levels. Its theme is laws that originally [*ba-rishonah*] were one way but then were changed "for the sake of the public welfare" or "for the sake of peace." While divorce is never mentioned as one of these rules that was changed for the public welfare or for the sake of peace, it is thematically the prime candidate.

In the Gospel of Mark (10:2–12, discussed in more detail below), Jesus challenges the Pharisees (i.e., the predecessors to the rabbis) on the law of divorce in Deuteronomy 24. Basing himself on the creation story ("male and female he created them" [Gen 1:27] and "For this reason a man shall leave his father and mother and be joined to his wife, and the two shall become one flesh" [Gen 2:24]), Jesus argues that two people whom God has joined, no man should put asunder. The Damascus Document in the Dead Sea Scrolls is only slightly more lenient. Interestingly, it too uses Genesis 1:27 to argue against divorce (or, more accurately, against remarriage), stating, "[They] are caught twice in fornication: by taking two wives in their lives, even though the principle of creation is 'male and female he created them' (Gen 1:27). And the ones who went into the ark 'went in two by two into the ark' (Gen 7:9)."[20] As Lawrence Schiffman has argued, the addition of the words "in their lives" implies something more than just a proscription against polygamy. The additional words would seem to imply that a person should only marry one person in their lifetimes. While this may not be a proscription against divorce in general (the Temple Scroll [54:4], for example, acknowledges the existence of divorcées without making an issue of it), it does seem to proscribe remarriage by either party should the couple separate.[21] Similarly, Paul prefers that husbands and wives not separate (*mē chōristhēnai;* 1 Cor 7:10), but if they do, he exhorts the woman to remain unmarried (*menetō agamos;* 1 Cor 7:11). Likewise, in Mark 10:2–12 (cf. Matt 9:3–9) Jesus is quoted as saying, "Whoever divorces his wife, except for unchastity [*mē epi porneia*], and marries another, commits adultery [*moichatai*]" (Matt 19:9).[22] Thus, even as the early Christian sect and the Dead Sea sectarians allowed for some couples to divorce (i.e., to separate, at least in cases of *porneia*), they seem to counter one of the key elements of mishnaic divorce: that the wife (both parties, really) be completely free to remarry (Mishnah *Gittin* 9:1–3).

I would argue that the Mishnah is subtly using the section on policies that change for the sake of peace and for the public welfare as a way to respond to Jews such as Paul, Jesus in the Gospels, and the Dead Sea sectarians, arguing that indeed, originally marriage (and not divorce) was the correct law for the divorcing couple, but their circumstances changed (they no longer get along), and now a corrective is needed for the sake of peace, for the public welfare. That is on the individual level. On the national level, I would argue that the Mishnah is using this central theme coupled with the overriding theme of the tractate to demarcate the people. Originally those boundaries were broader, but for the sake of the public welfare the Mishnah is now marking who is in and who is out. Thus, this section culminates with Mishnah *Gittin* 5:9, pointing to the groups who are outside the bounds of the rabbinic community:

A. A woman may lend her fellow, who is suspected when it comes to sabbatical year produce, a *nafah*-sieve, a *kevarah*-sieve, a millstone, or an oven; but she may not winnow or grind with her. The wife of a Fellow may lend the wife of an *'am ha'aretz* [a Jew who is not a member of the rabbinic fellowship][23] a *nafah*-sieve, a *kevarah*-sieve, and she may winnow, grind, and sift with her; but, once she pours water [on it], she may not touch it with her, because one may not encourage those who commit sin.
B. And all of these they only said for the sake of peace.
C. One may encourage gentiles on the sabbatical year, but not Jews. And one may inquire about their welfare for the sake of peace.

In ever widening circles, section A delineates relations first between properly and not properly practicing rabbinic Jews, broadening to delineate relations between rabbinic and non-rabbinic Jews. Section C finally widens to delineate relations between Jews and gentiles, all for the sake of peace. I would argue that it is not happenstance that the focal section of the tractate ends by prescribing rulings for the sake of peace between rabbinic and non-rabbinic Jews and between Jews and gentiles, pointing to what I believe is the larger national agenda of this tractate. The tractate opened by delineating what was in and what was out of the land of Israel, and mishnah 5:9 points us to those who are in and out, first of the *ḥavurah,* the rabbinic community, and finally of the people of Israel.

The final mishnah of the tractate (9:10) points us even further to who would seem to be one of the key groups intended here. That passage contains one of the only parallels in all of the Mishnah with the New Testament. When the School of Shammai states that "A man should not divorce his wife unless he found in her a matter of unchastity [*devar 'ervah*], as it is said, 'if he found in her an unchaste matter [*'ervat davar*]' (Deut 24:1)," this directly parallels the position attributed to Jesus in the Sermon on the Mount: "I say to you that whosoever divorces his wife, except for a matter of unchastity [*logou porneias*], makes her an adulteress" (Matt 5:32; cf. Matt 19:9). While the Gospel of Matthew sets this up as being in conflict with Deuteronomy 24:1 (Matt 5:31), the School of Shammai's exegesis in the final mishnah of our tractate demonstrates that this position was as easily derived from the verse as it was in opposition to the verse. Indeed, the Greek *logou porneias* can be read simultaneously as the direct equivalent of both the School of Shammai's Hebrew *devar 'ervah* and the biblical *'ervat davar,* which the latter interprets through the reversal of the construct (if we read according to the printed edition of the Mishnah).[24] In fact, while the parallel in the Gospel of Luke ("Anyone who divorces his wife and marries another commits adultery, and whoever marries a woman divorced from her husband commits adultery")[25] lacks the exception regarding unchastity that connects the ruling both to Deuteronomy 24:1 and the School of Shammai, it also lacks the claim that Jesus stated this in opposition to the biblical law, leaving open the possibility that the law was developed from rather than in opposition to Deuteronomy 24:1. Indeed, even in Mark 10:2–9 (and its parallel in Matt 19:3–9), Jesus only counters the Pharisees' plain reading of Deuteronomy 24:1 by explaining it (midrashically) in light of Genesis 1–2:

> Some Pharisees came, and to test him they asked, "Is it lawful for a man to divorce his wife?" He answered them, "What did Moses command you?" They said, "Moses allowed a man to write a certificate of dismissal and to divorce her." But Jesus said to them, "Because of your hardness of heart he wrote this commandment for you. But from the beginning of creation, 'God made them male and female' (Gen 1:27). 'For this reason a man shall leave his father and mother and be joined to his wife, and the two shall become one flesh' (Gen 2:24). So they are no longer two, but one flesh. Therefore what God has joined together, let no one separate."

Even here in Mark, the Pharisees' position can be read in line with the School of Hillel in Mishnah *Gittin* 9:10 (And the School of Hillel say, "Even if she ruined his dinner, as it says, 'because he found in her an unseemly matter [*devar 'ervah*]'"[26] [Deut 24:1]), and Jesus's position could still be quite close to that of the School of Shammai, making this conflict no greater than the internal rabbinic debate. Thus, in this nascent period for both Christianity and rabbinic Judaism, the two may have converged more than they diverged, at least regarding the laws of divorce and their derivation from the Bible.[27]

CONCLUSION

What I would like to argue from the structure of the Mishnah is that when we read the beginning, middle, and end of the tractate together, the redactor would seem to be claiming that this period of commonality was an earlier period [*ba-rishonah*], before the corrective was needed.[28] When these three key sections of the tractate are brought together, two pictures thus form—one on the individual level and the other on the national. The individual level is a case for divorce (contra the Mishnah's contemporary Christian interlocutors), basing it in the general position that sometimes earlier rulings and transactions—even when made with the best of intentions—are flawed and need to be fixed, with the national level delineating what and who is in and outside of the land and people of Israel. In other words, this tractate would seem to be attempting to establish a parting of the ways from non-rabbinic Jews (Christians among them), arguing that while perhaps these non-rabbinic Jews and their positions were once considered within the boundaries of Israel (as evidenced, for example, by Jesus's position on divorce generally conforming with that of the School of Shammai), a corrective is now needed for the sake of the public welfare: non-rabbinic Jews, including Christians, ought henceforth to be considered outside the bounds of Israel. Interestingly, even by using the dispute on the interpretation of Deuteronomy 24:1 as a way of both engaging non-rabbinic Jews and Christians in the internal dialogue and simultaneously rejecting them as outside the bounds of the community, Mishnah *Gittin* may be only further continuing its uncanny likeness to the Gospels, especially the Gospels of Mark and Matthew. Mishnah *Gittin* 9:10 and Mark 10:2–12 (and its parallel in Matt 19:3–12) use the dispute (between the Schools of Shammai and Hillel and between the Pharisees and Jesus, respectively) on the context in which to read Deuteronomy 24:1 as both the way of including Jesus and the Pharisees/rabbis in the same exegetical world yet simultaneously as the way to reject the Pharisees/Jesus as outside of acceptable exegesis and practice.

In other words, both the Mishnah and the Gospel of Mark are using this exegetical dispute as a way to demarcate their ideological community and to reject the other as outside those bounds.

In 2003, Adam Becker and Annette Yoshiko Reed edited an important book that challenged the long-standing notion that Jews and Christians had "parted ways" by the second century CE. In this iconic volume *The Ways That Never Parted: Jews and Christians in Late Antiquity and the Early Middle Ages,* they and a number of other scholars argue that Jews and Christians continued to interact and intermingle and mutually to affect another long after the supposed "parting of the ways" in the first and second centuries.[29] The present essay does not attempt to answer whether Jews (rabbinic and non-rabbinic, Christian and non-Christian) were interacting with one another *in actu.* How the communities were behaving is beyond the scope of this essay. What this essay does attempt to show is that in the late second and early third centuries, the redactor of Mishnah *Gittin* attempted to use the theme of divorce as a way of mapping out the boundaries of Israel both geographically and metaphorically, the land and the people.

And in this sense, the author should be seen as a parallel to his near contemporary, Justin Martyr, whom Daniel Boyarin has argued was one of the first to use the notion of heresy as a way of marking the ideological boundaries of his community.[30] Boyarin has already argued that the Mishnah ought to be read in light of Justin Martyr's heresiology as itself attempting to mark its ideological territory.[31] I would here like to add Mishnah *Gittin* to the places and ways in which the redactor of the Mishnah is attempting to create those boundaries and separate the rabbinic community from non-rabbinic versions of Judaism. Interestingly, Ishay Rosen-Zvi has argued that Mishnah *Gittin* 9:10 better reflects the ideology of the second century CE than that of the first century, which it claims through its attributions to represent.[32] This modification would make the ideology behind that Mishnah contemporary with Justin Martyr and thus date it to precisely the time in which Boyarin has argued that the notion of heresiology and attempts to bound communities based on ideology were developing among some Christians and rabbinic Jews.

One final comment: we should note that we are interpreting a text about gender (divorce) as addressing the national and the political. Here, gender and the marital couple are being used as a metaphor for the nation, and national boundaries are being drawn through the description of marital boundaries. That is, gender is never merely gender, and the act of defining who is a Jew is never genderless. What are traditionally seen as gender-related topics concurrently transcend gender. That is, in much of rabbinic literature, gender is inextricably part and parcel of rabbinic ideologies and modes of thinking that range far beyond what is traditionally considered a gender-related topic.

NOTES

1. For scholarship on divorce in the Bible, see, e.g., Alexander Rofé, "Divorce in the Hebrew Bible and the Meaning of Sefer Keritut," *Tarbiz* 78 (2009): 437–46 (Hebrew), and Bernard S. Jackson, "The 'Institutions' of Marriage and Divorce in the Hebrew Bible," *Journal of Semitic Studies* 56 (2011): 221–51.

2. Unless otherwise stated, all translations are my own.

3. This is also the interpretation of Alexander Rofé. See Alexander Rofé, *Deuteronomy: Issues and Interpretation* (London: T&T Clark, 2001), 188–89.

4. Other verses also allude to a written bill of divorce being given by the "husband" (albeit metaphorically, see Isa 50:1 and Jer 3:8), but these too do not preclude the possibility that divorce could be initiated in other ways as well, including by oral declaration or even by the wife. Indeed, the divorce in the story of Samson makes no mention of a written bill of divorce (Judg 14–15, though this too is not dispositive). On the question of how to read Deuteronomy 24:1–4, see Rofé, *Deuteronomy,* 188–89, and Arie Toeg, "Does Deuteronomy 24:1–4 Incorporate a General Law of Divorce?" *Dine Israel* 2 (1970): 5–24. In his commentary on Deuteronomy for the *JPS Torah Commentary* (Philadelphia: JPS, 1996), 220, Jeffrey Tigay titles this section "Forbidden Remarriage," explaining that "The laws of divorce are not prescribed in the Torah. They were undoubtedly the subject of customary law. What little we know about them comes from indirect references in prophecies, narrative, and laws like the present one. Talmudic texts subject the present law to a very close reading in order to extract as much guidance about divorce as possible."

5. The words inside the brackets were added above the line.

6. *TAD* B3.3, translated by B. Porten. The complete contract can be found in Bezalel Porten, *The Elephantine Papyri in English* (Leiden and New York: Brill, 1996), 208–11. See also Joseph Fitzmyer, *A Wandering Aramaean: Collected Aramaic Essays* (Atlanta: Scholars Press, 1979), 243–71; Abraham Mann, "The Jewish Marriage Contracts from Elephantine: A Study of Text and Marriage (Egypt, Aramaic)" (Ph.D. diss., New York University, 1985); Yochanan Muffs, *Studies in the Aramaic Legal Papyri from Elephantine* (Leiden and New York: Brill, 2003).

7. On divorce in the Mishnah, see Judith Romney Wegner, *Chattel or Person? The Status of Women in the Mishnah* (New York and Oxford: Oxford University Press, 1992), esp. 45–50; Judith Hauptman, *Rereading the Rabbis: A Woman's Voice* (Boulder, CO: Westview, 1998); Ishay Rosen-Zvi, "Even If One Found a More Beautiful Woman: An Analysis of Grounds for Divorce in Rabbinic Literature," *Jewish Studies, an Internet Journal* 3 (2004): 1–11 (Hebrew).

8. *TAD* A4.7 (Porten, *The Elephantine Papyri in English,* 139–44). On the temple at Elephantine, see Stephen G. Rosenberg, "The Jewish Temple at ELEPHANTINE," *Near Eastern Archaeology* 67:1 (March 2004): 4–13; Gard Granerød, "The Former and the Future Temple of YHW in Elephantine: A Traditio-Historical Case Study of Ancient Near Eastern Antiquarianism," *Zeitschrift Für Die Alttestamentliche Wissenschaft* 127:1 (March 2015): 63–77.

9. Of related interest is Papyrus Se'elim 13, although whether to read the crucial passage in that text as a female-initiated divorce is the subject of much debate. See, e.g., Ada Yardeni and Jonas C. Greenfield, "A Receipt for Ketubba," in *The Jews in the Hellenistic-Roman World: Studies in Memory of Menahem Stern* (ed. Isaiah M. Gafni, Aharon Oppenheimer, and Daniel Schwartz; Jerusalem: Zalman Shazar Center for Jewish History and the Historical Society of Israel, 1996), 197–298 (Hebrew); Hanna M. Cotton and Ada Yardeni, *Aramaic, Hebrew, and Greek Texts from Nahal Hever and Other Sites with an Appendix Containing Alleged Qumran Texts (The Seiyal Collection, II)* (Discoveries in the Judean Desert 27; Oxford, UK: Clarendon, 1997), 65–70; Adiel Schremer, "Papyrus Se'elim 13 and the Question of Divorce Initiated by Women in Ancient Jewish Halakha," *Zion* 63 (1998): 377–90 (Hebrew); Tal Ilan, "Notes and Observations on a Newly Published Divorce Bill from the Judaean Desert," *Harvard Theological Review* 89 (1996): 195–202; Tal Ilan, "The Provocative Approach Once Again: A Response to Adiel Schremer," *Harvard Theological Review* 91 (1998): 203–4.

10. I.e., outside of the land of Israel.

11. R. Meir includes Akko within the land of Israel (Mishnah *Gittin* 1:2).

12. Alternatively, R. Eliezer may be attempting to mark off the western border at Lod (Mishnah *Gittin* 1:1), though why he marks a boundary in that precise location has vexed scholars for centuries.

13. See especially the work of Avraham Walfish, particularly as articulated in his dissertation "The Literary Method of Redaction in the Mishnah Based on Tractate Rosh Hashanah" (Ph.D. diss., Hebrew University of Jerusalem, 2001). See also Avraham Walfish, "Approaching the Text and Approaching God: The Redaction of Mishnah and Tosefta Berakhot," *Jewish Studies* 43 (2005–2006): 21–79. Similarly, I have shown that Massekhet Kallah (albeit a slightly later text) is also carefully structured (David Brodsky, *A Bride without a Blessing: A Study in the Redaction and Content of Massekhet Kallah and Its Gemara* [Tübingen: Mohr Siebeck, 2006], 87–175).

14. All translations from 2 Maccabees are from the New Revised Standard Version.

15. For more on 2 Maccabees and its structure and purpose, see Robert Doran, *Temple Propaganda: The Purpose and Character of 2 Maccabees* (Washington, DC: Catholic Biblical Association of America, 1981); Jan Willem van Henten, *The Maccabean Martyrs as Saviours of the Jewish People: A Study of 2 and 4 Maccabees* (Leiden: Brill, 1997); Jan Willem van Henten, "2 Maccabees as a History of Liberation," in *Jews and Gentiles in the Holy Land in the Days of the Second Temple, the Mishnah and the Talmud: A Collection of Articles* (ed. Menahem Mor, Aharon Oppenheimer, Jack Pastor, and Daniel R. Schwartz;

Jerusalem: Yad Ben-Zvi Press, 2003); 62–86; Daniel R. Schwartz, *2 Maccabees* (Berlin: De Gruyter, 2008).

16. All translations from the book of Jubilees are from O. S. Wintermute, "The Book of Jubilees," in *The Old Testament Pseudepigrapha* (ed. James Charlesworth; New Haven: Yale University Press, 1983), 2.52–142.

17. Indeed, my former colleague Vivian Mayer first pointed out to me several years ago this structure within the Mishnah, and it is to her that I owe the credit for this observation. She pointed it out in particular regarding Mishnah *Shabbat,* among other tractates. In several important works, Avraham Walfish has pointed to aspects of this structure. Thus, he has shown that the first and last chapters of Mishnah *Qiddushin* work together to frame the text (Avraham Walfish, "Creative Redaction and the Power of Desire—A Study of the Redaction of Tractate Qiddushin: Mishnah, Tosefta, and Babylonian Talmud," *Jewish Studies, an Internet Journal* 7 [2008]: 31–79 [Hebrew]). Walfish has also shown that individual chapters evince this envelope style (Walfish, "The Literary Method of Redaction in the Mishnah Based on Tractate Rosh Hashanah").

18. Walfish also sees those mishnayot that ostensibly seem most out of place as of particular importance to the theme and structure of the Mishnah (Walfish, "The Literary Method of Redaction in the Mishnah Based on Tractate Rosh Hashanah").

19. Using the classic rabbinic hermeneutic of *heqesh* [bringing together two texts by means of a common feature].

20. CD 4:20–5:1 (translation from Florentino García Martínez, *The Dead Sea Scrolls Translated* [Leiden: Brill, 1994], 36).

21. Lawrence Schiffman, *Reclaiming the Dead Sea Scrolls: Their True Meaning for Judaism and Christianity* (Philadelphia: Jewish Publication Society, 1994), 130. For a full bibliography of secondary scholarship on this passage broken down by their respective interpretations, see Adiel Schremer, "Qumran Polemic on Marital Law: CD 4:20–5:11 and Its Social Background," in J. M. Baumgarten et al. (eds.), *The Damascus Document: A Centennial of Discovery,* Studies on the Texts of the Desert of Judah 34 (Leiden: Brill, 2000), 148–49nn3–6. More recently, see Vered Noam, "Divorce in Qumran in Light of Early Halakhah," *Journal of Jewish Studies* 56 (2005): 206–23.

22. Mathew 5:32. Much has been made of the word *porneia.* See the scholarship cited in note 27 below.

23. The term *'am ha-'aretz* went through major definitional change from the Mishnah to the Babylonian Talmud and beyond. In later literature, it came to mean someone who was ignorant and uneducated. In the Mishnah, however, it is consistently used to refer to Jews who are not members of the rabbinic fellowship. Thus, they adhere to general Jewish practice but not to the details of the law as delineated by rabbinic law. For this reason, the best definition for this term is "a non-rabbinic Jew."

24. Alternatively, the School of Shammai's exegesis may rest on the emphasis on the word *'ervah,* depending on how we read Manuscript (MS) Kaufmann (and MS Parma).

We should note that MS Kaufmann of the Mishnah has *'ervat davar* [an adulterous matter], with the word *davar* added in the margin, and MS Parma has *'ervah* (without the additional word *davar*), making the parallel to the Sermon on the Mount perhaps slightly less conspicuous. It is not entirely clear what the "original" language was in the Mishnah, but in any case, the School of Shammai in the Mishnah and Jesus in the Sermon on the Mount both hold the same basic legal position, and both use language that is directly reminiscent of Deuteronomy 24:1, suggesting that both derived their rulings from their exegesis of this biblical passage.

25. Luke 16:18. Unless otherwise stated, all translations from the Gospels are from the New Revised Standard Version.

26. MS Kaufmann has the word *'ervah* missing in the body and the word *ervat* added in the margin. MS Parma has the word *davar* without the word *'ervah.* The printed edition has the full phrase, *devar 'ervah.* Following the manuscripts, Rosen-Zvi ("Even If One Found a More Beautiful Woman," 1–2) has argued that the School of Hillel is focusing on the word *davar* [matter] outside of the context of the word *'ervah* [nakedness/sexual sin]. While this may be true, even following the printed edition and the marginal correction in MS Kaufmann, their exegesis may simply settle on how sexual to take the word *'ervah,* with the School of Shammai taking it to imply adultery and the School of Hillel taking it to refer to any unseemly matter.

27. Most New Testament scholars consider this thesis in the Sermon on the Mount to be in opposition to Deuteronomy (as it ostensibly claims). See, for example, Rudolf Bultmann, *History of the Synoptic Tradition* (trans. J. Marsh; Oxford, UK: Blackwell, 1963), 135–36; M. Jack Suggs, *Wisdom, Christology and Law in Matthew's Gospel* (Cambridge: Harvard University Press, 1970), 110–15; Joachim Jeremias, *New Testament Theology* (trans. J. Bowden; New York: Scribner, 1971), 1:251ff.; Robert Guelich, "The Antitheses of Matt 5:21–48: Traditional and/or Redactional?," *New Testament Studies* 22 (1976): 444–57; John P. Meier, *Law and History in Matthew's Gospel: A Redactional Study of Mt. 5:17–48* (Rome: Biblical Institute Press, 1976), 12–61. But note that Asher Finkel sees it as exegetically derived from Deuteronomy 24:1 (Asher Finkel, *The Pharisees and the Teacher of Nazareth: A Study of Their Background, Their Halachic and Midrashic Teachings, the Similarities and Differences* [Leiden: Brill, 1974], 164). The evidence from the Mishnah (coupled with its absence in Luke) suggests the distinct possibility that this opposition was a later addition to the Matthean tradition (i.e., that it is redactional rather than traditional, to put it in terms of the scholarly literature on the topic). In any case, the parallel with the position of the School of Shammai is striking, and I believe that the Mishnah is consciously referencing the Gospels here. The bibliography on the topic of divorce in the New Testament (including how to understand the key word *porneia*) is too vast to list here. For a few key articles, see, e.g., Thomas V. Fleming, "Christ and Divorce," *Theological Studies* 124 (1963): 106–20; David R. Catchpole, "The Synoptic Divorce Material as a Traditio-Historical Problem," *Bulletin of the John Rylands Library* 57 (1974): 92–127; Joseph Fitzmyer, "Matthean Divorce Texts and Some New Palestinian Evidence," *Theological Studies* 37 (1976): 197–226; Bruce Vawter, "Divorce

and the New Testament," *Catholic Biblical Quarterly* 39 (1977): 528–42; Evald Lövestam, "Divorce and Remarriage in the New Testament," *Journal of Late Antiquity* 4 (1981): 47–65.

28. For more on the relationship between the Sermon on the Mount and Mishnah *Gittin* 9:10, see Rosen-Zvi, "Even If One Found a More Beautiful Woman"; Phillip Sigal, *Halakah of Jesus of Nazareth According to the Gospel of Matthew* (Atlanta: Society of Biblical Literature, 2007), 105–43; Reinhard Neudecker, "Marriage and Divorce: The Pharisees and Jesus in the Light of Early Rabbinic Literature," *Sacra Scripta* 11 (2013): 262–86; Eben Scheffler, "(The Markan and Matthean) Jesus' Appropriation and Criticism of the Torah: The Question of Divorce," *Hervormde Teologiese Studies* 67:1 (March 2011): 1–6.

29. Adam Becker and Annette Yoshiko Reed, eds., *The Ways That Never Parted: Jews and Christians in Late Antiquity and the Early Middle Ages* (Tübingen: Mohr Siebeck, 2003); see especially the introduction by Becker and Reed.

30. Daniel Boyarin, *Border-Lines: The Partition of Judeo-Christianity* (Philadelphia: University of Pennsylvania Press, 2004), 37–73.

31. Ibid., 74–86.

32. Rosen-Zvi, "Even If One Found a More Beautiful Woman."

All in the Family: Ancient Israelite and Judahite Families in Context

Cynthia Shafer-Elliott

INTRODUCTION

Today we often hear about the decline of the modern family. Ask any politician and he or she will provide you with statistics on divorce, abuse, consumerism, and lack of parental involvement—just to name a few. However, when we think of family, typically several images come to mind: we think of the members of our own family, family meals and get-togethers, and the occasional conflicts that arise at them. We all have stories we could tell about the last family holiday or dinner that ended in disaster, but we also think about those moments when joy and sorrow are shared among related people who care about each other.

Many disciplines study the family, and I am pleased to say that within the fields of biblical studies and archaeology, the family has become a subject of research. I have long been interested in the study of ancient Israelite and Judahite families,[1] but my academic curiosity about the subject grew with the expansion of my own family. I found that considering the ancient Israelite family not only aids in our understanding of ancient Israel and Judah but also helps us appreciate our own family and its traditions more fully. The scope of this essay is not to argue for or against any particular aspect of the ancient family; rather, in this essay I describe the context of the ancient Israelite and Judahite family. More specifically, I address who was considered part of the family, how they lived, and what their daily lives consisted of. The sources used for this discussion include textual descriptions from the Hebrew Bible and archaeological remains viewed through the lens of household archaeology.[2]

DEFINING THE ANCIENT ISRAELITE FAMILY

Before a discussion of who was part of the ancient Israelite and Judahite family can occur, the terminology used must be clarified. Within the Hebrew Bible, there are several terms that denote various degrees of "family." The largest social group was the tribe [*shebet, matte*], while the smallest social group was the *bayit 'ab* or *bayit 'em,* translated as "house of the father" or "house of the mother." The middle social group was the *mishpachah,* and this term is used in a variety of ways: in reference to nations or large social groups (e.g., Gen 10:5, 32; 12:3; Amos 3:2), as species of animals (Gen 8:19), and of Israel as a whole (Amos 3:1), or separately as the northern kingdom of Israel and the southern kingdom of Judah (Jer 33:24). However, most of the occurrences of *mishpachah* within the Hebrew Bible indicate a clan or extended family (Exod 6:14, 25; Num 1:2).[3] J. Blenkinsopp further defines *mishpachah* as "a group of individual families or households forming a major unit of the tribe and claiming common, unilineal descent from a real or fictitious ancestor."[4] Rarely was a person considered an individual; rather, a person was considered in light of who he or she was connected to—the group the person was a part of: the person's *bayit 'ab* [or immediate family], *mishpachah* [extended family or clan], and *shebet* [or tribe].

A second clarification regarding families in ancient Israel and Judah also needs to be made. It is often thought that a household solely consists of immediate family members who live together; however, anthropologists and sociologists who study families in various geographical locations and chronological periods make a distinction between family and household. A family is defined by kinship, descent, and marriage, while a household is defined by coresidence and/or the sharing of domestic functions.[5] In other words, a family is a group of people who are related to each other either biologically or through marriage, but they may or may not live together. A household is a group of people who typically live and/or work together but may or may not be related. For instance, an ancient Israelite household could include immediate and extended family members but also nonrelated members such as slaves, guests, concubines, or hired workers. These same members of the household could live together in the same house or compound, while others (such as a hired worker) could live elsewhere but come to the household land to work.[6]

Ancient Israel and Judah practiced a social residence pattern that anthropologists refer to as "patrilocal." Patrilocal residence is when a married couple resides with or near the husband's parents or household. In other words, a son remains in his father's household [*bayit 'ab*] after reaching maturity and brings his wife to live with his family after marriage. Conversely, when a daughter marries she leaves her father's house and resides within the household of her husband's father or household. Most Israelite marriages were endogamous, which is the custom of marrying only within the limits of a local community, clan, or tribe, as opposed to exogamy, which is the custom of marrying outside the limits.[7]

The nucleus of the Israelite family, the *bayit 'ab,* could therefore be defined as a household, since it included related and nonrelated members who worked together and, more than likely, lived together. The *mishpachah* [clan] would have consisted of several of these households living within close proximity to each other, often forming their own village. Several clans that claimed a common ancestor made up a tribe and lived within the boundaries of their tribe's geographical territory. An example of an Israelite household can be found in Judges 17–21, where the household of Micah the Ephraimite is mentioned. Within this narrative, Micah is the patriarch of the household that includes his widowed mother, his sons, and more than likely their families (17:2, 18:22). The household expands when Micah hires a young Levite to serve as the household priest (17:10–12). The members of the household lived in several dwellings surrounded by a boundary wall (18:14–16, 22). This narrative helps illustrate the Israelite and Judahite household and its members and also introduces the second aspect of the household—the physical house itself.

THE ISRAELITE HOUSE

At present, who was part of the Israelite/Judahite household has been established, yet a description of what the houses may have looked like is just as important to include when attempting to understand the ancient family. Using archaeology to study the ancient household has become its own specialization called "household archaeology." Even though the household is the smallest and most common of the social groups, it is also the most plentiful. There are three main aspects of the household to study: (1) the material aspect, which consists of the dwelling, secondary buildings and features, areas where household activities took place, and its possessions; (2) the social aspect, meaning the members of the household and their relationship to each other; and (3) the behavioral aspect, which looks at the activities the household members performed.[8] Taking these aspects into consideration, household archaeology can be characterized as the archaeological study of a household's buildings, possessions, and members and the activities they engaged in. Through this investigation information regarding the activities and behaviors of the members of the household can be better understood, providing a more comprehensive picture of the daily life of the ancient Israelite and Judahite family.[9] While the social aspect of the household was discussed above, the material aspect of the physicality of the house needs to be addressed.

The Israelite/Judahite house itself has been extensively researched and has no shortage of analysis. In the 1970s archaeologists began to notice that the excavated houses from Israel's Iron Age (ca. 1200–586 BCE; i.e., the time of Israelite and Judahite kings) had a similar plan and common features. The typical house had two floors and a flat roof. The first floor consisted of a back broad room with one to three (oftentimes three) rooms running perpendicular to it. The first floor had wood or stone pillars supporting the second floor; these pillars often had short boundary walls between them to help segregate space. Houses were small but still ranged in size depending on whether the house was in an urban or rural environment.[10] For this reason, it is best to think of the Israelite house as being multifunctional, with several household chores and activities taking place in the limited space available. The first floor was used for a variety of domestic activities, including storage, production (such as pottery making), food preparation and consumption, and religious ritual. The second floor was the family's sleeping quarters and could also have been used for some light domestic activities, such as weaving. The flat roof of the house also served as a space in which to conduct production chores, such as drying flax (Josh 2:6), or for sleeping in the hot summer months.

What to call these houses is a matter of some debate. Some scholars call them "the four-room house" because the floor plan typically includes four rooms; other scholars call them "pillar houses," since most of them have pillars, while still others call them "the Israelite house." It must be said, however, that many of these houses had more or less than four rooms, and some had no pillars (at least not found); similarly, it is difficult to say with certainty if these houses were used only by the Israelites. What is known is that this style of house was the popular form in ancient Israel/Judah during the Iron Age; thus, perhaps it is best to call it the Iron Age house until proven otherwise.[11]

Regardless of what it is called, the basic features of the house during the Iron Age are consistent and would include space to conduct a variety of household activities. Household space on the bottom floor was multifunctional, with several household chores taking place in the limited space available. Some of the common features of an Iron Age house include stone floors, storage space, ovens, and courtyards. In many Iron Age houses, the perpendicular side room closest to the front door contained a stone floor. It has been argued that the location coupled with the stone flooring suggests that this is where some of the smaller herd animals, such as sheep and goats, were stabled. The stone floor would have withstood the heavy trampling of animal hooves and would also allow for easier cleanup.[12] Households were self-sufficient and needed space to store their grain, wine, and other household goods. When Iron Age houses are excavated, large concentrations of storage jars are often found in the other side room and/or the back broad room.[13] Ovens used for cooking and baking, called *tabun* or *tannur,* are often found in the central living space and in the outside courtyard.[14] It seems that most Iron Age houses had an open area or courtyard in front of the house that was used as a communal space to conduct household chores, especially in the hot summer months.

DAILY LIFE OF THE ANCIENT ISRAELITE AND JUDAHITE FAMILY

The final aspect of studying households is the behavioral aspect, which looks at the activities the household performed. The average ancient Israelite/Judahite household was the basic economic unit; whether a family lived in the city or the country, Israel and Judah consisted of agrarian communities where the household was the nucleus of everyday life. The household economy evolved from a simple subsistence level in the early Iron Age (ca. 1200–1000 BCE) to a more complex system under the monarchy in the Iron II period (ca. 1000–586 BCE). In the early Iron Age, Israel's household economics were agrarian and pastoral in nature and were generally free from taxation by a dominating class. However, with the establishment and evolution of the monarchy in the second Iron Age, the economics of the Israelite household changed as well. The Israelite household was still predominantly agrarian and pastoral, but the monarchy extracted surplus from households through taxation, unpaid labor, interest on debt, and rental fees.[15]

The daily concern of most ancient people was survival, and ancient Israel/Judah was no different. Subsistence economies rarely have the luxury of gender roles. Gender roles refer to the socially constructed roles, behaviors, activities, and attributes that a given society considers appropriate for men and women.[16] Each member of the ancient Israelite/Judahite household was expected to participate in their survival, regardless of sex, age, or other differentials. C. Meyers writes that the survival of any group is dependent upon three factors: procreation, protection, and production. The fertility of both the household's members and its land made the difference as to whether or not that household survived. The procreation factor was predominated by female biological factors, such as menstruation, pregnancy, birth, lactation, and weaning. Consequently, the procreation factor often fell under the female domain and dictated that her daily household activities oftentimes occurred within or near the dwelling. Similarly, the protection factor was managed by the household males, more often the patriarch of the household whose role it was to protect the members of the household, especially the females and children.[17] Production was the factor that certainly joined the household together in its daily activities, since all members of the household were required to participate. Production involved agriculture, animal husbandry, and the making of various goods, such as pottery. Certain times of year, such as planting and harvest, required that all able members of the household contribute. With that said, during times of war the women of the household were required to bear more of the production responsibilities.[18]

ROLES OF THE HOUSEHOLD MEMBERS

The ancient Israelite/Judahite household was a subsistence economy; hence, every member of it was important and vital to its survival. While this type of economy may not have had so-called gender roles, certain household members had more specific roles to perform: in particular, the role of the patriarch and matriarch, who possessed the most power and authority within the household. A brief look at these two important roles will further enhance our understanding of the Israelite/Judahite family and household.

THE PATRIARCH

The patriarch was the protector of the household. Employment of his authority included how the household would farm and herd and the power over life and death within the household. Even though the patriarch had this seemingly massive amount of power, his authority was not absolute; his authority was primarily over his wives, sons, and daughters. Issues of life and death would include officially adopting a baby into the household when it was born and being the household judge in cases of dishonor and disobedience. For instance, the commandment to "honor your father and mother" (Exod 20:12) may seem like a quaint rule to teach children, but in reality the commandment held more weight for adult children living within their household *bayit 'ab.* Children, even adult children and their families, were expected to obey their patriarch and matriarch by participating in the farming and herding of the household property and by having children. If the child, even as an adult, is unwilling to herd and farm as the patriarch dictates, it is the father's role to decide the outcome.[19]

Part of the patriarch's role of protector over his children included determining when they were eligible for marriage. Marriage in ancient Israel and Judah was more about political and economic issues and less about romance. In fact, V. Matthews and D. Benjamin describe marriage as

> a delicately negotiated covenant sealing a significant political or economic contract [that] was designed to bring together two households that were willing to exchange substantial goods and services with each other over a significant period of time. Marriage was more a matter of business than pleasure.[20]

When the patriarch decided that it was time for his daughter to marry (most likely soon after puberty), an arrangement was made typically within the household's clan [*mishpachah*] or tribe [*shevet*]. These types of endogamous marriages were intended to keep property within the clan or tribe. Given that ancient Israel and Judah were patrilocal societies, marriage of a daughter signified the loss of a contributing member of the household, which impacted its economy greatly. Consequently, a *mohar,* or a betrothal gift in the form of money, goods, land, or service from the groom's *bayit 'ab,* was given to the bride's *bayit 'ab* (Gen 34:8–17, Exod 22:16). Examples of bridal betrothal gifts in the Hebrew Bible can be found in the narratives of Dinah and Shechem in Genesis 34:12, Michel and David in 1 Samuel 18:25, and Gomer and Hosea in Hosea 3:2. Two of the three narratives have the patriarch requesting the betrothal gift as a service in the form of incapacitating the enemy (Dinah/Shechem and Michel/David), but the third narrative in Hosea provides a more realistic gift in that Hosea paid fifteen shekels of silver, a homer of barley, and a measure of wine (Hos 3:2).[21] The bride's household also gave a *shillukhim,* translated as a dowry or betrothal gift to the household of the groom, also in the form of money, goods, or transferable land (1 Kgs 9:16). However, the *shillukhim* was also seen as a way to provide security for the bride, who in theory maintained possession of it.[22]

THE MATRIARCH

The matriarch also possessed a great deal of authority within the household. A large aspect of production includes the preparation of food, which took place in the dwelling or its courtyard. As was mentioned earlier, because of women's reproductive roles it was often necessary for them to conduct household chores closer to the dwelling. One of the more important tasks conducted at the dwelling included the preparation of food and, consequently, was primarily under female control.

When Iron Age houses are excavated, artifacts such as cooking ovens, pots, grinding stones and slabs, pestles and mortars, bowls, and storage jars are found within the dwelling and its courtyard. The triad of the Israelite diet included olives, grapes, and cereals. Olive oil was essential in cooking and the lighting of lamps. Grapes were dried but, more important, were made into wine. Since fermented beverages were safer to drink than stagnant water, wine was an imperative foodstuff. However, it was the cultivation of cereals that became the most important part of the Israelite diet, so much so that the Hebrew word for bread, *lechem,* is synonymous with food. Cereals were used for a morning porridge or daily bread. Processing grain into an edible form involved a complex chain of activities: soaking, milling, and grinding grain into flour that would be made into dough—a process that would occupy at least two hours per day. Ovens are often found in a centralized location, which would enable women to conduct other household chores and the sharing of baking resources, such as the oven itself and dung used for fuel. A centralized location and the sharing of ovens also encouraged social relationships and cohesion among the group (Lev 26:26).[23]

The matriarch was in essence the manager of the household. She controlled the operations of the household, including the manufacture of such goods as soap, pottery, baskets, cloth, and tools. One of her most important tasks as the household manager was the authority over one of the major aspects of production: the preparation, storage, distribution, and consumption of food. It was the matriarch who dictated what and how much produce was to be prepared as a meal or prepared into and stored as other foodstuffs, such as beer, wine, oil, parched grain, and dried fruit. Who was going to perform these tasks and when were also under the command of the matriarch. In essence, it was she who decided who ate, when, what, and how much—the authority over the household food contained much power. The capable wife in Proverbs 31 sings the praises of the matriarch as the manager of the household:

> She is like the ships of the merchant, she brings her food from far away. She rises while it is still night and provides food for her household and tasks for her servant girls. . . . She looks well to the ways of her household and does not eat the bread of idleness. (Prov 31:14–15, 27)

Indeed, the matriarch's role as the manager was essential to the survival of her household and would have required exceptional skill, expertise, and diplomacy, resulting in a significant amount of household power and prestige.[24]

SUMMARY

This essay discussed the context of the ancient Israelite and Judahite family; more specifically, it addressed who was considered part of the Israelite family, how they lived, and what their daily lives consisted of. The study of the material, social, and behavioral aspects of an ancient household clarified what the daily lives of the average ancient Israelite/Judahite man, woman, and child would have looked like during Israel's Iron Age. Sources such as the Hebrew Bible and archaeological remains helped visualize the form and function of the household. To truly understand ancient Israel and Judah better, we must shift our attention away from what Carol Meyers calls "places of prestige," meaning the palaces, temples, and battlefields that hardly represent what daily life would have included for the average Israelite and Judahite; rather, our attention should shift to focus on the stage where daily life occurred—the home.[25] Could we even be so bold as to say that the concept of household and family meant more to the ancient Israelites than we could ever imagine? Indeed, every member of the household was imperative to its survival regardless of sex, age, or any other differential; the family and its members were highly valued. In today's world, where the importance of family is often overlooked or dismissed, perhaps we can look to the Israelite and Judahite family to remind us of the value and significance of family.

NOTES

1. When discussing ancient and biblical Israel, it is appropriate to mention both Israel and Judah, since both were official kingdoms starting ca. 922 BCE.

2. All passages from the Hebrew Bible are taken from the New Revised Standard Version.

3. Joseph Blenkinsopp, "The Family in First Temple Israel," in *Families in Ancient Israel* (ed. L. Perdue, J. Blenkinsopp, J. J. Collins, and C. Meyers; The Family, Religion, and Culture Series; Louisville: Westminster John Knox Press, 1997), 49–50.

4. Blenkinsopp, "The Family in First Temple Israel," 50.

5. Jack Goody, "Fission of Domestic Groups among the LoDagaba in the Developmental Cycle in Domestic Groups," in *The Developmental Cycle in Domestic Groups* (ed. J. Goody; Cambridge, Cambridge University Press, 1958), 53–91.

6. Cynthia Shafer-Elliott, *Food in Ancient Judah: Domestic Cooking in the Time of the Hebrew Bible* (Oxford, UK: Routledge, 2014), 12–14.

7. "Endogamy" and "Exogamy," Oxford Dictionary Online, http://www.oxforddictionaries.com/us/definition/american_english.

8. Richard R. Wilk and William L. Rathje, "Household Archaeology," *American Behavioral Scientist* 25 (1982): 617–39.

9. Shafer-Elliott, *Food in Ancient Judah,* 14.

10. Four houses the author analyzed measured 10.5 x 12.9 meter, 10 x 8 meters, 7.5 x 6.75 meters, 9 x 9 meters. See Shafter-Elliott, *Food in Ancient Judah,* 109.

11. For a sample of work on the origin, form, and function of the Israelite house, see Yigal Shiloh, "The Four-Room House: Its Situation and Function in the Israelite City," *Israel Exploration Journal* 20 (1970): 180–90; Yigal Shiloh, "Elements in the Development of Town Planning in the Israelite City," *Israel Exploration Journal* 28 (1978): 36–51; Yigal Shiloh, "The Casemate Wall, the Four-Room House, and Early Planning in the Israelite City," *BASOR* 268 (1987): 2–15; Lawrence E. Stager, "The Archaeology of the Family in Ancient Israel," *Bulletin for the American Schools of Oriental Research* 260 (1985): 1–35; Israel Finkelstein, *The Archaeology of the Israelite Settlement* (Jerusalem: Israel Exploration Society, 1988); Avraham Faust, *Israel's Ethnogenesis: Settlement, Interactions, Expansion, and Resistance* (London: Equinox, 2006); Frank Braemer, *L'architecture domestique du Levant à l'Age du Fer* (Paris: Editions Recherché sur les civilisations, 1982); J. David Schloen, *The House of the Father as Fact and Symbol: Patrimonialism in Ugarit and the Ancient Near East* (Studies in the Archaeology and History of the Levant 2; Winona Lake: Eisenbrauns, 2001); James Hardin, *Households and the Use of Domestic Space at Iron II Tell Halif: An Archaeology of Destruction* (Reports of the Lahav Research Project at Tell Halif, Israel Series 2; Winona Lake: Eisenbrauns, 2010); Ehud Netzer, "Domestic Architecture in the Iron Age," in *The Architecture of Ancient Israel: From Prehistoric to the Persian Periods* (ed. A. Kempinski and R. Reich; Jerusalem: Israel Exploration Society, 1992), 193–201.

12. Hardin, *Households and the Use of Domestic Space,* 93, 263; Stager, "The Archaeology of the Family in Ancient Israel," 13.

13. See Shafer-Elliott, *Food in Ancient Judah,* chap. 3.

14. For a fuller discussion on cooking ovens, see Shafer-Elliott, *Food in Ancient Judah;* Alison Mcquitty, "An Ethnographic and Archaeological Study of Clay Ovens in Jordan," *Annual of the Department of Antiquities Amman, Jordan* 28 (1984): 259–67; Alison McQuitty, "Ovens in Town and Country," *Berytus* 39 (1994): 53–76; Shira Gur-Arieh et al., "The Taphonomy and Preservation of Wood and Dung Ashes Found in Archaeological Cooking Installations: Case Studies from Iron Age Israel," *Journal of Archaeological Science* 46 (2014): 50–67.

15. Norman K. Gottwald, "Social Class as an Analytic and Hermeneutical Category in Biblical Studies," *Journal of Biblical Literature* 112:1 (1993): 6–8; Cynthia Shafer-Elliott, "Economics—Hebrew Bible," in the *Oxford Encyclopedia of the Bible and Gender Studies* (ed. Julia M. O'Brien; New York: Oxford University Press, 2015), 119–25.

16. Definition of gender roles as in "Gender, Women, and Health," World Health Organization, http://www.who.int/gender/whatisgender/en/.

17. Victor H. Matthews and Don C. Benjamin, *Social World of Ancient Israel: 1250–587 BCE* (Grand Rapids: Baker Academic, 1993), 12.

18. Carol Meyers, "Procreation, Production, and Protection: Male-Female Balance in Early Israel," *Journal of the American Academy of Religion* 51:4 (December 1983): 574–76.

19. Matthews and Benjamin, *Social World of Ancient Israel,* 9–11.

20. Ibid., 13.

21. Ibid., 17; Blenkinsopp, "The Family in First Temple Israel," 60.

22. Elaine Goodfriend, "Mishpatim: Rules for Life in a Covenant Community," in *The Torah: A Women's Commentary* (ed. T. Cohen Eskenazi; New York: WRJ Press, 2008), 427–43; Drorah O'Donnell-Setel, "Exodus," in *The Women's Bible Commentary* (ed. C. A. Newsome and S. H. Ringe; Louisville: Westminster John Knox Press, 1992), 26–35; Tikva Frymer-Kensky, "Virginity in the Bible," in *Gender and Law in the Hebrew Bible and the Ancient Near East* (ed. V. H. Matthews, B. M. Levinson, and T. Frymer-Kensky; *Journal for the Study of the Old Testament Supplement Series* 262; Sheffield: Sheffield Academic Press, 1998), 79–96.

23. Aubrey Baadsgaard, "A Taste of Women's Sociality: Cooking as Cooperative Labor in Iron Age Syro-Palestine," in *The World of Women in the Ancient and Classical Near East* (ed. B. Alpert-Nakhai; Newcastle upon Tyne: Cambridge Scholars, 2008), 13–44, esp. 42; Jennie R. Ebeling, *Women's Lives in Biblical Times* (London: T&T Clark, 2010), 32–33; Carol Meyers, "Engendering Syro-Palestinian Archaeology: Reasons and Resources," *Near Eastern Archaeology* 66:4 (2003): 185–97; Carol Meyers, "The Family in Early Israel," in *Families in Ancient Israel* (ed. L. G. Perdue, J. Blenkinsopp, J. J. Collins, and C. Meyers; Family, Religion, and Culture Series; Louisville: Westminster John Knox Press, 1997), 25; Shafer-Elliott, "Economics and Gender—Hebrew Bible," 119–25.

24. For more on ancient Israelite women, see Ebeling, *Women's Lives in Biblical Times;* Meyers, "Procreation, Production, and Protection," 569–93; Carol Meyers, *Discovering Eve: Ancient Israelite Women in Context* (Oxford: Oxford University Press, 1988); Meyers, "The Family in Early Israel," 1–47; Carol Meyers, *Rediscovering Eve: Ancient Israelite Women in Context* (Oxford: Oxford University Press, 2013).

25. Meyers, *Discovering Eve;* Meyera, "The Family in Early Israel"; Meyers, *Rediscovering Eve.*

Family Values and Biblical Courtship and Marriage: Spanning the Time Barrier

Charles David Isbell

INTRODUCTION

The importance of family[1] within the broader community of Judaism has its roots in some of the most significant narratives of the Hebrew Bible, and in each case marriage is portrayed as the cornerstone of the biblical family. And marriage is very much in the news these days. From one end of the political spectrum comes an impassioned plea for the legalization of gay marriage, which, we are repeatedly assured, is the only way to provide full enfranchisement to the homosexual segment of our population and thus a moral and legal imperative.[2]

Those at the opposite end of this spectrum warn that such a legal move is certain to usher in the apocalypse. Especially significant is the accompanying view that this particular apocalypse could easily be avoided by the administration of a few doses of "reparative therapy."[3] Equally prominent at the apocalypse-fearing end of the religio-socio-political spectrum, and a close ally of the opposition to homosexual marriage, is the simplistic position of those who call for a return to biblical marriage, which, we are assured with deadly fervor, is among "the fundamental unchanging truths that have been ordained by God in the Bible"[4]—and thus another of those monolithic and immutable scriptural principles upon which Christian America was founded.

Were they not so morbidly serious, we might be tempted to chuckle at our fundamentalist friends when they pound on the Bible regarding marriage. But at the least, these proponents of biblical marriage should be required to spell out exactly what parts of marriage they intend to import from the world of the Bible into modern society. And since they insist on being fully dedicated to their proposal, we should be allowed to ask some basic questions, beginning with this one: If biblical marriage is the goal, should biblical customs of courtship also be followed?

BIBLICAL COURTSHIP CUSTOMS

Do proponents of biblical marriage support the courtship method used to find a wife for Isaac?[5] His father dispatched to a friendly tribe in the home country a trusted emissary at the head of a ten-camel cavalcade laden with gold, an ample supply of those alluring and ever-popular nose rings, and other visible symbols of the family's great wealth. Launching his search at a popular drinking establishment, the faithful servant quickly located an appropriately beautiful and healthy female, whom he showered with expensive gifts and effusive compliments before cleverly finagling an invitation to spend the night at her family home. The vulgar show of wealth proved to be highly effective, for when the young lady returned home and her older brother "spied the expensive nose ring and the bracelets on the arms of his sister" (Gen 24:30), he rushed back to the oasis to find the emissary. There he not only repeated the invitation of his sister to spend the night with the family but also invited the man to supper with warm and friendly words: "Come in, O blessed of the LORD. Why are you standing outside? I have already prepared the house [for you], and even a place for your camels" (24:31).

The biblical narrative clearly implies that Laban lacked adequate time to complete a full background investigation or even a cursory credit check on Isaac, and this fact leads Rashi to explain that the phrase "All the good stuff of his master in his hand" (Gen 24:10) refers to a written document[6] from Abraham signing over "all his possessions to Isaac, so that they should be eager [*yiqpətzu*] to send their daughter to him." This accords well with the statement later in the narrative that the servant, seated in the family home of Nahor, described the wealth of Abraham in detail but assured his hosts that "he [Abraham] has given him [Isaac] everything he owns" (24:36).[7] Clearly, with or without the midrashic explanation of Rashi, the force of the story is that the opportunity to marry his sister to an ostentatiously wealthy suitor, even a man whom no one in the country had ever seen, provided adequate biblical grounds for big brother Laban.

Perhaps modern marriage should begin with the type of biblical courtship illustrated by the actions of Jacob and Moses. Both of these men fled from the land of their birth, one to escape a murderous twin brother (Gen 27:41) and the other to avoid prosecution as a murderer (Exod 2:15). Arriving in a foreign land, both men followed the biblical precedent set by the emissary of Abraham and headed immediately to the local watering hole to meet chicks.

Jacob moved to the head of the eligible bachelor line, waited for the appropriate moment, and showed off his physical prowess by rolling a huge stone from the entrance to the communal well of water (Gen 29:10). This proved to be precisely the kind of testosterone exhibition guaranteed to impress the lovely Rachel and intimidate all other potential suitors.

Moses, dressed as an Egyptian (Exod 2:19) rather than a fleeing felon or a lowly Hebrew slave, faced down the local tough guys who regularly stole water from hapless female shepherdesses (2:17) in his own display of masculinity. Two significant aspects of Mosaic courtship stand out. Not only did he present himself as an Egyptian aristocrat who would obviously be considered wealthy, but he also combined his appearance of wealth with a display of the kind of physical prowess that had proved so successful for Jacob.

Soon after their showy displays, Jacob and Moses each married the prettiest girl in town, and each man took a job with his new father-in-law. In fact, as a reward for his faithful service in the family business, Jacob was awarded two wives!

Maybe the biblical courtship custom our conservative friends are pushing is chronicled in the narrative about the marriage of Dinah to the son of the regional prince, Ḥamor (Gen 34). After he had raped her, Shechem now wanted to marry Dinah (34:4),[8] and we can only hope that this is one biblical custom that modern proponents of biblical marriage will have difficulty in reviving. Swayed in part by the promise of an unusually hefty bridal price (34:12), the brothers of Dinah agreed to the marriage but insisted that not only the prospective bridegroom but also every other male in the city of Shechem be circumcised. They then waited until the men of the town were recovering from surgery and slaughtered them all (34:25). They even killed the new groom and his father before bringing their sister back to the family home, of course without returning the bridal price (34:25–26)! Finally, they seized the material wealth, the children, and the wives of the slaughtered males (34:29).[9]

Perhaps the biblical template for courtship leading to marriage is to be found in the example of Ruth and Boaz. Here, we recall, a saucy widow tarted herself up a bit and hied off to waylay the slightly inebriated Boaz in the middle of the night, boldly uncovering his genitals ("feet") before hopping into bed with him in what was clearly an audacious marriage proposal from a determined young lady to the wealthiest bachelor in town.[10] This was not only sex before marriage but sex employed to induce marriage. What could be more biblical?

Yet another biblical courtship custom appears in the account of the union between Michal and David. According to the narrative recounted in 1 Samuel 18:20–29, the prospective father-in-law (King Saul) was not happy with the idea of having David in the family. So, he proposed that the young suitor bring one hundred Philistine foreskins in place of a dowry, certain that the attempt would result in the death of David (18:25c). David, perhaps aware that Saul would have preferred a nice Jewish doctor instead of a humble shepherd for his daughter (18:23), presented his future father-in-law with double the requested number of Philistine foreskins (two hundred instead of merely one hundred), thereby earning his way into the royal family (18:27).[11]

BIBLICAL MARRIAGE: ROMANTIC LOVE OR JUST GOOD BUSINESS?

Surely the plea for biblical marriage cannot be referring to Abraham, the righteous father of us all. We need not tarry over the open marriage arrangement he enjoyed with Sarah that allowed him to impregnate her female slave Hagar.[12] But we cannot ignore his polygamy in the context of the discussion about current marriage customs. I refer here to the marriage of Abraham and Keturah, the wife who produced six sons with Abraham (Gen 25:2). Since Abraham, falling down laughing, had noted forty years earlier that he was too old to sire children (Gen 17:17), since the discovery of Viagra was still some years in the future, and since the notation of the marriage to Keturah in Genesis 25:1 simply notes that "Abraham took another wife" without specifying a time frame, biblical scholar Nahum Sarna believed that the account of his marriage with Keturah did not "relate to a time subsequent to Sarah's death and Isaac's marriage, but to many years before."[13] This would be consistent with the rabbinic dictum that *'eyn mûqdam ûmə'ûḥar ba-tôrah* [there is no early or late in the Torah]—that is, that the narratives of the Torah are not always in strict chronological sequence. But it also makes Abraham the husband of two women at the same time and the father of children by both wives as well as one slave girl.[14]

These narratives about some of our most famous ancestors, especially the report of the marriage between Abraham and Keturah, require that we examine the legitimate purposes of marriage in biblical times. Only then can we ask whether any of those purposes still obtain in the twenty-first century.

We note first that romantic love, as popularly understood in the modern world, plays virtually no role in the biblical institution of marriage.[15] Proposals did not occur in the moonlight between two young people who were scarcely mature enough to distinguish the difference between being in love and being in heat. Most frequently, they were arranged as a business or political transaction between the heads of two families that shared mutual interests, customs, and culture.

The fact that the name of Abraham's second wife is linked with the word for "spices" [*kətoret*] lends plausibility to the idea that the Keturah tribes were involved in the production, shipment, and distribution of spices, a precious commodity and a valuable source of income. Of the six Keturah tribal leaders, three bear names well known from nonbiblical sources and are associated with oases along the international trade routes.[16] Thus, the linkage of Abraham and Keturah secured a vital connection between the Abraham tribes and other important members of the economic cartel in the region.

This leads to a second observation about the biblical concept of marriage. Not only does the Torah regularly describe an economic and political linkage between two groups of people friendly to each other, but such alliances are also often described in familial terms "arranged in a genealogical pattern."[17] That is, terms such as "brother," "son," "father," "sister," etc., often referred to the social standing of the persons described rather than simply to the biological cellular unit. Thus "brothers" or "sisters" were social equals, "sons" or "daughters" ranked below "fathers" or "mothers," and so forth. Clearly the relationship between Abraham and Keturah is better understood as an economic alliance between the "family" of Abraham and at least six tribal groups affiliated with Keturah rather than as a marriage between one male and one female.[18]

Third, apart from the existence of an economic, military, or social alliance between groups of people with mutual interests, the primary purpose of marriage was the production of offspring. And this is indicated in multiple ways, not least of which is the biblical conception of feminine beauty. Rivkah is a clear example. Not only did she come from an acceptable family headed by a "brother" of Abraham (Gen 24: 15), but her physical ability to draw enough water to satisfy ten thirsty camels that had just completed a long journey leads directly to the biblical description of her as "beautiful." This was no mere slip of a lass, no delicate flower of femininity, but a woman hardy and healthy enough to do strenuous physical labor and above all to bear children.

THE CORE VALUES EXEMPLIFIED IN BIBLICAL MARRIAGE

What I am suggesting is that it is impossible to draw directly upon the biblical customs of marriage as templates for our own day. The world has changed radically from their time to ours, and it is necessary to look not at the external customs with which the biblical personalities were familiar and comfortable and instead to probe more deeply into the core values of family and social constructs that were important to them, apart from the ways in which those core values were expressed externally in their era. Clearly, biblical marital compatibility was defined in ways that we have difficulty comprehending.

And yet, the biblical ideas of marriage have much to teach us about responsibility to a goal larger than our own selfish interests. To limit the idea of marital love to physical compatibility alone is perhaps the height of arrogance on our part. We see daily the results of a system that allows marriage to begin in the deceptive glow of moonlight, only to end when the moonlight fades and the temporary physical attraction it induced no longer exists. The dashing suitor whose body is ravaged by illness or the stunning beauty whose body succumbs to gravity and time are realities that cannot be avoided. If a relationship is built solely on the physical, age or disease can dull the ardor of both partners and can ultimately render meaningless all thoughts of a "better or worse" clause. To put it bluntly, when moments of illness or physical deterioration arrive, something more is required than romance and moonlight. Seen in this manner, it would be well for us to examine once again the biblical concern with the creation of a unit that serves the larger societal development. I submit that there are at least three aspects of biblical marriage worthy of our careful consideration.

First, it should not be unthinkable that the choice of appropriate partners might be made, or at least assisted, by adults whose experience and wisdom can see past the external markers of physical beauty and who are not bewitched by the moon, bothered by alcohol, or bewildered by physical characteristics that will change with time all too quickly. In other words, our modern ideas about the basis or proper foundation for marriage need to be reexamined.

Second, there can be no question about the sad fact that when a modern marriage fails because it was built on a shaky foundation or because the two principals grow in different directions, it is the children who suffer the most. We surely owe it to our world to emphasize the responsibility of a marital partnership to the nurturing of children who will enhance society and advance the moral and ethical ideals of Judaism and indeed of all humanity. This should not mean a simplistic rule forcing two people to remain married "for the sake of the children," but it surely requires the acknowledgment of the fact that the dissolution of a marriage is almost never an issue that involves only two people.

DIVORCE

These concepts lead us to examine the biblical and rabbinic views of divorce. The key verse from Scripture is Deuteronomy 24:1: "If a man takes a woman and marries her, and she does not find favor with him because he finds something obnoxious about her, he may write a bill of divorce for her and send her away." Now, "something obnoxious" is the difficult Hebrew phrase *'ervat davar* [literally, a matter of nakedness], which the Septuagint renders by *aseksemon pragma* [a dishonorable deed], itself as ambiguous as the Hebrew it translates. Matters of nakedness or deeds of dishonor could include adultery, of course, but would not be limited to that single example.

The Mishnaic discussion of divorce[19] ends by citing three competing rabbinic opinions about the meaning of this Hebrew phrase *'ervat davar.* (1) The conservative School of Shammai ruled that "a man may not divorce his wife unless he has found unchastity in her," specifically citing Deuteronomy 24:1 and interpreting *'ervat davar* to mean adultery.[20] (2) The liberal School of Hillel ruled that divorce was permissible "even if she spoiled a dish for him" and cites the same biblical phrase as its authority![21] (3) Rabbi Akiva offered yet a third ruling, still more liberal than that of Hillel, authorizing divorce even if a man found another woman who was prettier, which he also links to Deuteronomy 24:1 but from which he highlights a different phrase: "she has not found favor in his sight."[22]

There is yet another Hebrew phrase in Deuteronomy 24:1 that demands attention: "a writ of divorce" [*sepher kərî tût*], a term not discussed specifically by the three rabbinic authorities.[23] The rabbinic word for this phrase is *geṭ,* and the Tanna'im considered it such an important issue that they devoted a complete tractate (*Gittin*) to the subject. But to understand the rabbinic views of divorce, we must turn to a related tractate devoted entirely to the matter of marital agreements, *Ketubbot.* A *ketubbah* was/is a marriage contract that a man was required to give to his bride at the time of the betrothal, similar in many ways to a modern prenuptial agreement. It sets forth in writing the obligations to a wife that the groom agreed to fulfill, including his legal obligation to her if he should decide to divorce her. Adultery by the wife, of course, could invalidate the entire marital contract and trigger a release of the husband from his obligation to continue to support her. This is the context in which Shammai offered such an apparently restrictive opinion about the rights of a man to divorce his wife. But if the reason of a husband were only that he did not like a wife's cooking (Hillel) or that he had found someone more attractive (Akiva), he would be required to complete all of his financial obligations to her set forth in the *ketubbah.* Because the *ketubbah* would have been negotiated before the wedding and thus before anger or disillusionment with the relationship had begun, and because the bride would have been represented by a person who was committed to protecting her (a father or a brother), her security would virtually always be safeguarded. Lacking a reason to invalidate the *ketubbah,* such as adultery or a comparable act of lewdness or prostitution, the unsatisfied husband could gain his divorce but would have no legal way to avoid his continuing financial responsibilities.

Modern Jewish wives may well wish to quarrel with the uncomplicated exit from marriage available only to a husband, and many modern Jewish authorities have expressed a concern to provide comparable exit strategies for a wife who is dissatisfied, perhaps because her husband has burned the supper once too often.[24] Yet from the perspective of our spiritual ancestors, surely our practice of turning to secular courts to settle the dispute between estranged Jewish partners would be hardly more satisfactory at the end of a relationship than our facile acceptance of sexual attraction as the major basis for its beginning, especially when at the end of the dispute it is often only the lawyers for both sides who profit financially from the quarrel while husband, wife, and children are left with far less to divide among themselves. Especially if it could be expanded to include equality of opportunity to both partners, the classical rabbinic idea of an agreement negotiated before anger and disillusionment begin to eat away at the partnership quite conceivably could mitigate the economic losses typically faced by the wife and children and thus serve the larger community far better.

CONCLUSION

No, the external customs of biblical courtship and marriage are not the crux of the matter, and frantic calls for a return to biblical marriage simply obscure the real issues. But the value of developing customs resulting in appropriate partnerships that contribute positively to family and society is a biblical example worth following. We may find it necessary to modernize and reformulate these time-bound biblical customs, and that is as it should be. Each generation should be granted such freedom to express itself. But we need not abandon the goal of marriages that are (1) formed to serve the moral values of the larger human community, (2) produce children who contribute to the growth and survival of society, and (3) result in unions that endure because they consist of two partners who share values that have stood the test of time.

NOTES

1. The exact referential fields denoted by the biblical terms *bayit, mišpaḥah,* and *ševeṭ* must be teased out contextually. For *bayit* and its allomorph *beyt-'av,* meanings as diverse

as an actual physical dwelling place or the people who reside in it are possible, as are the ideas of a royal dynasty (David) or a family that survives through numerous generations (the midwives in Exodus). For *mišpaḥah,* reference is sometimes to a cellular family, but at other times it implies an entire clan (including slaves and their children), (foreign) hired servants, and concubines or second wives and their offspring as well. Sometimes it describes a collection of several clans that have formed a political and social alliance. A third biblical category to be defined is *ševeṭ,* usually translated as "tribe." Its relationship to "house" and "family" is difficult to describe simply, but *ševeṭ* must be examined as a third major social unit in biblical Israel. All three terms presume the importance of marital relationships that serve to ensure the continuity of the group as well as to foster the inculcation of moral and spiritual values to successive generations.

2. I have yet to hear an impassioned plea for the inalienable right of the gay community to experience the joy of bitter and costly legal disputes once the gild is off the lily and divorce rears its ugly head. In addition, while it may not be doubted that granting true legal equality to all citizens is a worthy goal that has been too long delayed, we might be excused also for worrying about the unintended consequences of foisting in-laws on people who have surely suffered enough already.

3. This is the term adopted into its party platform by Texas Republicans at their 2014 annual convention in Fort Worth. In the section "Celebrating Traditional Marriage," homosexuality is defined as "a chosen behavior that is contrary to the fundamental unchanging truths that have been ordained by God in the Bible." The following platform plank boasts the actual title "Reparative Therapy" and notes that the Texas GOP recognizes "the legitimacy and efficacy of counseling, which offers reparative therapy and treatment for those patients seeking healing and wholeness from their homosexual lifestyle." The complete platform is available at www.texasgop.org.

4. See note 3 above.

5. See Genesis 24.

6. Literally, "a gift deed" [*šəṭar mattanah*].

7. This is the point where Rashi has the servant show the family the "gift deed."

8. This is the remedy called for in Deuteronomy 22:28–29. But note the comment of Robert Alter on this motif in the ancient world: "Rape was a dire fate, but one which could be compensated for by marriage, where the violated virgin rejected and abandoned by her violator was an unmarriageable outcast, condemned to a lifetime of 'desolation.'" See Robert Alter, *The David Story* (New York: Norton 1999), 269–70.

9. Although the physical evidence at the site is somewhat unclear, archaeologists have speculated that the attorney handling this divorce might have based his fee on a body count rather than on the standard contingency basis.

10. See my "Nice Jewish Girls: Liquor, Sex, and Power in Antiquity," in *Women and Judaism: Proceedings of the Fourteenth Annual Symposium of the Philip M. and Ethel Klutznick Chair in Jewish Civilization, October 28 and 29, 2001* (Studies in Jewish Civilization 14;

ed. Leonard Greenspoon, Ronald A. Simkins, and Jean Cahan; Omaha: Creighton University Press, 2003), 23–32.

11. Although this particular biblical custom has much to commend it, I am not optimistic about its chances of becoming federal law. The Philistines are well represented in Washington, and their powerful anticircumcision lobby would easily defeat any proposal involving foreskins.

12. This was a custom that may have had legal precedents in the area of Mesopotamia, where Abraham was born.

13. Nahum Sarna, *Genesis: The JPS Torah Commentary* (Philadelphia: JPS, 1989), 172.

14. The text is interesting. In Genesis 25:1, Keturah is clearly labeled a "wife" [*'ishah*], precisely the designation applied to Sarai in Genesis 11:29 and also to Hagar in 16:3. But 25:6 mentions "concubines" in the plural [*pî lagšî m*] as having born children to Abraham. JPS *Tanakh* translates *'ishah* as "concubine" in Genesis 16:3, apparently anticipating that the plural in Genesis 25:6 appears to link Keturah and Hagar together. Thus, either Abraham (a) was married with three women (all designated by *'ishah*) at the same time, (b) he impregnated concubines during the time he was married to Sarah, or (c) he was married with two wives simultaneously and also fathered a child with Hagar. Neither Hagar nor Keturah is dubbed a "concubine" [*pî legeš*] in the text, and except for the notation in 16:3 calling her a "wife" [*'ishah*] Hagar is referred to either as a "maidservant" [*šifḥah*] or a "[female] slave" [*'amah*]. Regardless of the way the text describes them, Abraham fathered children with all three ladies in the same time period. I suspect that this biblical custom will have trouble achieving legality in at least forty-nine of the fifty states.

15. See the essays on love in *Love—Real and Ideal—in the Hebrew Bible and the Jewish Tradition: Proceedings of the Eighteenth Annual Symposium of the Klutznick Chair in Jewish Civilization—Harris Center for Judaic Studies, September 18–19, 2005* (Studies in Jewish Civilization 18; ed. Leonard Greenspoon, Ronald A. Simkins and Jean Cahan; Omaha: Creighton University Press, 2008).

16. Sarna, *Genesis,* 172.

17. Ibid., 171.

18. Parenthetically, this concept brings modern Jews great relief by helping us to realize that Isaac did not marry his biological first cousin but rather the daughter of a tribal leader who was the social equal of his own father Abraham (see Gen 24:24).

19. See Tractate *Gittin.* The citations of Shammai, Hillel, and Akiva are in *Gittin* 9:10.

20. This was the position later espoused by Jesus, according to Matthew 5:31.

21. Shammai and Hillel lived only about fifty years before Jesus, and it is likely that he would have been aware of their schools of thought and teachings.

22. It is clear that while the ruling of Jesus was radically different from those of Hillel and Akiva, the conservative Shammai had interpreted the Hebrew text of Deuteronomy itself in a manner very close to what Jesus appears to teach in Matthew. And, as we know from

rabbinic discussions of other issues, there was no movement among the rabbis to decide once and for all among the three opinions of Shammai, Hillel, and Akiva, all of whom were well-known and respected authorities. Contrary to an assumption sometimes made about the teachings of Jesus serving to loosen the strictures of Jewish law, we may note that both Shammai and Jesus are offering not a more liberal but a far more restrictive and conservative interpretation.

23. And although it is cited from the Septuagint in the Greek text of Matthew, it likewise receives no comment or explanation from Jesus.

24. The excellent book of Perry Netter, *Divorce Is a Mitzvah* (Woodstock: Jewish Lights, 2002), addresses concerns of this nature. The title of the book was suggested to Netter by a phrase from Rashi, *mitzvah ʿalav ləgaršah,* commenting on Deuteronomy 24:1. The bibliography included by Netter is also invaluable.

Presumptuous Halachah: On Determining the Status of Relationships Outside Jewish Marriage

Gail Labovitz

INTRODUCTION

When (now Rabbi) Amitai Adler and Rabbi Julie Pelc Adler stood together under the huppah, their wedding may not, at first glance, have looked especially different from other Jewish weddings most of us are familiar with. But once there, they did not ritually enact their union as might have been expected, through the giving of a ring and the traditional formula "Behold you are betrothed to me by this ring according to the law of Moses and Israel." Instead, they chose to create a binding relationship between them by means of the innovative ceremony of *B'rit Ahuvim,* or Lover's Covenant—devised, in fact, by the groom's mother, Rachel Adler, in her critical book of feminist theology, *Engendering Judaism*[1]—rather than by the traditional Jewish procedure known as *kiddushin.* The Lover's Covenant is constituted through a ritual/legal act in which the couple creates a partnership between them, modeled on Jewish laws of creating partnerships for business, trade, and other financial endeavors;[2] this is done by each putting something of value into a bag and then lifting the bag together. *B'rit Ahuvim* is also enacted by means of a document in which the couple asserts their intent to make a covenant of commitment and fidelity between them and delineates emotional and practical obligations they agree to take on toward each other; the language is both poetic (including biblical and rabbinic citations) and legal.

The document drafted and signed by this bride and groom contained an intriguing additional provision, however, as follows:

> This Lover's Covenant is not *kiddushin,* and the sexual relations of the groom and the bride are not with the intent of *kiddushin,* and not with the intent of licentiousness, but only and solely with the intent of the expression of love. In the event, God forbid, that the groom and the bride should want or need to undo this partnership, it will be undone by means of mutual agreement between them, by a document and their own signatures and the signatures of two valid witnesses, before a just *beit din* [rabbinical court]; or by the declaration of the desire of one of them, and his/her own signature and the signatures of two valid witnesses, before a just *beit din.* . . . And all of this is without the need for a *get* of divorce.

> Therefore, this partnership is established on the condition that no *beit din* in Israel, in the event that the groom or the bride want or need to undo this partnership, will call this partnership *kiddushin* out of doubt, and rule that the groom and the bride require a *get* of divorce for the *kiddushin.* But if this condition is met, then this partnership will be annulled retroactively.[3]

It is the purpose of this essay to explore, and eventually explain, one key reason why this couple might deem such a provision necessary.

According to Jewish law and practice since at least the time of the Mishnah (approximately 200 CE), the legal basis for Jewish marriage is the act of *kiddushin,* a unilateral process in which a man "acquires" a woman. As Mishnah *Kiddushin* 1:1 has it, there are three methods by which this is accomplished:

> A woman is acquired in three ways, and acquires herself in two ways. She is acquired by money, by document, and by sexual intercourse. By money—Beit Shammai say by a *dinar* (a silver coin), or by the equivalent of a *dinar;* and Beit Hillel say by a *p'rutah* (a copper coin; the smallest unit in rabbinic currency), or by the equivalent of a *p'rutah.* . . . And she acquires herself by a divorce document, and by death of the husband.

The mechanics of each of the methods is further spelled out in the Tosefta, a collection structurally parallel to the Mishnah and containing materials roughly contemporaneous with those of the Mishnah.[4] In the first three paragraphs of *Kiddushin* in this work, each of the methods is explained:

> Halachah 1
> By money how (*is the acquisition effected*)? He gave her money [or the equivalent of money], [and] he said to her "Behold, you are betrothed [*m'kuddeshet*] to me," "Behold, you are betrothed [*m'oresset*] to me," "Behold, you are a woman/wife to me," she is *m'kuddeshet.*
>
> Halakhah 2
> And by document? . . . even if he wrote (the document) on a potsherd and gave it to her, [or] on blemished parchment and gave it to her, she is *m'kuddeshet.*
>
> Halakhah 3
> And by sexual intercourse? Any act of sexual intercourse that is for the sake of *kiddushin,* she is *m'kuddeshet;* that is not for the sake of *kiddushin,* she is not *m'kuddeshet.*

The common elements are that (a) the man conveys the appropriate item (an item of value or a document) or performs the appropriate act (consummating the relationship), and (b) the man specifies his intent to betroth the woman by his act. Once this occurs, the woman is *m'kuddeshet*—betrothed, legally bound to the man in a form of inchoate marriage. That is, although the couple still needs to undergo the ceremony of *nissu'in*—full marriage marked by the recitation of the *Sheva Berachot,* the seven blessings—and are not yet expected to cohabitate, once *kiddushin*/acquisition is performed, any sexual encounter the woman has with another man would be considered adulterous, and the relationship can be severed only by the man giving the woman a *get,* a divorce document. Divorce in Jewish law, it should also be noted, is thus constructed in the same manner, as a unilateral act that mirrors and reverses betrothal; at the core of Jewish divorce procedure and document (the *get*) is a statement from the husband: "Behold you are permitted to any man" (see Mishnah *Gittin* 9:3). Since it is he who "acquired" her, it is he who must release her.

The challenge of *kiddushin* from a feminist perspective is thus both practical and fundamental. On the practical level, because a man must grant a halachic divorce of his own free will, it is within his power to withhold the divorce or set onerous conditions, effectively "ransoming" the *get* and the woman's freedom to remarry. Such cases in fact occur with some frequency, particularly in Orthodox communities and in Israel where marriage and divorce are adjudicated under (Ultra-)Orthodox interpretations of Jewish law. A great number of proposals have therefore been put forth and debated to ameliorate the worst effects of this imbalance of power (though far fewer have found general acceptance and been put into practice).[5] But on a more foundational level, marriage by a unilateral act, one that is furthermore constructed through metaphors of acquisition and ownership of the female partner[6] and nonreciprocal exclusive sexual access to her, is simply not a model that can be made to comfortably fit with feminist ideals of equal and egalitarian commitments and obligations between life partners.[7] One of my areas of personal scholarly interest over the last several years has thus been in studying newly developing proposals—such as *B'rit Ahuvim*—that reflect the intent of their creators to devise ceremonies that do not meet the halachic requirements of *kiddushin* (although they may bear some resemblance to *kiddushin*) and that will not be taken as such by others.[8]

PRESUMPTUOUS HALACHAH

Any attempt to disentangle Jewish marriage from the gendered categories of the traditional halachic system is complicated by some important additional factors built into halachic conceptualizations of marital and other sexual contact between Jewish men and women. In order to understand how this is so, let us begin by taking a further look at Tosefta *Kiddushin* 1:3. What I would now like to highlight is that this passage considers the possibility of a sex act *not* for the sake of creating betrothal between a Jewish man and a Jewish woman who are otherwise permitted and free to be married to each other. What Tosefta *Kiddushin* 1:3, along with many subsequent legal and other sources, therefore indicates is that rabbis and halachic decisors have long been aware of the possibility and reality of Jewish men and women engaged in relationships involving sexual relations and/or long-term commitments to one another outside the rubric of *kiddushin*. These include relationships initiated through what the rabbis deemed to be (toraitically) ineffective *kiddushin,* through legal or ceremonial means other than *kiddushin* (such as through the rites and rituals of another religion or by civil marriage) or through no set rite or legal act at all (as in the Tosefta).

Rabbinic authorities were, over the course of Jewish history, called on to evaluate the nature of these relationships and their status under Jewish law. A great deal has been written on this topic—both in actual halachic analyses and arguments and codes and rulings themselves, and in secondary studies of the responsa and related literature. There are thus many lenses through which scholars could and have analyzed rabbinic treatments of marriage outside the bounds of *kiddushin*—considering, for example, how they reflect decisors' theories of the nature of marriage or sociological conditions that have influenced decision making. It is therefore not my intent to try to cover all or even a significant portion of this vast body of material—an impossible task. Rather, I will focus on what I see as one critical factor that recurs regularly in the multiple approaches by which halachic authorities of the past and present have attempted to address the halachic status of committed heterosexual relationships between Jews, even given the multiple forms that these relationships have taken over history. This factor is yet one more element that emerges from Tosefta *Kiddushin* 1:3, in which the evaluation of a sex act as effective betrothal hinges on a matter of intent (whether the act is "for the sake of *kiddushin*" or not)—thereby raising the question of how intent is to be determined. I will then conclude by addressing how this factor becomes relevant to the possibility of creating new ceremonies and forms of Jewish marriage today.

I am guided here most significantly by the work of Rachel Adler, who has addressed in depth the feminist critique of classical halachah in her aforementioned work of Jewish feminist theology and theory, *Engendering Judaism.*[9]

Adler also elaborates and expands on this topic in an article in which she analyzes the writings of Rabbi Zvi Schachter in opposition to the phenomenon of "women's prayer groups" in Orthodoxy, which I will also cite below.[10] Based on these works, I would like to highlight two concerns in particular that I find relevant to my inquiry here. First, Adler notes the ways in which classical halachic discourse is prone to prioritizing certain questions and issues while rendering others invisible: "The method . . . determines the choice of questions, rather than the questions determining the choice of method. Questions that do not conform to the system's method and categories are simply reclassified as non-data and dumped out."[11] She continues: "The presumptions select the questions. The categories shape them."[12] To the extent that the arbiters of the halachic system did recognize these forms of relationship outside of *kiddushin,* Adler's analysis would suggest that a strong impulse existed (and still exists) to frame them in such a way that they fit the preexisting categories and methods of the classical halachic system. To some degree, of course, this sort of process is necessary to and representative of any legal system, as not all cases that will arise could ever be anticipated, and the system must use what resources it already has to assimilate them. The concomitant risk, however, is that this process may facilitate a tendency to distort the circumstances of the case in question and the issues it raises into ill-fitting but already known categories if the decisor is reluctant to innovate new categories and understandings or if using the preexisting categories advances the interests of the decisor.[13]

What is more, Adler elaborates an additional related concern in "Innovation and Authority": "The male elite who claim responsa literature as their domain continue to converse only with one another and to render anonymous the outsiders whose acts provide the content for the elite conversation."[14] In the context of women's prayer groups, this means that even though the women who first contributed to the development of these groups are known and identifiable and that they themselves and/or their writings on this subject could be consulted, instead "There is a 'gentlemen's agreement' to converse *about* rather than *with* these mothers of inventions so that their accomplishments may be reframed for the purposes of the responsa literature as problems detected by one rabbi and referred to another for solution."[15] Thus, although the creators of and participants in ceremonies through means other than *kiddushin* (such as Adler's son and daughter-in-law) potentially stand before halachic authorities to explain their decisions, choices, and intents, this phenomenon identified by Adler suggests that they cannot presume that they will actually be granted such opportunities or be properly heard and understood if they are. Thus, to think about alternatives to *kiddushin* and how they are likely be received by the legal experts and arbiters of halachic communities[16] first necessitates consideration of the varying ways in which the more established halachic system might be able to absorb marriages enacted by such ceremonies into its existing categories and the ways in which decisors have already attempted to absorb (or not) and interpret other forms of non-*kiddushin*–based relationships into halachic categories. To this end, in the remainder of this essay I will demonstrate that halachic literature addressing the multiple questions of marriages and relationships established without the rituals of *kiddushin* is rife with assumptions, generalizations, and rabbinic principles that claim to interpret and speak for the motives of the parties, particularly the male party, involved.

WHAT DOES A MAN INTEND? FURTHERING THE RABBINIC PICTURE OF *KIDDUSHIN*

First, a bit of critical background for what follows is necessary: it should be noted that a number of rabbinic passages strongly imply that marriage via *kiddushin* is ideally the only context in which Jewish men and women should engage in sexual relationships with each other. In the very next paragraph in Tosefta *Kiddushin* after those considered above (1:4), for example, Rabbi Lazar [Elazar] interprets Leviticus 19:29—“Do not degrade your daughter and make her a harlot, lest the land fall into harlotry and the land be filled with depravity”—to refer to sexual relations between unmarried partners without marital intent. In the tannaitic midrashic commentary to Leviticus, *Sifra* (*Kodashim* perek 7), the same verse receives a similar exegesis, in this case anonymously and as an uncontested view:

> I spoke only of defilement that is for the sake of licentiousness. And which is this? This is one who hands his daughter over to his fellow without the intent of marriage, and similarly the one who hands herself over without the intent of marriage.[17]

This source also designates sex without marital intent as a form of *zenut,*[18] meaning “licentiousness” or “fornication”; in rabbinic Hebrew, this term encompasses a broad range of sexual acts that take place outside of rabbinically sanctioned parameters even if they do not violate explicit biblical prohibitions such as the incest laws of Leviticus 18 and 20.[19] That is, according to the *Sifra,* any intimate relationship between a man and a woman for which intent to create *kiddushin* had not been explicitly specified would fall under this rubric.

Thus, based even on just this source and others seen above so far, those authorities addressing the status of relationships outside of *kiddushin* would confront the dilemma expressed by legal scholar David Novak:

> In the rabbinic sources there seem to be only two possible heterosexual unions between Jews: either Jewish marriage [*kidushin*], or fornication [*be'ilat zenut*]. . . . In working up from these sources one has basically two options: (1) everything which is not explicitly *kidushin* is, therefore, fornication; (2) everything which is not explicitly fornication is, therefore, *kidushin*. At this level the argument can move, with equal ease, in either direction. On the one hand, one can argue that Jewish marriage requires that one's intention be for Jewish marriage and *all* that it entails. . . . On the other hand, one can argue that a couple, who have taken upon themselves the public responsibility of living together as husband and wife, can hardly be equated with a couple spending some time together in private lust.[20]

As already noted, a number of factors could and did influence the reasons and means by which individual rabbis and scholars over time have decided to pursue one approach or the other, including personal inclinations and understandings of the nature of marriage, historical circumstances in which decisors found themselves, and the unique details of each specific case that came before a decisor. In order to understand some of the later legal history relevant to this question, several important implications of the sources we have already seen need to drawn out and a few additional rabbinic sources considered. In particular, I would like to highlight those that relate to the intent of the parties to a marriage or other relationship.

First is the Talmudic elaboration on the theme of male agency in enacting *kiddushin,* known in subsequent halachic literature as the requirement of *natan hu v'amar hu*—"he gives, and he speaks." After citing the definition of betrothal by money as in Tosefta *Kiddushin* 1:1, the Babylonian Talmud, *Kiddushin* 5b, adds a discussion of several permutations of actions and statements between the two parties:

> But if she gave (an item of value to him), and she said, "Behold, I am betrothed [*m'kuddeshet*] to you," "Behold, I am betrothed [*m'oresset*] to you," "Behold, I am a woman/wife to you"—she is not *m'kuddeshet.*
>
> Rav Pappa objected to this: The reason (why she is not betrothed) is (because we require that) he gave and he spoke, but if he gave and *she* spoke, she is not betrothed.

> But take note of the latter part (of our opening tradition): But if she gave to him and she said (one of the formulas)—it is not (binding) *kiddushin*. This implies that if he gave and she spoke—it would be *kiddushin*! . . .
>
> Rather, this is what it means to say: If he gave and he spoke—it is obvious that it is *kiddushin*. If he gave and she spoke—it becomes as if she gave and she spoke and it is not *kiddushin*.
>
> And if you like I can say (as an alternate answer): If he gave and he spoke—it is *kiddushin*; if she gave and she spoke—it is not *kiddushin*; if he gave and she spoke—it is a doubtful case, and we are concerned on the level of rabbinic (rather than Torah) law.

Only regarding a betrothal in which the man is the sole and fully active party—initiating the betrothal and stating the intent that his actions create a betrothal—is it certain that a binding betrothal has taken place.

This is not to say that the will and intent of the woman are immaterial, as an earlier Talmudic passage on 2a–b makes clear—although here too the discussion is framed around male agency and the question of why the mishnah is worded in such a way that the woman is the grammatical subject of a passive verb ("is acquired") rather than specifying that the man actively acquires her:

> If it had taught "he acquires," I might have said even without her consent. [Since] it teaches "A woman is acquired" (this indicates that) by her consent—yes (she is betrothed); without her consent—no (she is not betrothed).

However, in keeping with the rule just noted that the man is the one who acts and speaks in the optimal betrothal procedure, it may be no surprise to find that the woman need not overtly state or mark her acceptance. Short of a purposeful, discernible rejection of the *kiddushin* (for example, immediately discarding the item given to her), the woman is usually deemed to have freely consented to become betrothed. As we shall thus see, because *kiddushin* is fundamentally a unilateral act in which the man acquires the woman, but not vice versa, it will be the will and intent of the man—and rabbinic presumptions about the will and intent of the man—that become central to much of the discussion on this topic.

One of the key instances in which this kind of attention to the man's intent becomes apparent is in a discussion found in Bavli *Gittin* 81b. The mishnah to which this passage is commentary describes a couple who has previously been married and divorced, who then (after the divorce) share a room in an inn. Beit Hillel and Beit Shammai disagree as to whether the woman needs a second divorce document (Beit Hillel rules yes, Beit Shammai no):

> And Rabbi Yohanan holds like this tanna, as it was taught: Rabbi Shimon ben Elazar said: They Beit Hillel and Beit Shammai did not dispute about [a case in which] they did not see that she engaged in sexual intercourse—that [in that case] she does not need a second divorce document. About what did they dispute? When they did see that she engaged in sexual intercourse, for Beit Shammai say that a man may intend his sex act to be licentious (i.e., nonmarital) sex, and Beit Hillel say a man does *not* intend his sex act to be licentious sex.
>
> And as for the Mishnah, which we established as referring to [a case in which] they did *not* see that she engaged in intercourse—about what did they dispute? When there are witnesses to the seclusion (the man and woman being alone together) and there are not witnesses to sexual intercourse—Beit Shammai hold [that] we do *not* say that witnesses to seclusion are equivalent to witnesses to sexual intercourse, and Beit Hillel hold [that] we *do* say that witnesses to seclusion are equivalent to witnesses to sexual intercourse.

The case hinges on the question of whether there is reason to be concerned that the couple has reestablished *kiddushin* and their marital relationship by means of sexual intercourse. As the Gemara analyses the dispute in the mishnah, it thus considers these factors: (1) Is it possible to presume intent (notably the man's intent) for *kiddushin* even when not explicitly stated? (2) If there is credible evidence that the couple was alone together such that sexual intercourse could have or even was likely to have taken place but no definitive evidence that it did take place, should it nonetheless be assumed that it did?

Given that Jewish law has typically followed Beit Hillel, two things thus emerge from the passage, each framed as a broad legal principle. The first of these is the legal presumption *ein adam oseh be'ilato be'ilat z'nut;* that is, a man does not intend his sex act to be licentious sex. This principle also appears a few additional times in the Babylonian Talmud in a few additional distinct circumstances.[21] As in this case, the issue at hand in each is the possibility that the couple, and more particularly the man, was of the intent to initiate *kiddushin* through sexual intercourse. Since the alternative is to define the sex act as *z'nut,* outside the bounds of proper Jewish behavior, the proposal here is to give the man the "benefit of the doubt" through a presumption that his intentions instead must certainly have been legitimate, that is, marital. Second is Beit Hillel's assertion that *hen hen edei yihud v'hen hen edei bi'ah,* or witnesses to seclusion of a man and a woman together are deemed equivalent to witnesses to sexual intercourse between them. Even though it is not known for certain that a sexual encounter took place, the seclusion itself is sufficient grounds to be concerned, or even presume outright, that one did. Putting these two factors together, the legal result is that at least in this case there do not need to be either witnesses to the sexual act itself or an explicit statement of intent in order to establish a reasonable concern that *kiddushin* may have taken place; rather, if the couple has been in seclusion together in circumstances conducive to sexual contact, there is at minimum a suspicion and at maximum a legal presumption that (a) sexual intercourse has taken place and (b) that the man intended the intercourse as an act of betrothal. The woman's understanding of what is happening during the seclusion and/or sex acts is not considered directly. Perhaps her participation alone is taken as her consent.

When subsequent authorities begin to develop their legal stances on (heterosexual) sexual relationships between Jews outside of *kiddushin,* it is considerations about the scope of this case (and others like it) and most particularly the legal principles that emerge from it that take center stage. To recap, at this point several key points and presumptions have been established:

1. *Kiddushin* is an act of male agency, and not a mutual process; a Jewish couple does not "get married to each other." Put another way, *kiddushin* is enacted through a model of acquisition. The man "takes" or "acquires" the woman, and in doing so he becomes entitled to exclusive sexual access to her; she has no reciprocal legal entitlement to his sexual exclusivity.

2. Acquisition must be done with his intent and her consent. Therefore, because sexual intercourse between two parties who are free to become husband and wife is a means of initiating *kiddushin,* knowing the intent of such a sex act is critical.

3. A sex act without marital intent is classified as licentiousness, improper behavior not to be engaged in by Jews observant of the rabbinic halachic system. Therefore, we presume that a Jewish man would certainly not engage in licentiousness. At least under certain circumstances, then, if he did have sexual relations with a woman not already legally his wife, it may be further presumed that his intent was for *kiddushin* instead [*ein adam oseh be'ilato be'ilat z'nut*].

4. If there is a reasonable possibility that a couple might have had sexual relations, although proof is lacking, this is sufficient to be concerned that such an act took place [*hen hen edei yihud v'hen hen edei bi'ah*] and may be grounds to impose the legal ramification of that sex act at least as a measure of caution.

POST-TALMUDIC DEVELOPMENTS: RESPONSA AND CODES

It is in the post-Talmudic period that we begin to have records of rabbis attempting to apply this set of principles and legal assumptions to actual cases that are brought before them. These cases are also then considered by others through the lens of their theoretical underpinnings and in the process of codification in works such as the *Mishneh Torah* of the Rambam. I will single out here just a few cases and rulings that are especially critical in terms of their impact on the development of halachic jurisprudence on this topic and the deployment of some of the rabbinic principles and presumptions about marriage, sexual conduct, and (male) intent surveyed just above.

In the course of answering a question on a related topic, Hai Gaon, a leading scholar of the Babylonian Jewish community at the turn of the millenium, makes reference to a cause célèbre that roiled the Jewish Babylonian community in the seventh century (and had continuing ramifications for several generations after). In the case at hand, the Resh Galuta, the "Head of the Exile" and representative of the Jewish community to the Arabic/Muslim authorities, had fathered a son by his slave woman (who had been given to him by the Arabic king).[22] The question arose as to the status of the child. It is a general principle in Jewish law (as in many other, but not all, slave systems) that the child of a slave woman has the status of the mother (i.e., is also a slave) and as such has the status of a possession that would be inherited by his biological siblings as part of his biological father's estate. Jewish law and tradition also, however, discourages if not outright prohibits sexual contact between a free Jewish man and an enslaved woman (and similarly or all the more so an enslaved man and a free Jewish woman); by law there can be no binding *kiddushin* with a woman who is enslaved. Hence, by the understandings of nonmarital sex already discussed above, sexual contact under such circumstances would necessarily be understood as *z'nut* [licentiousness]. Thus, the geonic authorities of the time were presented with a social, moral, and quite possibly political quandary: could it be that the political leader and representative of the Jewish community would act in this manner?

Some geonic authorities of the time thus invoked the principle of the Talmud, *ein adam oseh be'ilato be'ilat z'nut,* to propose a novel "solution":

> However, this is a dispute on the matter among the later Geonim, and the root of it is [the case of] Bustanai the Resh Galuta (who is the same [person] as Haninai[23]) who had sexual intercourse with his slave woman, the daughter of Kansari the king of Persia, given

> to him by Amar son of Katav, king of the Ishmaelites as a gift, and she gave birth to a son, and he [Bustanai] died, and his [the child's] brothers rose up to sell him. And the sages of the *yeshivot* disputed over this. There were those among them who said, so long as he [Bustanai] did not free him [the son], he is a slave and needs to be freed by his brothers. . . . And there were those among them who said: Bustanai was a head of the community, and it was in his power to free her, and if he had not freed her he would not have had sexual contact with her, since Beit Hillel held that a man does not intend his sex act to be licentious sex, and all the more so the head of the community.[24]

Since it is within a man's power to free his slaves, if Bustanai wanted to have a legitimate relationship with his slave woman he could free her and immerse her in a *mikvah* [ritual bath], at which point she would become a legitimate convert to Judaism (and eligible for Jewish marriage). Given the principle that a man will seek to avoid licentious sex—read quite broadly—and since it was within Bustanai's power to make the sex legitimate, some geonic authorities argued that one must allow for the possibility that this is precisely what Bustanai did; moreover, as a result, both she and the child must be considered as full Jews at least out of doubt that this happened.

It should not be difficult to see, though, that the logic of this case—and the way in which the principle that presumes the righteous intent of Jewish men has been deployed here to "resolve" it—could be readily expanded from the original circumstances to cases of other men who fathered children by their slave women (which was the context in which Hai Gaon considered the issue) and well beyond. Thus, it is not surprising to find that while some contemporary and later authorities cited and/or adopted the reasoning of this case, others expressed significant resistance. Most notable of these is the great codifier of Jewish law Moses Maimonides (the Rambam), who took up this issue in conjunction with the case of the couple at the inn in his explication of the laws of divorce (*Mishneh Torah,* "Laws of Divorce" 10:19):

> Some of the Geonim ruled that any woman with whom a man had sexual intercourse in the presence of witnesses needs a divorce document, on the presumption that a man does not intend his sex act to be licentious sex. And they expanded and added to this matter that arose in their minds such that they ruled that [in the case in which] one who has a child by his slave woman, we are concerned regarding him . . . lest perhaps he freed his slave woman and [only] afterwards

> had sexual intercourse with her, and there is one who rules that he certainly freed [her] since a man does not intend his sex act to be licentious sex. And all these things are extremely far-removed in my eyes from the ways of proper ruling and it is improper to rely on them. For the sages did not articulate this presumption except regarding his wife whom he divorced . . . since she is [has been] his wife, and it is with his wife (e.g., only with a woman with whom he has already had a marital connection) that it is presumed of him that a man does not intend his sex act to be licentious sex, until he specifies that it is licentious sex. . . . But with all other women, every fornicator is under the presumption that he had sexual intercourse for the purpose of licentiousness, until he specifies that it is for the purpose of *kiddushin.*

In the Rambam's understanding, if the principle is taken to its logical extreme,[25] we would have to be concerned about the possibility of *kiddushin* any time there was reasonable evidence of sexual contact between an unmarried Jewish woman and a Jewish man—which we also know from Bavli *Gittin* 81b means evidence not necessarily of the sex act itself but even seclusion of the couple together [*hen hen edei yihud . . .*].

While the Rambam did not explicitly spell out the ramifications of such a position, his rhetoric does suggest that it does not comport with reasonable conclusions about human behavior. While it might be nice to suppose that all Jewish men had "honorable" intentions when engaging in sexual relations outside of already established marriages, such an assumption stretches the boundaries of credulity. Rather, the Rambam argues, the Bavli invoked this principle only in a small set of circumstances, all of which share a common feature: that is, that some form of marital relationship had already been established at some time between the couple. Only when there is reason to suspect that the man's thoughts and intentions are already focused on a marital relationship can we legally presume that his intent in this sexual encounter is for the sake of (re)establishing marriage. And indeed, this reading is confirmed in the Rambam's discussion of the status of the slave child in regard to his father's estate (is he an heir to it or part of it?) in the laws of inheritance (*Mishneh Torah,* "Laws of Inheritance" 4:6):

> One who had a slave woman and fathered a child from her, and acted towards him [the child] in the manner of [legitimate] children, or if he says "He is my son and his mother has been freed"—if he were a scholar or a man of good reputation who is very punctilious

> in the details of the commandments, then this [child] inherits from him. . . . But if he were from among the other ordinary folk—and it goes without saying if he was among those who act freely in this [type of behavior]—then this [child] is under the presumption of being a slave in all matters, and his [biological] brothers from his father may sell him.

Although the Rambam does not invoke the principle of *ein adam* . . . directly here, he is clearly trying once again to limit the scope of its applicability by distinguishing cases in which the father was known to be a scholar and/or a religiously scrupulous man, whereas other more "ordinary" Jewish men do not get presumptions of having acting in a proper manner.

Finally, in this portion of our discussion there is the highly influential responsum of Rabbi Yitzhak ben Sheshet, known as the Rivash (*Responsa of the Rivash,* 6), which would come to be cited in nearly every analysis of this question that followed. This responsum discusses the case of a female forced convert from Majorca during the Inquisition who had married another forced convert under Catholic rites. The woman bore a child, but the husband subsequently went abroad and disappeared. The woman was eventually able to return to a Jewish community and Jewish practice. Since both parties were Jewish by birth, were there grounds to consider the marriage between them a Jewish marriage, *kiddushin* at least after the fact, in which case the woman would need to (locate the man and) get a divorce before being allowed to remarry in the Jewish community? The Rivash musters a number of arguments to deny any halachic significance to the marriage, and I cannot review them all here. But what I would like to emphasize is how he assembles together many of the considerations we have already been discussing to bolster his argument.

The Rivash begins with the claim that only relationships established knowingly and intentionally as *kiddushin,* through the recognized and correctly performed procedures of *kiddushin* (the couple is eligible for *kiddushin,* the *kiddushin* is properly witnessed, etc.), thereby have the status of *kiddushin:*

> There is no doubt that the betrothal or marriage, call it what you wish, which were done in the religion of idolaters and by the priests of their gathering places—there is not even a suspicion of *kiddushin* in them, even if there were valid witnesses at them, because [the requirement of] "he gave and he spoke" was not fulfilled by them (the rites performed). . . . And in any case, in this situation he did not give her anything; rather only the priest blesses them aloud and gives a ring to each one.

The Rivash quickly moves on, however, directly to the question of whether the presumption *ein adam . . .* should be relevant here. It was, after all, known to others, including other originally Jewish forced converts, that the couple lived together as husband and wife. Under the additional principle of Beit Hillel in Bavli *Gittin* 81b—witnesses to seclusion are equivalent to witnesses to sexual intercourse—perhaps that knowledge of cohabitation between the man and the woman (not to mention her pregnancy!) should be sufficient to presume sexual contact between them:

> But rather, what needs to be looked into is that he was secluded with her in a publicly known way, and she "stood under him" (lived as his wife) and became pregnant from him. . . . And according to their words (i.e., the views of those Geonim who ruled broadly), in a case such as this where they are familiar with each other, and also he took her to be his wife, it would seem at first glance that she needs a *get* because there are witnesses that he was secluded with her, even though there are no witnesses to a sex act [itself]. And in a case of this sort, we say witnesses to seclusion are equivalent to witnesses to sexual intercourse, and since she engaged in sexual intercourse, we say that he had sex with the intent of *kiddushin,* because a man does not intend his sex act to be licentious sex.

Can it therefore be presumed (or at least possible) that the sexual act was done with the intent of legitimate (Jewish) marriage, that is, *kiddushin*?

The Rivash's response, however, is to turn to the Rambam's argument (and those of others as well) against a broad application of the *ein adam . . .* principle:

> However, the Rambam, *z"l,* deflected this ruling with all his power (literally: with both hands). . . .
>
> For even according to the view of those Geonim *z"l* who held that in general we say that he had sexual relations for the purpose of *kiddushin,* here this man under consideration did not have sexual relations for the purpose of *kiddushin.* For since they married in marriage rites under the law of the idolators and at their gathering place by the word of the priest, it is as though they made clear that their intent was not for *kiddushin* according to the laws of Moses and Jewish women, but rather for the ways of idolaters, who are not under the law of *kiddushin* and *gittin.* And if this is so, she is not like a (Jewishly) married woman. . . .
>
> And in the case under consideration, certainly you do not have more brazen people than these, who go of their personal desires to

> idolatry to bow down there, and their acts demonstrate their brazenness and their irreverence.

The fact that the wedding took place as a Catholic ceremony does not mean only that the rites were substantially different from Jewish marriage. Rather, entirely other presumptions about the actions, motives, and intent of the parties emerge. The choice of ceremony in the rites of another religion is to be understood as an active rejection of *kiddushin* as the basis of the marriage; the nature of the ceremony itself creates a presumption that the man had no intent at any time to create a Jewish marriage between himself and the woman. Indeed, if, as the Rambam ruled, only a person of good reputation and Jewish practice can even perhaps be presumed to have engaged in a sex act with only legitimate intent, then participation in Catholic—in the words of the Rivash, "idolatrous"—rites itself removes one from possible consideration on this account and in fact creates the opposite presumption: that the intent was of brazenness and disregard for proper Jewish sexual morals.

CIVIL MARRIAGE

The concept of civil marriage—that is, marriage overseen through secular governmental authority—first appeared in Holland in 1580 but did not immediately attract rabbinic attention. The apparent first published responsum addressing the topic is dated to 1741.[26] The challenge of civil marriage is that it takes place outside the framework of Jewish marriage by means of *kiddushin* but, seemingly, also does not take place within the framework of any other religion or set of theological assumptions immediately antithetical to Judaism. Frequently, the two coexist: a couple is legally required to be civilly licensed or married under the law of the state but is not prevented from having a religious ceremony of their choice as well; it may even be that the officiation of a clergy person also fulfills the civil requirement. When couples both follow the procedures of the state and marry through *kiddushin,* there has been relatively little halachic concern; the couple is married Jewishly, and she will need to receive a *get* for the Jewish marriage to be severed, since marriage by *kiddushin* can be severed only by the *get* process.

Yet the existence of civil marriage allows a couple a new option for marrying—and severing that marriage—outside of any Jewish framework. What is the status of a marriage enacted only through civil procedures, without a Jewish ceremony? If living together as husband and wife by virtue of a civil marriage in some way creates at least a doubtful *kiddushin* after the fact, then from within the halachic system it should not be severed merely by a civil divorce degree, and any subsequent marriage of one of the parties—especially the wife—to another Jew is potentially adulterous. This set of questions has generated a vast body of literature and a multiplicity of views among those who have addressed it. Among the decisors who have taken it up, some have written responsa of great length and/or multiple responsa and have also responded to each others' views in additional writings. Thus, following Gedsel Ellinson, author of the thorough study *Non-Halachic Marriage,* I will state now that "It is not our aim to put in order the responsa on the topic; we will consider only the halachic foundations, in the course of investigation of a selection of rulings."[27]

A starting point for many of these responsa and analyses is the ruling of the Rivash discussed just above. Its applicability, however, can be understood in very different and even opposite ways. That is, if one wants to apply or extend the reasoning of the Rivash regarding the forced converts (and of other decisors considering other similar cases), one must come to a personal judgment: is the critical factor in that case that the marriage rites were something other than *kiddushin* and did not meet the criteria for valid *kiddushin,* or is it the very "choice" of Catholic rites in particular—that is, the rites of a religion contrary to Judaism—that negates any validity under Jewish law? Put another way, is civil marriage religiously neutral, in which case it can be evaluated in terms of other factors such as its content, the legal rights and responsibilities it entails, and/or the social expectations regarding the commitments the couple are making to each other—and the correspondences or lack thereof with Jewish understandings of marriage? Could such a couple subsequently lend a Jewish character to their union ex post facto through their open life together as husband and wife and the reasonable assumption that they have consummated their relationship? Alternately, does the very choice to enter a civil marriage while foregoing *kiddushin* and Jewish rites carry religious significance? Does such a choice indicate something about the desire of the couple, and particularly of the man, not to establish their relationship as *kiddushin*—or, going a step further, perhaps even indicate something about their lack of connection to Judaism and lack of commitment to "proper" Jewish practice?

In fact, it is intriguing to see the way in which both decisors and those who have analyzed their decisions yet again turn to the discourse of what presumptions may be made about the intent of those entering into civil marriage without also participating in a Jewish ceremony of *kiddushin* (among other considerations). As Ellinson summarizes one strand of thinking found in some of the more recent responsa of the twentieth century, "We are concerned for [the possibility] of *kiddushin* through sexual intercourse, even if the parties did *not* intend Toraitic *kiddushin.* There are those who hold that for the requirements of *kiddushin,* it is possible to suffice with the intent of the parties to create between them fixed marital bonds."[28] Orthodox authorities often cited in association with this view include Rabbi Yosef Eliyahu Henkin and Rabbi Yosef Rosen (also known as the Rogatchover), both active in the early part of the twentieth century prior to World War II. While there are some important difference in their approaches and they come to somewhat different conclusions, both make one central point in their arguments: the presumption that parties to a civil marriage—and once again, most particularly the man—expect that a critical commitment of marriage is sexual exclusivity. The husband's expectation that through marriage he has exclusive rights to sexual access to his wife is similar, both argue, to the legal condition created by *kiddushin.* Any relations between them are thus more like his ownership of (understood as exclusive sexual access to) her through *kiddushin* than licentious relations, *z'nut,* and must be evaluated as such. Such a marriage should be severed by a *get,* at least out of doubt that it might fulfill the requirements of *kiddushin.*[29] Nor is this approach limited to Orthodox thinkers. As Rabbi Isaac Klein, a leading halachic authority of the Conservative movement and author of the responsum that guides Conservative practice to this day, wrote in 1938, "Our experience is that the moral standards of those who have become united through civil marriage, as far as marital fidelity and the purity of their family life is concerned, compares very favorably with the standards of those who have had the benefit of a religious marriage."[30]

On the other side—that is, among those who hold that civil marriage has no Jewish standing—rulings often hinge on presumptions about the intents and desires of the parties vis-à-vis Judaism and Jewish marriage. The choice of a civil marriage, no less than the choice of a marriage in a religion other than Judaism, is understood as a conscious and willing rejection by the couple of Jewish marriage and *kiddushin* and indeed a rejection of a commitment to Judaism altogether. This view was expressed, for example, in several responses to Rabbi Henkin's responsum, as in the following from Rabbi Shlomo Zalman Auerbach, who emphasizes the secular nature of civil marriage: "just as they don't worry and think that she might not be betrothed to him according to the religions of the Christians and the Ishmaelites, thus to our great sorrow he doesn't care at all that she is not betrothed to him according to our holy Torah."[31] The very point of civil marriage alone, he suggests, is that it represents a rejection of any religion. It should be noted that even according to this view some rabbis, Rabbi Moshe Feinstein being a notable example, have ruled that it is still preferable to have a *get* given where possible to resolve any doubt, but they would allow the woman's remarriage without a Jewish divorce when circumstances make insisting on a *get* problematic. It is also possible to make the exact opposite presumption, as does Rabbi Klein of the Conservative movement: "Let us see what the mental attitude is of the parties that go through a civil marriage. Is it a matter of *l'hakhit* ('spite'), or just a passive disregard of the requirements of the Jewish law? In most cases it is safe to assume that the parties do not object to a religious marriage. . . . In many cases it is sheer case of ignorance. . . . Under these circumstances, we surely cannot assume that the parties have definite objections to being married *k'Dat Mosheh v'Yisroel.*"[32]

CONCLUSION

In conclusion, we return to the wedding of the Adlers, and the strange provision in their marital document, and to the question of how the traditional halachic system is likely to approach newly developing alternatives to *kiddushin* such as, but not limited to, *B'rit Ahuvim.* What the Adlers, both of whom are rabbinically trained and versed in many of the complexities discussed in this essay, intuited is that when the arbiters of traditional halachah come to consider a ceremony such as theirs, those arbiters will come with a tradition full of presuppositions and presumptions that may be imposed on a marriage and the couple who entered it. In the sources surveyed here, we have seen that exclusive and binding relationships between heterosexual partners, initiated by marital processes other than *kiddushin,* may be brought under the rubric of *kiddushin,* such that they must be severed by the (unilateral) *get* process.

It is certainly possible, based on sources here, that to use a ceremony such as *B'rit Ahuvim* is to state clearly, in a way that civil marriage may not, that the couple is deliberately foregoing *kiddushin* and that their marriage should not be evaluated as such. Alternately, the choice of a ceremony that retains elements of Jewish language could as easily be taken as a desire not to reject Jewish forms and proper Jewish behavior, something that is more doubtful in the case of civil marriage. Knowing that their motives will be scrutinized and defined by others, the Adlers are attempting to the best of their abilities to make their own assumptions about their marriage, their relations, and their intents explicit, to forestall the possibility that other assumptions might be imposed upon them. In this, I would suggest that the couple has identified an important challenge that anyone seeking alternatives to *kiddushin* must consider and attempt to address, as they have.

NOTES

1. Rachel Adler, *Engendering Judaism: An Inclusive Theology and Ethics* (Philadelphia: Jewish Publication Society, 1998). See particularly Chapter 5, "*B'rit Ahuvim:* A Marriage Between Subjects," 169–207.

2. See Tosefta *Ketubot* 10:4; Maimonides, *Mishneh Torah,* "Laws of Agents and Partners," 4:1.

3. "Lover's Convenant, Brit Ahuvim Ceremony" [Heb.], Amitai Adler and Julie Pelc Adler, shared in private communication with this author. All translations of primary and secondary sources are my own unless otherwise noted.

4. Among recent works on the relationship of Mishnah and Tosefta, see, for example, some of the essays in *Introducing Tosefta: Textual, Intratextual, and Intertextual Studies* (ed. Harry Fox and Tirzah Meacham; Hoboken: Ktav, 1999); Judith Hauptman, *Rereading the Mishnah: A New Approach to Ancient Jewish Texts* (Tübingen: Mohr Siebeck, 2005); Robert Brody, *Mishnah and Tosefta Studies* (Jerusalem: Hebrew University, Magnes Press, 2014).

5. See my discussion in Gail Labovitz, "Behold You Are [Fill in the Blank] to Me: Contemporary Legal and Ritual Approaches to *Qiddushin,*" in *Love, Marriage, and Jewish Families Today: Paradoxes of the Gender Revolution* (ed. Sylvia Barack Fishman; Waltham: Brandeis University Press/University Press of New England, 2015), 221–39.

6. See Gail Labovitz, *Marriage and Metaphor: Constructions of Gender in Rabbinic Literature* (Lantham: Lexington Books, 2009).

7. It may also be noted, although this is not my primary focus here, that marriage by *kiddushin* is built on heteronormative assumptions.

8. In addition to the sources already referenced above, see Gail Labovitz, "Engendering Halakhah: Rachel Adler's Berit Ahuvim and the Quest to Create a Feminist Halakhic Praxis," in *Revisioning Ritual: Jewish Traditions in Transition* (ed. Simon J. Bronner; Oxford: Littman Library of Jewish Civilization, 2011), 165–89, and "*Qiddushin,* Marriage, and Egalitarian Relationships: Making New Legal Meanings," in *Association for Jewish Studies Perspectives* (Spring 2013): 46–47.

9. Adler, *Engendering Judaism.*

10. Rachel Adler, "Innovation and Authority: A Feminist Reading of the 'Women's Minyan' Responsum," in *Gender Issues in Jewish Law: Essays and Responsa* (ed. Walter Jacob and Moshe Zemer; New York, Oxford: Berghahn Books, 2001), 3–32. Within these groups, women gather to pray together. The groups generally do not consider themselves to constitute or function as a minyan, a prayer quorum, since Talmudic and later

(premodern and more recent Orthodox) halachah typically insists that only men can form such a community, and the groups therefore omit from their services certain elements of the liturgy that are deemed to require a minyan [known as *d'varim she'b'kedushah*]. Other than maintaining this restriction, however, the participants generally pray all or specific parts of a typical prayer service, including the reading of the Torah.

11. Adler, *Engendering Judaism,* 28.

12. Ibid., 29.

13. As David Novak writes, using civil marriage as "a paradigm for how modern halakhists have confronted the uniquely modern phenomenon of secularity": "In such situations the employment of classical sources by modern halakhists must be by analogy rather than by the strict identification with a previous precedent, or the strict subsumption of a case under a specific rule. . . . Analogies involve the selective judgment of the authority deciding the new case at hand. If his selective judgment is not to be capricious, then it is clear that in the absence of definite halakhic precedents and rules in this area such judgment will stem from philosophical criteria. . . . [H]is judgment will be to *select* from what the sources already present for his analogies. . . . [H]e will have formulated a concept of what essentially characterizes marriage *and* what essentially characterizes Jewish marriage. Although recognizing differences between the two, he will certainly not characterize them as mutually exclusive." David Novak, "The Marital Status of Jews Married under Non-Jewish Auspices," *Jewish Law Association Studies* 1 (1985): 62.

14. Adler, "Innovation and Authority," 5.

15. Ibid. Adler notes that this can be true even of those whose intent is to defend the permissibility of prayer groups. In a similar vein, if a different context, Ronit Irshai writes that "my contention that halakhah is markedly masculine and that gender biases are often a feature of halakhic decisions *does not refer exclusively or even necessarily to those areas where there appears to be actual discrimination against women.* . . . [T]he ideological underpinnings of halakhic decision making in these areas [issues related to reproductive technologies] reflect essentialist concepts of gender that often relate to women as objects rather than subjects and fail to take their interests and perspectives adequately into account." Ronit Irshai, *Fertility and Jewish Law: Feminist Perspectives on Orthodox Responsa Literature* (Waltham: Brandeis University Press, 2012), 17, my emphasis.

16. Which need not be Orthodox. See, for example, the responsum on civil marriage by the Conservative movement scholar Rabbi Isaac Klein, cited and briefly discussed below: Isaac Klein, *Responsa and Halakhic Studies* (New York: Ktav, 1975), 1–12.

17. And see also Bavli *Sanhedrin* 76a. In a later period this view would be expressed especially strongly by Maimonides in Mishnah Torah, "Hilchot Ishut," 1:4.

18. Although the verse in Leviticus uses two verbal forms of this root: *l'haznotah, tizneh.*

19. Or, in Michael Satlow's words, "*Znut* . . . is a [vague] grouping, roughly translating into 'licentiousness,' and usually indicates non-biblically prohibited sexual liaisons that are strongly condemned by the rabbis. . . . The use of *znut* almost always refers to some kind

of non-marital, non-adulterous sexuality." Michael L. Satlow, *Tasting the Dish: Rabbinic Rhetorics of Sexuality* (Brown Judaic Studies; Atlanta: Scholars Press, 1995), 140. See also my article "Consent, Agency, and the Semantics of Sexuality in the Babylonian Talmud," 25–28, available at http://www.brandeis.edu/projects/fse/judaism/docs/articles/consent.pdf.

20. Novak, "The Marital Status of Jews Married under Non-Jewish Auspices," 63.

21. Other relevant passages/cases are found in Bavli *Yevamot* 107a (but see Elyakim G. Ellinson, *Non-Halachic Marriage: A Study of the Rabbinic Sources* (Tel Aviv: Dvir, 1975, 116n4 [Heb.]), on differences between this case and the others) and 109b–110a, *Ketubot* 72b–73a, and *Kiddushin* 65a–b.

22. Other versions of the episode suggest that there was more than one child born from the relationship and that their father raised them as legitimate sons. Ellinson (*Non-Halachic Marriage,* 117, n6) discusses this case briefly. See also Simha Assaf and Leah Bornstein-Makovetsky, "Bustanai ben Haninai," in *Encylopaedia Judaica,* Vol. 4 (2nd ed.; ed. Michael Berenbaum and Fred Skolnik; Detroit: Macmillan Reference USA, 2007), 316–17, and the sources (primary and secondary) referenced there.

23. Or Bustanai was the son of Haninai; see note 22.

24. Responsa of the Geonim (*Sha'arei Tzedek, helek* 3, *sha'ar* 1, *siman* 17).

25. It is true that the rhetoric of the Rambam suggests in some ways the opposite: first the Geonim ruled that any sex act between two legitimate Jews might count as *kiddushin,* and then they expanded the logic of that ruling to ridiculous extremes in the case of the slave mother. But it is actually only this latter case (the slave mother) that appears in Geonic sources known to us, either in the original or as citations by later authorities and commentators. Ellinson (*Non-Halachic Marriage,* 119) suggests that the former "ruling" was thus Rambam's own extrapolation from the Geonic discourse about the slave mother.

26. Following Abraham Hayyim Freimann, *The Order of Betrothal and Marriage after the Completion of the Talmud* (Jerusalem: Mosad ha-Rav Kook, 1964), 362 [Heb.], citing a responsum in the collection "*Pri Etz Hayyim.*"

27. Ellinson, *Non-Halachic Marriage,* 175–76.

28. Ibid., 179.

29. On the views of these two decisors, see Freimann, *The Order of Betrothal and Marriage,* 370–71, 374; Ellinson, *Non-Halachic Marriage,* 179, particularly n40; Novak, "The Marital Status of Jews Married under Non-Jewish Auspices," 70–73; Ariel Picard, "'According to the Law of Moses and Israel': The Essence of Marriage According to the Halakhic Decisors of the Twentieth Century; Civil Marriage as a Test Case," *Democratic Culture in Israel and in the World* 12 (2011): 157–64, 180–84.

30. Klein, *Responsa and Halakhic Studies,* 11.

31. Translation taken from Picard, "'According to the Law of Moses and Israel,'" 165.

32. Klein, *Responsa and Halakhic Studies,* 10.

Agunot, Immigration, and Modernization, from 1857 to 1896

Haim Sperber

INTRODUCTION

This essay investigates the phenomenon of *agunot* (explained below) in the second half of the nineteenth century. Since then, and especially during the first two decades of the twentieth century, this has become one of the most discussed issues on the social and cultural Jewish agenda. Although referred to sporadically in nineteenth century Jewish social history research, this issue has not been extensively investigated. This essay offers an introduction to this topic.

The essay's main objectives are to

1. sum up the research to date,
2. estimate the magnitude of the phenomenon,
3. discuss the available databases,
4. formulate certain conclusions based on research on all the known cases of *agunot* between 1857 and 1896, and
5. provide insights on the effect of the phenomenon of *agunot* on
   A. the status of nineteenth century Eastern European Jewish women,
   B. the changing role of rabbis in Eastern European communities, and
   C. the complex relationship between absconding husbands and immigration.

DEFINITION OF *AGUNOT*

The term *agunot* (sing. *agunah*) refers to Jewish women who are unable to divorce because they have been abandoned by their husbands. The word literally means "anchored," suggesting that such women are chained to their marriages, since according to Jewish law only the husband is able to grant the wife a *get* [writ of divorce]. Although in the past most *agunot* were abandoned wives, there are various other ways of attaining this status.

The traditional way of coping with the phenomenon of *agunot* was to ask the rabbis for advice. A rabbi usually alerted other rabbis about the absconding husband as part of the effort to find him and obtain a *get* for the abandoned wife. Rabbis were also very instrumental in offering legal aid to *agunot.*[1] This changed with the advent of Jewish journalism in the mid-nineteenth century. Women began to search for their absconding husbands by placing advertisements in newspapers and other journals. With these new avenues open to them, women no longer depended solely on rabbinical help for finding a solution to their plight.

THE STATE OF RESEARCH TO DATE

Historical research of the phenomenon in the second half of the nineteenth century is virtually nonexistent.[2] However, much more has been written about *agunot* in the early twentieth century, especially in North America.[3]

CheaRan Freeze devoted thirteen pages to *agunot* in her pathbreaking research on Jewish divorce and marriage in the Russian Empire in the late nineteenth century.[4] She was the first to regard it as an important aspect of the nineteenth century Jewish family history. Arthur Hertzberg and, recently, Gur Alroey probed this phenomenon as part of their research of Jewish immigration.[5] Margalith Shilo investigated *agunot* in the small Jewish community in Jerusalem in the nineteenth century.[6]

Mark Baker is the only researcher who primarily focused on this topic, but his work covers only four years, from 1867 to 1870, and is limited to only one source, the Hebrew Newspaper *HaMagid*.[7] In her Ph.D. dissertation, Noa Shashar relates only to the period before 1850.[8]

The research results in this essay are the first exclusively dedicated to *agunot* in the late nineteenth century.

THE EXTENT OF THE PHENOMENON

All the data for the scope of the phenomenon of *agunot* are estimates. Most *agunot* were not reported as such due to either shame or despair. Furthermore, although most *agunot* lived in Eastern Europe, much of the data refer to post-migration reports, particularly to North America and the United Kingdom, in the late nineteenth and early twentieth centuries.

Mark Baker suggests that the *agunot* reported in Jewish newspapers represented only 1 percent of all the cases, based on Ephraim Deinew's statement in a footnote in *HaMagid* (April 21, 1869): "Readers of the Jewish journals need not think that the published cases of *agunot* in newspapers are all the cases. In fact if all *agunot* would wish to publish their troubles, all the journals would not suffice. In fact only one in a hundred is mentioned."[9]

Arthur Hertzberg claimed that during the period of the Great Immigration (1881–1924) one hundred thousand Russian Jews deserted their wives and families, but he did not cite his sources.[10] ChaeRan Freeze doubts this estimate.[11]

However, figures given by Jewish organizations in Great Britain and the United States might give some further hints. The British Jewish Board of Guardians' report for 1870 gives the number of *agunot* as 103.[12] Their report for 1871 refers to 105 cases.[13] These are huge numbers, if the size of the Jewish population in Great Britain (fewer than 300,000 in 1870) is taken into account. In the 1880s, the figures were much higher. The report for 1881 cites 151 cases,[14] and the 1886 report cites 214 cases.[15] The numbers for the 1890s was even higher. The report for 1892, for example, gives 353 *agunot.*[16]

As far as North America is concerned, Hertzberg's figures are indirectly supported by a report by Morris D. Waldman to the Sixth Conference of the National Jewish Charities in the United States in 1909. Waldman reported on deserted women requesting aid from charities in various cities: 78 in St. Louis, 90 in Baltimore, 204 in Chicago, and 1,046 in New York.[17] Waldman also quoted research from 1901, with the number of deserted Jewish women in Boston given as 105 for the same year.[18]

In 1908–1909, the records of the United Hebrew Charities of New York (UHCNY) showed that 652 out of 1,046 women were deserted for more than a year, including 130 for more than a decade. Waldman provided figures of deserted women assisted by the UHCNY from 1903 to 1909 (1,052, 970, 1,124, 1,040, 106, 1,049, and 1,046, respectively).[19] It seems that in New York alone, there were at least a few hundred new *agunot* per year. As early as 1871, a report of the Hebrew Benevolent and Orphan Asylum Society of New York, published in the *Jewish Messenger* on May 5, 1871, refers to 78 deserted wives supported by the society in 1870 alone.

All these figures do not include Eastern Europe. However, most *agunot* found in the present research came from the Russian and Hapsburg Empires, and figures do not exist for them. Rather, research on East European *agunot* relies heavily on qualitative rather than quantitative sources

THE SCOPE OF THE RESEARCH

This essay is based on research on over forty-seven hundred cases of identified *agunot,* most of them from Eastern Europe. Most information on *agunot* can be found either in newspapers (mostly Jewish newspapers in Hebrew or Yiddish)

or in rabbinical responsa books and other sources. As shown here, these two main databases portray different *agunot* narratives. The basic assumption is that at least one hundred thousand Jewish *agunot* lived in Eastern Europe during the second half of the nineteenth century. Although there is some information relating to anonymous *agunot,* especially in the rabbinical sources, this research concentrates solely on those identifiable by either name or place.

CATEGORIES OF *AGUNOT*

Based on research of forty-seven hundred cases of *agunot* in the nineteenth century, seven basic types were identified.[20]

1. Women Deserted by Husbands Who Disappeared

Isaac Waldorf is probably the most notorious case of desertion. After deserting his wife in Vienna, he went to New York and remarried. When his second wife died, leaving three young children, he appointed an eighteen-year-old girl, who came from Vienna, to look after his children, and later he married her. The bride invited her mother from Vienna to come to New York. The mother recognized her son-in-law as the husband who deserted her. The daughter/third wife was born a few months after Waldorf's desertion.[21]

In most of the known cases, the husbands were not found. There were also a few cases of wives deserting husbands.[22] However, deserted husbands who were still married could apply for a *heter meah rabanim* [permission, signed by one hundred rabbis (from three countries)] to marry another wife. Men would look for rabbis willing to sign such permissions. In a peculiar case, in 1857, Itzik Walershtein from Hungary went on a mission to collect one hundred rabbis' signatures for another man whose wife was insane. However, Walershtein disappeared, making his own wife an *agunah.*[23]

According to Jewish law, wives could not receive such permission. This created a problem in countries where bigamy was illegal.[24] In some cases of couples married according to Jewish law but without having recorded the marriages by the state, husbands would deny the marriages altogether.[25] However, since they were married according to Jewish law, the wives would remain *agunot,* although the whereabouts of the husbands were known.

Since women could not receive *heter meah rabanim,* their only option was *heter agunah* [permission to the *agunah*], which is discussed later in this essay. Desertion was the most common reason for women becoming *agunot* (see Table 1).

2. *Women Who Refused to Receive or Were Not Granted a* Get

Some husbands who refused to grant their wives permission for divorce were imprisoned or deported. The cases of imprisoned or deported women unwilling to receive a *get* were much fewer,[26] while some refused to receive it for other reasons, particularly economic considerations.[27] Not many cases of the latter were found, although this later became more widespread.

3. *Widowed Women Whose Brothers-in-Law Refused to Grant Them Permission to Marry Others*

According to Jewish law, when a husband dies and has a surviving brother, the widow, if she does not have children, is obliged to marry the brother unless she is released from this duty. This is done through a ceremony called *halitza* [Levirate marriage] in which the widow takes off the brother-in-law's shoe, whereby she receives the brother-in-law's permission to marry another man. Thus, he is released from the obligation to marry her, and she becomes free to marry whomever she desires. In one peculiar case, a brother of a deceased man went to give his sister-in-law *halitza* but disappeared, and his own wife thus became an *agunah* as well.[28] Sometimes the brother-in-law could not be found,[29] refused to give permission,[30] or demanded payment for it.[31]

4. *Women Whose Husbands' Bodies Have Disappeared*

Such instances include husbands' deaths by drowning[32] or by natural disasters while traveling. The difficulties in such cases could be that a husband's body was not found or was mutilated beyond recognition.[33] In such instances, women could not remarry until the husbands were officially pronounced dead. There were many instances in which husbands had been taken into the armed forces and died during their service, but their bodies were missing or mutilated.[34] In some cases enlisted husbands did not return home, sometimes by choice.[35] In other cases they were missing in action, but the rabbis refused to accept the army death reports.[36] In one case the husband had been murdered but the body was discovered only much later,[37] and during all the intervening years the woman remained chained to the marriage.

5. *Improperly or Incorrectly Written* Get

The divorces of women with such a *get*[38] could not be finalized.[39] In some cases, the *get* was deliberately written in an improper way.[40]

This issue was the subject of a number of literary works, mainly in nineteenth century Russia. Among the most famous of such pieces was Yehuda Leib Gordon's poem "Kotzo shel Yod" [קוצו של יוד].[41]

There were also some cases in which women refused to receive the *get* because the husband tried to serve it by using force or intimidating the woman.[42] In other cases, rabbis refused to accept the *get* written by rabbis who were appointed by the state but whose ruling was deemed improper because they did not have rabbinical training and formal rabbinical education.[43]

6. Women Whose Husbands Became Mentally Ill and Were Not Competent to Grant a Get

In such cases, women had to apply for *heter beth din* (התר בית דין) [permission of the rabbinical court] to be released from the marriage.[44] Similarly, women who had become mentally ill were not considered competent to receive a writ of divorce,[45] and the husbands became chained to such marriages. Such matters could be adjudicated by rabbis using *heter meah rabanim,* as mentioned above.

7. Women Refused a Get *by Jewish Converts to Christianity or Islam*

Some of the converts to Christianity became anti-Jewish agitators, such as Israel Aaron Birman, also known as Dr. Yustus.[46] In such cases, the divorces still had to be granted according to Jewish law. In the event that converts refused to grant a *get,* the women became *agunot.*[47]

The most famous instance involving conversion was of Sarah Leah, the widow of Mechel Alter Gener of Odessa in the Russian Empire, who became an *agunah.* Both of Mechel Alter Gener's brothers converted to Christianity and were not willing to grant Sarah Leah *halitza.* She needed special rabbinical permission to remarry. The case was much debated in newspapers, rabbinical responsa, and civil courts in Odessa. The rabbinical debate was conducted by Rabbi Avraham Yoel Abelson of Odessa. The correspondents included Avraham Yoel Abelson, Israel Issar Shapira, Aaron Zeev Wolf Wail, Itzhak Elhanan Spector, Mordechai Aarom Gimple, Leib Frankel, Yosef Zechaia Shtern, Naphtali Tzvi Yehuda Berlin, Shimon Arie Schwabacher, and Shmuel Mohaliver—many of the most important rabbis in Eastern Europe.[48]

HOW *AGUNOT* COULD OBTAIN PERMISSION TO REMARRY

In cases (categories 2–6) in which a husband was not found for a few years or was declared insane, in a coma, or unable to function, the rabbis could release the *agunah* from her chains by the *heter aguna* [התר עגונה]. To gain

Table 1. Data on the Categories of the Known Cases of Agunot

	Agunot	*No.*	%
1	Deserted by husband or wife	3,012	
1a	Serial deserting husband (2 or more deserted wives)	150	
	Total deserted wives Total deserted by wife Total desertions	2,987 175 3,162	 68.09
2	Refusing to grant or receive a *get*	128[1]	2.54
3	*Halitza* issues	202	4.28
4	Husband suspected dead (one case of a wife)	608	12.50
5	Improper *get*	235	4.59
6	Mental or severe illnesses	274[2]	5.79
7	Conversion	80	1.71
8	Undefined and other cases	23	0.50
	Total	4,712	100.00

1. Among those cases, 24 women refused to receive the *get.*
2. Including 13 males [*agunim*] and 249 females [*agunot*].

such permission was the principal goal of *agunot.* However, rabbis could grant such permission only within the framework of Jewish law.[49] In many cases, the newspapers applied pressure on the rabbis to be more liberal and issue written permissions to remarry more frequently.

Table 1 divides the known cases of *agunot* into various categories. About 30 percent of the women researched became *agunot* for reasons other than desertion by their husbands. Furthermore, the two major sources on *agunot,* which are discussed below—namely Jewish newspapers and responsa books—offer two different narratives regarding *agunot.* While the newspapers dealt mainly with deserted women, the responsa dealt mainly with women whose husbands were deceased as well as with 6 *halitza* cases and *get* and mental health issues. Thus, out of 1,584 cases of *agunot* cited in responsa, 1,121 (70.8 percent) were women not deserted by their husbands, while 2,260 out of 2,560 cases (88.3 percent) reported in the Jewish newspapers were women deserted by husbands (see Table 5 later in this chapter). The reason for this is explained in the next section.

THE SOURCES

The sources describing such phenomenon are vast, but most have not been researched until now. There are four main databases on *agunot:* newspapers, especially Jewish ones; rabbinical sources, especially responsa books; official Russian rabbinical documents; and letters and documents in private archives.

As mentioned earlier, the different sources offer alternative and sometimes conflicting narratives regarding *agunot.* This is demonstrated in the analysis of the various sources.

I. JEWISH NEWSPAPERS

While the Jewish newspapers are mostly in Hebrew, there are some in Yiddish[50] and in various local Jewish newspapers.[51]

Much information regarding *agunot* is found in the Jewish newspapers. Indeed, the first Hebrew newspaper, *HaMagid,*[52] published from 1856 to 1903 initially in Lyck, Prussia, and later in other places, put the matter of *agunot* very high on the agenda. While Mark Baker's research on *agunot* in *HaMagid* is restricted to the years between 1867 and 1870,[53] the current research investigates all the issues of the newspaper.

Information on *agunot* is also available in other Jewish newspapers, particularly in those published after 1880.[54] Information on *agunot* in the newspapers appeared in two main forms: advertisements and news reports.

The advertisements, placed by women or their relatives, mostly fathers, sought information on the whereabouts of husbands. They were published only after the editors verified the validity of the information.

The editors were very much aware of possible manipulation by the parties concerned. On June 28, 1871, the editor of *HaMagid* reported on some instances of women approaching the newspaper a few weeks after husbands went away on business, and by the time of publication the husbands had returned. To avoid such problems, the newspapers specified the information that advertisements should include and stated that "We will not advertise any advertisements concerning *agunot* if the matter is not presented to us by the rabbi or communal officials of the place where the *agunah* resides."[55] The usual procedure was to ask the local rabbi to confirm the woman's version, after the editor of *HaMagid* (June 23, 1869) wrote that he had been deceived by two people a few years earlier. He decided that advertisements would not be published without rabbinical consent.[56]

In many cases the rabbis would write the advertisements,[57] which were then posted as letters from the rabbis to the editor. In other cases, advertisements were written by newspaper correspondents or community officials.

Two typical examples of advertisements are the following:

1. This first advertisement was published in *HaMagid* (June 16, 1866, and September 9, 1866). It relates to a woman deserted by her husband five years earlier. In most such advertisements there is much information regarding the deserters, while information on the abandoned wives is rare:

   A woman Necha, the daughter of Haim David of Warsaw, was betrayed by her husband five years ago. Last year, he wrote to his family that he was in Suez, Egypt, and has not been heard from for nine months now. The man is tall and has a black beard and hair. He is about 34 years old and is a roofer by profession. Some years ago he was in the Caucasus. The address he sent is in Suez under the name of Moritz Greenwald. The person who would do the good deed of meeting him and receiving the *get* from him will be well rewarded, as our late Sages have proclaimed many times. Please, as soon as the editor should learn anything, let him inform the great genius, our teacher, Rabbi Doberosh Meizlish, may his light shine, the head of the Beth Din of Warsaw. I hope that all our fellow sons of Israel, wherever they are, will try to find out the whereabouts of this man.

   Benjamin David, Secretary, Warsaw Sacred Community

2. The second advertisement refers to two women left by the same man. Again, there is much information about the deserter and very little concerning the deserted wives. The advertisement appeared in *HaMagid* (August 20, 1873):

   A WOMAN'S CRYING VOICE

   A woman [named] Pesia, daughter of David Levy, is seeking Israel Baer, born in Berditsov, Russia. [Baer is] the son of Yehoshua Heschel Shapira, grandson of the famed Leah Menasche. Having married in the town of Hamla, Galicia, [the said Baer] lived in Yassi, Romania, for a number of years but ran off, not to be found. I have been traveling for three and a half years, looking for him without success. Therefore, I beg all those who have a connection with *HaMagid* to try and make him send a *get* to his above-named wife. This is how he looks: He is about forty-four years old, of medium height; his hair and beard are black [giving his face] a round [appearance]. On one foot, he has a [birth] mark, and, on his lower [back . . . a scar from] a healed blow. He took along Yaacov, his [now] 15-year-old son from this marriage. The son is

> bleary-eyed and has a dark, dappled face due to blisters; he has thick lips. Now I know, as a matter of certainty, that this betrayer has abandoned another wife in the city of Tchernowitz, Romania. Her name is Yenta, and she is divorced from her first husband, Mihel Tandetnik. She resides at a baker's place near the military hospital. It is a religious commandment to force him to release both his wives from their chains. A *get* for each of them should be addressed to me, care of my aid Yosef ben Itzhak or care of the rabbis in the above-mentioned cities.
>
> Itzhak Aizik Shor, Chief Rabbi of Bucharest

In most cases the advertisements were published free of charge.[58] In some cases the advertisement was published in more than one newspaper,[59] but in most cases they appeared only in one. If a woman wanted to publish a series of pleas, she had to pay for the advertisements. The best-known case of paid advertisement is of Bassia Freizetova, who published her requests in three newspapers in 1883. Freizetova also tried other routes, such as appealing to rabbis and local Russian authorities.[60] In some cases women would publish an advertisement and, after a decade or more, publish another one.[61] Occasionally a woman or her relatives offered financial rewards.[62] However, offers of rewards were rare.

Another way a woman's plight would become known was through the publication of her story by a newspaper correspondent. A good example is the case of Shlomo Braham. The story was initiated and followed up by a *HaMagid* correspondent. Many correspondents helped to trace deserting husbands across borders, notably Ber Dov Goldberg in Paris, David Fishman in Tiberias, and Shlomo Behor Hutzin in Bagdad.[63]

The editors encouraged their correspondents to pursue elusive husbands. Such was the case of Libbe Marcus. David Meyer Marcus left his wife Libbe twice. In the second abandonment, he emigrated from Russia to France. The Paris correspondent of *HaMagid,* Ber Dov Goldberg, was very helpful in finding Marcus and preparing the *get.* The editor helped Libbe reach Paris and receive the *get.*[64] In some cases readers added information that helped with the deserters' apprehension,[65] or the pursuit might have begun with an advertisement but was then followed by a newspaper investigation.[66]

Sometimes the editors published incorrect information in attempts to locate the deserter. Such was the case with Ithzhak, the son of Moshe the Cohen. An advertisement was published in *HaMagid* (January 17, 1884). The publication detailed the route Itzhak took in 1881 from Breslau through Italy, England, and Egypt. In his final letter to the family, he stated that he intended to go to Bombay, India. After late 1881, all contact with him was lost. The advertisement was published in early 1884, and meanwhile the family moved from Breslau to Serbia. On April 3, 1884, the *HaMagid* correspondent in San Francisco wrote that Itzhak came there from the East Indies and then moved to Los Angeles. However, the original advertisement was republished on September 24, 1884. A possible explanation is that despite the further information, he did not return or send a *get.* Another explanation may be that since the name "Itzhak the son of Moshe the Cohen" is very common, the San Francisco correspondent was reporting on another Itzhak. In my view the second explanation is more feasible, since some details were added that were different from those given in the original advertisement.

In some instances, the newspaper editors were quite eager to publish stories of *agunot.* This was the case regarding the alleged deserting husband Yehuda Kahalan, who was accused of abandoning Rachel Friedel. The newspaper published both sides of the story: the wife accused Kahalan of desertion, and Kahalan himself denied the accusation. However, the newspaper kept on insisting that it was a desertion case even after it became clear that Kahalan had not deserted his wife.[67]

The editors were clearly looking for *agunot* even if there were none, and they were much criticized for this. As a result, from 1879 onward *HaMagid* published far fewer dispatches about *agunot* and only if the editors were certain that the wives were indeed deserted.[68]

In rare instances, the Hebrew newspapers cited cases published earlier in other Jewish newspapers.[69] The editors also referred cases to rabbis, encouraging them publicly to help the *agunot.*[70] They even published articles condemning rabbis who were reluctant to do so.

Special attention was drawn to cases of serial deserters. For example, Zeev Margaliot abandoned seven wives (see *HaMagid,* February 24, 1874, and *HaLebanon,* March 25, 1874, and August 26, 1874), and his namesake Alexander Sender Margaliot deserted three wives (see *HaMagid,* July 6, 1859; August 30, 1859; October 6, 1859; December 7, 1859; and March 21, 1860).[71]

Awareness of the issue of *agunot* in the public sphere had side effects. Some dishonest people would try to make a living from such a matter. Moshe Goldstein of Cairo, Egypt, claimed that he was carrying a *get* from Itzhak Finkel to his wife Ester Zissel. Goldstein claimed that Finkel asked him deliver a *get* to his wife. According to the Jewish law, a *get* has to be sent via a messenger if the husband and wife were living in places far away from each other. Finkel was supposed to be living somewhere near the Caspian Sea, while Ester lived in

Russia. In each city Goldstein passed through, he requested that Jews pay for his expenses, since he was performing a mitzvah [holy commandment].[72]

Similarly, the above-mentioned case of Bassia Freizetova became so famous that two criminals, presenting themselves as her father and husband, tried to profit from her plight. The older one, who posed as Bassia's father, asked Jews for money to help him take the deserter back to his deserted wife.[73] For some professional criminals, such as Hirsch Denmark, wife desertion was just one of an assortment of criminal activities.[74] Some deserters were actually engaged in trafficking women.[75]

Another indication that the phenomenon of *aguno*t was becoming an important issue among the Jewish public was that some husbands threatened to leave their wives without granting a *get,* thus making them *agunot.*[76]

HEBREW NEWSPAPERS AND THE ISSUE OF *AGUNOT*

The newspapers dealt mainly with the first type of *agunot*—wives deserted by husbands. The issue of *agunot* was mainly addressed in Hebrew newspapers and rarely in the Yiddish ones. For example, between 1862 and 1872 while *Hamelitz* published sixty-five advertisements on *agunot,* its Yiddish edition *Kol Mevaser* published only five. American Yiddish newspapers, which began to appear only in late 1870, published more information, mostly referring to North American *agunot.*[77]

Eliezer Lipman Zilbermann (1819–1882), the publisher and first editor of *HaMagid* (founded in 1856), brought the issue of *agunot* to the forefront of the Jewish social debate. As Baker has shown, Zilbermann made this issue one of the most important topics in *HaMagid.*[78]

On September 13, 1865, in a very long editorial, Zilbermann proclaimed that *agunot* were one of the most important matters that should be discussed in the Jewish press. He also stated that *HaMagid* would put pressure on rabbis who hesitated in taking up the cause.[79]

Orthodox newspaper editors disagreed with, in their view, the overemphasis of the issue, especially Yehiel Brill, the editor of *HaLebanon,*[80] who accused Zilbermann of reporting on *agunot* even in simple marriage disputes between husband and wife. In July 1879, Brill published another editorial in which he stated that the issue should be dealt with exclusively by the rabbis, and not in the media.[81]

In the late 1870s and early 1880s, David Gordon became the new editor and publisher of *HaMagid,* promoted from deputy editor, in which position he had served since the mid-1860s. Gordon was more concerned with the

Jewish national movement and the settlement of Jews in Palestine and less focused on social issues.[82] After Gordon's death in 1886, his son Dov, who was the editor until 1890, continued his father's editorial policy. In 1890, Yaacov Shmuel Fux became publisher and editor; he continued along those lines until *HaMagid* closed down in 1903. Under Fux's leadership, *HaMagid* concentrated solely on cultural and political issues, altogether neglecting the social problems in the Jewish community.[83]

From 1880, *HaMelitz* (which was founded in Odessa in 1860 and later moved to St. Petersburg)[84] and *Hatzfira* (founded in Warsaw in 1862)[85] became the leading newspapers to spread the word about the issue of *agunot.* Both *HaMelitz* and *Hatzfira* became daily newspapers in the late 1880s, giving the matter widespread coverage.[86]

Table 2 analyzes all information found in the Jewish newspapers on *agunot* between 1857 and 1896.[87]

As the analysis clearly shows, in the four decades investigated, about 75 percent of the mentions in media sources on *agunot* were advertisements. However, the advertisements dropped from 88.9 percent in the first decade to 60.2 percent in the fourth decade. On the other hand, the number of news reports on *agunot* rose from 31 in the first decade to 330 in the fourth, possibly reflecting the professionalization of Jewish media.

II. RESPONSA

Agunot became an ardent issue in the Jewish community, mainly in Eastern Europe, as evidenced by the vast amount of information on the subject in nineteenth century published responsa and rabbinical questions and answers.[88] Even more information is found in unpublished responsa, which can be located in rabbinical archives.[89] While this issue became prominent in responsa in the nineteenth century, it was a major topic of discussion in rabbinical literature long before.[90] In traditional Jewish society, family issues were usually handled privately and discreetly (although, of course, the disappearance of husbands was known in the shtetl and the community).[91] A unique feature of nineteenth century responsa was their reaction to the public challenge, including the leaders of nineteenth century Jewish community, and the high profile of the issue of *agunot* in the Jewish press. The rise of journalism offered *agunot* a new way to try to solve their situation. Requesting the aid of rabbis was practically the only avenue open to the abandoned wives until the mid-nineteenth century.[92] Thereafter, the public

Table 2. Analysis of Newspaper Information Concerning *Agunot*

Total advertisements (ads)	*Total*	*Papers and other sources*	*News reports*	*Multiple mentions*	*Papers and response*	*More than one paper*	*One newspaper ad*			*Years*
							Ads and follow-up	*Many ads*	*Single ad*	
275 (88.9%)	393	2	30	25	14	13	44	20	156	1857–1866
598 (89.3%)	670	0	76	31	10	32	44	57	422	1867–1876
487 (70.4%)	710	1	224	12	8	51	19	73	322	1877–1886
495 (60.2%)	841	4	341	8	3	48	20	88	330	1887–1896
1852 (74.5%)	2,560	7	671	76	35	144	127	238	1,231	Total
	229	General newspapers								
	2,789	Total								

spotlight on the issue of *agunot,* not only in newspapers[93] but also in Hebrew and Yiddish literature,[94] affected rabbinical literature in general and responsa in particular.[95]

Some examples of the effect of the new public scene on the major rabbis in Eastern Europe are presented below. Rabbi Naphtali Tzvi Yehuda Berlin, head of the famous Volozin Yeshiva, referred to *HaMelitz* of 1887 as a source of information on *agunot.*[96] In another instance, Rabbi Berlin referred to *Hatzfira.*[97] However, he stated that rabbinical decisions should not appear in the newspapers unless absolutely necessary.[98] Rabbi Hayyim Berlin, the son of Rabbi Naphtali Tzvi, referred to *HaLebanon* (a less surprising reference, since it was an Orthodox journal that published an addendum of rabbinical literature).[99] Rabbi Hayyim Berlin also mentioned his father's habit of reading the debates about religion in the newspapers, which he claimed was a common thing to do on Shabbat.[100] The well-known Rabbi David Friedman referred to several mentions of *agunot* in *HaMagid* of 1873.[101]

Rabbi Shalom Mordechai Shvedron, in a responsum on the *agunah* Hava Sateshny, even based his decision on information he found in a newspaper.[102] In the case of the *agunah* Reizel Laysten (1895), whose husband drowned in a ship on its way to America, Rabbi Shvedron also relied heavily on newspaper reports, even claiming that had the husband survived, he could have sent a note via the newspapers.[103] Rabbi Yosef Shaul Nathanson as well as other rabbis published their requests regarding *agunot* in *HaMagid.*[104]

In fact, the most important rabbis in Eastern Europe, such as Shlomu Kluger (1785–1869),[105] Itzhak Elhanan Spector (1817–1896),[106] Yosef Shaul Nathanson (1810–1875), and many others, wrote responsa on *agunot.*

However, information in the responsa is partial in many cases and does not provide precise data regarding persons and places involved in some cases. In many of the cases, even the date is not specified. Another methodological problem is that many responsa books were not published by the authors and appeared only long after they were written.[107] Responsa literature mostly deals with the second, third, and fourth categories of *agunot,* that is, involving *halitza,* identifying the dead, and *get* completion issues. There are also many other responsa on *agunot.*

Many other cases than those found in the responsa have been analyzed in this research. All the cases of *agunot* mentioned without a date or clear timing in the responsa were ignored in this research. The following methodology was adopted: cases in which a year is not mentioned were ignored and left out of the database, whereas instances in which only a place or a name was missing went into the database, while if both the place and name were missing, they were not included. There are two other databases, but they have much less information on *agunot.*

III. OFFICIAL RABBINATE PAPERS ESPECIALLY IN RUSSIA

From 1844 onward, officially recognized rabbis of the community became officers of the state in the Russian Empire. Many communities continued to employ unofficial rabbis alongside the official ones. However, many of those living in Jewish communities were prepared to assent to administration by the official state rabbis.[108] This occasionally created a new category of *agunot:* women thought to have married and divorced not exactly according to Jewish law.[109] However, research on these sources is just beginning.

IV. LETTERS AND OTHER INFORMATION CONCERNING IMMIGRANTS

This applies particularly to East European immigrants to the United States and England.[110] Such important sources can be found in the records of women's benevolent societies and of social workers. Most of these records relate to the early twentieth century and are thus outside the scope of this research.

This essay considers data mostly from Jewish newspapers and responsa. The information collected is analyzed in Tables 3–8.

Table 3 shows a constant rise in the number of cases reported in each decade. The reasons for this were the rising awareness to the issue of *agunot* as well as the increase in the number of newspapers, which also became more widespread. *Agunot* became a hot issue that helped to sell the newspapers.

Although 96 percent of the reported cases were deserted women, the numbers of deserted men might be higher than was known. In a patriarchal society, many men were reluctant to publicize the fact that they were deserted. Many of the cases of deserted men portrayed the deserting women as either out of their minds or unfaithful, which seems have been somewhat misleading.

Most information on the known cases of *agunot* comes from the media. The information published in the newspapers is also much fuller in details, and many cases can be followed for long periods of time. However, all sources have much more information (usually descriptions) about the absconding men and much less about the women.

Many cases of *agunot* were related to immigration. Furthermore, although in many cases the deserted did not go to other countries, others left their

Table 3. Identified *Agunot* from 1857 to 1896

Years	*Cases*	*Incidents*[1]
1851–1856	49	63
1857–1866	728	1,043
1867–1876	1,122	1,517
1877–1886	1,254	1,875
1887–1896	1,553	2,315
Total	4,712	6,813

1. Some cases appeared in several sources, hence the difference between the number of cases and the number of incidents.

Table 4. Gender Division of *Agunot*

	Number	*Percentage*
Males[1]	218	4.6%
Females	4,494	95.4%

1. A deserted man is one who could not be served a *get* because his wife left or became mentally ill. He might ask to rabbis to grant him permission to marry another wife, which was denied in most cases.

Table 5. Sources of *Agunot* Cases

Sources	
Jewish newspapers	2,560
General newspapers	229
TOTAL NEWSPAPERS	2,789
Responsa (Only 36 incidents appeared both in the responsa and in the newspapers. Rabbis who published advertisements about *agunot* did not discuss those cases in their responsa.)	1,584
Others[1]	339
TOTAL	4,712

1. Others in Table 5 refer mainly to archival records; for example, the *Jewish Board of Guardians*, MS173, Hartley Library, the University of Southampton.

Table 6. Breakdown of Cases

Percentage	*Number*	
40.24%	1,896	Immigration-related cases
40.91%	1,928	Nonimmigration-related cases
18.85%	888	Not clear if related to immigration

shtetls, villages, or cities for other places within the vast Russian and Hapsburg Empires. Another research finding is that toward the end of the nineteenth century, many couples or families migrated, and the desertions took place after immigration. The author is currently investigating this phenomenon.

Table 7 clearly shows that *agunot* were mostly an East European phenomenon: 4,024 out of 4,712 known cases (85.3 percent) were in Eastern

Table 7. Geographical Dispersion from 1857 to 1896

Number	*Place*
2,198	Russian Empire[1]
1,164	Habsburg Empire (including Galicia, but excluding Hungary)
367	Congress Poland
155	Romania
145	Hungary
135	Eretz Israel
134	United States
119	England
105	German states
44	Turkey
36	Morocco
35	Iraq
13	France
11	Syria
11	Caucasus
10	Egypt
6	Sweden
6	Persia
5	Algeria & Tunis
2	Australia
3	Denmark
1	Bulgaria
1	Canada
4,712	Total cases identified

1. On the geographical complexity of Eastern Europe, see Shaul Stampfer, "The Geographical Background of East European Jewish Migration to the United States before World War I," in *Migration across Time and Nations: Population Mobility in Historical Contexts* (ed. I. A. Glazier and L. De Rosa; London and New York: Holmes & Meier, 1985), 227–28, and "Patterns of Internal Jewish Migration in the Russian Empire," in *Jews and Jewish Life in Russia and the Soviet Union* (ed. Y. Ro'i; Ilford, Essex, and Portland: F. Cass, 1995), 37. Internal migration was the cause of many *agunot* cases.

Table 8. Destinations[1] of Known Immigration-Related Cases of Agunot

Destination	*1851–1866*	*1867–1876*	*1877–1886*	*1887–1896*	*Total*
United States	57	101	195	401	763
England	17	55	61	124	257
German states	16	55	35	16	122
Russian Empire	02	37	25	27	109
Congress Poland	25	34	16	15	09
Habsburg Empire (including Galicia excluding Hungary)	61	22	81	26	28
Romania	22	28	16	12	78
Hungary	21	14	11	13	59
France	8	9	25	5	47
Eretz Israel	32	19	31	21	67
Turkey	71	10	9	6	42
Australia and New Zealand	12	10	4	6	28
India	6	7	5	3	21
Egypt	3	4	1	12	20
Sweden	4	7	3	1	15
Argentina	0	1	1	13	15
Caucasus	0	6	4	5	15
Holland	2	1	4	2	9
South Africa	0	1	4	3	8
Syria	2	1	1	4	8
Brazil	0	0	1	6	7
Iraq	4	1	1	1	7
Italy	4	1	1	1	7
Canada	0	0	1	4	5
Morocco	0	1	1	2	4
Algeria	0	0	1	1	2
China	1	0	1	0	2
Mexico	1	1	0	0	2
Persia	0	0	2	0	2
Denmark	0	1	0	0	1
Portugal	1	0	0	0	1
Total	228	473	459	719	1,896

1. See Lloyd P. Gartner, "Jewish Migrants en Route from Europe to America: Traditions and Realities," *Jewish History* 1:2 (1986): 49–67.

Europe. However, since the 1890s, the number of cases in immigration countries (especially the United States) rose.

Table 8 shows that 1,293 out of 1,896 cases (68.2 percent) of husbands left for distant foreign countries (especially on the American continent), while 603 (31.9 percent) left for nearby countries (for example, from the Russian Empire to Romania or the Hapsburg Empire).

CONCLUSION: *AGUNOT,* IMMIGRATION, AND MODERNIZATION

Various conclusions can be drawn from this research:

1. The role of rabbis as the sole decision makers in the Jewish community, and in particular as far as women were concerned, was diminished by the Jewish media, which played a major role, as well as by other factors. Women, and *agunot* in particular, took advantage of this. Rabbis based their decisions on halachah [Jewish Law]. Rabbis could be more lenient toward women's needs on certain occasions. However, since the status of women in halachah was inferior, rabbis could not provide them with much help. As the phenomenon of *agunot* became more extensive, the rabbis became more helpless in supporting the women's cause.
2. Deserted women could not rely on the rabbinical establishment or other communal institutions. They came to realize that women needed to help themselves. Publishing advertisements was only one of the avenues open to women in dealing with their plight. The fact that religious Jewish women were now turning to the newly formed public arena was probably the most significant change. This also reflected women's deep understanding of the modern public sphere, especially with regard to the role of the media in modern society. The wide public airing given to the issue of *agunot* in the nineteenth century was an important indicator of East European Jewry's modernization.

   This research does not manage to give a satisfactory answer as to why desertion of wives became more widespread. Possibly, demographical parameters, such as the age difference between husbands and wives, particularly at the time of marriage, should also be taken into account in attempts to explain the issue.[111] Another explanation might be the effect of immigration, as discussed in the next point.

3. Immigration was among the major reasons behind the phenomenon of *agunot* in the nineteenth century. The sense of being in constant motion created a cultural environment that encouraged many men to desert their wives and families. But was the issue of *agunot* part of the immigration process,[112] or did immigration just exacerbate the matter?[113] Although in my view immigration certainly played a role, it was not causal. Rather, it was an added complication, together with other radical changes in Jewish family life and the role of women in Jewish society in nineteenth century Eastern Europe.[114]

With massive immigration, the desertion of women became a much greater predicament. In fact, immigration changed the nature of desertion. During the period of large-scale immigration, there were many more cases of husbands deserting their wives and families after arriving at their new destinations.

NOTES

1. See Noa Shashar, "1648–1850, עגונות וגברים נעלמים במרחב האשכנזי" [*Agunot* and the Men Who Disappeared in the Ashkenazi Realm, 1648–1850] (Ph.D. diss., Hebrew University of Jerusalem, 2012).

2. The halachic [Jewish legal] aspects have been much researched, especially by the Agunot Research Unit at the Centre for Jewish Studies at the University of Manchester, http://www.manchesterjewishstudies.org/agunah-research-unit/. See also Aviad HaCohen, *The Tears of the Oppressed: An Examination of the Agunah Problem; Background and Halachic Sources* (New York: Ktav, 2004).

3. For example, Anna R. Igra, *Wives without Husbands: Marriage, Desertion, and Welfare in New York, 1900–1935* (Chapel Hill: University of North Carolina Press, 2007); Reena Sigman Friedman, "Send My Husband Who Is in New York City: Husband Desertion in the American Jewish Community," *Jewish Social Studies,* old series, 44:1 (1982): 1–18; Ari Lloyd Fridkis, "Desertion in the Jewish Immigrant Family: The Work of the National Desertion Bureau in Cooperation with the Industrial Removal Office," *American Jewish History* 71:2 (1981): 285–99.

4. ChaeRan Freeze, *Jewish Marriage and Divorce in Imperial Russia* (Hanover and London: Brandeis University Press, 2002), 230–42.

5. Arthur Hertzberg, *Jews in America—Four Centuries of an Uneasy Encounter: A History* (London and New York: Columbia University Press, 1989), 198–99; Gur Alroey, *המהפכה השקטה*; [The Quiet Revolution: Jewish Emigration from the Russian Empire, 1875–1924] (Hebrew) (Jerusalem: Zalman Shazar Center, 2008).

6. Margalith Shilo, *Princess or Prisoner? Jewish Women in Jerusalem, 1840–1914* (Hanover and London: Brandeis University Press, 2005), 190–97.

7. Mark Baker, "The Voice of Deserted Jewish Women, 1867–1870," *Jewish Social Studies,* new series, 2:1 (1995): 98–123, reprinted in Anna Rosner Blay, ed., *Eshkolot: Essays in Memory of Rabbi Ronald Lubofsky* (Melbourne: Hybrid Publishers, 2002), 73–92.

8. See note 1.

9. Baker, "The Voice of Deserted Jewish Women," 98n4.

10. Hertzberg, *Jews in America,* chap. 10.

11. Freeze, *Jewish Marriage and Divorce in Imperial Russia,* 231.

12. Ms 173 1/12/2, 1870, 11, Special Collection, Hartley Library, Southampton. See also *Jewish Messenger* (May 25, 1871).

13. Ms 173 1/12/2, 1871, 37.

14. Ms 173 1/12/4. 1881, 45. See also "Runaway Husbands," *Jewish Messenger* (October 22, 1880).

15. Ms 173 1/12/4, 1886, 51.

16. Ms 173 1/12/5, 1892, 42.

17. Morris D. Waldman, "Family Desertion," in *Sixth Biennial Session of the National Conference of Jewish Charities in the United States* (St. Louis, May 17–19, 1910) (Baltimore: Press of Cohn & Pollock, 1910), 56 (available at http://www.bjpa.org/Publications/downloadPublication.cfm?PublicationID=1400).

18. Ibid., 59. Walman refers to Lee K. Frankel, "Report of Committee on Desertion," in *Fourth Biennial Session of the National Conference of Jewish Charities in the United States* (Philadelphia, May 6–8, 1906) (Baltimore: Press of Cohn & Pollock, 1907), 54 (available at http://www.bjpa.org/Publications/downloadPublication.cfm?PublicationID=2788). See also E. Tobenkin, "Deserted Wives in Ghetto Find Work in Junk Shops," *Chicago Tribune* (April 28, 1907), which refers to 150 deserted wives, many of them *agunot,* in Chicago. He even used the term *aguna* [*sic*!]. See also his follow-up article, "How the Deserted Wives of the Ghetto Try to Woo Back Their Husbands," *Chicago Tribune* (May 30, 1909), in which he claims that the "numbers [of *agunot*] Run into [the] Thousands."

19. Waldman, "Family Desertion," 72–73. The *Chicago Tribune,* as early as 1879, quoted a report by the local United Hebrew Relief Association, mentioning "twenty-one women, who have been deserted and left destitute." *Chicago Tribune* (September 23, 1879).

20. This categorization differs from the one by Michael Broyde, who researched the issue from a halachic perspective. See Michael J. Broyde, *Marriage, Divorce and the Abandoned Wife in Jewish Law* (New York: Ktav, 2000), 73–74. Freeze, *Jewish Marriage and Divorce in Imperial Russia,* 231, offered another categorization, which in my view does not cover all cases of *agunot.*

21. The case was much publicized: *HaMagid* (August 2, 1888), *HaMelitz* (July 31, 1888), *Hatzfira* (July 30, 1888), *Hatzvi* (August 17, 1888) (all in Hebrew); *American Israelite* (July 20, 1888), *The Ledger* [Warren, Pennsylvania] (July 13, 1888). Most references in

the American press were in newspapers published in Iowa: *Sioux County Herald* (July 19, 1888, and August 9, 1888), *Sioux Valley News* (July 19, 1888, and August 9, 1888), *Le Mars Semi-Weekly Globe* (July 21, 1888), *Summer Gazette* (July 19, 1888), *Carroll Sentinel* (July 27, 1888, and August 10, 1888), *Northern Vindicator* (July 20, 1888, and July 27, 1888), *Emmet County Republican* (July 19, 1888), *Van Wert Republican* [Ohio] (July 19, 1888), *Burligton Hawk-Eye* [Iowa] (July 12, 1888). See also the *Ottawa Daily Citizen* (July 11, 1888), *Aurora Daily Express* (July 11, 1888), *Chicago Daily Tribune* (July 11, 1888), *Omaha Daily Bee* (July 12, 1888), *Washington Critic* (July 12, 1888), *St. Paul Daily Globe* (July 11, 1888), *Atlanta Constitution* (July 13, 1888). Even the New Zealand newspapers published the case: see *Wanganui Chronicle* (September 6, 1888). Most of the New York press ignored the case with the exception of the *New York Tribune* (July 11, 1888).

22. Haya Brayne deserted Leib Berger in 1871 (*HaMagid* [May 5, 1874]), and Leah, Isaac Bloch's wife, was found in New York ten years after eloping from Poland (*New York Times* [June 1, 1878]). Fruma Leah, the wife of Yehoshua Naphtalewitz, disappeared in 1871, taking with her a son and a daughter (*HaMagid* [July 12, 1871]).

23. See the responsa book by Yosef Shaul Nathnson, *Shoel u-Meshiv* (שואל ומשיב), 1st ed. (Lemberg [Lvov], 1865; reprint, New York: Klilat Yofi Publishing, 1980), answer 279. For a typical *heter meah rabanim,* see Itzhak Tzioni, *Sefer Shelot ve-Tshuvot Olat Itzhak* [ספר שאלות ותשובות עולת יצחק] (Vilnius [Vilna in Hebrew]: Avram Tzvi Katzanekboyigen Press, 1885), sign 191.

24. Examples include the case of Ludwig and Auguta Cohen, *New York Times* (July 30, 1886), and the case in Russia cited in *HaMelitz* (February 1, 1886).

25. See the case described by Rabbi Avraham Borshtein, *Avnei Nezer* [אבני נזר] (Piotrkow Trybunalski [Peterkove in Hebrew], 1912; reprint, New York: Avraham Tzvi Friedman Press, n.d.), sign 134.

26. In 1885, a woman sent to prison for four years refused to receive a *get.* Yaacov Widenfeld, *Kohav me-Yaacov* [ספר שאלות ותשובות כוכב מיעקב] (New York: Moshe Aarom Kempfeler Publisher, 1958), sign 40.

27. In 1869, there was a case of a wife who refused to accept a *get* for such reasons; see Eliahu Gutmacher (Yosef Shmuel Kriger, reproduced from manuscript), אדרת אליהו, שאלות ותשובות* חידושים* ביאורים בש"ס ובארבעת חלקי שלחן ערוך [*Aderet Eliahu,* Part 2], אבן העזר וחושן משפט ועניינים שונים[Even Ha-Ezer and Other Matters] (Jerusalem: Rabbi Kook Institute, 1984), sign 43. The husband's request to marry another wife was refused. For a case of a woman who refused to take a *get* sent from America unless she received payment, see Shlomo Yehuda Tabak, ספר שאלות ותשובות תשורת ש"י [Hebrew: *Sefer Shelot ve-Tshuvot Tshurat Shay*] (2nd ed.; Sighetu Marmatiei [Sigat in Hebrew], 1905; reprint, New York: Grossman Publishing House, n.d.), sign 60.

28. See the Hebrew newspaper *Havatzelet* (January 29, 1886) and (February 5, 1886).

29. See the cases of Gitel in *HaMagid* (April 21, 1879); Raize Kaufman in *HaMelitz* (May 31, 1869); and the much publicized case of Leah, the widow of Israel Brahan, who tried

to locate her brother-in-law Itzik, in *HaMagid* (October 20, 1880; October 27, 1880; November 3, 1880; November 10, 1880; and November 17, 1880) and *HaTzfira* (June 22, 1880; June 29, 1880; July 13, 1880; and July 20, 1880).

30. *HaTzfira* (November 28, 1893, and December 1, 1893) and *HaMelitz* (July 23, 1894).

31. See the case of the widow of Yoel Yosefson in Rabbi Itzhak Elhanan Spector, עין יצחק, כולל שאלות ותשובות על ארבעה חלקי שלחן ערוך [Hebrew: *Eyn Itzhak*], Vol. 1 (Vilnius, 1889; reprint, New York: Hayim Ve-Bracha Publishers, 1965), sign 32.

32. For example, *HaMagid* (July 9, 1873) and *Hamelitz* (February 28, 1888, and March 28, 1889).

33. Avraham Tzvi Komineayer was killed by a building that collapsed, and his body could not be identified. See the responsum of Hayym Halbershtam, ספר שאלות ותשובות דברי חיים [Hebrew: *Sefer Shelot ve-Tshuvot Divrei Hayym*], Vol. 2 (Lemberg, 1872; reprint, Krakow, 1892, and New York: Bobover Yeshiva Bnaei-Zion, 2002 [the last edition was used here]), sign 53. The case was also discussed by Rabbi Avraham Tzvi Teomim, ספר חסד לאברהם [Hebrew: *Sefer Hesed le-Avraham*] (2nd ed.; Lemberg, 1898; photocopy, New York: Goldenberg Brothers, n.d.), sign 15.

34. For example, Shildel's husband, Dov ben Yeruham, a soldier in the Austrian Army, disappeared while fighting in Italy. See Rabbi Avraham Yehuda HaCohen Schwartz, שאלות ותשובות קול אריה [Hebrew: *Shelot ve-Tshuvot Kol Arie*] (Szilagysomlyd [Shimloy in Hebrew and Yiddish], Hungary, 1904; reprint, New York: Yeshivat Kol Yehuda, 1967), sign 87.

35. *HaMagid* (November 12, 1873, and November 19, 1873) and *HaMelitz* (May 2, 1884).

36. There is very little research on the phenomenon of *agunot* of soldiers in the nineteenth century. The only exception hardly refers to pre–World War I agunot: Sarah Gavriella Berger, *Sentenced to Marriage: Chained Women in Wartime* (Penn Humanities Forum on Travel, Undergraduate Mellon Research Fellows, 2006–2007), http://repository.upenn.edu/cgi/viewcontent.cgi?article=1001&context=uhf_2007.

37. The case of Shmuel Mivchem, in *HaMelitz* (June 10, 1865).

38. Spector, *Eyn Itzhak,* sign 40.

39. See the case of the *get* given by Issashar Kaminsky in *HaMagid* (April 1, 1868, and May 13, 1868).

40. Like the *get* given by Ishaya ben Yoel of Austria, see the responsa of Itzhak Aaron Itinga HaLevy, שו"ת מהרי"א הלוי [Hebrew: *Shut Maharia Ha-Levy*] (Lemberg: Uri Zeev Wolf Salat Press, 1893), part 2, sign 12.

41. Michael Stanislawski, *For Whom Do I Toil: Judah Leib Gordon and the Crisis of Russian Jewry* (London and New York: Oxford University Press, 1988), 127–28. See also Stanley L. Nash, "Kotzo Shel Yod" [The Tip of the Yod], *CCAR Journal: A Reform Jewish Quarterly* 53:3 (2006): 107–88.

42. Like the wife of F. See Rabbi Moshe Teomim, ספר שאלות ותשובות דבר משה [Hebrew: *Sefer Shelot ve-Tshuvot Devar Moshe*] (Lemberg: Uri Zeev Wolf Salat Press, 1864), question 79.

43. See the notes of Rabbi Shmuel Mohaliver in Yehuda Leib HaCohen Maimon, ed., שו"ת מהר"ש מוהליבר, שאלות ותשובות וחקרי הלכה [Hebrew: *Shut Marash Mohaliver*] (Jerusalem: Rabbi Kook Institute, 1980), part "Even Ha-Ezer," answer 4.

44. Spector, *Eyn Itzhak,* 172.

45. Nathnson, *Shoel u-Meshiv,* answer 122.

46. On Yustus, see *HaMagid* (January 8, 1885, and February 26, 1885) and *American Israelite* (July 25, 1884). On conversion and its effect on the family, see CheaRun Freeze, "When Chava Left Home: Gender, Conversion, and the Jewish Family in Tsarist Russia," *Polin* 18 (2005): 153–88.

47. For example, the case of Gitle Mogiovskia; see Freeze, *Jewish Marriage and Divorce in Imperial Russia,* 238. See also *HaMelitz* (December 6, 1895).

48. Freeze, *Jewish Marriage and Divorce in Imperial Russia,* 266, 365n171. The issue was discussed mostly in *HaMelitz* (April 12, 1886; April 30, 1886; May 10, 1886; May 14, 1886; June 11, 1886; December 4, 1889; and March 27, 1890) and *HaTzfira* (March 25, 1890). The rabbinical exchange was republished in 1985. The debate took place in 1885 and 1886. Avraham Yoel Abelson, תקנות עגונות (ב׳ חלקים) שו"ת בדין חליצת מומר [Hebrew: *Takanot Agunot*] (part 1: Odessa, 1885; part 2: Odessa, 1887), reprinted by Yehoshua and Itzhak Yaacov Abelson; ספר עץ חיים. שו"ת, חדו"ת וחקרי הלכה מתורתם של ג׳ דורות לבית אבלסון ובו נכללו שו"ת וחדו"ת נדירים מגאוני עולם בדורות האחרונים [Hebrew: *Sefer Etz Hayym*] (Hadera and Jerusalem: Published by the family, 1985). The responsa were published originally in Odessa in 1885 (Part 1) and 1887 (Part 2). Part 1 includes eight letters from rabbis, and Part 2 includes forty-six letters.

49. Bernard S. Jackson, "*Agunah* and the Problem of Authority" (text of lecture, delivered in London on March, 13, 2001, under the auspices of the Institute of Advanced Legal Studies, the Oxford Centre for Hebrew and Jewish Studies, and the Jewish Law Publication Fund Trustees), http://static1.1.sqspcdn.com/static/f/784513/11612709/1302164223207/BSJ+Agunah+and+the+Problem+of+Authority+2001.pdf?token=rW58WKgckihjG1wxP8zcAMZb5gM%3D.

50. Most advertisements concerning *agunot* were published in Hebrew; very few were published in Yiddish, although Yiddish was the most common spoken language among the Jews. Thus, in the Yiddish newspaper קול מבשר [*Kol Mevaser*], only five advertisements from *agunot* were found for the years between 1862 and 1872.

51. On Jewish journalism especially in Eastern Europe, see Susanne Marten-Finnis, *Vilna as a Centre of the Modern Jewish Press, 1840–1928: Aspirations, Challenges and Progress* (Oxford: Peter Lang, 2004); Gideon Kouts, *The Hebrew and Jewish Press in Europe: Selected Problems in Its History* (Paris and London: Suger Press, 2006); Oren Soffer, "The Case of the Hebrew Press: From the Traditional Model of Discourse to the Modern Model," *Written Communication* 21:2 (2004): 141–79.

52. Menucha Gilboa, לקסיקון העיתונות העברית במאות השמונה עשרה והתשע עשרה [Hebrew: *Hebrew Newspapers' Lexicon in the Eighteenth and Nineteenth Centuries*] (Tel Aviv: Mosad Bialik, 1992), 119–35.

53. Baker, "The Voice of Deserted Jewish Women."

54. A total of seventeen Hebrew newspapers and seven Yiddish newspapers were consulted, and eight local Jewish newspapers were screened.

55. See also editorial notes, *HaMagid* (August 7, 1862), and general response, *HaMagid* (August 14, 1862, and June 14, 1865).

56. Editorial in *HaMagid* (June 23, 1869).

57. For example, *Hamelitz* (February 9, 1865), signed by Rabbi Yaacov Yosef of Oddessa; *Hamagid* (May 6, 1866), signed by Rabbi Moshe Shor of Yassi, Romania; *Hamagid* (July 5, 1865), signed by Rabbi Avraham Kluger of Brody; *Hamagid* (April 13, 1870), signed by Rabbi Isaac Shor of Bucharest, Romania; *Hamagid* (July 28, 1875), signed by Rabbi Shmuel Mohaliver of Radom, Poland.

58. Most papers stated this at the top of the front page. On February 12, 1858, and September 12, 1860, *HaMagid* announced that advertisements on *agunot* would be free of charge.

59. The case of Yocheved was rare, since her advertisement for her husband Avraham Meyer Aphter was published in Hebrew as well as in German. See *HaMagid* (June 11, 1872; September 11, 1872; May 28, 1873) and *Der Israelite* (January 20, 1875). The advertisement in the German Jewish Orthodox newspaper was published two years after the Hebrew one. The advertisement in *Der Israelite* was a rare reference to *agunot,* the only one in the newspaper in that year. In 1909 Elias Tobenkin, in a report on *agunot,* claimed that advertisements were very useful in finding the runaway husbands; "How the Deserted Wives of the Ghetto Try to Woo Back Their Husbands," *Chicago Tribune* (May 30, 1909). However, advertisements seem to have been less effective in late nineteenth century Russia.

60. Freeze, *Jewish Marriage and Divorce in Imperial Russia,* 235–36.

61. *HaMagid* (July 17, 1872, and June 28, 1876). And after thirteen years, three additional advertisements in *HaMelitz* (September 7, 1889; September 9, 1889; and October 2, 1889).

62. Tzila Beyla offered twenty-five rubles to cover the expenses of finding her husband Yaacov Kantiger (*HaTzfira* [June 7, 1881]). Tzipa Abramovitz offered five hundred rubles as a payment to her husband in exchange for her release (*HaMagid* [June 25, 1873, and August 30, 1873]). Miriam Tabirsky offered fifty rubles to anyone who would help her find her runaway husband (*HaMagid* [January 27, 1874]).

63. *HaMagid* (October 22, 1873). The story was initiated and followed up by *HaMagid.* On Hutzin, see Lev Hakak, אגרות הרב שלמה בכור חוצין [Hebrew: *Igrot Ha-Rav Shlomo Behor Hutzin*] (Tel Aviv: Ha-Kibutz Ha-Mehuhad Publishing, 2005).

64. *HaMagid* (June 10, 1864; September 7, 1864; December 12, 1864; February 1, 1865; and June 21, 1865).

65. In the case of Frieda and Levy Itzhak Frankel, an advertisement was published in *HaMagid* (April 19, 1865, and April 26m 1865), and then the local rabbis asked for assistance in *HaMagid* (May 2, 1865, and February 7, 1866). The final piece of information was provided by a reader (*HaMagid* [March 21, 1866]).

66. For example, *HaMagid* (January 17, 1884, April 3, 1884, and September 24, 1884).

67. The first piece accusing Kahalan of desertion was published in *HaMagid* on July 18, 1878. The publication originated from Vilnius. On November 20, 1878, the newspaper published a retraction by the board of the Jewish community of Teltz (Telšiai in Lituanian). On January 29, 1879, the Vilnius version of the story was published again, with many more details. On April 30, 1879, another retraction, this time from New York, appeared in *HaMagid.*

68. There is a decrease from an average of forty-five incidents per year in the preceding decade to an average of twenty in the years 1879–1881. The Kalahan affair was not the main reason for downsizing in references to *agunot* in *HaMagid.* The policy of the new editor, David Gordon, was the main reason for this, as discussed later.

69. The article "America" in *HaMagid* (December 18, 1862) quoted the *Jewish Record,* misspelling the name of the newspaper. Another article by the same name in *HaMagid* (August 29, 1886) was translated from the *Hebrew Observer.*

70. See the public appeal by the editor of *HaMagid* to Rabbi Shlomo Kluger of Brody in *HaMagid* (July 11, 1866). In an earlier instance, Rabbi Kluger responded to the challenge by *HaMelitz* with a very long letter in *HaMelitz* (April 25, 1864, and August 3, 1864).

71. On serial deserters, see Table 1.

72. *HaMagid* (March 10, 1869).

73. *HaMelitz* (January 5, 1885); *HaMagid* (December 18, 1884).

74. *HaMagid* (August 17, 1864; September 13, 1865; and September 28, 1870). Hirsch Frankel was another professional criminal who deserted his wife; see *HaMagid* (May 26, 1874, and October 21, 1874).

75. *HaLebanon* (April 9, 1873).

76. See many examples of this in the responsa of Naphtali Tzzvi Yehuda Berlin, משיב דבר [Hebrew: *Meshiv Davar*], Part D, sign 38 (Warsaw: M. I. Halter Press, n.d.; 2nd ed., New York, n.p., 1950).

77. For more on *agunot* in the Jewish newspapers, see Haim Sperber, "The Phenomenon of *Agunot* in East European Jewish Society as Reflected in Jewish Newspapers, 1857–1896," *Kesher* 40 (2010): 102–8 (in Hebrew).

78. Baker, "The Voice of Deserted Jewish Women." As a rule, Zilbermann emphasized various aspects of social life in *HaMagid.* See Mark Baker, "Diagnosing the Jewish

Condition: Medical Discourse and Social Reform in *Hamagid,* 1860–1881," in *History on the Edge: Essays in Memory of John Foster (1944–1994)* (ed. M. Baker; Melbourne: University of Melbourne Press, 1997), 117–40.

79. Editorial, *HaMagid* (September 13, 1865, and June 23, 1869).

80. *HaLebanon* (March 21, 1870).

81. *HaLebanon* (July 17, 1879).

82. Yosef Salmon, "David Gordon and '*Ha-Maggid*': Changing Attitudes toward Jewish Nationalism, 1860–1882," *Modern Judaism* 17:2 (1997), 109–24; Carol Diament, "The First Hebrew Newspaper [*Ha-Maggid*]: Early Hebrew Journalism and Its Political Roles," *Journalism History,* 30:1 (2004): 31–39.

83. Gilboa, *Hebrew Newspapers' Lexicon.*

84. *HaMelitz,* with Alexander Zederboim as the editor, was published in Odessa. On Zederboim (sometime referred to as Zederbaum), see Steven J. Zipperstein, *The Jews of Odessa: A Cultural History, 1799–1881* (Stanford: Stanford University Press, 1985), 81–82; Stanislawski, *For Whom Do I Toil,* 81–82 and 218–19. Zederboim was also the initiator and publisher of the first Yiddish weekly, *Kol Mevaser,* published in Odessa between 1861 and 1872. However, *Kol Mevaser* made very little mention of the issue of *agunot.* See Shmuel Versses, "[The] Woman's Voice in the Yiddish Weekly *Kol Mevaser*" [Hebrew], *Huliot* 4 (1997): 53–82. On *HaMelitz,* see Gilboa, *Hebrew Newspapers' Lexicon,* 138–49. Between 1881 and 1889, Zederboim published another Yiddish weekly, *Yudishes Folksblatt.*

85. Gilboa, *Hebrew Newspapers' Lexicon,* 167–81.

86. Ella Bauer, "The Race for a Hebrew Daily: How Did '*Hatzfira*' Become a Daily Newspaper" [Hebrew], *Kesher* 32 (2002): 87–96.

87. Including the following newspapers. In Hebrew: *Hayom, Havatzelet, HaCarmel, HaLebanon, HaMagid, HaMevasher, Hamelitz, Hamitzpe, Haperach, Hatzvi* (appeared sometimes as *HaOr*), *Hatzfiea, Hashahar, Mahazikei Hadat, Kol Mahazikei Hadat, Moriya, Nesher* (appeared sometimes as *Hanesher*), *Ivri Anochi,* and *Aley Haperach.* In Yiddish: *Das Folksblatt, Di Tzukunft* (appeared in 1884 as *Der Poilisher Idel), Der Yidisher Express, Haynt, Warshaver Yudisher Tzeitung, Yiddishes Tageblatt* (appeared sometimes as *Der Morgenshtern*), *Kol Mevaser,* and *Forverts.* In English: *American Hebrew* (sometimes appeared as the *Hebrew American*), *American Israelite, Jewish Chronicle, Jewish Messenger, Jewish Standard, Jewish World.* In German: *Allgemeine Zeitung des Judentums* and *Der Israelite.*

88. Much of the responsa literature can be traced using the Responsa Project Database of Bar Ilan University, www.responsa.co.il.

89. For example, the archives of Rabbi Moshe Nahum Yerushalimski at the Schocken Institute in Jerusalem, http://www.schocken-jts.org.il/library4.htm. See Haim Sperber, "Responsa Books as a Source for Investigating *Agunot* in Jewish Society" [Hebrew], *Quntres: An Online Journal for the History, Culture, and Art of the Jewish Book* 2:1 (2011): 47–48, https://taljournal.jtsa.edu/index.php/quntres.

90. See Shashar, "*Agunot* and the Men Who Disappeared in the Ashkenazi Realm." The Responsa Project gave 1,608 citations of *agunah,* 1,524 citations of *igun* (עיגון), 792 citations of *agunot,* 276 citations of *agun* (עגון), and 633 citations of *iguna,* retrieved on May 2015. Many citations reflect pre–nineteenth century cases, but many are post-1896, the year in which the research ends.

91. Shashar, "*Agunot* and the Men Who Disappeared in the Ashkenazi Realm."

92. Ibid.

93. On the role of the media in changing the Jewish public sphere, see Derek J. Penslar, "Introduction: The Press and the Jewish Public Sphere," *Jewish History* 14:1 (2000): 3–8.

94. Naomi Seidman, "Gender and the Disintegration of the Shtetl in Modern Hebrew and Yiddish Literature," in Steven T. Katz, ed., *The Shtetl: New Evaluations in Its History and Character* (New York: New York University Press, 2007), 193–210.

95. See Sperber, "Responsa Books."

96. *Meshiv Davar,* Part B, sign 8.

97. Ibid., Part D, sign 49.

98. Ibid., Part B, sign 9.

99. See Hayyim Berlin, ספר נשמת חיים—דרשות, מאמרים ומכתבים בענייני ציבור, חיזוק הדת ומערכות ישראל [Hebrew: *Sefer Nishmat Hayyim*] (ed. Yaacov Kosovsky-Schahor; Bnei Berak: n.p., 2003), sign 137. On *HaLebanon,* see Roni Be'er-Marx, "Halevanon': Zur Neuinterpretation eines Orthodoxen Organs," in *Die jüdische Presse im Europäischen Kontext, 1686–1990* (ed. Susanne Marten-Finnis and Markus Winkler; Bremen: Edition Lumiere, 2006), 89–99.

100. Berlin, *Sefer Nishmat Hayyim,* sign 24. See also Eliezer Brodt, "Corrections and Clarifications on Two Editions of R. Chaim Berlin's Responsa: An Egregious Example of Censorship," *The Sofrim Blog* (October 12, 2009), www.sofrim.blogspot.com.

101. David ben Shmuel Freidman, ספר שאילת דוד [Hebrew: *Sefer Sheilat David*] (Piotrkow Trybunalski [Petrkove in Hebrew]: Mordechai Tzederboim Press, 1913), part of *Even Ha-Ezer* (in Hebrew), sign 16.

102. Shalom Mordechai Shvedron, ספר שאלות ותשובות מהרש"ם [Hebrew: *Sefer Shelot ve-Tshuvot Maharsham*] (Jerusalem: Hatam Sofer Institute, 1974 [first published in 1902]), Part 7, sign 40.

103. Ibid., Part 1, sign 8. In the case of Hannah Golda, again in 1895, he encouraged her to advertise her case in the newspapers (ibid., Part 7, sign 150).

104. *HaMagid* (June 22, 1858; June 20, 1860; July 3, 1861; August 28, 1871; and October 1, 1871); so did Rabbi Mordechai Weisman Hayut in *HaMagid* (July 28, 1860, and August 14, 1867), Rabbi Hayyim Nathan Dambitzer in *HaMagid* (August 21, 1862), and Rabbi Shlomi Kluger, via his son Avraham Beyamin Kluger, in *HaMagid* (September 21, 1864, and September 28, 1864).

105. Haim Gartner, "New Uses of an Old Tool—The Scope of Influence of 19th Century Galician Rabbis according to Statistical Analysis of Responsa Literature" [Hebrew], in *Papers of the 12th World Congress of Jewish Studies* (Hebrew Section), Vol. 2 (Jerusalem: World Congress for Jewish Studies, 1990), 127–36.

106. Aaron Rakeffet-Rothkoff, "Rabbi Yitzhak Elhanan Spektor of Kovno, Spokesman for *Agunot*," *Tradition* 29:3 (1995): 5–20.

107. Shmuel Glick, "Changes, Omitting and Inner Censorship in Responsa Books" [Hebrew], *Quntres: An Online Journal for the History, Culture and Art of the Jewish Book* 1:1 (2009): 40–76, https://talijornal.jtsa.edu/index.php/quntres/article/viewFile/40/8.

108. See Michael Stanislawski, "Reflections on the Russian Rabbinate," in *Jewish Religious Leadership: Image and Reality*, Vol. 2 (ed. Jack Wertheimer; New York: Jewish Theological Seminary, 2004), 429–46.

109. See the case of Finkel and Shmuel Oppenheim, (Mohaliver, Shut Marash Mahaliver, Even Ha-Ezer, sign 4).

110. The list of sources is huge, including records at the Yivo Archives, the American Jewish Historical Society Archives in New York, the American Jewish Archive in Cincinnati, and the Jewish Board of Guardian Records in the Southampton University Archive, among many others. Some of the early twentieth century letters were published by Gur Alroey, *Bread to Eat and Clothes to Wear: Letters from Jewish Migrants in the Early Twentieth Century* (Detroit: Wayne State University Press, 2011).

111. Tables A.4, A.5, and A.7 in the appendix to Freeze, *Jewish Marriage and Divorce in Imperial Russia.* See also the case of the Jews of Mitau in Andrejs Plakans, "Age and Family Structures among the Jews of Mitau, Kurland, 1833–1834," *History of the Family* 8:4 (2003): 545–61 and Table 4, 553. On the parallel structure of families in Russia, see Matti Polla, "Family Systems in Central Russia in the 1830's and 1890's," *History of the Family* 11:1 (2006): 27–44.

112. Olive Anderson offers a useful discussion on the subject, although the English scene was much different than the East European one; see Olive Anderson, "Emigration and Marriage Break-Up in Mid-Victorian England," *Economic History Review* 50:1 (1997): 104–9.

113. See the different views of G. Alroey, "'And I Remained Alone in a Vast Land': Women in the Jewish Migration from Eastern Europe," *Jewish Social Studies,* new series, 12:3 (2006): 39–72, and Lloyd P. Gartner, "Women in the Great Jewish Migration," *Jewish Historical Studies* 40 (2005): 129–39.

114. On Jewish family life in the preceding era, see Freeze, *Jewish Marriage and Divorce in Imperial Russia,* and Tamar Salmon-Mack, "Marital Issues in Polish Jewry, 1650–1800" [Hebrew] (Ph.D. diss., Hebrew University of Jerusalem, 2002).

II. THE PRESENT

Lost, Hidden, Discovered: Theologies of DNA in North American Judaism and Messianic Judaism

Sarah Imhoff and Hillary Kaell

Family Tree DNA, a commercial personal genetic testing company, advertises its services by appealing to a Jewish past: "Your ancestors left clues in your DNA which you can use to determine your deep ancestral origins and to link you with others in recent times. We can compare your results with our database—the largest of its kind in the world—and tell you whether those clues indicate possible Jewish ancestry and whether you match others who are Jewish."[1] The company subtly markets itself to both Jews and non-Jews, suggesting that DNA testing can help a person understand something fundamental about oneself and one's relationship to others.

In her work on Native Americans and DNA, Kim Tallbear uses the phrase "gene talk" to refer to "the idea that essential truths about identity inhere in sequences of DNA."[2] She shows how people use the interpretations of DNA sequences to make legal and political claims but also to understand themselves more deeply. In all of these processes, Tallbear notes, gene talk often takes interpretation for fact and can even mislead. In our respective research on Jews and Messianic Jews we have found similar kinds of gene talk, though the political stakes are quite different than for Native Americans. Like Tallbear, we focus less on the science itself than on how people make social meaning out of technological possibilities.

Gene talk permeates American culture at large. From the 1970s television miniseries *Roots* to Henry Louis Gates's recent PBS show *Finding Your Roots,* Americans have sought out and embraced their distinctive versions of ethnic heritage. In *Roots Too,* Matthew Frye Jacobson shows how white U.S.-born Americans embraced Irish, Italian, Polish, and other European ethnic pasts. This "ethnic revival," a legacy of the 1960s, birthed a new way of talking about identity—a "new syntax of nationality and belonging,"[3] as Jacobson writes. This syntax of belonging is very much still with us, and now gene talk participates in discourses of belonging right alongside talk of food, grandparents, art, and music.

The scholarly literature that analyzes gene talk and white ethnic revival, however, has a tendency to overlook religion or relegate it to being merely another marker of cultural difference. It positions gene talk as a discourse about ethnicity and place in society without noticing that it can also be about place in a theological or cosmic narrative. The phenomena we analyze here participate in something that looks like "ethnic revival." That is, we might have said that gene talk and DNA testing form a new wave—or a new tool in the toolkit—of contemporary ethnic revival. And while this is true, it is not the whole story. In these Jewish and Messianic cases, gene talk and its power construct much more than just an ethnos. They participate in constructing religious identities, and they make theological claims. Even in the case of secular Jews, as we will see, a secularized version of a theological narrative underwrites gene talk and its significance.

Based on research conducted on North American Judaism and Messianic Judaism, this essay explores how gene talk operates as parallel phenomenon for these two groups. That is, gene talk shares certain traits, yet the reasons behind it ultimately diverge. We begin by analyzing what we mean by "gene talk," where it happens, and what it sounds like in each of these communities. We then consider the implications for ideas of family, specifically how this includes notions of "lost" relatives and "hidden" roots as well as the interaction between gene seekers and their family members. After noting how the two sets of vocabularies and reasons for appeal seem quite similar, we conclude by clarifying how gene talk does quite different authorizing work for Jews and Messianics.

GENE TALK AND JEWISH COMMUNAL NARRATIVES

North American Jews talk a lot about DNA. "I haven't done a DNA test yet," explained a Jewish man, but I want "to test to help solve the mystery of my great-grandfather's family."[4] "Jews whose great-grandparents were chased from their Russian shtetls," announced a magazine article, "leave molecular scars adhering to our DNA."[5] And many Jews have their DNA tested even when they assume that they already know the results. As one woman posted in an online group, "I got my DNA results. . . . I'm 99% Ashkenazi. No surprise there!"[6] A confirmation of Jewish heritage like this can make people feel connected to the past, imagine closeness with ancestors, and narrate rich stories about personal histories. When it provides a sense of rootedness and ethnic distinctiveness, this Jewish gene talk reflects the larger trends of white ethnic revival. But gene talk in the Jewish community also reflects a distinctively Jewish set of ideas and history.

DNA is on the radar of many Ashkenazi Jews because of their distinctive role in the history of science. Historically, Ashkenazim have been a relatively endogamous population—that is, they largely married and had children with one another. This relative endogamy meant that they became an early interest of geneticists. And many geneticists were Ashkenazi themselves. The result was that Ashkenazim were overrepresented in the people studying and the people being studied. Moreover, the prevalence of Tay Sachs and other heritable diseases, such as Gauchers, in Ashkenazi populations led to Jewish public health campaigns promoting DNA testing of partners before marriage or planning children. Recent testing for BRCA1 and BRCA2 genetic mutations, also somewhat more prevalent in people with Ashkenazi ancestry, have likewise contributed to increased awareness of genetics for North American Jews.

Even so, the deepest appeal and meaning of gene talk in Jewish communities is not the scientific facts that it offers Jews. It's not even disease awareness. The deepest appeal of gene talk is the narrative it helps create: DNA functions as a trope in a narrative about the coherence of Jewish identity and peoplehood. Jews talk about "our ancestors," "our people's history," and "our own families' forebears" as imprinted "in our DNA."[7] A recent headline proclaimed "Genetic Study Proves Jews Are a People."[8] After his DNA test, a Canadian-born Jew explained that "One of the reasons I made aliyah is because I believe I am actually from this area [Israel/Palestine], and I do feel like I'm returning home."[9] All this gene talk suggests fundamental and scientific interconnections among Jews across history and an ancestral homeland. These ideas of historical and religious memory living in genetic material, as we will see, are similar to the way that Messianics engage in gene talk. But the underlying reasons for this gene talk, which depends on theological and religious ideas, diverge for the two groups. We argue that for Jews, gene talk can serve as a confirmation—or, for nonreligious Jews, as a secular substitution—for the theological idea of peoplehood. Whether or not it is scientifically accurate—and in many cases it is not—gene talk provides support for the idea that Jews are a fundamentally connected, cohesive, and distinctive people.

When North American Jews are interested in genetics and DNA, they often go where most Americans get their information: the Internet. As with any topic, the Internet offers scientific rigor and clear lay interpretations of technical material, as well as poor, utterly wrong, or misguided information. It is not our interest here to police erroneous information about Jews and genetics. Rather, we seek to clarify what information people are encountering and how they interact with it.

Many Jews get information about Jews and genetics from websites with specifically Jewish content or missions. Two large Jewish religious websites,

Chabad.com and Aish.com, both affiliated with observant forms of Judaism, are popular locations for curious Jews. Because these websites offer the most comprehensive online resources for many religious topics, many Jews, even the nonobservant, find themselves getting their information from these sites. The response to an Aish.com article titled "The Cohanim—DNA Connection" included more than twenty accounts with personal interest stories or stories about the links between DNA and Jewish identity. One man wrote that "I never understood what it meant to be a cohain before this article." Several shared the results of their own tests, such as the man who had just been DNA tested by Family Tree DNA and had the Cohen Modal Haplotype.

Another, likely a non-Orthodox Jew, wrote that "In my temple [a word for synagogue used by Reform Jews but not others], before the evening prayers, there are discussions about origins," which he connected to DNA. Another commenter, who may or may not be Jewish, framed her response in religious terms: "I am so thrilled to see yet again of God's handiwork that he has kept the priesthood line of Aaron!" Non-Jews too get information from these sites. The same Aish article, for instance, included a comment from a Finnish person about "Jewish roots among Finnish people"; he wondered if DNA testing could help uncover the true history.[10]

MyJewishLearning.com, a religiously unaffiliated website, also features several articles about DNA.[11] They contain more scientific information and less traditional exegesis than those on Chabad.com and Aish.com, but they still aim to make the genetics comprehensible to nonexperts. The comment sections for many articles—"Ashkenazim, Sephardim, Mizrahim," "Native Americans and Jews," and others—overflow with commenters announcing or puzzling through their own DNA. Here too, commenters include non-Jews ("I am non Jewish but very interested,"[12] "I'm America Indian on my father's side, my daughter and I have a love for Israel and want to live there one day. Deep down we feel we are Jewish"[13]) and Jews ("I am from the Tribe of Levi. . . . We Jews go back a few thousand years"[14]). There are far fewer participants who frame their questions or comments in terms of Torah observance, but the relationship of genetic information to biblical history is still a major source of conversation on nonreligious sites. On all of these Jewish content websites, then, gene talk abounds.

Jews also go to the websites of DNA testing companies themselves to understand "Jewish genetics" and DNA. Many of these companies have specifically designed their websites, explanations, and even tests to appeal to Jews. 23andme, Family Tree DNA, DNA Consultants, and Roots for Real all have specific tests marketed toward Jews. Family Tree DNA has hosted webinars, or online seminars, specifically for Jews doing genealogical research. As these for-profit companies suggest, there is a growing and profitable industry focused on DNA, genetics, and Jewishness. And it is in these companies' interest to market DNA as though it tells essential stories about personal history and identity. If they framed DNA as merely a sequence of chemical compounds, then far fewer people would be interested in their own DNA results.

There are also a growing number of discussion groups for Jews interested in DNA, genealogical research, and family histories. The "Tracing the Tribe—Jewish Genealogy on Facebook" group had nearly 7,000 members as of December 2014. The discussion groups on the website JewishGen, which explains that it is designed to "ensure Jewish continuity" by presenting resources for genealogy, support thousands of posters. JewishGen, one of the largest Jewish genealogy websites, is affiliated with both the Museum of Jewish Heritage and Ancestry.com, and its "Family Tree of the Jewish People" currently includes information on over five million individuals submitted by more than forty-five hundred Jewish genealogists.[15]

As the commenter who said that the members of his temple talked about "origins" and DNA before evening prayers suggests, gene talk takes place offline too. While many of these conversations happen spontaneously, some occur in settings more formal than synagogues. Since its 1981 inception, the International Conference on Jewish Genealogy has grown significantly, and it includes popular sessions focused on DNA. At the 2013 conference, for instance, Family Tree DNA sponsored sessions, led by its founder Bennett Greenspan, called "Understanding, Interpretation, and Use of DNA Results" and "Haplogroups: What They Are and What They Mean for Jews." Seven other sessions also focused on DNA.

Jews from all religious affiliations as well as nonaffiliated Jews participate in gene talk. Orthodox Jews tend to be particularly aware of DNA because of public health campaigns promoting the awareness of and testing for genetic diseases. A genetic testing company called Dor Yeshorim (Hebrew for "the generation of the upright"), for instance, has become very popular among young adult Jews considering marriage. The company screens each partner and then tells them whether they are compatible or not; that is, whether both partners are carriers of the same recessive gene that could lead to children with these diseases.

But observant Jews also use gene talk in realms well beyond that of the medical concerns for potential children. Chabad connects DNA evidence to religious practice, using the former as an argument for pursuing the latter. "Ashkenazi, Sephardi, Yemenite and Italian *kohanim* can actually trace their backgrounds back to the Jews of the Exodus. And if modern science has given us the tools to prove common ancestry, isn't the next obvious step to dedicate ourselves to our common purpose—G-d's Torah and mitzvot?"[16] They even use it as evidence for the historical moral uprightness of Jews: "But almost 100% of all men with family tradition of priesthood *do* descend from *kohanim.* Generation after generation of Jewish women were faithful to their husbands and their tradition. What a proud record of fidelity. . . . This devotion to our spouses and our G-d has always been the way of the Jew."[17] For religiously observant Jews, then, gene talk can be about continuity, as Dor Yeshorim and its mission demonstrate. It can also be about affirming religious practices and theological concepts, as Chabad shows.

Nonreligious Jews also participate in gene talk. Unlike the Chabad article, they do not frame genetic connections as a reason to do mitzvot, but these connections are nevertheless meaningful for them. One commenter on MyJewishLearning.com identified as secular and celebrated how "DNA testing has been able to show how many genes we have are Jewish," which he equated with "direct blood," though he was careful to say that he welcomed converts too.[18] Others ask explicitly how to understand their identity, given their genetic and historical knowledge. A commenter to the historical article "Who Are the Semites?" reprinted on MyJewishLearning.com wrote that "My Jewish ancestors are from Lithuania, Russia and Poland. My sister sent in my Dad's DNA. Came back showing Sephardic connections. . . . [H]ow do I find out my race?"[19] Nonreligious Jews, then, also assume that DNA can tell them something essential and meaningful about themselves. They imagine that DNA holds clues to their identity and social place.

GENE TALK IN MESSIANIC JUDAISM

Messianic Judaism is a movement of congregations that incorporate aspects of Jewish ritual into evangelical or charismatic Christian worship. Its current form dates to the late 1960s, when young Jewish converts to Christianity, often associated with California's Jesus movement, joined the "Hebrew Christian" descendants of earlier converts to form congregations and then denominational associations that retained aspects of their Jewish heritage.[20] Today, estimates of the number of Messianic Jews vary widely—anywhere from 30,000 to 2.5 million—but it is clear that the movement is growing rapidly.[21]

Messianic Jewish leaders view the movement as by and for people like them, "ethnic" Jews who believe in Jesus. Jewish men are favored for congregational and denominational leadership; "ethnic" Jews comprise the movement's public face as authors, musicians, Davidic dance teachers, and televangelist talk show guests or hosts. Yet upwards of 70 percent of congregants are in fact "gentile believers" (GBs), as they are known in the movement, a fact almost completely ignored by scholars.[22] With growing numbers of GBs, congregations are also becoming increasingly diverse and include Americans of African, European, and Hispano origin as well as immigrants from across the globe.

Most congregants, gentile or Jewish, arrive from Pentecostal or charismatic churches that follow some form of premillennialist theology.[23] They believe that contemporary Jews are the genetic descendants of biblical Israelites and are thus crucial because, first, they are of the same lineage as Jesus, and thus their rituals and prayers most closely approximate what Jesus knew during his incarnation on Earth. And second, Jews are understood to have a key role to in the End Times that will presage the Messiah's return. To be a Jew is thus to be situated at the very center of biblical and apocalyptic narratives.

Gene talk, though largely stifled by the ethnic Jewish leadership, remains so prevalent that GBs often encounter it shortly after their arrival. Unlike North American Jews, however, few GBs actually test their DNA. Gene talk is thus a space of imagined possibilities, filled with discursive weaving and dodging: "I don't know that I have any Jewish heritage. But maybe there is. . . . I don't say that I'm not but I don't say that I am."[24] This kind of talk hints at a complicated question: is Judaism inherited or not? Most GBs associate certain essentialized traits with Jewishness, ranging from the physiognomic (big noses) to the societal (community oriented, book smart).[25] Yet they are circumspect about labeling Jews a race, which they define as "scientifically" inalienable—that is, rooted in one's DNA. The supposed fixity of racial categorizations belies how GBs understand their own spiritual biographies, where they discovered a "heart" for Jewishness—their own and Jesus's—as they grew with God following the radical self-transformation that is central in evangelicalism (being "born again"). Yet fundamentally, GBs still believe that you cannot convert to being a Jew as you can to a religion, such as Christianity.[26]

This paradox between (racial) fixity and (spiritual) discovery is a central feature of the gentile experience in Messianic Judaism, reinforced by the movement's leaders, who strongly discourage gentile conversions and have generally denied the validity even of those considered halachic by Orthodox Jews.[27] As a result, most GBs attempt to distinguish bloodlines from beliefs by drawing a tripartite schema. Although the terminology varies, effectively it runs as follows: the "Hebrews" (or Israelites) are a race physically descended from Abraham and the twelve tribes, a bloodline flowing through all contemporary Jews. Being "Jewish," on the other hand, is to be part of a religion that has failed to understand the Word of God. And last, "Israel" is the people of God, which includes all believers in Jesus grafted together into a single lineage or, in Messianic terms, one "new man" (Eph 2:15). GBs follow Messianic leaders in rejecting the idea that anyone can or should convert to Judaism the religion, since it would require renouncing Jesus as the Messiah, which they rightly understand to be alien to it. Yet many of them also want to be more than spiritually "grafted"—they want to be part of the bloodline.

One way to claim this lineage is to draw on a tradition of biblical exegesis that traces the roots of contemporary people-groups to an ancestor in the book of Genesis. Scholars of U.S. religion have examined how, for example, Native Americans were viewed as descendants of the Ten Lost Tribes and African Americans were viewed as descendants of Noah's son Ham.[28] Though GBs reiterate a number of these theories, most commonly they trace their roots back to Abraham, thereby broadening the Jewish "line" to encompass nearly everyone. "God said to Abraham that he'd have many descendants," notes Donald, a fifty-year-old white man who attends Melech Israel, a congregation in the southern United States. "I was not brought up Jewish. I don't know that I have any Jewish heritage at all. But I *may* have Jewish ancestry but that far back, I won't know it. And so I don't say that I'm not but I don't say that I am."[29]

To speak in such generalities rarely generates controversy in Messianic congregations. The second way to trace lineage is more specific and thus is potentially open to refutation: clues within one's own makeup or actions become visible proof of a particular DNA. In Messianic gene talk, someone else, generally a stranger or distant relative, is the first to call attention to the fact that a GB may have Jewish roots. GBs describe being told that they "look" Jewish or that their aptitude for learning Hebrew must be genetic. Then GBs begin to piece together other clues, such as an elderly relative who mysteriously whispered certain prayers under her breath or had an inexplicable familiarity with Jewish rituals or ideas.[30] For example, Sharyla, a forty-nine-year-old African American in the same congregation as Donald, notes that her mother's father, a Baptist pastor, had Hebrew books. She says, "I know a lot of Baptist preachers who *don't* study Hebrew. So I don't know. Because they were *old* books so I don't know how long [our family] had them."[31] Gene talk always hints—never declaims—a key distinction between Jewish and Messianic Jewish contexts.

The most important clue, however, comes from within the believer herself: a deep calling to the Jewish people. Donald concludes his discussion about descent from Abraham by emphasizing that while anyone may have this lineage, he and other GBs almost certainly do: why else would God have called them to Messianic Judaism? Here, notions of scientific objectivity dovetail with the pietistic heritage of evangelical Christianity, wherein believers are expected to create and sustain intimate, emotionally immersive relationships with Jesus, God, and—in the case of premillennialists—God's people, the Jews. The intensity of these connections leads GBs to deduce that perhaps they have a calling in their blood. Karyn, an African American woman in her late fifties, is typical: "I've always questioned [if I might be Jewish]," she says, "because of the love and the commitment being so deep, and even my family, when I was going [to Messianic services], they used to tell me I was strange. So I know that I'm not 'the typical person' culturally speaking." Later, she notes that Jewish-style worship "felt like coming home. This is the other half that has been missing. I'm just coming in touch with my Jewish roots."[32] While "roots" could be taken metaphorically, Karyn, like many GBs, implies an intuition perhaps borne of "genetic memory," the DNA of their ancestors within them.[33]

HIDDEN LINEAGES AND LOST RELATIVES

Both Jews and Messianic Jews use the language of discovery in gene talk. But the two groups differ when it comes to what is unknown and might be uncovered. When Family Tree DNA and other DNA testing companies talk about "lost" relatives, they are not lost in the sense that they have disappeared from the Jewish people. "If you are looking for that long-lost relative or ancestor," the Family Tree DNA website explains, "or if you feel that some day, someone may use a DNA repository to look for long-lost relatives, you should consider doing this simple DNA test. Your ancestors left clues in your DNA which you can use to determine your deep ancestral origins and to link you with others in recent time."[34] In some sense, these lost relatives are not properly lost at all; rather, it is the familial connections that have been lost. Persecution and forced migration obscure or sever connections in this language of lostness.

But they do not obscure a person's own Jewishness from herself. She knows she is Jewish, and so do her relatives, even when she does not know all the connections in her lineage. "Finding" these lost relatives and ancestors appeals because it creates connections, which add to the branches and roots of the family tree. It adds to the tester's knowledge of her identity and to her story. It may create a greater sense of connection to other Jews and to the Jewish people. But except for people outside the Jewish community who use DNA to discover their own Jewish ancestry, it does not transform the tester's self-understanding.

Rather than "lost," Messianics often talk about what is "hidden." This idea fundamentally redounds to the self: the true nature of one's blood is unknown even to oneself often because an ancestor hid the truth, which was then forgotten over time.[35] This idea derives in part from the mainstream Jewish community, where there has been a surge of popular and more scholarly media about "hidden" or "secret" Jews, most often the "anusim" descendants of Spanish or Portuguese Jews.[36] Typical is Jewish writer Gloria Golden's *Remnants of Crypto-Jews among Hispanic Americans,* marketed with the tagline "Hidden deep in the heart of the American Southwest among the larger Hispanic population are descendants of the Sephardim, Jews from Spain and Portugal."[37] These books began to appear frequently in the 1990s and early 2000s, just as more gentiles were joining the Messianic movement. While these two events are not causal, their confluence has popularized an authoritative narrative upon which GBs now draw.

Talk of *anusim* circulates widely among Messianics online and also provides one of the few contexts when "gene talk" is promoted by congregational leadership. Lana, a forty-year-old woman of mixed-race ancestry, describes how "*A lot of times* people hid their Jewish identity. And as time went by, as generations went on, they didn't tell anyone. . . . We've had guest speakers here [at Melech Israel] that have said that they discovered Jewish sects in Africa and in Asia—and all over the world—India. I mean, these people were hidden off but they came from Spain after the Inquisition."[38]

Stories of "hiddenness," as opposed to "lostness," mean that some GBs can make stronger claims to Jewish lineage than others. Lana self-identifies as a person of black, white, and Asian blood, but in her southern milieu she is commonly seen as African American. In Messianic terms, African Americans have the most difficulty making claims to Jewish descent that are accepted by other congregants, although they are sometimes successful if they follow recognized typologies of the "hidden" Jew, such as when Lana hints that she may share blood with these newly discovered sects. African immigrants are usually more successful, assuming that they claim descent from well-known groups such as the Beta Israel or Lemba. GBs of East European descent also make strong claims based on the perception that with so many Jews in these regions, there was certainly intermarriage and hidden identities.[39]

The most accepted of these "racial shifters" are Hispanics and others with a plausible *anusim* identity.[40] Congregations in the southwestern United States include a growing number of people in this category. Rabbi Silvio estimates that when he arrived at Beth Yeshua, in a mid-sized southwestern city, only 10 percent of the congregants were Jews. About five years later, that number has risen to 25 percent mainly due to the inclusion of newly discovered *anusim*—including Silvio himself. He discovered his roots during his pastoral training at a Pentecostal seminary. Embracing this definition of himself, he married the daughter of a well-known gentile leader in Jewish evangelism and began a Messianic ministry.[41] People such as Silvio are accepted into congregational leadership as Jews and are even celebrated by the largely Ashkenazi opinion makers at the denominational level. In short, it is vitally important to leaders (and most congregants) that Messianics, but especially public figures, claim Jewish blood in ways that converge with acceptable discourses in mainstream Judaism, such as the *anusim.*[42] Thus, Messianics reiterate their self-understanding as Jews and retain a claim to legitimacy in the eyes of American Jews and the evangelical Christians who support them as Jewish-run ministries.

The gene talk one hears in congregations is the result of a rather solitary process of searching, most of which takes place online. Like Christian prophecy seekers, GBs carefully compile disparate pieces of information (indeed, many GBs are already familiar with such methods of piecing together dates and places regarding the apocalypse).[43] The most popular lineage search is built around a kind of "Hebraized name lore": onomastics or, more precisely, anthroponomastics, the study of personal names.[44] GBs scan lists of Jewish-associated names, picking out those in their own family trees and looking for phonological concurrences.

Take, for example, Nora, a fifty-six-year-old white woman raised in a Methodist church. Like many GBs, she recalls always feeling "called" to Judaism. "Every Jewish person has like a spark in them," she says, "And even if somebody is descended from Jews and they don't know it, they can still have the spark."[45] She encountered gene talk at a now-defunct Messianic congregation in a large northeastern city. Shortly after, she recounts, "because I had an ancestor whose middle name was Sevilla, the light bulb went off. That's Seville! That's a city where a lot of Jewish people lived." She began to hunt online for clues about this mid-eighteenth century ancestor, Enis Sevilla Sloy:

> And I found that the name Sloy is sometimes a Jewish name. . . . One of the Arabic ways of saying Solomon is Sloymon. That's one theory. Or Sloyal. It was a Belarusian word that means jar. And Jewish merchants used jars like that. That's another possibility. This name is [also] in one of these books with Jewish surnames. And in Krakow, Poland, there's a name Slojman. And Krakow is a city where Sephardic Jews settled after the expulsion.[46]

Nora notes that Sloy might also be Gaelic, however. As is typical, she evaluates etymological clues according to how they match her "genetic memory"—that "spark" she feels. Thus, she gathers multiple potential correlates that all seem to point in one direction: the presence of Sephardi blood.

Although the process by which GBs decide what evidence to accept is largely idiosyncratic, there are nevertheless limits as to what can be hidden and discovered. Judy, a seventy-year-old woman from Texas who attends a Messianic congregation in the Southwest, described it as "a quandary." She would dearly like to be Jewish, as one of her uncles claims. However, his evidence, culled from a website ancestry search, traces the family's lineage back to King Hezekiah in the eighth century BCE, one of the most prominent kings of Judah who is also mentioned in Jesus's genealogical line recounted in the Gospel of Matthew. Given that the first Temple was destroyed, she reasons, it is unlikely that he uncovered substantive genealogical records. Without ruling it out, Judy hesitates to make such an ancient and extravagant claim.

For American Jews, gene talk and family tree building is meant to bring families together—sometimes only conceptually, sometimes virtually, and occasionally even physically. The motto of the International Jewish Genealogical Society is "Without the past, there is no future. Reach out."[47] When Jews send in their DNA to Family Tree DNA for genetic testing, for example, one of the most popular options they choose is called "Family Finder." This option lets the user "Discover unknown family connections" and "Connect with living relatives." 23andme advertises "Contact your DNA relatives across continents or across the street" and has a popular "Relative Finder" option.[48] And when they get these matches, many Jews try reaching out to their "DNA matches."

Genealogist Elise Friedman's webinar, hosted by Family Tree DNA, gives advice for contacting potential "matches" via e-mail.[49] Sometimes the connections happen on social media. In the "Tracing the Tribe" Facebook group, members often "meet" distant cousins they have seen on their "Family Finder" result in the comments. In one comment thread, a man wrote "Hi, Sam, just checked my Family Finder on ftdna.com and it appears that we are possible 4th cousins." Sam replied. In the same thread, a woman wrote to contact another commenter after seeing her name in the thread: "Hi Sarah! Any idea how we are related? You're a pretty close match to me on GEDMATCH (100 cM, 5 gens)."[50] Some Jews—though not all—use their DNA results to contact potential family members. And the vast majority of Jews who see "Relative Finder" and "Family Finder" results get evidence for genetic connection beyond the family members they know. Author A. J. Jacobs decided to hold the "biggest family reunion ever" when a fan from Israel wrote him to say that the two were related. Using genetics and genealogy paired with family tree websites, Jacobs identified seventy-seven million relatives and extended an open invitation to the June 2015 family reunion.[51]

GBs' gene talk, on the other hand, may create or aggravate tensions with their family members and rarely, if ever, leads to new connections. Nearly all GBs come to the movement as single adults or couples without children (including grown children).[52] Most see themselves as spiritual mavericks who follow God's calling and describe feeling different from their families, as Karyn does above. In part, this perspective reflects the evangelical Protestant emphasis on each adult's responsibility for his or her own faith. It also adheres to a biblical typology: when potential followers of Jesus asked for leave to bury a father or say goodbye to kin, they were rebuked. No one who looks back, Jesus told them, is fit for the Kingdom of God (Luke 9:59–62).

GBs are aware that family members, especially their grown children, may feel ambivalent about their new Messianic Judaism. By practicing Jewish-like rituals, GBs reorient their social calendars away from Sunday church and family meals. They generally refuse to celebrate Christmas. They give up beloved family dishes, such as Easter ham. More existentially perhaps, GBs also often have difficulty reconciling themselves to their parents, who brought them up in Christian churches. Some dismiss their parents' faith altogether. Others imply that their parents knew about their Jewish roots. Inspired by the *anusim* speakers at Melech Israel, Lana decided to trace her genealogy until her mother made her promise not to. Like most GBs, Lana construed this rather inexplicable request as hinting at a secret lineage her parents are trying to protect. Last, some GBs gloss over difference altogether. Eva, a co-congregant of Lana's, denies any true theological disjuncture with her Baptist family: "But our parents, I believe they wanted the same thing [as us]. Even though—bless them and their hearts—they knew Jesus was a Jew but they [failed to recognize it]. Their heart was still 'People are people. We love the Lord.'"[53]

RECOGNIZING GENE TALK'S RELIGIOUS ROOTS

Previous studies of Messianic Judaism have posited that gene talk arises from two sources: GBs seek to become Jews in order to advance within the movement's leadership, and they are caught up in the broader "white ethnic revival" that speaks to a sense of postmodern rootlessness. Jewishness gives them an identity.[54] Yet these conclusions fail to explain why GBs spend so much time "gene talking" without ever insisting on being accepted as Jews and thus never benefiting directly in institutional terms. Further, it leaves unclear why GBs from all races, not just "white ethnics," speculate about their lineage.

Similarly, scholarship on Jews has suggested that gene talk is about either disease, especially Tay Sachs, BRCA1, and BRCA2, or ethnic identity. But companies such as 23andme and Family Tree DNA are legally limited in their ability to make medical claims or offer medical interpretations of DNA results. They comply with these legal mandates and sometimes even announce them on their websites, so the Jews who test through them are not primarily seeking medical advice. Furthermore, many Jews who test are already secure in their personal Jewish history. Finding an ethnic identity to claim was not at stake for the woman who wrote that "I got my DNA results. . . . I'm 99% Ashkenazi. No surprise there!"[55] Something else motivates these Jewish DNA testers to engage in gene talk.

To understand its appeal to both Jews and GBs, we need to take the religious dimension of this activity seriously. Gene talk appeals to North American Jews for several related reasons. In addition to providing roots, history, and distinctiveness for a group of mostly white Americans, as Jacobson and other expositors of white ethnic revival would have it, Jewish gene talk also does crucial religious and communal authorizing work. These three reasons for the appeal of Jewish gene talk—providing scientific support for tradition, seeming certainty in questions of who is a Jew, and redemption of Jewish history—all point to the idea of Jewish peoplehood. This idea of peoplehood, or even chosenness, has foundations that are religious, theological, and biblical. And for religious Jews, it remains important in these contexts. But gene talk can also offer a secularized version of peoplehood that emphasizes connection, family, history, and distinctiveness while avoiding charges of chauvinism that can plague the concept of chosenness.

This gene talk emphasizes that like the "begat" verses in Genesis 10, lineage matters. Who your ancestors are matters a little. But what matters a lot are the fact that you have ancestors, that family trees connect Jews together, the idea that

Jews share DNA, and the idea that Jewishness is somehow biological. Gene talk at once assumes and reinforces the idea that Jews are a people and that peoplehood is fundamental to Jewishness. Whether this functions as a justification for religious tradition and practice or functions as a secularized version of a theological connection, gene talk cements the idea of Jewish community.

First, gene talk and interpretations of DNA can provide "scientific proof" of religious traditions. The most popular instance of this occurs around what people call the Cohen gene, a sequence of alleles on the Y chromosome of some men who identify themselves as cohanim. In its explanation of the Cohen gene, the official Chabad website asks "Are these tribal affiliations [Cohanim] just a matter of folklore and tradition? Can such claims actually be proven?" and then answers that "Today they can, and the key is DNA testing."[56] According to Chabad's interpretation of this DNA evidence, men can scientifically "prove" their status as Cohanim. In this article, Chabad values DNA tests above "just" tradition. This is quite remarkable because of Chabad's intense commitment to Jewish tradition.

Aish.com offers a similar question-and-answer structure for discussing genetic findings. The article begins by introducing Karl Skorecki, the Canadian Jewish geneticist who participated in the earliest research of the Cohen Modal Haplotype. "Dr. Skorecki considered, 'According to tradition, this Sephardi Cohen and I have a common ancestor. Could this line have been maintained since Sinai, and throughout the long exile of the Jewish people?' As a scientist, he wondered, could such a claim be tested?" Later the Aish.com article proclaims that "The research findings support the Torah statements that the line of Aaron will last throughout history."[57]

But it is not only the Jewishly devout who tell this story of the scientific proof of an ancient priestly line. One DNA testing company markets the possibility of identifying a person's "ancient tribe."[58] Immediately after hearing explicitly that presence of the "Cohen gene" in men is halachically irrelevant and utterly inconclusive—about half of men who self-identify as cohanim have it, and some men who do not also have it—one man said, "But I want to have a DNA test anyway. Just to be sure." In a 2010 lecture, secular journalist Jon Entine calls the Cohen gene "a remarkable story of genetic witness to the traditions of Judaism and the Israelites. Absolutely amazing."[59] Entine uses the religiously coded language of "witness," more commonly a Christian idiom (from Isa 43:12), for the way that genetics vindicates theological and textual Jewish traditions. Gene talk here supports textual and ritual religious traditions.

Second, in addition to playing a strong supporting role in religious narratives about priestly tribes, gene talk seems to provide scientific data about who is and who isn't a Jew. Scientists all agree that there is no genetic sequence common to all Jews and absent from all non-Jews. And yet, Jews still talk of "Jewish genes." Jewishness is "embedded in my genes, my DNA," explained a man who identifies as Jewish after receiving the results of his DNA test.[60] An Aish article titled "Jewish Genes" says that "There is now new and exciting DNA evidence for common Jewish origin—not just among Cohanim, the Priestly Class, but among Jews scattered all over the globe."[61] In the summer of 2013 the Israeli Ministry of the Interior even requested a DNA test of a potential birthright traveler in order to prove she was Jewish.[62] Positioning DNA as an arbiter of Jewishness appeals to Jews because Jewish identity is, we might say, really messy. The Reform movement's acceptance of patrilineal descent, halachic standards that differ even from one another, Israeli criteria about who qualifies for *aliyah,* differing conversion processes, and intermarriages all contribute to an increasingly confusing landscape of Jewish identification. Science, in contrast, seems to provide clear criteria. This kind of gene talk purports to provide a factual answer to the complicated question of who is a Jew.

Third, gene talk appeals to a sense of connection and continuity in the face of recent Jewish history. Some of these projects explicitly refer to the Holocaust. JewishGen officially calls itself "A Living Memorial to the Holocaust" and offers both a Yizkor Book of "lists of Holocaust martyrs"[63] and a Holocaust Registry. The registry relies on information supplied by professional and amateur genealogists, including that which they have discovered through genetic testing. "As more people add records and search the database," the website explains, "it is our hope that this registry will help bring about reunions with loved ones."[64] The DNA Shoah Project, whose mission is "building a database of genetic material from Holocaust survivors and their immediate descendants in hopes of reuniting families disrupted by the Shoah . . . and, eventually, assist in the forensic identification of Holocaust-era remains."[65] JewishGen and the DNA Shoah Project assert that genetics can help people rediscover ancestors, and they also suggest that DNA might help bring justice to Jewish history.

Beyond these explicit links to the Holocaust, popular gene talk and DNA testing marketing also allude to the ways genetics can heal past injustices of Jewish history. Family Tree DNA, one of the largest personal DNA testing company, has a Jewish founder and markets itself specifically to Jews. A marketing video proclaims that "Many Jewish families have been separated due to forced migration and persecution over the last several centuries. Now thanks to Family Tree DNA, you may rediscover lost roots and cousins."[66] Drawing on inquisition and Holocaust narratives of lost Jewish relatives, this suggests a redemptive capacity of family history. Gene talk can recover and redeem Jewish connections after historical persecution worked to destroy them.

While much of the gene talk in Jewish communities may sound similar to the gene talk in Messianic Jewish communities, it is incorrect to assume that their reasons for doing so are identical. In order to understand GB gene talk, one must first take theological changes into account. Since the nineteenth century, Western Christians have begun to view Jesus's earthly life as a major tool for creating an intimate relationship with him. Jesus as Jew mattered. Among evangelicals, this notion dovetailed with an equally important shift: the premillennialist view of contemporary Jews as the "genetic" descendants of Israel and thus as "genetically" linked to Jesus as well.

Gene talk also corresponds to how evangelicals read the bible "literally," meaning that for them it is an accurate rendering of historical events and of typologies with present-day application. The Hebrew Bible, in particular, continually authenticates through lineage. In the book of Numbers, for example, the Lord commands the Israelites to take a census, tracing each person back to their "original" tribe. Read in light of the Gospels, this becomes even more significant: Jesus's own lineage is traced back to David in order to authenticate his Messiahship. This kind of interpretive logic parallels gene talk, where the full implication of GBs' interior "selves"—the deep love they feel for the Jews and their sense of belonging to the Jewish people—may be explained fully by tracing descent.

Yet we still fall short of explaining why gene talk rather than genetic testing is appealing. The answer, we believe, relates to how gene talk is a practice, in Pierre Bourdieu's terms. It takes place over years, cementing congregational members in a shared discursive tradition that reflects and contributes to the hermeneutics that matter to them. Engaging in gene talk strengthens their conviction not that they are Jewish (necessarily) but that lineage matters: it matters that Jesus was a "genetic" Jew, that North American Jews are "genetic" descendants of Israelites, that one's spiritual growth may reflect what lies hidden within one's DNA. Further, gene talk that follows recognized patterns among mainstream Jews—related to the *anusim,* for example—is more accepted and valued. Thus, ironically, by engaging in gene talk without doing DNA testing, Messianics find a way to participate in the Jewish community by contributing to its authenticating discourse.[67]

In fact, actually undertaking genetic testing entails significant risk. We don't mean that it may reveal that GBs are not "actually" Jewish (for there are many ways to construe genetic data). Rather, the risk is an ontological one. Judaism-as-religion, according to Messianics, is incorrect in two fundamental ways: because it denies the Messiah, it also ignores the radical nature of Jesus's claim that, first, there is no longer a difference between "Jew and Greek" and, relatedly, Greeks (i.e., gentiles) are now grafted into the Jewish people. To dig too hard for Jewish roots—to move talk into action—risks negating the central Gospel promise of new life and togetherness in Jesus. In short, evangelical theology propels GBs toward claiming a Jewish identity and also problematizes it. To focus on race as an inalienable attribute has the potential to directly undermine the theology that undergirds Messianic Judaism and evangelical Christianity as a whole.

Clearly, DNA means something much more than just the science behind it. Gene talk holds great appeal for both Jews and Messianic Jews because it has the ability to extend narratives of self and authorize certain ways of belonging. In these contexts, gene talk is not simply another kind of discourse about ethnicity and place in society. It is also about place in a cosmological sense, operating alongside and within religious practices and ontologies. Jews and Messianic Jews share a fascination with DNA testing and yet differ in how and why they engage in gene talk, differences rooted in their divergent theologies.

NOTES

1. "Discover Your Jewish Ancestry—Family Tree DNA" (accessed October 1, 2014), https://www.familytreedna.com/landing/jewish-ancestry.aspx.

2. Kim Tallbear, *Native American DNA* (Minneapolis: University of Minnesota Press, 2013), 4.

3. Matthew Frye Jacobson, *Roots Too* (Cambridge: Harvard University Press, 2008), 6.

4. Post on "Tracing the Tribe" Facebook group, October 16, 2014, 2:59 p.m. (accessed October 20, 2014), https://www.facebook.com/groups/tracingthetribe/.

5. Dan Hurley, "Grandma's Experiences Leave a Mark on Your Genes," *Discover Magazine* (June 11, 2013), http://discovermagazine.com/2013/may/13-grandmas-experiences-leave-epigenetic-mark-on-your-genes.

6. Post on "Tracing the Tribe" Facebook group, October 20, 2014, 6:32 p.m. (accessed October 20, 2014), https://www.facebook.com/groups/tracingthetribe/.

7. Jerome Epstein, "Setting an Example for Future Generations," *Jewish Exponent* (September 13, 2007), http://jewishexponent.com/setting-an-example-for-future-generations.

8. "Genetic Study Proves Jews Are a People," *Shavei Israel* (September 15, 2014), http://www.shavei.org/featured_articles/ashkenazijews/?lang=en.

9. Michelle Alperin, "A Different Kind of Roots Journey," *Jewish Week* (October 22, 2014), http://www.thejewishweek.com/special-sections/healthcare/different-kind-roots-journey.

10. Yaakov Kleiman, "The Cohanim-DNA Connection," *Aish* (accessed September 15, 2014), http://www.aish.com/ci/sam/48936742.html.

11. Alex Joffee, "Jewish DNA Speaks," *My Jewish Learning* (accessed September 15, 2014), http://www.myjewishlearning.com/beliefs/Theology/Who_is_a_Jew/Types_of_Jews/jewish-dna.shtml.

12. Comments to Alexander Joffee, "Jewish DNA Speaks," http://www.myjewishlearning.com/beliefs/Theology/Who_is_a_Jew/Types_of_Jews/jewish-dna.shtml.

13. Comments to David Koffmann, "Native Americans and Jews: The Lost Tribes Episode," http://www.myjewishlearning.com/history/Modern_History/1700-1914/America_at_the_Turn_of_the_Century/Regional_Judaism/Peddlers_and_Frontier_Judaism/Native_Americans_and_Jews.shtml.

14. Ibid.

15. "Family Tree of the Jewish People," *JewishGen* (accessed September 5, 2014), http://www.jewishgen.org/gedcom/.

16. Elisha Greenbaum, "The Kohen Gene," Chabad.org (accessed September 8, 2014), http://www.chabad.org/parshah/article_cdo/aid/652568/jewish/The-Kohen-Gene.htm.

17. Ibid.

18. Comments to Deborah Jiang-Stein, "For Crying Out Loud, It's a Culture, Not a Race!," *My Jewish Learning* (accessed January 2, 2015), http://www.myjewishlearning.com/blog/jewish-and/2014/04/.

19. Comments to Bernard Lewis, "Who Are the Semites?," My Jewish Learning (accessed January 2, 2015), http://www.myjewishlearning.com/beliefs/Theology/Who_is_a_Jew/Types_of_Jews/Semites.shtml.

20. David A. Rausch "The Emergence of Messianic Judaism in Recent American History," *Christian Scholar's Review* (1983): 44–45; Yaacov Ariel, *An Unusual Relationship: Evangelical Christians and Jews* (New York: New York University Press, 2013), 218–21.

21. The number of Americans who attend Messianic congregations each week is very difficult to ascertain; estimates range from 30,000 to more than 2 million. Its impact is much broader online and through book sales. In one of the field sites, for example, there were about 150 attendees per week, about 300 online attendees, and about 1,500 weekly visitors to the congregation's online store. It is often unclear whether "membership"

counts include most GBs, many of whom are not viewed as full members. For that reason, the word "congregants" rather than "members" is used here.

22. Clearly, a more thorough demographic study is needed of this wide-ranging movement. However, based on a five-site comparison (which included attendance at two other congregations), the number of GBs is persistently underestimated at 40–60 percent. Earlier studies also focus almost exclusively on the ethnic Jewish minority of congregations, in part because it is they who matter most to the movement's leadership. See Hillary Kaell, "Born-Again Seeking: Explaining the Gentile Majority in Messianic Judaism," *Religion* 45:1 (2015): 43n3. Typical estimates of the GB population appear in Jeffrey S. Wasserman, *Messianic Jewish Congregations: Who Sold This Business to the Gentiles?* (Lanham: University Press of America, 2000), 73–76, 159; Rausch, "The Emergence of Messianic Judaism," 51; Carol Harris-Shapiro, *Messianic Judaism: A Rabbi's Journey through Religious Change in America* (Boston: Beacon, 1999), 29; Shoshanah Feher, *Passing Over Easter: Constructing the Boundaries of Messianic Judaism* (Lanham: AltaMira, 1998), 47–50; Daniel Juster and Peter Hocken, *The Messianic Jewish Movement* (Ventura: Toward Jerusalem Council II, 2004), 10, http://www.messianic jewishonline.com/essays.html.

23. About 85 percent of U.S. Messianic Jews are charismatic, as are 65 percent of congregations, according to Peter Hocken, *Challenges of the Pentecostal, Charismatic and Messianic Jewish Movements: The Tensions of the Spirit* (Abingdon: Ashgate, 2009), 97. Four out of five leaders in this multisite study received ordination from Pentecostal seminaries. Evangelicals, Pentecostals, and charismatics share similar roots in Protestantism and believe in salvation through Jesus Christ, biblical inerrancy, and the necessity of being born again when an adult believer experiences spiritual rebirth (John 3:3). A key difference is that Pentecostals also recognize gifts of the Holy Spirit (e.g., speaking in tongues). We use the term "charismatic" to signal adherence to Pentecostal beliefs without necessarily denominational affiliation.

24. Hillary Kaell, interview with "Donald," July 15, 2013.

25. Janet Jacobs notes similar ideas among American crypto Jews, or *anusim*. Janet Jacobs, *Hidden Heritage: The Legacy of the Crypto Jews* (Berkeley: University of California Press, 2002), 141, 174n20. For a broader discussion of physiognomy and (constructed) ethnicity, see Mary C. Waters, *Ethnic Options: Choosing Identities in America* (Berkeley: University of California Press, 1990).

26. Though congregations diverge somewhat regarding who is considered a "Jew," all retain the idea that it is a bloodline. At one northeastern congregation in this study, a Jew was limited to someone raised by "ethnically" Jewish parents who had later accepted Yeshua. More typical of the movement as a whole, another congregation defined as Jews people with any type of Jewish heritage, those who had discovered hidden roots, or someone married to a person in those categories.

27. Conversion is very contentious in Messianic Judaism and is currently rejected by both denominations (the Messianic Jewish Alliance of America and the Union of Messianic

Jewish Congregations). John Fisher and Chaim Urbach, "Messianic Conversion: Is it Viable?," *Kesher* 6 (Winter 1998): 30–49.

28. Sylvester Johnson, "The Rise of the Black Ethnics: The Ethnic Turn in African American Religions, 1916–1945," *Religion and American Culture* 20:2 (2010): 125–63; Henry Goldschmidt, "Introduction: Race, Nation, and Religion," in *Race, Nation, and Religion in the Americas* (ed. Goldschmidt and Elizabeth McAlister; New York: Oxford University Press, 2004), 3–34.

29. All names are pseudonyms. Donald, personal interview, June 15, 2013.

30. Kaell, "Born-Again Seeking," 17.

31. Sharyla, personal interview, June 4, 2013. GBs usually focus on the maternal line, because although few Messianics adhere to rabbinic guidelines on descent, it is still viewed as more authoritative.

32. Karyn, personal interview, June 12, 2013.

33. Circe Sturm, *Becoming Indian: The Struggle over Cherokee Identity in the Twenty-First Century* (Santa Fe: School for Advanced Research Press, 2010), 41.

34. "Discover Your Jewish Ancestry—Family Tree DNA."

35. One exception is the reference to the "lost tribes." People who identify as crypto-Jews also often describe reclaiming religious knowledge that was "lost" to them. Jacobs, *Hidden Heritage,* 84. On comparable notions about "hidden" blood that compels spiritual discoveries, see Sturm, *Becoming Indian,* 32–34, 72; Seth D. Kunin, "Juggling Identities among the Crypto-Jews of the American Southwest," *Religion* 31:1 (2001): 41–61.

36. The list is long but includes Trudi Alexy, *The Marrano Legacy: A Contemporary Crypto-Jewish Priest Reveals Secrets of His Double Life* (Santa Fe: University of New Mexico Press, 2003); Stanley M. Hordes, *To the End of the Earth: A History of the Crypto-Jews of New Mexico* (New York: Columbia University Press, 2005); Barbara Ferry and Debbie Nathan, "Mistaken Identity? The Case of New Mexico's 'Hidden Jews,'" *The Atlantic* (December 2000); David M. Gitlitz, *Secrecy and Deceit: The Religion of Crypto-Jews* (Santa Fe: University of New Mexico Press, 2002). The *Journal of Spanish, Portuguese, and Italian Crypto Jews,* edited by Abraham D. Lavender, began publication in 2009.

37. Gloria Golden, *Remnants of Crypto-Jews among Hispanic Americans* (Mountain View: Floricanto, 2005).

38. Lana, personal interview, June 8, 2013.

39. In the interviews and fieldwork for this project, GBs never traced similar stories to relatives hidden during the Holocaust. When it was broached, they agreed that it was an interesting idea but not part of their history. It is hard to know why they drew this distinction; perhaps it is because the Holocaust is more recent or because it seems sacrosanct.

40. Sturm, *Becoming Indian,* 41.

41. The importance of this lineage depends on the congregation. In Pastor David's congregation, for example, he frowns on talk of "hidden" *anusim.* Although still prevalent, it is discussed much less openly than in Silvio's congregation.

42. The idea that there are *anusim* has been embraced by many Jews, though not without controversy. See Judith Neulander, "The Crypto-Jewish Canon: Choosing to Be 'Chosen' in Millennial Tradition," *Jewish Folklore and Ethnology Review* 18 (1996): 19–59; Kunin, "Juggling Identities among the Crypto-Jews," 43.

43. Timothy Weber, *On the Road to Armageddon: How Evangelicals Became Israel's Best Friend* (Ada: Baker Academic 2004), 45–66; Ariel, *An Unusual Relationship,* 142–52.

44. Neulander, "The Crypto-Jewish Canon," 43. Neulander notes a similar process in the Southwest related to place-names (43–45). We have never heard Messianics refer to places. They focus on their own family history. Abraham Lavander, "The Distinctive Hispanic Names (DHN) Technique: A Method for Selecting a Sample or Estimating Population Size," *Names: A Quarterly Journal* 40 (March 1992): 1–16, and "Hispanic Given Names in Five United States Cities: Onomastics as a Research Tool in Ethnic Identity," *Hispanic Journal of Behavioral Sciences* 10 (June 1988): 105–25.

45. Nora, personal interview, November 14, 2012. The idea of a "spark" to which Nora refers comes from kabbalistic Judaism and circulates quite widely among GBs and others who discover Jewish roots. See, for example, Rachel Lehmann-Haupt, "The Hidden Jews," *Daily Beast* (16 June 2009), http://www.thedailybeast.com/articles/2009/06/16/the-hidden-jews.html. For background, see Louis Jacobs, "The Doctrine of the 'Divine Spark' in Man in Jewish Sources," in *Studies in Rationalism, Judaism, and Universalism: In Memory of Leon Roth* (ed. Raphael Loewe and Kegan Paul; London: Routledge, 1966), 87–114; Henry Goldschmidt, "Religion, Reductionism, and the Godly Soul: Lubavitch Hasidic Jewishness and the Limits of Classificatory Thought," *Journal of the American Academy of Religion* 77:3 (2009): 547–72.

46. Nora, personal interview, November 14, 2012.

47. "About IAJGS" (accessed January 6, 2015), http://www.iajgs.org/blog/about/about-iajgs/.

48. "Find Out What DNA Says about You and Your Family," *23andme* (accessed January 6, 2015), https://www.23andme.com.

49. "Understanding DNA Results in the Context of Ashkenazi Ancestry," *YouTube* (September 17, 2014), https://www.youtube.com/watch?v=BCjQnOONT8I&feature=youtu.be.

50. Post on "Tracing the Tribe" Facebook group, October 24, 2014, 7:18 p.m. (accessed October 24, 2014), https://www.facebook.com/groups/tracingthetribe/.

51. "Are You Related to AJ Jacobs? Author to Host Biggest Family Reunion Ever and You're Invited" (July 17, 2014), http://abcnews.go.com/Lifestyle/author-aj-jacobs-organizes-global-family-reunion-genealogy/story?id=24554792.

52. Kaell, "Born-Again Seeking."

53. Eva, personal interview, January 6, 2013.

54. Harris-Shapiro, *Messianic Judaism,* 73; Feher, *Passing Over Easter,* 48.

55. Post on "Tracing the Tribe" Facebook group, October 20, 2014, 6:32 p.m. (accessed October 20, 2014), https://www.facebook.com/groups/tracingthetribe/.

56. Lorne Rozovsky, "Raise Your Hand If You're a Kohen," *Chabad.org* (accessed June 15, 2013), http://www.chabad.org/library/article_cdo/aid/762109/jewish/Raise-Your-Hand-If-Youre-A-Kohen.htm.

57. "The Cohanim—The DNA Connection," http://www.aish.com/ci/sam/48936742.html (accessed Nov 2, 2014). Aish.com is a popular resource for North American Jews, though it also reflects Israeli religious discourse at times. Jerusalem-based rabbi Yaakov Kleiman, for instance, authored this particular article. Kleiman has written two English-language books about DNA and Judaism: *DNA and the Bible: the Genetic Link* (Springdale: Lightcatcher Books, 2004) and *DNA and Tradition: Genetic Link to the Ancient Hebrews* (New York: Devorah Publishing, 2004).

58. "Are You Jewish?," *iGenea* (accessed September 5, 2014), http://www.igenea.com/en/jews.

59. "Jewish DNA: The Kohenim Gene and the Lost Tribes of Israel," *YouTube* (accessed September 5, 2014), https://www.youtube.com/watch?v=ioYAjdDALqk.

60. Jon Entine, *Abraham's Children: Race, Identity, and the DNA of the Chosen People* (New York: Grand Central Publishing, 2007), 15.

61. Yaakov Kleiman, "Jewish Genes," *Aish* (accessed January 6, 2015), http://www.aish.com/ci/sam/48937817.html.

62. "Teen Told She Can't Join Birthright without DNA Test," *Times of Israel* (July 28, 2013), http://www.timesofisrael.com/teen-told-she-cant-join-birthright-without-dna-test/; Asher Zeiger, "Russian-Speakers Who Want to Make Aliyah Could Need DNA Test," *Times of Israel* (July 29, 2013), http://www.timesofisrael.com/russian-speakers-who-want-to-immigrate-could-need-dna-test/.

63. "The JewishGen Yizkor Book Necrology Database," *JewishGen* (accessed January 6, 2015), http://www.jewishgen.org/databases/yizkor/.

64. "JewishGen Holocaust Global Registry" (accessed January 6, 2015), http://www.jewishgen.org/registry/.

65. DNA Shoah Project (accessed January 6, 2015), http://www.dnashoah.org.

66. "FTDNA—Discover the Story of You," *YouTube* (accessed January 6, 2015), https://www.youtube.com/watch?v=r_WwNfdPESk.

67. Sturm, *Becoming Indian,* 7.

Contemporary Modern Orthodox Guidance Books on Marital Sexuality

Evyatar Marienberg

Young women and men who are about to be married in *haredi* [Ultra-Orthodox] communities are encouraged to have a few meetings with a person of the same sex, designated as a groom/bride teacher, whose role is to instruct them about married life, the laws of menstrual impurity, and the marital act itself. This is also the case in some parts of the Modern Orthodox/National Religious world. Some young couples, especially those who are on the right side of this world, really need such instruction, as indicated by this rather honest, but not unique, statement: "I am a rabbi-teacher in a Yeshiva and alumnus of a serious Yeshiva myself. My wife is a teacher, and alumna of a prestigious yeshiva for women. I describe our background in order to explain why we have no knowledge in this domain."[1]

In addition to this oral and hopefully individualized guidance, a wide range of specialized books and booklets are available for newlyweds (or engaged) couples from these groups. In recent years, manuals were also written for parents to help them explain sexuality to their young children. Schools are also slowly starting to realize that they need to deal with these issues, and a growing number of curricula target this market. More advanced works, aiming to help already-married Orthodox adults solve problems in their own sexual life, are also available now. These various works present a broad view of the ways marital sex is explained and prescribed in the contemporary Jewish Orthodox world. My plan in this essay is to examine several Modern Orthodox works of these various kinds, published in Israel and in the United States in the last few decades. I will not discuss publications that aim explicitly, by their nature, style, or content, at *haredi* Jews and that are less likely to be of interest for Modern Orthodox couples.

MODERN ORTHODOXY

The term "Modern Orthodoxy" is a very problematic one especially in recent decades, when this supposedly clearly defined branch of Orthodox Judaism grew significantly in numbers and, not incidentally, also in diversity.

Orthodox Judaism itself is hard to define. One can probably say that generally, officially, Orthodox Jews are those Jews who believe that the Torah is divine, that it was handed from God to Moses as is, that the Talmud and later authoritative sources are the only legitimate interpretation of the laws in it, that modern notions should have a minimal impact on these laws, and that one must make a great effort to follow these laws as explained by the rabbis. These laws should shape one's daily life.[2]

Some people might object to the definitions suggested above, saying that some Orthodox Jews do not think of the Torah as literally divine or that some Orthodox Jews believe that modern concepts can and should impact Jewish practices. Others might say that some Conservative Jews hold that the rabbinic laws should shape their own daily life as well. All of this is true, but such people are on the fringes of their own respective groups (even if often they think, or pretend, they are not). In most cases, I believe that the definitions above cover the vast majority of Orthodox Jews and eliminate the vast majority of non-Orthodox Jews.

It has become commonplace for at least the past several decades to divide the Orthodox world into *haredi,* previously referred to as Ultra Orthodoxy, and Modern Orthodoxy. It is obvious, though, that just as the very definition of Orthodoxy is problematic, any definition of its subgroups is also complicated. In both cases, it is probably better to speak of a certain spectrum, situating Modern Orthodox Jews between *haredi* Jews and Conservative (or in Israel, traditionalist or secular) Jews. Modern Orthodox Jews will be those Orthodox Jews who believe in the importance of Jewish practices in daily life but also give positive value to secular culture.

A major question today is if those on the right side of so-called Modern Orthodoxy, known as National *haredi, Hardal,* Radical Religious Zionism, or Toraniyim [Torah Oriented], should be considered Modern Orthodox at all, considered as a type of *haredi* Judaism, or dealt with as a category of itself. There is no consensus on the answer.

KNOWLEDGE ABOUT SEXUALITY

There are many ways to transmit knowledge about sexuality. It can be done visually, orally, or in written form. It can be done formally, in class, or informally, from peers, partners, family members, and newspapers as well as on the Internet and in numerous other ways. In this essay I will focus only on formal, written, published material in book form of two types, written by and aimed at people located within the wide spectrum of Modern Orthodoxy: books written for parents, trying to help them find the right way to transmit such information to their children, and books written for people who are about to get married. I will not deal with *haredi* books, and I will not deal with oral guidance.

BOOKS FOR PARENTS

In 2009, a little booklet of 68 pages titled *Talking to Your Children about Intimacy: A Guide for Orthodox Jewish Parents* was published by Sara Diament. Diament is a Modern Orthodox woman herself. According to her self-description, she lives in New Jersey and holds master's degrees in Jewish studies and health and behavior studies. The book is very clearly written "from within," using the language, codes, and assumptions of American Modern Orthodox Jews. The book discusses the importance of parents talking with their children about sexuality while of course adapting it to the child's age, maturity, and interest in the matter. The text is peppered with Hebrew and Yiddish words that are commonly used in American Modern Orthodox circles and provides some examples of how adults in this community might explain these issues to children. The following is an example of instructions and ideas given by Diament:

> While you should never say anything that is not truthful, you need not give *complete* information at all times. When my children were very young, and they asked my husband and me how parents have a baby, our first line of response was always, "The first thing you do is *daven* [pray] to Hashem [God] to help you have a baby." This response was both truthful and imparted our *hashkafah* [religious point of view] and was usually quite satisfactory, at least initially. I remember that when my son was about nine, he asked me, "If non-Jewish people don't *daven* to Hashem how can they have a baby?" I answered him truthfully (but not completely) that a man and a woman could have a baby without *davening* to Hashem, but that was something that Jewish people did. My son didn't probe any further. But if he had, I would have explained that beyond *davening* to Hashem, there was something that *Immas* and *Abbas* [mothers and fathers] do together to help make the baby, and answered any further questions that arose.[3]

Toward the end of her book, Diament provides an imaginary report by a brother and sister, aged ten and eleven, of the information they learned from their parents (father to son, mother to daughter). Diament says that letting children read it alone or together with their parents can help the discussion. The text is an interesting mix of explicit content together with theology:

> When Hashem [God] created Adam and Chava [Eve] the first thing that He instructed them was, "Peru u'revu—Be fruitful and multiply," which in regular English means "Have children!" [Mom] also told me that while it is true that Abba [Dad] and she davened [prayed] to Hashem [God] to have us, that there is a special part that parents play alongside Hashem in creating a baby. . . . Abba explained to me that because an Abba and Imma [father and mother] love each other, when they are alone together at night in bed they like to be close. Sometimes, they might just hug and kiss each other. Other times, they take their clothes off to feel very close in a way that only Immas and Abbas do. They may also decide to have sexual relations. Abba said that he needed to explain what that was—because beside being a nice way of being close, it is also what an Imma and Abba have to do to play their part in creating a baby. He told me that when a man and a woman have relations the man comes very close to the woman. By then, from thinking about all the cuddling they are doing, his penis has become firmer than usual. This makes it easier for the man to put his penis inside a special opening in the woman's vagina. My Abba told me not to worry—it doesn't hurt the lady—in fact it feels very nice. Hashem wanted to make sure that it was something pleasurable to do so that married people would want to do it. He said that it's one of the ways that a husband and wife can show their love for one another, even when they aren't going to create a baby from it. After a man puts his penis inside a woman's vagina, he rubs it back and forth so he can release from it a little bit of liquid called semen. In the semen, there are something called sperm, though they are too small to see—you'd need a microscope. The sperm have something like a tail so they can travel, in a swimming kind of way, deeper into the vagina.[4]

In this text, children learn that God is in charge but also learn about penises, vaginas, erections, and sperm. In fact, the actual act is explained clearly and accurately, without any obvious censorship, though, of course, adapted to the age of the children and described as something religiously kosher.

A few years later in 2012, another book of the same type, *Talking about Intimacy and Sexuality: A Guide for Orthodox Jewish Parents,* was published by Yocheved Debow. Debow describes herself as a Modern Orthodox American-born Israeli woman who wrote her doctoral dissertation on the matter.[5] The book, 342 pages long, does not contain as much Orthodox jargon as Diament's book and is by far more comprehensive. Whether this is a good or bad thing depends on the reader's expectations. Diament's book can be read quickly by busy parents and provides ready-made recipes on how to deal with the issue. Reading Debow's book demands more time, although it is written in a very accessible way. Like Diament, Debow uses both scientific and Jewish literature and concepts, but obviously Debow's more voluminous work includes by far more of both. At the same time, Debow's book at times feels more apologetic. Very often it compares "Judaism" to a "Western Approach." "Judaism," according to Debow, is spiritual, while "Non-Judaism" is materialistic and commercial and supports immediate gratification.[6] In its essence, the attitude that the book expresses is not different from Diament's. Parents should speak with their children, adapting, of course, to age and personality; actual scientific terms should be used to refer to the sexual organs; lack of explanation is not a good idea (or as Debow puts it, even a bad explanation is better than no explanation); and when the time is appropriate and the child is, or seems to be, interested in the matter, the basic details of the sexual act should be explained honestly and accurately.

Debow's work is a by-product of her involvement in creating a curriculum on the matter under the auspices of Yeshiva University, the flagship academic institution of American Modern Orthodoxy. It was published jointly by two respected organizations in the Modern Orthodox world: the publishing house Ktav and Orthodox Union Press. It is hard to imagine better credentials from a Modern Orthodox perspective. On the other hand, this strong identification with Modern Orthodoxy, which is also very central in the content, might push away Orthodox parents who are located more on the right side of the Orthodox spectrum, closer to the National *haredi* or *haredi* worlds. Diament's booklet, although Modern Orthodox in many ways, is less explicitly so and thus might be possibly consulted by such parents.

The two books of Diament and Debow represent a watershed in dealing with the matter in American Modern Orthodoxy. One slim, the other comprehensive; one practical, the other more theoretical; one published independently, the other under the auspices of major institutions. Both provide English-reading Modern Orthodox parents with specific guidance of how to speak about the matter with their children in a manner that is in line with the current recommendations of professional organizations while, at the same time, being adapted to Modern Orthodox sensitivities, wishes, beliefs, and practices. Guidance to children should be given, according to them, with implicit or explicit understanding that they should not engage in sexual relations or any sensual contact before marriage. In addition, the entire sexual act is described as an act with religious meanings. No drawings of body parts are provided.

Would an average Modern Orthodox person follow the instructions of these two books? I do not know. The books by Diament and Debow show that it is possible to find a way to explain the fundamentals of the sexual acts to children while respecting core concepts of Modern Orthodoxy. On the question of whether this actually happens in the real world, I have no answer. At the time I wrote these lines, neither of these two books had been translated to Hebrew. As far as I know, there is no comparable work written originally in Hebrew. Non-English-speaking Modern Orthodox parents in Israel do not yet have a guide of this kind to help them.[7]

BOOKS FOR BRIDES AND GROOMS

Several dozen Modern Orthodox marital guides for young couples have been published in Hebrew and in English, in Israel and in United States, in recent decades. Though one can find a few works of this type from the 1970s, maybe even from the 1960s, these works were isolated cases and did not yet constitute a distinct genre. The real wave of Modern Orthodox publications on marital life started around 1985 and continues today in full force.[8]

Most of these books are of little relevance to this study due to the fact that they contain theoretical, theological, or ideological discussions of married life but not a significant explicit section on sexual relations. From those books that can be categorized on the more or less Modern Orthodox spectrum and that contain a significant section on marital sex, I consider about half a dozen to be particularly interesting. Here, I will explore three of them.

SHLOMO AVINER'S *ETZEM ME-ATZAMAI* [BONE OF MY BONES]

Shlomo Aviner is an Israeli rabbi who was born in France in 1943 and moved to Israel in 1966. For many years he has been a leading figure in the national religious community, especially among the settlers. He is one of the founders and leaders of the national-religious branch known, among other titles, as "National *haredi*."[9] This is a group that grew out of the national-religious movement; some might consider it to be outside of the so-called Modern

Orthodox spectrum. Among other things, this group is characterized by what its adherents see as stricter observance in some domains, particularly women's dress. It also accords a more central place to men's study of rabbinic texts and promotes separation from the secular world.[10]

Aviner is not an uncontroversial person even in his own branch of National *haredi,* something which is perhaps not surprising: in radical groups, people are considered kosher or nonkosher because of nuances that might look insignificant to an outsider. Still, he remains a prominent figure, well known outside of his immediate circles. He has published dozens of books and has had weekly broadcasts and columns in various media venues affiliated with the religious Right. He or his disciples also operate multiple websites with hundreds, perhaps thousands, of videos featuring his lectures and answers to questions in both Hebrew and French.

Aviner is extremely interested in issues related to sexuality and *tzinut,* which literally means "modesty" but in reality is connected almost entirely to the regulation of women's dress and to relations between the sexes.[11] It is thus not surprising that he is the author of several books on these matters.

The most relevant book to our discussion is *Etzem me-Atzamai* [Bone of my Bones], published in 1984 with a new edition in 2001.[12] It is partially structured as questions and answers: "What should be done when there is incompatibility between the spouses regarding copulation?";[13] "Sometimes the woman desires the union more than the man. Must he abide, or should she give up?";[14] or "What should a man do if he gets aroused very fast, while his wife gets aroused more slowly?"[15] Whether the questions are ones that Aviner was actually asked or are his own creation I do not know, though I tend to believe that many are crafted by him as a literary tool.

On the cover of *Etzem me-Atzamai* one finds that it is "For Married Couples Only," though in the "warnings" opening of the book it is said that brides and grooms can consult it a few days before the event. Aviner declares that *Etzem me-Atzamai* is only for those who have difficulties with their sexual life. Those who do not should not consult it. It is also only for simple people who have to fight their evil inclination. Holy people do not need the advices of the book.[16]

Aviner considers himself a champion of women's rights and honor.[17] Women are gentle and sensitive, and their husbands must continually take this into consideration. On the other hand, because women are superior beings to men in many aspects, they also have some serious obligations toward men. For example, women should be "givers": they should devote their lives to "giving" to their husband. If, for example, the woman is not enjoying marital relations, this is still okay. Many women never enjoy sexual relations, says Aviner. "Many couples are made in such a way that the women cannot reach physical enjoyment, and one must not insist on it. This is vain. It is more important for the wife that her husband loves her and hugs her, and that his enjoyment is important for her. This is enough."[18] "The fact that you do not enjoy," says Aviner in response to a real or crafted question from a woman, "is not critical. There are women who did not enjoy [sex] in their entire life, and this did not bother them, but it was all with great love [to their husband]."[19] The woman has "an inner enjoyment from the closeness, from the love, friendship, and peace. She does not need the physical enjoyment." What is important, he declares, is that she at least does not suffer.

When engaging in marital relations, lights must be off, even though it is permissible to leave a small light on during foreplay. Talking is very important, especially for the woman. The husband must show her warmth by talking to her and making her happy. One is not allowed, though, to speak about unrelated issues, and Aviner even warns women that this is not the time to raise concerns of various kinds.[20] Gentle touch is also important. There is no place the husband is forbidden to touch, although those who are particularly pious might decide to create some limits. Aviner does not seem to be thrilled with the possibility of the husband touching his wife's genitalia. He rarely mentions this possibility, nor does he tell his readers about its importance if the woman's satisfaction is a goal. In the same vein, the idea that a woman experiences pain in her first instances of intercourse seems to him to be a given. Considering the fact that he does not instruct his readers about foreplay, he might indeed be right with regard to what happens in the bedrooms of those following his guidance. To put it bluntly, for couples who follow his guidance, the chances that the woman will reach sexual satisfaction are indeed quite low.

Aviner is aware that problems can occur. He mentions in particular male impotence and premature ejaculation. These happen "especially for the most modest grooms." The couple should not feel too much guilt and should try again later. Holy thoughts, relaxation, and reducing the excitement can solve most problems. The bride must not expect enjoyment from the first union. In fact, for Aviner, as we saw earlier, even if the woman never enjoys marital relations, nothing is wrong.[21] With such a view, it is no surprise that Aviner does not spend much time, if at all, on female physiological problems. The woman, anyway, should not expect pleasure from the act. Aviner does not mention the option of reaching for professional help, and one can imagine that for him, as long as the couple succeeds somehow to conceive and the husband is happy, the situation is satisfactory.[22]

ELYASHIV KNOHL'S *ISH VE-ISHAH* AND *ET DODIM*

Some years after revised versions of Aviner's book appeared, another book, *Ish ve-Ishah* [Man and Woman], by Elyashiv Knohl, entered the same market.

Elyashiv Knohl, born in 1948, is a rabbi of a religious kibbutz and was educated in some of the same rabbinic circles as Aviner. Unlike Aviner, though, who remained on the conservative side of the national religious world throughout his career, Knohl was for many years a senior faculty member in charge of training students for the rabbinate in a yeshiva that was known to be—although unquestionably Orthodox—on its progressive side.[23]

Knohl's book initially appeared in 2003, with a subsequent thoroughly revised second edition in 2005 and a third edition in 2014.[24] An English edition was released in 2008.[25]

Many of the Modern Orthodox contemporary works on the matter speak to both husband and wife and try to guide readers in ways that the authors believe take into consideration women's concerns as well. In reality, many of these texts, and not only those by Aviner, might still seem to be, for an outsider, very problematic from a feminist or egalitarian perspective. Knohl does it dramatically better than most others. In fact, one of the most outstanding characteristics of his book is its commitment to an as-egalitarian-as-possible treatment of both partners, expressed in its very language. In Hebrew, a language with clear distinctions between feminine and masculine verbs and nouns, writing or talking in inclusive language is extremely hard. Knohl makes a real effort to do so in every sentence and in every term used.

Knohl's book deals mostly with issues that are not related to our specific interest. In its scope it is similar to countless other guides to marital life published in the Orthodox world. What makes it so essential for us is a separate thin brochure titled *Et Dodim: A Guide to Marital Relations from a Torah Perspective,* which is attached to the sealed book.[26]

One of the central threads in Knohl's booklet is the idea that the man and the woman have the same obligations and rights with regard to sexual relations. Everything should be done with mutual consent, and no side has more rights or obligations than the other. If the Talmud and halachic [Jewish legal] literature say, for example, that a man "can do with his wife whatever he desires," it means of course with mutual consent. If the Talmud suggests ways to enhance the chance that the newborn will be male, the Talmud did not mean it scientifically but just as a way to encourage the enjoyment of both partners in time past, when male children were more appreciated by some. Needless to say, this is not the way the regulations have been presented and prescribed for centuries. And yet, being an Orthodox rabbi writing to orthodox readers, Knohl does not present his interpretations as a break from a long tradition but instead presents them as the "true" meaning of Jewish texts on the matter throughout history.

Knohl devotes significant time to discussing problems that might occur, such as premature ejaculation, male impotence, and vaginismus. He explains that these phenomena are common, and the couple should not develop anxiety over them or feel embarrassed. He offers some possible solutions and explains that if after a while the couple still feels that things are not right, they should seek professional advice. In particular at the beginning of their relations, couples should be aware that the difficulties are normal. Unlike most traditional guides, Knohl admits that the couple might not succeed in having full relations in their first night together. In fact, he even says that if this seems to them inappropriate, they do not have to try. Postponing it for a while is acceptable.[27] One should remember that at least some of the couples whom Knohl addresses are indeed young men and women who never had any physical contact with a member of the other sex, and some of them did not even touch their spouse until the wedding ceremony, which happened only a few hours earlier. For them, having to go immediately "from nothing to everything," as some put it, can indeed be traumatic. Knohl tells them they do not have to. His unapologetic permission is remarkable in the Orthodox context and shows again that Knohl puts the couple's well-being very high.

It is hard to summarize Knohl's work in a few words, but it is correct to say, I believe, that the technical content in it is outstanding and would have been appropriate and useful for probably any young person of any culture and background who is about to begin experiencing heterosexual relations. Of course, Knohl weaves this practical guidance with halachic considerations, but it is clear that he puts the mutual enjoyment of the couple as the utmost priority: almost all regulations are presented as tools to achieve this goal. Obviously, being Orthodox, if the law is clear and Knohl does not know of loopholes to get around it, the law is the last word.

JENNIE ROSENFELD'S AND DAVID S. RIBNER'S *ET LE'EHOV*

In 2011, an English booklet (ninety-two pages long) titled *Et Le'Ehov: The Newlywed's Guide to Physical Intimacy,* written by Jennie Rosenfeld and David S. Ribner, appeared.[28] A parallel Hebrew edition was published in 2013. With these two versions, the book became available in the first two languages of the vast majority of the world's Jews. I discuss here the original English version, which was the one actually written by these two American-born immigrant-to-Israel authors.

Rosenfeld holds a Ph.D. in English, and her dissertation dealt with sexual ethics in the Modern Orthodox world. She was active for several years in projects regarding sexual education in such communities. Ribner is a professor of social work at Bar-Ilan University in Israel, a certified sex therapist, and an ordained Modern Orthodox rabbi.

The book does not include a rabbinic approbation of any kind, nor does it include any mention of consultation with a known rabbinic authority (even though some of those mentioned in the acknowledgments are rabbis). Obviously, the fact that Ribner himself is ordained can be seen by some as giving it some rabbinic authority. It mentions some connections with Yeshiva University, the same institution that contributed to the works of Debow described above, and uses the vague term "Torah-Observant" to describe its intended audience. It is hard to believe that the authors never consulted major rabbis on issues discussed in the book, but one can understand the possible reasons why they decided not to mention explicitly such consultations. It is probable that some of these rabbis did not want to be openly associated with their project, even if they agreed with its content and even supported its cause. Moreover, the authors probably wanted to make it clear this is a book written from a professional perspective, not a religious one, even if the intended readers and the authors themselves are Orthodox. Last but not least, giving an approbation from one rabbi can always mean that the book might be dismissed by those who do not highly regard that particular rabbi. Instead, Rosenfeld and Ribner chose to open the book with an extremely pious preface, one that should speak to readers of all shades of Orthodoxy: "At every step in the creation of this manual, we keenly felt the presence of the *Borei Olam* [Creator]. We have ventured into sensitive waters and we pray that what we have produced here does not deviate in any way from our obligation to sanctify the Name of Heaven."[29]

The book consists of an introduction, eight chapters, and appendices of various kinds. In the introduction, the authors say that they wrote it for brides, grooms, and those teaching them. The authors justify the book's existence by stating that "This kind of information was once passed from parent to child; our impression is that this is no longer the norm."[30]

The level of detail in the book might be surprising to outsiders. And yet it should be remembered that some of their readers might actually have little to no knowledge about the physiology of members of the other sex and even little understanding of their own: "For the new *Kallah* [bride], seeing her husband's erect penis can be confusing. . . . When erect, the penis can become a deep red and almost purple. . . . These changes are normal and should not be a cause of concern."[31]

Trying to serve as well as possible even such readers, the book explains the appearance and functions of male and female genitalia, preparation for the couple's first sexual experience, kissing, foreplay, orgasm, and, understandably, intercourse.[32] It mentions the possibility for newlyweds to postpone the first intercourse. Rosenfeld and Ribner present it not only as acceptable but also as common.[33] Several times in the book they inform and remind readers that other Jewish Orthodox couples have similar problems and that the advice they may have received from pious instructors may not be something everybody else agrees with. The question of the first night is one example. Another is with regard to the observance of the laws of *niddah* [menstrual impurity]. Rosenfeld and Ribner admit that it can have serious negative implications for the couple's intimacy, even though the common party line with regard to this topic is that it enhances intimacy by giving the couple a "time-out" to do other things.[34] In the same way, Rosenfeld and Ribner acknowledge that the idea that couples will always have desire for intimacy when the wife returns from the ritual bath, following the *niddah* period, is also often detached from mundane reality.[35]

The core of heterosexual sexual relations, vaginal intercourse, is described at considerable length.[36] The authors explain that intercourse should not come without any foreplay, emphasize the importance of natural or artificial lubrication, and warn that it takes some time for couples to do the "fine-tuning" that will make it enjoyable. They explain very meticulously how penetration happens, how each of the spouses should position himself or herself, and how one should move. They give special attention to the missionary position, though they do not say that it is particularly recommended. They only mention the probable fact it is "the manner that is used most often around the world." They also tell couples that a wet spot on the sheets following intercourse is to be expected.

In a subsequent chapter, the authors discuss briefly what they call "Alternate Intimacies." Because some of these acts—for example, oral sex—might not be deemed perfectly kosher by all rabbis, the authors add a warning: "Though this guide has been prefaced with the caveat that it is not meant to serve as a halachic resource, this point deserves to be reiterated here. We have chosen to include below a wide range of sexual activities. However, some of the actions below may not be sanctified by your individual halachic authority (*posek*)."[37]

The book's final sections discuss, like other books we saw, physiological and psychological problems that may affect sexual relations. As in some other works, the authors recommend consulting a professional if the problems persist. Two other elements that also appear at the end of the book are relatively unusual. One of them is a rather extensive list of resources on sexuality, including books, websites, and companies that sell sex toys. The other appendix is a sealed envelope with the following warning: "Note: This envelope contains illustrations that are meant to accompany the text and to clarify certain points with regard to male and female sexual anatomy and sexual positions. These illustrations are therefore explicit, and each person should take this into account before viewing the drawings."

Inside the envelope, five illustrations are again preceded by the same warning, with a further note that the illustrations have been commissioned specifically for the book and that "they attempt to balance the necessary sensitivity with the need for clarity and accuracy." Two of the illustrations show the female and male genitalia, and three of them show sexual positions: missionary, woman on top, and rear entry. Indeed, they are very minimalistic. Ribner, in an online audio interview,[38] explains that some of his clients, and eventually readers, might need such detailed depictions. After all, many of them have no television at home, do not go to movies, and have never seen a sexual act in a film, be it even a nonpornographic one. As a result, some of them might not know how, for example, to position their legs.

CONCLUSION

I have explored five complex books, written by people who could be described as part of the large spectrum of Modern Orthodoxy, with Aviner on its right margin. Based on my study of these books and many others, I think it is fair to say that there is currently a revolution in the way marital sexuality is presented in some Modern Orthodox works. The changes are mostly due to the increasing impact of feminist ideas and the way academic scholarship in general, and social sciences in particular, penetrate the internal discussion. The first two books we examined were written by women immersed in current scholarship on the matter. I do not think that this is a coincidence: Modern Orthodox women often have higher academic education than men. Obviously, not all women are so enlightened and open. Some of the most disturbing texts on the matter, not explored here, were written by women, such as Rachel Neriyah. Aviner also includes in one of his books a section that he claims was written by a woman, and its content is essentially identical to texts that are officially his. At the same time, not all men write books that ignore modern knowledge. The most we can say is that in some places some women bring outside scholarship into the system. This is not different from what we know happened during the period of Jewish Enlightenment [Haskalah], for example. Women are not expected to devote their time to Jewish sources, their education is less controlled and restricted, and they are expected to be a bridge, mostly for financial reasons, between the closed Jewish world and the outside.

The fourth book, by Knohl, was written by a male rabbi who does not have formal training in the field but admits repeatedly and clearly that he has consulted extensively others who do, including women. The fifth book was written by a man and a women, both having academic training in the field. On the other hand, Aviner's book, the third on my list, lacks any of this knowledge and reflects not much more than a repetition of old rabbinic ideas cast in modernized language. Aviner should be credited with starting the revolution by speaking frankly on the matter and writing about it. Knohl took a further step by taking serious consideration of the social sciences when writing his rabbinic manual. Diament, Debow, Rosenfeld, and Ribner took yet another step by gaining full academic training in the field and by trying to adjust the traditional religious ideas of Modern Orthodoxy to what they know from academia, not the other way around.

NOTES

1. Puah Institute, http://puah.org.il/ViewShut.aspx?ArticleId=7552. Question asked December 28, 2010. The context, content, and style make it clear that the couple is not *haredi.*

2. A non-Jewish female undergraduate student who took a course on Judaism with me defined Orthodoxy in this way in a paper: "While many religions allow individuals to fit the religion into their lives, the strict followers of Jewish law show that their lives have to be fit around Judaism. The Jewish law impacts every part of their life." I would like to thank B. Williard for permission to mention this definition, which I find very pertinent.

3. Sara Diament, *Talking to Your Children about Intimacy: A Guide for Orthodox Jewish Parents* (Bloomington: Xlibris, 2009), 37.

4. Ibid., 51.

5. Yocheved Debow, *Talking about Intimacy and Sexuality: A Guide for Orthodox Jewish Parents* (New York: Ktav and OU Press, 2012).

6. See, for example, ibid., 20–21. The same theme appears in almost any section of the book that defends Modern Orthodox concepts.

7. A different genre—books aimed at young readers, mostly boys and young men, that try to help them deal with the challenges of the conflict between their sexual maturity and the religious prohibitions related to sexual activity of all kinds—is not of relevance for us, as these books do not speak about the "how to" of intercourse. One of the most impressive books in this genre in recent years is Eli Sheinfeld, *Ha-Yetzer, ha-Lev, ve-ha'adam* [The Urge, the Heart, and the Person] (Jerusalem: Sifriyat Bet-El, 2010).

8. Very justly, this is what Reuven P. Bulka writes in the introduction to his book *Jewish Marriage: A Halakhic Ethic* (New York: Ktav, 1986), xv: "This book was written in . . . Israel, in 1983–1984. . . . That the subject of marriage is of immediate moment was driven home to me quite forcefully in the first few months [of that year]. Every week of those initial months, a new volume concerned with marriage [from the context, I assume that Bulka refers to 'religious' books] appeared on the bookstalls." Learning from other scholars, such as Amy DeRogatis, that a boom of evangelical marital guides started in the United States in the 1960s, it is not a wonder that it took a generation until the same phenomenon appeared on the Israeli eastern shores of the Mediterranean and in American Modern Orthodox circles.

9. Members of this group often refer to themselves as *toraniyim* [Torah oriented] or *emmuniyyim* [faith oriented].

10. In several places, Aviner admits that many see his writing as close to the *haredi* world. He rejects this claim, saying that what he writes is pure halachah [Jewish law], but the very fact that he feels he has to distance himself from the *haredi* world is a good hint that the line separating his halachic rulings in some matters from parallel rulings in the *haredi* world is rather thin. See another book by Shlomo Aviner, *Ahoti Kalah* [My Sister Is a Bride] (Jerusalem: Sifriyat Hava, 2002), 25. On the "National *haredi*" world, see, for example, Shlomo Fischer, "Fundamentalist or Romantic Nationalist: Israeli Modern Orthodoxy," in *Dynamic Jewish Belonging* (ed. Harvey Goldberg, Steven Cohen, and Ezra Kopelowitz; Oxford, UK: Berghahn, 2011), 91–111.

11. See the important article of Yossef (Yoske) Ahituv, "Modesty—From a Myth to an Ethos" [Hebrew], in *A Good Eye—Dialogue and Polemic in Jewish Culture: A Jubilee Book in Honor of Tova Ilan* (ed. Nahem Ilan; Tel Aviv: Hakibbutz Hameuchad, 1999), 224–63.

12. Shlomo Aviner, *Etzem me-Atzamai* [Bone of My Bones] (Beth El: Sifriyat Hava, 2001).

13. Ibid., 15.

14. Ibid., 19.

15. Ibid., 94.

16. Ibid., 7.

17. On some aspects of this, see also Julia Schwartzmann, "Constructing a New Type of Jewish Woman—The Power Concept in the Women-Oriented Literature of Rabbi Aviner," *Modern Judaism* 28:1 (2008): 64–78.

18. Aviner, *Ahoti Kalah,* 67. See also Aviner, *Etzem me-Atzamai,* 34.

19. Aviner, *Etzem me-Atzamai,* 81.

20. Ibid., 15–17 and 24–25, for example.

21. Aviner, *Ahoti Kalah,* 58–67.

22. Aviner, *Etzem me-Atzamai,* 19–38.

23. Full disclosure: I was a student in that yeshiva (Yeshivat ha-Kibbutz ha-Dati of Ein Tzurim in Israel) at the time Knohl was there, though I had rather limited interactions with him. I believe that my assessment of his book is not influenced by this biographical fact. It is tempting to see a few words on page 22 of Knohl's brochure, which we will discuss later, as related to Knohl's attachment to this yeshiva. The manner in which he speaks about the editors of the Talmud is a type of thinking that was common in that institution but is not typical of many other less progressive ones.

24. *Ish ve-Ishah* (Ein Tzurim: Yeshivat ha-Kibbutz ha-Dati, 2003, 2005, 2014). The first edition was twenty-four pages long. The second and third editions are fifty-one pages long.

25. Elyashiv Knohl, *The Marriage Covenant: A Guide to Jewish Marriage* (trans. Kaeren Fish and Eli D. Clark; Ein Tzurim: Yeshivat ha-Kibbutz ha-Dati, 2008).

26. "Time of Love," based on Ezekiel 16:8.

27. It should be remembered, though, that the couple's first intercourse, if they assume that the wife is a virgin, has significant implications for the coming days. If the couple had intercourse, even if hymenal blood was not visible, they must keep eleven or twelve days of separation, very similar to the separation that is required due to menstruation.

28. Jennie Rosenfeld and David S. Ribner, *Et Le'Ehov: The Newlywed's Guide to Physical Intimacy* (Jerusalem and New York: Gefen Publishing House, 2011). The words "Et le-Ehov" mean "A Time to Love"; see Ecclesiastes 3:8.

29. Rosenfeld and Ribner, *Et Le'Ehov,* 7.

30. Ibid., 10.

31. Ibid., 21.

32. Ibid., 17–41.

33. Ibid., 28.

34. Ibid., 46–48 and 80–82, for example.

35. Ibid., 69–70 and 74, for example.

36. Ibid., 30–33.

37. Ibid., 42.

38. "Hidden Jerusalem: Sex Therapist David Ribner," *Tablet Magazine,* http://tabletmag.com/podcasts/119984/hidden-jerusalem-sex-guide.

Challah from Abba: The Modern Jewish Father

Joshua Brown

> God, slow to anger and abounding in kindness; forgiving iniquity and transgression; yet not remitting all punishment, but visiting the iniquity of fathers upon children, upon the third and fourth generations.
>
> —Numbers 14:18

Since its birth, Judaism has been concerned with the effects of one generation's actions upon another. In this particular verse the rabbis understand not only that every generation is different but also that each generation is dependent upon the ones that came before it and those that come after it:

> Consider the implications of this verse by analogy with a four-level storehouse, one level above the other; on one there is wine; on another oil; on still another, honey; and on still another, water. If a fire starts on any one of the levels, what is above it will extinguish the fire. But if all four levels should have oil on them, all four will burn down. Likewise, if children persist, generation after generation, in the wicked ways of their forefathers, punishment will be visited upon them. But if the generations alternate, one generation righteous and the next wicked, and so on, then "the fathers shall not be put to death for the children, neither shall the children be put to death for the fathers" (Deut 24:16). Hearing this, Moses rejoiced, saying, "In Israel, no one is a malicious destroyer of grapevines just because his father was a malicious destroyer of grapevines."[1]

There are two assumptions made by this passage that are important to the study of the modern Jewish father. First, the rabbis are clear that fathers are influential in their children's lives. The second assumption is that children should strive to be different from their fathers in order to be righteous. Both assumptions are telling of the issues that fathers have faced throughout time. In this essay I look at the modern father and the many challenges he faces as he enters his home and works to become an active parent. In particular this essay focuses on four challenges facing fathers in the twenty-first century as they are informed by modern psychology:

1. The challenge of being Other in the child's life.
2. The challenge for the father to provide basic needs for the child.
3. The challenge for the father to introduce the outside world to the child.
4. The challenge to spend time that is of high quality but also time parenting the child.

Some of these challenges are ancient and have continued from generation to generation, while others are arising as unique to the modern era.

While less notable than the challenges, there are benefits that fathers bring to their children's lives. The latter portion of this essay will focus on these strengths that fathers have brought to parenting throughout the generations and finally the unique role fathers could play for the future generations of children.

CHALLENGES: THE OIL THAT BURNS FROM GENERATION TO GENERATION

If Abraham was the father of our biblical world, then Sigmond Freud has been the father of the psychoanalysis of the relationship between parents and their children. Like Abraham, whether the oedipal relationship speaks to us or not, it is the standard that all other theories are measured against and therefore will be the primary model I address in this essay.

CHALLENGE #1: FATHER AS AN OTHER TO THE CHILD

The Oedipus complex in Freudian psychoanalysis refers to a stage of psychosexual development in childhood whereby children of both sexes regard their father as an adversary and a competitor for the exclusive love of their mother.[2] Fathers, like oil, are an entity that is infinitely separated from the family in which they reside. This has been a major challenge for fathers to overcome throughout all of time, and according to current psychologists it has not receded. Moreover, as dual-earner families become the norm in our society, men are faced with a struggle to help fill the void of what was once a full-time stay-at-home job while being considered an other or outsider.

The father as Other impacts the family in a variety of ways. We will explore the complex nature of this outsider status through the relationship between the father as one excluded from the mother-child relationship:

> The pediatrician and psychoanalyst Donald Winnicott argued that "the infant and the maternal care together form a unit." Good enough mothering "includes fathers, but fathers must allow me to use the term maternal to describe the total attitude to babies and their care. The term paternal must necessarily come a little later than maternal." Winnicott held that the father's role in early infancy was to support the mother in her state of primary maternal preoccupation, to enable her to provide a holding environment and to avoid unnecessary impingements on the baby . . . when the infant is in the state of absolute dependency on the maternal holding.[3]

As Winnicott explains, the mother and child form a unit. The father falls outside of this unit and is not privy to the connection formed between the child and the mother. Notice that this is a relationship focused not on time but rather on dependency. The child is dependent upon the mother and not the father. While it is possible for the father to hold, care for, and even feed the baby, both society and biological factors often place the mother into the role of primary caregiver. The father becomes the alternative to mom, or Other.

Not only is this dependency fulfilling the child's needs, but it is also providing the child with pleasure. "Good experience is usually associated with need fulfillment—when it is in the presence of the mother in tune with its needs, which usually means a mother in the act of attending to them."[4] Fathers, perhaps without even knowing that it is happening, may find themselves outside the child's source of need fulfillment and even happiness in the early stages of life.

But need fulfillment can come from fathers as well. Technology has blessed us with bottles and other tools that help the father fill the biological roles of mother. For instance, in the cases of single-parent families in which the mother is absent, we can imagine that a child's needs are met by a man. But we should not be fooled into thinking that our modern postfeminist society is as egalitarian in the home as it is in the workplace. While women have moved into the professional world, they often do not relinquish their domestic role. Wendy Mogel, a noted family therapist and author of *The Blessing of a Skinned Knee,* spoke with me about this reality. She believes that "women today are trying to be perfect men as well as perfect women."[5]

The intent is not to point fingers at mothers but rather to illuminate the complexities of the love triangle that exists between parents and their child. Mothers, whether full-time parents or CEOs for corporations, continue to feel the pressure of being primary caregivers or "perfect women," as Mogel stated.

The father's challenge is to overcome the lack of space and find a balance between his partner's emotional need to be a "perfect" parent and his need to be a professional father.

But this otherness raises a wide range of emotions in the child. It is not only that the father is not the mother. We must also concern ourselves with how the child views the father in relation to the mother. The father is a necessary Other. This other often serves as a response or alternative to the mother. According to the French psychologist Jacques Marie Emile Lacan, "The child's sense of identity develops from seeing himself reflected in the other—the mother. . . . The father is seen as another brother wishing to take the child's place with the mother."[6]

In this case the father takes on the role of what we would term a brother. The child relates to father as one would relate in a sibling rivalry competing for the other parent's attention. This is heightened even further as we consider the sexual relationship often present among parents.

The oedipal relationship is a love triangle. Traditionally it occurs when two people in relationship create a third object, the child, to love. For the newcomer with needs from one and possibly both of the parents, their love for each other can be viewed as another challenge. This challenge is particularly problematic for fathers, as their children believe that their primary caregiver, the mother, often abandons them to seek the father.

"In fantasy, separation is always experienced as the mother retreating to the other room—the parental bedroom—with the second object, the father."[7] In this aspect of the oedipal theory the child becomes envious and even angry with the father. "The father is the hated depriving object, and this requires the father to have a capacity to be hated. The father has to accept that the central nurturing relationship involves the mother, and that he is excluded from the mother-infant couple."[8] And while the child is of primary concern, each member of this love triangle may feel similarly. "Essentially, the task for the mother, father and infant involves tolerating the link between two people they desire and which excludes them."[9]

CHALLENGE #2: PROVIDING BASIC NEEDS

Fathers are not mothers, and they face a challenge in breaking into the relationship between mother and child. The second challenge that fathers face focuses on whether it is even possible for fathers to provide basic needs for their child. Perhaps it is only the mother who can fill the needs of her child.

As we explore this second major challenge, we find that fathers may face a tremendous disadvantage, as their biological necessity seems to be diminishing with the progression of modern science in the field of fertility. "Winnicott reminded us that there is no baby without a mother."[10] One of the advances that modern science teaches us quite clearly is that men do not need to be present for childbearing or child rearing: "The acceptance of a whole new mode of procreation, ranging from 'do it yourself turkey-baster' inventions to sophisticated in vitro conception techniques, has contributed to the appearance that fathers are redundant beyond donating sperm."[11]

Women have a freedom that is biologically absent for men. Whereas a woman can birth to her child without a surrogate, a man must find a woman should he want to have a child alone. But it is not the biological limitations that provide the real challenge for fathers. Most fathers find themselves in a relationship. The biological needs are covered by their spouse. Rather, the social and psychological implications of not being a necessary part of the biological creation of a child are significant as we consider challenges facing fathers. This challenge stems from biology but is certainly made more difficult by the progressive nature of our society that often avoids gender differentiation:

> From the 1960s onwards, the women's liberation movement steered a difficult path between, on the one hand, stressing the equality of and importance of women, and at the same time on the other hand seeing motherhood as a potentially disadvantageous role in the battle for equality. There is little doubt that the new ideas on the importance of women . . . had the result that, in the second half of the twentieth century, there was an increasing loss of confidence in the value of the received sense of manhood and fatherhood.[12]

Feminism raised a question that we continue to ask and often fail to answer today: Are men necessary for child rearing? But asking for, needing, and receiving assistance in childbirth is not a new phenomenon. Abraham and Sarah laugh at God when they are told they will have a child. When Isaac marries Rebekah, he seeks help in becoming a father to help Rebekah get pregnant. "Isaac pleaded with God on behalf of his wife, because she was barren; and the LORD responded to his plea, and his wife Rebekah conceived."[13] Seeking help in fertility is an old challenge. What is unique about this challenge for our generation is that a woman can turn to God or to a fertility doctor without need for a man.

The question then becomes, what necessary role does the father play in his child's development? Within the oedipal context, the father is an Other often viewed as secondary. But there is more to raising a child than carrying it to term.

Viewed in a broader context, any attempt to understand the respective roles of mother and father has to take into account three immutable facts:

1. That the woman has the essential procreative role,
2. That the physical and psychological survival of the human infant requires the care of one other person, and
3. That the transformation of a biological baby into a fully functioning member of human society (i.e., socialization) involves more than mere physical and psychological survival.[14]

To push the father aside because he cannot fulfill the first fact above is to ignore a holistic perspective of child rearing. Children need another person to help socialize them and integrate them into society. As is discussed at the end of this chapter, fathers are ideal candidates for these needs.

CHALLENGE #3: THE CHALLENGE OF OPENING DOORS TO THE OUTSIDE WORLD

The previous challenges may be viewed as disadvantages that men face in our society due to their gender. Perhaps the third challenge can be considered an opportunity available primarily to the person taking on the role of the Other. This is the challenge of the father representing the outside world. One psychologist understands this in multiple stages: "There are three possible stages for the father. In the first stage, known as the mirror stage, the father is not distinct. In the second stage, the father intervenes and cuts the link between mother and child. And in the third stage, the child wishes to be like the father rather than to be the lover of mother."[15] Cutting the link between the mother and the child is an important stage for the child, but it can be a difficult transition for the father. This cutting of the link is one of the key actions a father can take as the representative of the outside world.

For Freud, "the concept of reality is bound up with the father." But this also allows "the father [to] appear mainly as a powerful figure to be fought or to whom we must submit."[16] This stage of fatherhood is therefore closest to the traditional role of the father as the patriarch of the family. In his book *Becoming the Kind Father,* Calvin Sandborn, a lawyer by trade, chronicles the struggle that this challenge presents. In telling his personal story, Sandborn relates the long tradition in masculinity of the man as an outsider to the intimate nature of domestic life. In this sense, fathers are beings of doing what is outside, such as work, politics, and fighting, and not feeling what is inside the home, such as love, peace, and comfort. For him, man has remained a knight in armor. "In fairy tales, the hero wears emotional armor as well as real armor. While he slays the dragon and saves the princess, he must always be brave. She shows emotions, but he doesn't. Instead, he is cool, powerful and 'in charge.' He's like Davey Crockett, 'The King of the Wild Frontier' . . . the man who knew no fear. . . . Many, like Batman, Green Hornet, the Lone Ranger and Zorro, actually wear masks to hide their faces and feelings."[17]

Sandborn believes that fathers leave masks and armor for their sons to adopt. This is his version of the burning oil present in every generation of men. He explains in his story that it is not only through fairy tales and comic books that this armor is transferred. It is also in very real life-changing moments that patriarchy has denied men the opportunity to express their emotions.[18]

One of these moments took place when Sandborn lost his father at the age of thirteen. He recounts the interaction among his brothers immediately after hearing of his father's death:

> I choked like I had a bone in my throat; and for a brief moment I cried. . . . Gasping, almost retching, I stumbled down the sidewalk with Tom. When we got to the corner, David suddenly stopped, took a deep breath, and looked back at me. He braced his shoulders and spoke authoritatively, in his Marine voice, "We're men in this family now, boys. We have to take this like men." He snapped the twig in his hands in two, and threw it to the ground. . . . "We've got the girls to take care of. We all have a job to do. . . . Think about it—Dad would want you to be strong champ," he said to me. "Don't worry, Tom's the oldest now, so he's in charge. He'll take care of you." He slapped the dust off of his hands, and strode quickly back into the house. By the time David slammed the door, I had stopped crying. I didn't cry again—or mention my father—for 15 years.[19]

Sandborn refers to this moment as a Boy Code Lesson and later explains how it turned his view of a knight in shining armor into a tin man with buried emotions. This is the challenge of representing the outside world. It is a system in which the father is the authority of the outward-focused image. He does not have the freedom or even the capability to be a master of his inside, emotional world. In Sandborn's words, "Patriarchy has denied men the opportunity to speak their feelings."[20]

While overcoming the biological barrier of giving birth to a child is impossible, taking off the emotional mask of patriarchy is open to men. Moreover, as the Other, the man has the ability to become another source of emotional support for his child:

> When the baby arrives what it needs is a carer, who for a while, can devote themselves to the child. . . . Whoever takes on this role should, if possible, have a state of mind encompassing several aspects described by Winnicott as "primary parental preoccupation," by Bion as "reverie." An adult in this state has unconsciously opened themselves up to the baby in a way that enables them to be deeply responsive to the baby's communications.[21]

Men cannot choose their sex, but some psychologists believe that men can choose to overcome the long burning oil of being emotionless. Sandborn explains that in order to build this relationship we must overcome a patriarchal competitive nature of win/lose mentality and replace it with a sense of love for ourselves. In his book, which reads much like a memoir, he explains:

> Too often men attack ourselves. I'm often shocked at how mean men can be when they talk about themselves. It's commonplace to hear men describe themselves harshly: "I'm such a no good bastard; Really, I'm just a stupid sonofabitch." As a young man told me, "I say things to myself that, if somebody else said it, I would punch them in the face."[22]

Sandborn believes that this is some of the oil that we inherit from our fathers. Personally, I did not relate to Sandborn's perspective until I recently observed it in action. At a retreat for fathers and sons at a camp outside of Los Angeles I supervised a friendly game of soccer: sons versus fathers. The game was mildly competitive, with high fives after every goal and a sense of comraderie among the two groups. Fathers would cheer for sons and vice versa. At one point in the game a twelve-year-old boy was passed the ball and had the opportunity to score. He pulled his leg back far and struck the ball with what looked like all his might. When the ball missed the goal, the boy, standing not so far from his father, fell down, hitting the ground with his hand. "I'm so stupid . . . such a screw up," he said.

Missing the goal was not a big deal, and it happened many times over the course of the game, but for this son it was a letdown, a sign of being a loser and not a winner. His father only a few feet away, along with the rest of the men, did not really notice the boy's disappointment. It is a normal reaction among men in a competitive setting. I was struck at both the intensity of the boy's reaction over a simple missed opportunity and the almost ambivalent response of more than twenty men. It was a sign to me that men, even at a very young age, may in fact be too harsh on thenselves.

Was this child's disappointment really his father's voice inside his head saying "How could you miss that shot?" I don't know. What is evident is that none of the men felt the need to react to this emotional outrage of hitting the ground with self-deprecating words. None of the fathers comforted the child or were even shocked by his outward disappointment. Rather, we all acted as knights in an armor that protects our vulnerabilities. It is a norm in male behavior, as Sandborn points out. "We're only a couple of generations removed from King George V's declaration that the father's proper role is to frighten his children. Even today, half of all Americans agree that 'the father must be master of his own house.' And in this traditional patriarchy, the father-son relationship has been one of dominance and submission, not of emotional connection."[23]

CHALLENGE #4: TRAVELING TOGETHER BUT GETTING NOWHERE

The fire in the storehouse of fatherhood reaches back through generations of men to biblical patriarchy. It is a reality that has been studied by psychologists and experienced by fathers and children such as Calvin Sandborn. But as the rabbis teach in their commentary, every generation is not only like the previous one; it is also unique to its own time. We are not only burning the same oil of biblical patriarchy. There are also new challenges that modern fathers must face.

As I mentioned in our discussion of Abraham, one of the primary traits of biblical fathers was their mission to be on a journey, constantly traveling. In my discussion with Mogel, she reminded me that modern fathers are also known to be travelers with their children. Recounting her own experience with her father, she remembers the importance of this traveling and reflects on the new challenges men face in the twenty-first century:

> I walked to school every day with my father. We lived in Manhattan and we walked together every day and we talked about his business. But also my father always wanted to know everything about my life. Even today, he wants to know the ages of the children that my daughter baby-sits for while she is in college. This is

> the beauty of the Jewish man—that he wants to know about his granddaughter's job.
>
> So one place fathering happens is in the car. . . . But I just went to the car show and I was shocked. There are big screen TVs in cars today. We saw these cars with large plasma screen televisions in them and then everyone is plugged in so you can't connect because you are connected. It is an erosion of the places where parenting takes place.
>
> The car used to be great. Driving to soccer practice or a b-day party you would process. I don't know what percentage now, but these tools to shut kids up—these machines are the plug and everyone is all stopped up and isolated. And the daddy, completely the odd man out. He is losing out the most because he doesn't have a unique role. He doesn't provide something essential for the system.[24]

As I teach twenty-first century teenagers, I realize that the television in the car is only the beginning of the new lover in our family triangle. Ipods, cell phones and GPS units are distractions in our lives that often prevent conversations. Mogel believes that these challenges affect the father in particular because occurrences such as riding in the car are not viewed as quality time. Sandborn adds a different perspective that is directed specifically at men trying to overcome the masked emotions of patriarchy:

> When something impacted me emotionally—when the boss dumped on me, when I had an argument with my wife, when one of the kids disappointed me . . . I would feel upset for a moment. But then I would immediately divert myself from the feelings. Like my brother David, I threw myself into the job at hand. I'd work long hours. Or I escaped into reading. Or, I'd turn off the feeling and turn on the TV.[25]

I empathize with Sandborn. On September 11, 2001, I arrived home just as the World Trade Center was struck by the terrorist planes. Like the rest of the country, I and the eleven other men in my house were in shock. For twenty-four hours our lives were at a standstill. Our world had been shaken in a way that my generation had never felt. Other generations recalled Pearl Harbor or President John Kennedy's assassination. We knew immediately that 9/11 would be our moment to remember where we were. But on day two and day three as emotions continued to flare, I noticed the men in my life becoming agitated: "When is sportscenter going to stop playing the news? When can I turn on sports again and get past 9/11?" We were not insensitive; in fact, a close friend barely survived the attack. But we did not want to experience the emotions; we wanted to turn those emotions off by turning on meaningless entertainment.

Technology is a new love in our lives, and men are known to be more interested in it than women. It can be a mask that we wear to hide our emotions and further disconnect us from relationships. But men face other challenges in expressing themselves. Sandborn claims that "intimacy with oneself prepares us for intimacy with others."[26]

Moreover, he explains that men are at a linguistic disadvantage in expressing these emotions:

> Men, unlike women, lack a broad range of words to describe various emotions. This lack of emotional vocabulary is a real deficit—it's part of the reason that almost 80% of men have difficulty identifying what they are feeling. I knew when I was angry or feeling something quite powerful, but I didn't have the words for subtler feelings such as disappointment, discouragement, insecurity, irritation or the like. . . . I would use words that either exaggerated the feeling ("I feel like crap") or minimized it ("It's nothing—I'm just tired"). As a result, I failed to experience the "disappointment"—because I was telling myself it was something else.[27]

Complicating this situation for fathers in particular is that the new role of the father expects him to be involved in the emotional side of the child's life to a greater degree than previous generations:

> In the modern, Western, nuclear family, mothers and fathers spend more time together than they did in the past and their roles are much less differentiated. Women no longer need to rely entirely on their husbands for material support or for obtaining power and status. Likewise, men now have social permission to be actively involved in parenting, and increasingly want to be given greater access to their children. . . . In the Western nuclear family we expect that fathers should be involved.[28]

With the changing role of women in our society, a space has been opened for the father to be more than just the one who communicates while driving the kid to school. Ironically, as the opportunities present themselves, the space is filled by new competition such as television and increasingly portable media. Adding to this concern is a long-held tradition of men's limited emotional vocabulary. Today, as my experience proved on 9/11, men often rely on distractions such as television to distance themselves from emotional opportunities. These opportunities may be our best tools in creating the relationships we wish to harvest with our children.

Mogel raises some other concerns about what prevents men from getting to journey with their children:

> What kind of parent does a Jewish father get to be. . . . I told you about how the men withdraw. It all seems as though the fathers are even wimpier now. I am thinking about the people I see in psychotherapy—the women are contemptuous about the men. Some of it is projection. What legs do men have to stand on now when the women can earn money and the emotional currency of women is overvalued. That women can relate to the children. He gets squeezed out and so what can he provide. And earning more money than the mom . . . big deal. We have this ambivalence toward money as it's dirty and we love it, so dad becomes that to us.[29]

The twenty-first century parent faces many competing interests. We have more dual-earner families, more distractions for our children, and more technology from our pockets, cars, and couches that can grab our attention. The expectations for fathers to be involved in their children's lives are possibly higher than ever before. Adding to the expectations are the "old" pressures to make money and the "old" ways of avoiding emotions by escaping to the television and sports. But it is not only society that wants dad to improve his role with children; it is the kids themselves. A Mori poll reported in *The Guardian* (April 10, 1997) showed that 20 percent of children eight to fifteen years old could not recall sharing an activity with their father in the previous week and that 80 percent want their father to spend more time with them.[30] At a North American Federation of Temple Youth workshop for male teens, camp director Bobby Harris asked young men to talk about love in their relationship with their fathers. Author Doug Barden recorded their responses:

> My father doesn't have a clue as to what is going on in my life.
> My father spends more time on his computer than he does with me.
> My father is a rabbi, and sometimes I feel he cares more about the congregation than he does about me.
> I wish my father would sit down more and talk with me about what's going on.

WRAPPING UP THE CHALLENGES

The role of the father is in transition. But we are sending mixed messages. On the one hand, our children are wondering where the father is in their lives, and on the other, the traditional role of the mother does not fit or may not even be available to the father. Add this to the struggle that men face sharing emotions, and we find that the father has an uphill battle in the family.

The picture painted by children is more complex as well. Mogel believes that our children have become entitled, and she worries for their future. This concern is intertwined with the challenges a father faces, as previously discussed:

> I was at a beautiful private school, and it is very progressive and casual and there were no seats left for the kids. And the teacher asked me if I minded sitting on the floor. So the teacher turned to a kid named Josh and said, "Josh do you mind sitting on the floor so Mogel can have a seat." And Josh responded to the teacher in a whiney voice, "No, but Lucy, you know I feel so much more relaxed when I sit on the couch."
>
> And I thought every issue is in there, and I immediately flashed to his first job interview and wondered if he will survive. His mother has taught him that his world revolves around his comfort. So the doting mother handicaps our kids.
>
> We have these young men—what is it going to be like when his wife is diagnosed with breast cancer? What is strength, maturity, leadership? What is the unique role of the father or the shared role? It's so much less clear.
>
> ME: What would you tell those parents?
>
> DM: Oh, I beat them up [jokingly]. Don't ask what's wrong. He comes home and complains about teachers and friends and being bored. Not getting the Nintendo Wii when other kids have it. Of course he wants the Wii; he has been brainwashed to want it. That's why we have Hannukah and birthdays and their own money. But when parents are worn down by life and then worn down by the kids' genius by lobbying, . . . this is also a challenge of how manipulative the children are. The kids, they're so powerful. And then the dads—what does he feel about the situation? Let's say he can't afford the Wii. He can't provide the Wii, and that is HIS role as father. Does he feel ashamed because the only thing he can contribute is the Wii because no one else pays attention to me?[31]

In this anecdotal story, Mogel highlights all of the challenges that I have raised for the modern father. He is a man struggling with his identity as it is associated with money. He is challenged to create a relationship with his children that values emotions, but he may not have the language and may feel more comfortable "buying" their love. The father also faces a complex competition with the mother, the primary lover of the children. Egalitarian parenting is possible, in my opinion, but only so long as we understand that this is one case in which fair may not be equal. A father cannot be artificially inseminated and carry the child to term, and the father cannot feed the child from his own body. Moreover, the mother can do these things, and even if she chooses not to, she remains a woman attached to a long tradition of gendered roles that pushes her to be the "perfect mother" and in today's world the "perfect man" as well. The position of the father seems somewhat lost, only able to react to the many changes and powerful forces that surround his desire to find a place in his family in which he can succeed and be a part of the team.

It is not my intent to paint a grim picture of the father. Family life is increasingly difficult for father, mother, and child. But it is significant that the father is such a missing person in the observed family, as it reflects one of the main problems and difficulties in becoming a father; that is, finding a role for him in the new family constellation.[32]

GOOD FATHERING IS NEEDED

Each generation of fathers faces challenges new and old. But this fatherly fire that the rabbis mentioned may also be a light for future generations. As discussed earlier, the role of the father, while complex and often difficult, is important and even necessary. In this last section of this essay I will address what fathers do to provide for their children's needs.

Fathers are an Other to their children. They are not the mother. But this Other plays an important role in the child's development. In the case of most families in which the father has not taken the place of the mother, the father becomes an important partner for the mother:

> If the mother is in this state of reverie, she needs another, usually the father, to manage the practical external demands and to act as a protector so that, for example, the mother is not too exhausted by relatives and friends or by her own anxieties about the baby. Father can settle the baby to sleep, change the baby, give a bottle so that the mother can rest and recover, encourage visitors to stay for a short while only, and contain and help think about the mother's and baby's emotional responses. The concepts of "holding in mind" and "containment" are both vital aspects of the relationship between child and father.[33]

It is not only important to note that the father is a protector and guardian of the mother and child but also that the father may have the ability to make the relationship between mother and child succeed. In this sense the father becomes a manager of mother and child. He is the person able to best understand their emotions and limitations. Standing just outside the immediate relationship between mother and child, the father may in fact have the best perspective on what steps to take next. But there is another important factor to keep in mind in this relationship. It is not competitive. Rather, it is symbiotic. The mother and father are a team working to keep each other in balance and to provide for the child.

Certainly this is good practice for relationships, but perhaps it is the role of the father to model this behavior for the child:

> The baby needs total care early on, but then steadily moves towards separateness, a wish to be alone and then to leave. This process means parents have, to some extent, to be left behind, discarded. For those adults who were uncertain of themselves, or who found in the baby an intense relationship they have had with no one else, there is a dread of losing the child and a painful wish to hold on. . . . Fathers have to both accept this themselves and help the mother separate and relinquish the child.[34]

Whereas we discussed the challenge that emotions place before fathers, there is a light that burns from this oil that is important for the child:

> The father, by virtue of being less involved emotionally, can relieve the situation through his access to a fresh perspective. Probably the commonest example of this is when an infant gets into an inconsolable state and, despite her best efforts, it is just impossible for the mother to soothe "her baby." . . . At such times a fresh parent with a fresh mind who, in the infant's perception, is not part of the persecuting situation, can step into the breach to rescue the situation. This can restore a calmer state. . . . When there is an actual father who can act in this way, we can think of him as performing a symbolic paternal function.[35]

The child needs the father in order to understand that his or her relationships are not limited to the mother but also that the mother's needs are not met solely by the child. This partnership of mother and father is one of the values that Mogel believes we need to emphasize the most and one that many couples are leaving behind:

> I would like for them to start with examining their actions in the light of the message that they send their kids of how much they respect each other. That's the core. We are worshiping idols, and the

> idols are our kids and their achievement. That has taken the place of God. It is so bad for the kids because it makes them so anxious and entitled. . . .
>
> I want the kids to see the parents cherishing each other—to see the mother really appreciating the father's strengths, his physical size, his experience in the outside world and bringing it into the inside world. I want the girls to see the fathers finding their mothers beautiful—potent antidote to the airbrushed world we live in.
>
> I want them to hear parents laughing together. My daughter once said to me when she heard my husband and I laughing in our room: "There is nothing that makes me feel more secure than to hear that sound." Parents don't realize this—they think it is all about the focus on the kid.
>
> Mothers need to think about what is unique about their husbands. I say to couples all the time, "Why did you marry him . . . has it really changed all that much?"
>
> Then they are totally poetic—but when they have kids the kids take such center stage, and I always say "the kids will be gone and if you haven't taken care of this relationship what is it going to be like."[36]

This is a challenge, but it is also an opportunity. And I believe that it is less complicated than overcoming years of patriarchal models or finding a way to break into the mother-child relationship. Sometimes it can even happen without any effort at all:

> A 13-month-old baby whose mother had recently returned to work was observed at the end of the day after he had been collected from his grandmothers. . . . He appeared to like nothing better than lying on a settee, apparently taking pleasure in his parents' conversation with each other as they went about their evening chores. This was his preferred activity at that time of night and it had an unmistakably settling effect on him. This baby seemed able to tolerate the awareness of his two parents having a relationship with each other and it is this that will form the basis of an internal space.[37]

Internal space is an important element in children forming their identities. What strikes me about this case in particular is that the child is passive and in the margins of the action. This marginal role is important for the kid, and it allows him to form an identity.

I believe that this is a light challenge, because in many situations the flame of a relationship is what brought the child into the world. The challenge is keeping the flame lit and making sure that the child does not replace the spouse.

The father represents a sense of power. Freud even described this as one of the strongest needs of a child. But the father also represents a sense of independence and the outside world:

> A key role for the father, which most men find they do intuitively, is to introduce the baby to the world. It is interesting to note that in general mothers appear to carry or sit holding their babies in the earliest weeks face to face, whilst fathers tend to hold the baby facing out into the world. . . . Many of the games fathers tend to enjoy playing with their children in a mutually pleasurable way tend to have elements of separation and return in them—a kind of losing/finding theme, perhaps enacting the necessary separation process.[38]

Fathers represent the world beyond the comforts of home to their child. They are the platform by which many children reach out into the world and discover themselves. This is a stark contrast to the mother, who holds her child close to her womb. Fathers not only bring the child to the world. They also bring the outside world into the home:

> The effect of "Daddy coming home from work" can bring relief to what can often be a stressful situation at the end of the day. . . . The father is also seen as instrumental in turning the baby's view towards the outside world away from the intense intimacy of the mother-child relationship, or as introducing the "third position" which is essential for healthy cognitive and emotional growth and development.[39]

The child needs to see that an outside world exists, and it is often the father who brings this reality into the house. As discussed earlier, our world is leveling the roles of mother and father, and it may seem as likely that the mother is the one "coming home from work." I accept this with one exception. Mothers continue to take maternity leave for a period of months. This trend is only beginning for fathers. The first paid family leave bill was passed in California only in 2004.[40] The Family Medical Leave Act does allow for any family member to take up to twelve weeks, but this is unpaid. This often leaves mothers, even those who work full-time, as the initial caretaker in the home and the father as the "coming home from work" model.

Fathers are often a bridge for their children to the outside world. They are also a bridge to the inner world of the child, giving the child a sense of independence:

> That is, the father is a child's primary experience of someone other than the mother. . . . The knowledge that someone else is thinking of and involved with the child frees the mother from her infant. It also frees the infant from the mother. It means that the child will have space to experience himself, can risk hating the mother, can even risk killing her in his mind, because there is someone else there to keep him alive.[41]

The child does not always need to hate the mother in order to gain from the father. But an overly obsessive relationship with the mother is unhealthy, and the father is the healthiest option to help children realize that they can depend on themselves as well as others. "Mother and infant need someone else to intervene to prevent them from remaining stuck in a merged, claustrophobic, potentially murderous relationship."[42]

Research shows that children benefit most when the mother and the father together help the child gain a sense of independence. "We found that while secure attachment in infancy to the mother predicted early development of emotional understanding, if attachment to the father was also secure, the child's development was even further enhanced."[43]

Again, the message is that of the parents as a team, working together to help the children adjust to their new environment. In fact, a number of large-scale studies have demonstrated that the greater the involvement of the father in an infant's early care, the more rapidly the infant develops and the more likely the infant is to withstand stress and to be socially responsive.[44]

Some studies have also shown that a father can be quite successful at raising his children as the primary caregiver, the role usually taken by the mother:

> Evidence for the overlap between the role of the mother and father comes from the work of Kyle Pruett. This is a longitudinal, in-depth study of 17 families where the primary caretaker was the father. The findings over eight years support the view that the "nurturing instinct" is not confined to females. Children develop extremely well in these families, and the child, far from demonstrating deficits in ego functions or object relatedness, seems more active, curious and less prone to pathological separation or stranger anxiety than infants whose primary dyadic relationship was with their mother.[45]

Unfortunately, we also know that not all people are good at nurturing their children. Calvin Sandborn's book is predicated on the anger of his father and his father's (and later his own) inability to be nurturing or what he terms "kind." In his process of self-change, Sandborn explains the steps that he took in order to become the "kind father" to himself. By looking at these steps, I believe that we can understand what a kind and nurturing father might look like:

1. Hold myself in friendly regard.
2. Pay attention to what I'm feeling.
3. Identify that feeling with accurate words.
4. Articulate the feeling to myself.
5. Give myself permission and support to actually feel it, grieve it if necessary.[46]

This emotional experience is what Sandborn lacked in a father. He writes the book under the premise that this is what fathers should be to their children and that when this is absent for men, they need to become this father for themselves. I am not sure that Mogel would agree:

> I just saw a family where they sing two songs and read two stories, then they have four kisses, then the dad comes in and reads a story and a song—it takes forty minutes every night. The parents hate it. But they are trying to be with their kids and love them. It has gotten way out of control because the ritual has gone sour. Its much too manicured and organized. It has become a huge power struggle. What is the definition of a book between the parents and kids?[47]

Her point, I believe, is that the emotions must be authentic and not rehearsed or scheduled. Sandborn wishes for men to go through a conversion that may not be possible. Certainly, men have the ability to love rather than hate, and I hope we can extend the vocabulary for men's emotions, but some people, men or women, are, I believe, less inclined to be extroverted in their emotional expression. Some people will never be warm and fuzzy. If they were to try, it would be putting on a mask of emotion, and I have to agree with Mogel: it would not work.

The final aspect of fatherhood worth mentioning for this thesis came as quite a surprise to me. For many years I have heard spouses talk about their husbands or fathers as though they were the "extra child" in the family. "I really have three kids," a mother of two children might say. To my surprise, this trait is not only common among men, but it is a welcome trait for them to hold within the family. Mogel explained that "A lot of the fathers I see are much more playful than the mothers."[48] This playful nature is not a coincidence. I already discussed the psychological significance of separation and return games that fathers often play with their children. Now, focusing specifically on some differences between fathers and mothers, many psychologists understand that a reaction to the "perfect woman" mother is the "playful father."

According to Mogel, there are two primary types of fathers in the traditional family structure:

1. The one who comes home and makes order, trying to make rules. Part of this is a reaction to feeling left out. One of those rules is to pay attention to me.
2. The second type takes time to play and be sillier than the mothers. Freud too writes about wit and humor. Sometimes the dads are more fun and funnier. The moms say that the dad is another kid.

These playful moments should not be minimized in their importance. The father, representing the outside world and an alternative to the mother, can provide his child with important memories that can help forge their identity. Mogel explained how this same theme arose as she asked women about their most vivid memories as a child:

> One woman recalled that her father was a diver, and when they spent time at the beach he would always dive and pick up starfish for her to keep. Another father took the kids on a hike one day, and when they got to a stream he said, "Boy I am thirsty." Turns out he had hidden some soda bottles under the bank of the river. He shocked his children when he reached down and pulled up these drinks out of the ground for his kids. Being the playful parent is important.[49]

Mogel was not interviewing these women about their relationships with their fathers. Unprompted, many of them referred to some of their strongest memories as memories with dad. Moreover, many of these memories were of dad doing playful things with them. Dad was having fun.

This is an exciting role for fathers to play as they look for models of fatherhood that are accessible to them, beneficial for their children, and not stepping on the toes of the mother.

CONCLUSION

Like oil in water, fathers are an important commodity that remains separated from its environment. As the rabbis explain, fathers can also be dangerous. Sandborn helps us understand the angry father and the man who wears the mask. Mogel points out that fathers are not separated always by their choice. They have a long, uphill battle to fight. And when they choose to fight it, they should do it with a great deal of love and respect for the child's mother. Finally, fathers bring some unique qualities to a family. They are guardians. They are Other and representative of the outside world. And they are playful, bringing a sense of fun into the family, creating memories that often last a lifetime for the children they help create.

NOTES

1. Midrash on Numbers 14:18 (Yalkut, *Shelah,* #744).
2. "Oedipus Complex," Wikipedia, http://en.wikipedia.org/wiki/Oedipal_complex.
3. Alicia Etchegoyen and Judith Trowell, *The Importance of Fathers: A Psychoanalitic Re-evaluation.* (New York: Brunner Routledge, 2003), 28.
4. Ibid., 77.
5. Interview with Wendy Mogel, 2008, Los Angeles.
6. Etchegoyen and Trowell, *The Importance of Fathers,* 30.
7. Ibid., 81.
8. Ibid., 85.
9. Ibid., 95.
10. Ibid., 93.
11. Ibid., xv.
12. Ibid.
13. Genesis 25:21.
14. Etchegoyen and Trowell, *The Importance of Fathers,* 83.
15. Ibid., 30.
16. Ibid., 24.
17. Calvin Sandborn, *Becoming the Kind Father* (Canada: New Society Publishers), 9.
18. Ibid., 63.
19. Ibid., 49.
20. Ibid., 63.
21. Etchegoyen and Trowell, *The Importance of Fathers,* 12.
22. Sandborn, *Becoming the Kind Father,* 30.
23. Ibid., 29.
24. Interview with Wendy Mogel, 2008, Los Angeles.
25. Sandborn, *Becoming the Kind Father,* 50.

26. Ibid., 60.
27. Ibid., 54.
28. Etchegoyen and Trowell, *The Importance of Fathers,* 93, 94.
29. Interview with Wendy Mogel, 2008, Los Angeles.
30. Etchegoyen and Trowell, *The Importance of Fathers,* 47.
31. Interview with Wendy Mogel, 2008, Los Angeles.
32. Etchegoyen and Trowell, *The Importance of Fathers,* 133.
33. Ibid., 12.
34. Ibid., 16.
35. Ibid., 77.
36. Interview with Wendy Mogel, 2008, Los Angeles.
37. Etchegoyen and Trowell, *The Importance of Fathers,* 81.
38. Ibid., 142.
39. Ibid., 132.
40. www.babycenter.com.
41. Etchegoyen and Trowell, *The Importance of Fathers,* 97.
42. Ibid., 98.
43. Ibid., 54.
44. Ibid., 51.
45. Ibid., 52.
46. Sandborn, *Becoming the Kind Father,* 60.
47. Interview with Wendy Mogel, 2008, Los Angeles.
48. Ibid.
49. Ibid.

"Jewish Education Begins at Home": Training Parents to Raise American Jewish Children after World War II

Joshua J. Furman

In 1954, the United Synagogue's Commission on Jewish Education published the first installments of *Your Child and You,* a pamphlet series on child-rearing issues facing the American Jewish parent. Azriel Eisenberg, the executive vice president of the Jewish Education Committee of New York, contributed a volume to the series titled *Talks with Parents* in which he advised mothers and fathers on the importance of Jewish education and the critical role that parents play in their children's development. He explained to his readers that "your children become what they are largely because of you, their parents. You are the most essential part of their world, for you are the first to create their world for them. As parents you give them not only your physical characteristics but also your outlook on life, your manners, your temperament." Even as he encouraged parents to enroll their children in religious schools and summer camps, Eisenberg stressed the central role that parents must play as "active partners" in their children's moral and spiritual growth.[1]

Echoing Eisenberg's call, numerous child-rearing authorities exhorted Jewish parents to take responsibility for their children's Jewish upbringing and to seek appropriate counsel toward this end, since, they argued, the act of raising children to identify as Jewish in a predominantly non-Jewish environment was no easy task. This view, held by many in the post–World War II American Jewish community, reflected a widespread sense of anxiety about the quality and authenticity of Jewish life in suburban environments. As the primary setting of Jewish family life transitioned in the 1940s and 1950s from urban immigrant neighborhoods of first and second settlement, rich with Jewish institutions and cultural life, to suburban neighborhoods that lacked an established Jewish infrastructure, communal leaders worried openly about the ability of Jewish parents to transmit Jewishness to their children in these new settings. For their part, many parents counted on rabbis and teachers to provide their children with Jewish role models.[2]

Nevertheless, Anna Bear Brevis, another author in the *Your Child and You* series, concurred with Eisenberg's view that parents could not rely on communal institutions alone to mold their children into knowledgeable, committed Jews. In her 1954 pamphlet *Jewish Education Begins at Home,* Brevis, a public school principal, noted that the vast majority of American Jewish children spent only a few hours a week engaged in formal Jewish schooling, as compared to thirty hours a week in public school, and they lived in communities largely devoid of Jewish cultural and religious activity. Therefore, she claimed, to ensure the successful transmission of Jewish heritage, mothers and fathers must give their children a home environment that inculcates a love and appreciation for Judaism. To train women toward this goal, Brevis called for and later helped create the Institute for Jewish Mothers in her native town of Buffalo, New York.[3]

Six years earlier, writing in the Conservative movement's publication *Women's League Outlook* in 1948, parent education specialist Rose Cahan argued that parents seeking to transmit a Jewish heritage to their children in America must contend with additional challenges beyond those faced by all mothers and fathers. "In a dual culture it is not easy to live a Jewish life," she wrote. "The Jewish way of life must be learned; it is not acquired at birth and parents have the primary responsibility of helping their children develop positive Jewish attitudes."[4]

Believers in the supreme power of nurture over nature, educators, rabbis, and psychologists looked to American Jewish parents to play a leading role in shaping the ethnic identity, religious practice, and moral compass of their children. Throughout the postwar period, they dispensed child-rearing advice to Jewish parents on a number of topics. In journals, magazines, pamphlets, sermons, and speeches, these child-rearing mentors urged Jewish parents to create the kind of home environment and instill the values that they believed would ensure a child's future happiness, loyalty to the Jewish people, and fitness for citizenship in a democratic, faith-centered United States.

This essay will examine Jewish parenting advice from the post–World War II era on topics specific to the needs and interests of Jewish parents, including information on how to celebrate Jewish birth rituals and festivals as a family and suggestions on how Jewish parents and their children should navigate the December holiday season. This generation of Jewish parents' interest in and need for such child-rearing advice is the result of several factors unique to this era. To a significant extent, this child-centered communal agenda reflected wider trends in American society at large. The postwar baby boom accelerated the pace of suburbanization as growing families sought greener pastures on the outskirts of cities in which to raise their children. Following fifteen years of economic deprivation and war, many Jews took advantage of new opportunities afforded them by the GI Bill and federal housing loans to purchase suburban homes.[5] As they took up residence in new neighborhoods away from the urban core, Jews and other middle-class Americans created greater physical and emotional distance between themselves and their parents. In many cases, grandparents no longer lived in the same neighborhood or city as their children and grandchildren. In their absence, new parents turned to another source of comfort and counsel: the child-rearing expert, whose recommendations stemmed not from Old World traditions or customs but instead from scientific research and psychological principles.[6]

Furthermore, at a time when American public culture embraced the notion of a Judeo-Christian heritage as a moral and political weapon in the nation's struggle against communism and the Soviet Union, Jews could prove their patriotic bona fides by embracing their religious traditions. Following World War II, in which Judaism earned newfound recognition and respect as one of America's three "fighting faiths," public performances of religiosity became a politically useful manner of simultaneously demonstrating faith in both God and the United States. In this newly ascendant "tri-faith America," as historian Kevin Schultz has described it, Jews joined synagogues and sent their children to Jewish schools in record numbers. They increasingly came to understand and define Jewish identity in terms of religion, although this shift in conception of Jewishness was not generally accompanied by an increase in ritual observance or synagogue attendance. Sociologist Marshall Sklare, analyzing the rise of the Conservative movement in the suburbs, argued that their synagogues functioned primarily as ethnic churches, facilitating opportunities around the premise of religion for Jews to meet and be around other Jews.[7] While contemporary observers and later scholars have critiqued the authenticity of this religious turn in American life, this historical context helps explain the motivation behind the plethora of books and articles aimed at introducing Jewish birth and holiday rituals to parents.[8]

As much as the recommendations from this cadre of experts drew upon insights and practices from the realm of Jewish tradition, external influences and historical circumstances also shaped the worldviews of Jewish parenting pundits in numerous ways. Their prescriptions for raising the perfect American Jewish child borrowed heavily from the fields of psychology and pediatric medicine and responded to the concerns and insecurities of an ethnic community adjusting to affluence and suburbanization.

While parenting advice books may appear to offer objective, timeless recommendations grounded in scientific evidence and empirical observation, the genre in fact reflects contemporary social and political tensions. Child-rearing advice, as a social and cultural construct, does not remain static over time; rather, the literature evolves and adapts in response to the needs and concerns of parents and society at a particular moment in history. Given that the task of parenting is intricately linked to the survival of a community and its cultural traditions, a critical reading of child-rearing literature reveals the tensions and insecurities at work within that particular social group.[9] Analyzing American Jewish parenting advice in the post–World War II decades helps us understand how American Jews have navigated between adherence to religious and cultural traditions and interest in new medical and psychological insights, articulated and encouraged particular notions of gender roles in the American Jewish family, and responded to changing socioeconomic realities since 1945, including suburbanization and embourgeoisement.

Even as American Jews enjoyed a period of unprecedented economic and social mobility, long-standing communal fears about antisemitism, acceptance, and Jewish continuity intensified and developed in new directions in the suburbs. To assuage these anxieties, authors of child-rearing literature sought to train parents in the art of raising sons and daughters who would embrace a Jewish identity in an American setting. They filled books for mothers and fathers with information about Jewish birth rituals and holidays so that parents could observe and preserve these traditions and pass them on to their children. They adapted the form and content of mass-market American baby books to produce similar volumes for Jewish audiences. They armed parents with guidance rooted in both traditional Jewish sources and modern psychology, arguing often that these two reservoirs of wisdom flowed together harmoniously. They argued that Jewish living was happy living, and that nothing could be so American as to live Jewishly.

USHERING THE CHILD INTO THE WORLD OF JUDAISM: RITUAL EDUCATION FOR PARENTS

In 1950, the Women's League of the United Synagogue of America, a group aligned with the centrist Conservative movement, published Sadie Rose Weilerstein's *Our Baby*, a scrapbook for parents to commemorate the milestones in a newborn's first years of life. Part record book and part explanatory volume, *Our Baby* included pages on Jewish rituals such as *brit milah* [circumcision] and *pidyon ha-ben* [redemption of the firstborn] as well as pages on which parents could document the place and time of the child's birth, the dates of various physical development milestones, the baby's feeding regimen and first words, and his or her medical and dental history.

Presented in soft pastel colors, Weilerstein's book closely resembled other keepsake volumes of the era produced for new American parents. Some suggestions to parents on what to record, however, pertained specifically to the baby's earliest encounters with Judaism, such as "First Visit to the Synagogue" and "Days for Gladness, Seasons for Joy" pages, which prompted the parent to describe the child's first experiences with each of the Jewish holidays in addition to Thanksgiving. On the page titled "A Tree for Baby," parents could attach a certificate in recognition of the planting of a tree in Israel by the Jewish National Fund in the baby's honor.[10]

The inclusion of these explicitly Jewish sections, alongside the generic sections about the baby's health and maturation found in similar publications for a general audience, signifies an effort on the part of the Conservative movement to encourage American Jewish parents to value their child's spiritual as well as physical growth. With the inclusion of a page for a Jewish National Fund certificate, Weilerstein and the United Synagogue also sought to persuade parents to instill an attachment to the land of Israel in their children. Through this and other forms of Jewish parenting literature, authors and speakers endeavored to teach mothers and fathers the knowledge and skills they would need to create a vibrant Jewish home environment for themselves and their children.

At the same time, the aesthetic and substantive resemblance of *Our Baby* to other books of its kind authored for a broad American audience suggests a desire, on the part of both publisher and purchaser, to render and receive information about Jewish child rearing in a thoroughly contemporary format.[11] This choice reflected a broader yearning on the part of most American Jews to blend seamlessly into American life and culture while simultaneously making some effort to retain Jewish distinctiveness. This effort to reconcile modernity and tradition, to strike a balance between acculturation and ethnic continuity, lies at the heart of American Jewish parenting advice literature.

Alongside *Our Baby,* a plethora of books and articles on Jewish birth rituals appeared beginning in the late 1940s, offering information and advice to parents on how to navigate a baby's induction into Judaism and Jewish peoplehood. Authors and producers of this literature operated on two assumptions: first, that American Jewish parents in fact desired to welcome their new son or daughter according to the principles and practices of Jewish tradition, and second, that they were at least partly, if not entirely, unfamiliar with what these traditions entailed. As such, consulting a concise and comforting reference guide could relieve parents of the guilt or embarrassment of having to ask a rabbi or relative for assistance.

Rabbi Reuben M. Katz, in the foreword to Conservative rabbi Hyman Chanover's 1956 book *Blessed Event,* noted that the arrival of a newborn baby is a time of intense mixed emotions, simultaneous excitement and apprehension. "American-Jewish parents are no different from other parents in sharing these rather universal emotions, the qualms, confusions and moments of ecstasy," he wrote. "And yet American-Jewish couples do have a tradition which provides for them a unique and socially desirable way of expressing their sense of awe, splendor, and dependence upon God during these sacred and memorable moments."[12]

Chanover's slim volume and others like it introduced Jewish parents to this array of birth rituals and advised them on the process of choosing a meaningful Hebrew and English name for their newborn child.[13] Parents could consult a number of books, including Chanover's *Blessed Event,* Nathan Gottlieb's *A Jewish Child Is Born* (1960), and Shonie Levi and Sylvia Kaplan's *Across the Threshold* (1959), for a carefully choreographed description of the *brit milah* ceremony for boys and the baby-naming synagogue ceremony for girls, along with other rituals such as the *pidyon ha-ben.* These works commonly included an English transliteration of the traditional Hebrew prayers, sometimes written entirely in capital letters with hyphens to signal syllable breaks, so that nervous fathers could practice their pronunciation of the lines they would be called upon to recite in public.[14]

Chanover also included newly composed English prayers for mother and father to recite in anticipation of the birth of their child, entreating God that the child should be born "sound in mind and body and with a happy nature," that the mother should be blessed with safety and strength during the delivery, and that both parents should "be privileged to raise this child to be a blessing to its loved ones, to Israel and all mankind."[15] These inclusions reflect a perception on the part of authors and publishers that many American Jewish parents of this era lacked fluency in Hebrew and would therefore appreciate, and likely require, alternatives and additions to the traditional Hebrew prayers recited at childbirth rituals. Furthermore, with the addition of English prayers, producers of child-rearing literature once again made an effort to contextualize Jewish birth rituals in a comfortable modern format for their target audience of acculturated Jewish parents.

BRIT MILAH AND THE THOROUGHLY MODERN MOHEL

The circumcision ritual, or *brit milah,* signifies the entrance of the Jewish male into the covenant between God and Abraham described in the book of Genesis. Circumcision functions in Judaism as an important marker of both ethnic and religious identity.[16] Discussions of the circumcision ceremony in these guidebooks and related sources, in addition to the step-by-step explanations of the ritual itself, frequently engaged in polemical discourse about the crucial religious importance of the act itself and the centrality of the mohel, or circumciser, to an authentic and valid execution of the ceremony. Commentators sought to alleviate the concerns of modern parents by presenting circumcision as a normal and medically safe procedure that would inaugurate the baby boy into Jewish peoplehood without risking his health or his status in middle-class American society. At the same time, authors differed according to their ideological roots as to how modern Jewish parents should navigate potential conflicts between Jewish customs and contemporary concerns.

Nathan Gottlieb, an Orthodox rabbi and mohel himself, devoted two separate chapters in his *A Jewish Child Is Born* to discussions of the ritual's religious meaning and the qualities of the modern mohel. "With circumcision," he wrote, "the child is made a Jew forever. . . . Through circumcision the newly born are dedicated to God, to His Torah, and to the highest moral and ethical code."[17]

Gottlieb proceeded to explain why circumcision is a practice completely in harmony with modern scientific principles but one that only a trained, pious mohel could perform. On the one hand, he claimed, "the technique of the modern mohel combines spiritual and surgical skill. The expert mohel is a specialist who has advanced this procedure to the most modern medical standards." Those who perform ritual circumcisions are capable of rendering the *brit milah* a painless procedure, thanks to a familiarity with and use of modern instruments and techniques. The circumcision ceremony itself reflects an intimate divine knowledge of pediatrics, Gottlieb argued, since by the eighth day—the day on which the commandment should be performed, according to Jewish law—the baby's blood-clotting factors are more developed and the potential health risks are greatly reduced.[18]

While *brit milah* thus accords with the latest and best medical practices, however, Gottlieb warned his readers that a physician—even a Jewish one—could not perform a halachic [valid according to Jewish law] circumcision unless he was also a religiously observant Jew trained in the laws and practices of this ritual, capable of performing the act accordingly. "Only the physical act of an expert mohel inspired by zeal for the Jewish religion renders a *brit milah* proper," Gottlieb cautioned. "If an ordinary physician not trained as a mohel performs circumcision, even if a rabbi is present and reads the prayers, what results is not *milah,* but only an act of surgery." He reassured parents that even Jewish doctors themselves prefer the services of a trained and devoted mohel to those of a surgeon.[19]

Other authorities, seeking to alleviate parental fears that circumcision might mark their sons as strange or harm them in some way, sought to remind parents that circumcision was a common practice around the world. Rabbi Morris Shoulson of Philadelphia, also a mohel, wrote in an essay for a volume on the Jewish family that between two hundred million and three hundred million people around the world lived in cultures that currently practice circumcision and that 92 percent of American males are circumcised. Even Prince Charles was circumcised at birth, Shoulson noted, when "the leading *mohel* of London" paid a visit to Buckingham Palace.[20]

Like Gottlieb, Shoulson also marveled at the harmony between the timing of the circumcision ceremony and the human body's development. Emphasizing the health benefits of Jewish ritual as an additional justification for its performance, he cited studies claiming that circumcised men carried a far lesser risk of developing penile cancer and that their wives would be less prone to cervical cancer as a result of never coming into contact with the foreskin.[21]

Several other authors from Conservative and Orthodox backgrounds echoed Gottlieb's insistence upon the indispensability of the mohel to an authentic and valid ceremony.[22] Authorities aligned with the more liberal Reform movement, however, such as Rabbis Levi Olan and Floyd Fierman, regularly assured their audiences that if a mohel could not be found or is not preferred by the parents, a doctor could perform a ritual circumcision so long as a rabbi or the father recited the appropriate Hebrew blessings and the baby's Hebrew name.[23] This scenario played out in dramatic form in *Covenants with the Lord,* a booklet of theatrical scripts written by members of the Temple Beth-El Sisterhood in Great Neck, New York, and published by the Reform-affiliated National Federation of Temple Sisterhoods in 1951 for broader use.

A collection of plays about Jewish life-cycle ceremonies from a Reform perspective, *Covenants with the Lord* followed three generations of the fictional Cohen and Gold families, marking the passage of time through various rituals. In the first play, a newborn boy is circumcised in the hospital by a doctor despite the objections of one of the boy's grandfathers, who insists that a mohel perform the procedure in the *sukkah,* as the boy is born during the holiday of Sukkot, when traditional Jews eat and sleep outside in temporary huts. The grandmothers politely but firmly explain to their husbands that the ceremony will be conducted indoors by a doctor, according to the new parents' wishes, so that the baby not catch cold outdoors or risk infection. "Our Jewish religion, thank God, is not a rigid one," the first grandmother explains, while the second adds, "True, a *mohel* today is just as sanitary as a doctor, but if the children insist—what could we do? That does not mean that we can't have a *mohel* or a rabbi to recite the [ritual blessings]. That our grandson starts his life as a Jew I took care of."[24] In the play, the grandmothers thus mediate between their husbands' desires to maintain tradition and their children's desire to conform to modern standards of health care and propriety, suggesting a model of ritual compromise for Reform Jews.

Whereas discussions of the circumcision ceremony revealed a deep current of anxiety about authenticity and ethnic status among the commentators, their overviews of the welcoming ceremony for girls, which centered on the announcement of the girl's Hebrew name during synagogue services, were much shorter and significantly less fraught. Naming ceremonies for girls in the synagogue, like the *brit milah* ceremony, reinforced traditional gender roles in the Jewish family, privileging the father's public presence as representative of the family and relegating the mother to the background.

"In the event your baby is a girl," Hyman Chanover wrote, "the welcoming rites will be quite simple. They will center about naming her." His chapter titled "If It's a Girl" described the mechanics of naming ceremonies for girls in Reform, Conservative, and Orthodox services. Regardless of the denominational setting, fathers played the public role of relating the baby's name to the rabbi and offering blessings in these ceremonies, while mothers remained largely invisible. Only in the Reform ceremony, according to Chanover, were mothers granted the opportunity to participate in offering prayers of thanks. Even in this case, however, the father retained the honor of announcing the child's Hebrew and English names and, through this and other declarations, "publicly accept[ed] the responsibilities of Jewish fatherhood."[25]

Across the denominational spectrum, these texts on circumcision emphasized the importance of the ritual as a symbol of the covenant between God and the Jewish people. Authors also highlighted the consonance between Jewish practice and scientific principles as a means of convincing wary Jewish parents of circumcision's many benefits and of framing *brit milah* as both an ancient religious tradition and a prudent medical intervention.[26] Whereas authorities from Conservative and Orthodox backgrounds emphasized the wisdom inherent in Jewish tradition insofar as it echoed and reinforced scientific findings, those writing from a Reform perspective praised Judaism's pragmatic flexibility and adaptability in response to situational considerations.

CHOOSING A NAME

The act of choosing English and Hebrew names for an American Jewish baby provided another opportunity for parents, and those offering advice to them, to weigh contemporary American tastes alongside Jewish practices. At the conclusion of the *brit milah* ceremony for boys, or in a separate synagogue ceremony for girls, most American Jewish parents bestow upon the baby a Hebrew name, important for use in Jewish ritual, in addition to an English name. According to Ashkenazi Jewish practice [roughly speaking, Jews originally from Central and Eastern Europe], the custom is to give a newborn the name of a deceased relative, thereby carrying on that relative's memory and expressing a desire that the baby inherit the qualities and character traits of his or her namesake. Sephardi and Mizrahi Jews, who trace their ancestry to the Iberian Peninsula, Italy, North Africa, and the Middle East, name children after living relatives, usually grandparents, for similar reasons.[27]

Accordingly, the practice of naming a Jewish child is tightly connected to the transmission of ethnic and cultural identity as well as expressions of acculturation. In a 1955 article in *Commentary* magazine, Rabbi Benzion Kaganoff declared that "[f]or Jews, first names are inevitably something more than convenient labels for identification. . . . Among us they take on a highly charged symbolic value."[28] Kaganoff and others writing on the subject of Jewish names suggested that a given name served multiple potential functions: a marker of either assimilation or fealty to Jewish tradition, an indication of the personal qualities that parents hoped their children would develop, and an opportunity to link past and future generations of Jews by virtue of carrying on the memory of a beloved family member.[29]

Rabbi Alfred Kolatch's 1948 *These Are the Names,* one of only a few books published on the subject of Jewish names before the 1970s, explored the history of Jewish naming practices from biblical times, weighed the merits and demerits of various approaches to selecting a Hebrew name for a newborn, and provided statistics on the most popular English and Hebrew names for children in addition to listing masculine and feminine names.[30] Kolatch and other authors encouraged Jewish parents to select English biblical names for their children, as opposed to those derived from French, German, and other sources. Simon Chasen, a Hebrew-language instructor at Weequahic High School and Rutgers University in New Jersey, noted in 1954 in the Conservative publication *Women's League Outlook* that many a great American political and literary figure dating back to colonial times carried a biblical name.[31] Therefore, Chasen argued, "if the American Jew really believes in his rightful place on the American scene, in his inalienable rights as an American, he will not fear to bear proudly names like Amiel, Boaz, Caleb . . . and others."[32]

Shonie Levi and Sylvia Kaplan echoed this view in their 1959 book for Jewish homemakers. Discouraging parents from selecting "so-called modern 'equivalents,' such as Stanley for Samuel, or Rhoda for Rebecca," the authors cheered the "revival today of the strong, colorful biblical names that are part of America's Puritan tradition."[33] That same year, in his landmark study *Jews in Suburbia,* Rabbi Albert Gordon noted with pleasure that the current generation of American Jewish parents was selecting such Old Testament names for their children with increasing frequency.[34]

While Gordon interpreted this development as a sign of growing ethnic pride among American Jews, Levi and Kaplan promoted the adoption of biblical names by arguing that traditional Jewish names were intrinsically American in both form and spirit. Returning to a theme prevalent in American Jewish thought since at least the nineteenth century, the notion that Jewish values from the Bible served as the inspiration for the American democratic system, these authors extended the argument to encompass the choice of a name. If names of Hebrew origin suited quintessential American figures such as Abraham Lincoln and Abigail Adams, they and others suggested, then parents should not fear that the choice of such a name will subject their child to discrimination.[35] This argument, linking adherence to Judaism with American patriotism, carried additional weight in a Cold War era characterized by increasing national acceptance of Judaism as an authentic American faith alongside Protestantism and Catholicism.[36]

HOLIDAYS FOR THE HOME

In addition to informing Jewish parents about birth rituals, rabbis and other authors of child-rearing advice also engaged in a concerted effort to educate their audience about how to celebrate Jewish holidays at home as a family. In May 1950, the Synagogue Council of America, which united all the main denominations of American Judaism, joined with Catholic and Protestant organizations to sponsor National Family Week, an initiative to promote family cohesiveness through religious education and worship. In a pamphlet announcing the program, the council endeavored to convince American Jews that religion was the best antidote for the fear and isolation brought on by social and economic dislocation and the ever-present threat of nuclear war.

Returning to a familiar postwar theme, the Synagogue Council of America and other communal leaders advocated the adoption of Jewish rituals in the home, as much for their own sake as for the psychological and emotional benefits that the family would reap as a result. If the Jewish family could be convinced to weave ritual observances into the fabric of their lives, the authors believed, children and parents would develop happiness, camaraderie, and emotional security; the family would rescue itself from disintegration and despair; and Jewish continuity would be ensured.[37]

Dr. Evelyn Garfiel, a psychologist and the national education chairman for the Conservative National Women's League of the United Synagogue of America, seconded these arguments in a 1953 article titled "The Sabbath and Jewish Family Living" published in the organization's magazine. As Garfiel explained to her readers, human beings need to acquire a sense of belonging to a group larger than themselves, and no group is more important in this respect than the family. Accordingly, Garfiel urged her readers to take advantage of the opportunities afforded by the Friday night Sabbath table rituals to cultivate familial fellowship. The act of joining together on a weekly basis to eat together, worship God, and bless one's children, she suggested, can instill "an intense feeling of being part of a self-sufficient group" upon the entire family.[38]

To help parents achieve this goal, rabbis and educators produced a wealth of how-to literature on Jewish holiday celebrations for parents in response to what they perceived as widespread unfamiliarity with these traditions among this particular generation of adults.[39] As with those rituals surrounding birth, authors of these holiday handbooks acknowledged that parents today "often find themselves unable to introduce the various home ceremonials and customs that are associated with our Festivals and Holy Days because they have long since forgotten the historic reasons for the observances, or because they never knew them."[40]

In light of this knowledge gap, many such guides aimed at multigenerational education, teaching parents so they could in turn teach and celebrate with their children. Rabbi Albert Gordon's 1947 *How to Celebrate Hanukah at Home,* along with companion volumes on the festivals of Passover and Purim, included an explanation of each holiday's origins, a program of Hebrew prayers and English readings, recipes for special dishes associated with each holiday, and a list of supplementary books and recordings. For children, Gordon included activities to entice their participation in the family ritual, such as a "Passover scavenger hunt," Passover-themed charades, songs, and poems.[41] Similarly, Rabbi Simon Glustrom's 1956 volume *When Your Child Asks* devoted a chapter to explaining how and why each Jewish holiday is celebrated. The author offered detailed answers for parents on questions their children might be tempted to ask about such topics as why Hanukkah is celebrated for eight days or why Jews eat only unleavened bread during Passover.[42]

Rabbis, psychologists, and educators counseled Jewish parents to observe holiday rituals and customs, both old and new, as a means of creating happy memories and giving children and adults a sense of belonging to both the Jewish community and American society at large. In the words of psychologist Kurt Lewin, such positive affirmations of Jewishness constituted "one of the few effective things that Jewish parents can do for the later happiness of their children." Possessed with a firm feeling of "group belongingness," Lewin and others believed, the Jewish child would be better prepared to cope with discrimination and the pressures of modern life. Domestic religious celebrations also offered American Jews an important opportunity to demonstrate their affinity for the shared values and beliefs at the core of Cold War American culture.[43]

DISSECTING THE "DECEMBER DILEMMA"

If postwar commentators viewed Jewish holidays as an invaluable opportunity to inculcate children and families with pride and security as Jews, then it is no surprise that they felt an urgent need to address the "December dilemma," the question of whether and to what extent Jewish parents should permit their children to participate in Christmas celebrations. In a new age of increased interfaith cooperation, in which public displays of religiosity carried significant political weight, and an era of increased sensitivity to children's mental and emotional states, the issue of Jewish engagement with Christmas took on new dimensions.[44] Seeking a balance between fostering goodwill with Christians and encouraging an intensification of Jewish family holiday observance, most rabbis delineated between public and private Christmas celebrations in recommending to parents what their children should and should not be allowed to do. In the process, they turned to religious, psychological, and social considerations in weighing how American Jewish parents should act.

Abraham Karp, a Conservative rabbi and author of the 1958 pamphlet *Our December Dilemma,* urged readers to resist the urge and social pressure to put up a Christmas tree in their home or to have their children participate in Christmas pageants and school celebrations. Karp's objection was rooted in both psychological and religious grounds. Such activities, he warned, could engender feelings of inferiority in the Jewish child, especially one who has not been raised to appreciate his or her Jewishness and the beauty of Hanukkah and other Jewish traditions. Moreover, Karp argued, when Jews decorate a Christmas tree or sing carols, they misappropriate Christian religious traditions in a manner disrespectful to believing Christians.[45]

Morris Landes, an Orthodox rabbi from Pittsburgh, put forward similar pleas to Jewish parents in a 1949 newspaper editorial in which he implored them to shun Christmas celebrations to protect their children's mental health and insisted that Christmas was a Christian holiday. The Jewish child who yearns to decorate a Christmas tree and receive a stocking full of gifts wants most of all to feel a part of something greater than himself, he argued. "To give him the tree without all the religious trimmings around it is to give him the shadow without the substance and to do irreparable harm to him psychologically," Landes wrote. "To give him both Christmas and Chanukah is to add confusion to psychic injury and to pave the way for maladjustments later in life."[46]

Like Karp, Landes turned to psychology to justify to Jewish parents why they must not celebrate Christmas with their children. He implored his adult readers to satisfy their children's emotional needs (and, implicitly, their own) through Judaism: "The child craves religion. Let him find it in Judaism. The child seeks status, the feeling that he belongs to something. Let him belong to the Jewish people." This notion of attachment could not be cultivated only in December, Landes argued, but is the result of regular engagement with Jewish holidays throughout the year—decorating a *sukkah,* or outdoor hut, in the fall; listening to the Exodus story at a Passover seder in the spring; and lighting the Hanukkah candles in the winter.[47]

The desirability of interfaith relationships also played a role as rabbis considered what Jewish parents and their children should and should not do at Christmastime. "It is the genius and greatness of America that differing religious groups live together in peace, harmony, and mutual respect," Karp wrote, appealing to a notion of American exceptionalism grounded in theological tolerance.[48] In this spirit, he and other rabbis did countenance certain interfaith activities at Christmastime, such as participating in a gift exchange or attending a holiday party, especially when done in a conscious spirit of goodwill between friends and neighbors of different religions. However, he cautioned, while this atmosphere of tolerance allows Jews to join with members of other faiths to mark national occasions, such as Independence Day and Thanksgiving, the same set of principles grant Jews the right to celebrate their own holidays as well.[49]

Given the strong pull of Christmas traditions for children, authors encouraged Jewish parents to give their children Hanukkah celebrations that matched the sensual and material festivity of the gentile holiday. Rose Goldstein, writing in *Women's League Outlook* in 1951, advised mothers to bring "bright lights and starry ornaments" into their home celebrations, with the use of electric menorahs to "satisfy the urge to illumine the blackness of winter nights." Goldstein described the process by which she converted a string of Christmas tree lights into a decorative assortment of paper flowers, lights, and six-pointed Stars of David, suitable for Hanukkah display. She also recommended that families exchange gifts for the duration of the holiday, which would add to the joy and excitement of the children, and that menorah-themed centerpieces and salads in the shape of the menorah be placed on the dinner table.[50]

She and others urged Jewish parents to elevate their family Hanukkah celebrations so as to mitigate the very temptation to participate in Christmas celebrations. Rabbi Albert Gordon explicitly reminded parents to "be mindful of the fact that your non-Jewish neighbors take time and pains to make Christmas an occasion of gladness. Unless you take equal pains with the Hanukah party," he warned, "you cannot hope to make the Festival a thrilling experience."[51] To address the religious and psychological issues at stake for Jewish children at Christmastime, Gordon and Goldstein called on American Jewish parents to invigorate their family Hanukkah celebrations with the introduction of festive decorations, games, food, and gift giving. Remaking the holiday in the image of the American Christmas, they reasoned, was the ultimate solution to the "December dilemma."[52]

CONCLUSION

On May 10, 1961, at the Park Schenley Restaurant in Pittsburgh, Lillian Friedberg addressed a local chapter meeting of Hadassah, a Zionist women's organization. Friedberg, the executive director of Pittsburgh's Jewish Community Relations Council, chose as her topic for the evening "Preparing Our

Children for Living in Today's World." Living in a predominantly Christian society, Friedberg declared, Jewish children needed a warm and comforting family environment, a strong education, and a solid foundation in the values of their religion, which she identified as democracy and human rights. Both the psychologists of today and the Jewish sages of old agree, she asserted, that the child raised in this manner is "fortified by his spiritual heritage . . . [and] strengthened by self-acceptance" and "embarked on a normal move toward a mature, useful and happy life."[53]

Friedberg's prescription for raising "a good American and a good Jew—a complete person"—exemplifies the central themes and arguments of postwar American Jewish parenting advice.[54] Friedberg and others offering child-rearing recommendations to American Jews relied heavily on psychological revelations about child development and mental health, a rhetorical strategy that framed the goal of Jewish continuity in appealingly secular and scientific terms. Authors of child-rearing literature also co-opted the ideological language of Cold War–era civic religion to convince Jewish parents that as good Jews and good Americans, they should choose biblical names for their children, celebrate religious holidays as a family, and take measured steps toward interfaith goodwill efforts at Christmastime. In an era when religious faith versus godlessness defined the gap between good and evil and between emotional security and spiritual despair, American Jewish parenting advisers urged mothers and fathers to make religious observance a hallmark of their family life. In sum, they offered American Jewish parents what many of them wanted: a means for bestowing their children with some measure of attachment to Judaism and the Jewish people in a manner that would not prevent their full entry and acceptance into mainstream American life.

NOTES

1. Azriel Eisenberg, *Talks with Parents: Your Child and You, a Pamphlet Series for Jewish Parents,* Vol. 31 (New York: United Synagogue Commission on Jewish Education, 1954), 1, 39.

2. Hasia R. Diner, *The Jews of the United States, 1654 to 2000* (Berkeley: University of California Press, 2004), 288–93; Riv-Ellen Prell, "Community and the Discourse of Elegy: The Postwar Suburban Debate," in *Imagining the American Jewish Community* (ed. Jack Wertheimer; Waltham: Brandeis University Press, 2007), 67–90.

3. Anna Bear Brevis, "Jewish Education Begins at Home," in *Your Child and You: A Pamphlet Series for Jewish Parents,* Vol. 3 (New York: United Synagogue Commission on Jewish

Education, 1954), 4. For more on a related project of Brevis's, "Judaism-in-the-Home," see Mrs. David A. Goldstein, "Looking Ahead with the Judaism-in-the-Home Project," *Women's League Outlook* (September 1951), 29.

4. Rose A. Cahan, "Your Child and You," *Women's League Outlook* (September 1948), 8.

5. Steven Mintz, *Huck's Raft: A History of American Childhood* (Cambridge: Belknap Press of Harvard University Press), 276; Elaine Tyler May, *Homeward Bound: American Families in the Cold War Era,* 20th anniversary ed. (1988; reprint, New York: Basic Books, 2008), 130–31; Diner, *Jews of the United States,* 282–91.

6. Peter N. Stearns, *Anxious Parents: A History of Modern Childrearing in America* (New York: New York University Press, 2003), 44–45; Julia Grant, *Raising Baby by the Book: The Education of American Mothers* (New Haven: Yale University Press, 1998), 201–5, 221; Mintz, *Huck's Raft,* 276–77. Stearns mentions, but does not cite, a survey from the 1940s in which a majority of American parents declared a desire to raise their children differently than their parents had raised them, suggesting a preference for expert child-rearing advice over the recommendations of family members.

7. Marshall Sklare, *Conservative Judaism: An American Religious Movement* (1955; reprint, New York: Schocken Books, 1972), 32–40, 132–45.

8. On the postwar religious revival and the rise of a Judeo-Christian American ethic, see Kevin M. Schultz, *Tri-Faith America: How Catholics and Jews Held Postwar America to Its Protestant Promise* (New York: Oxford University Press, 2011), 13–96; Jonathan D. Sarna, *American Judaism: A History* (New Haven: Yale University Press, 2004), 274–82; Will Herberg, *Protestant-Catholic-Jew: An Essay in American Religious Sociology* (1955; reprint, Chicago: University of Chicago Press, 1983).

9. Grant, *Raising Baby by the Book,* 1–5. See also Rima D. Apple, *Perfect Motherhood: Science and Childrearing in America* (New Brunswick: Rutgers University Press, 2006), 1–10; Ann Hulbert, *Raising America: Experts, Parents, and a Century of Advice about Children* (New York: Knopf, 2003), 3–10. Hulbert argues that while parenting advice evolves in response to new scientific developments and social concerns, in every period since the late nineteenth century child-rearing experts have fallen into the same opposing "nature" and "nurture" philosophical camps.

10. Sadie Rose Weilerstein, *Our Baby: A Record Book for the Jewish Child Covering the First Five Years* (New York: National Women's League of the United Synagogue of America, 1950). For an ad promoting the book as the perfect gift for the "mothers-to-be among your friends," see *Women's League Outlook* (March 1953): 31.

11. For parallels to Weilerstein's book for a general audience from this era, see May Farini, *Baby's Days and Baby's Ways* (Norwalk: C. R. Gibson, 1943); Estelle McInnes Upson, *Story of Our Baby: Year by Year* (Racine: Whitman Publishing, 1947); Phyllis Fraser and Phoebe Erickson, *Baby's First Five Years: Little Majesty Baby Record Book* (New York: Random House, 1948).

12. Reuben M. Katz, foreword to Hyman Chanover, *Blessed Event* (New York: Jonathan David Publishing, 1956), v.

13. The practice of adopting a secular name in addition to a Hebrew name, used primarily for ritual purposes, dates back to at least the Middle Ages if not earlier. See Aaron Demsky, "Double Names in the Babylonian Exile and the Identity of Sheshbazzar," in *These Are the Names: Studies in Jewish Onomastics,* Vol. 2 (ed. Aaron Demsky; Ramat Gan: Bar-Ilan University Press, 1999), 23–40; Rita Bredefeldt, "Naming Customs as an Indication of Assimilation: A Study of First Names in the Jewish Congregations of Stockholm and Malmö, 1895–1921," in *These Are the Names: Studies in Jewish Onomastics,* Vol. 4 (ed. Aaron Demsky; Ramat Gan: Bar-Ilan University Press, 2003), 77–89.

14. See, for example, the use of transliteration in Nathan Gottlieb, *A Jewish Child Is Born: The History and Ritual of Circumcision, Redemption of Firstborn Son, Adoption, Conversion and Choosing and Giving Names* (New York: Bloch Publishing, 1960), 41–46, 55–60, and 112–14, and the inclusion of English prayers for the circumcision ceremony (103–6); see also Chanover, *Blessed Event,* 20–21. Descriptions of the circumcision ceremony and naming ceremony, without the accompanying blessings, can be found in Shonie B. Levi and Sylvia R. Kaplan, *Across the Threshold: A Guide for the Jewish Homemaker* (New York: Farrar, Straus and Cudahy, 1959), 33–34. On the *pidyon ha-ben* ceremony, see Gottlieb, *A Jewish Child Is Born,* 51–60; Levi and Kaplan, *Across the Threshold,* 34–35.

15. Chanover, *Blessed Event,* 7. These innovative prayers were originally composed by Rabbi Max Klein, who served the Conservative-affiliated Congregation Adath Jeshurun of Philadelphia and was the author and translator of two prayer books. His papers are available in the Special Collections Library of the Jewish Theological Seminary.

16. Typically, the ceremony is performed when the Jewish boy is eight days old. For more on the religious significance of circumcision in Judaism, see Gottlieb, *A Jewish Child Is Born,* 87–91.

17. Ibid.

18. Ibid., 95–96. Other authors marveled at the harmony between the timing of the circumcision ceremony and the human body's development and cited studies claiming that circumcised men carried a far lesser risk of developing penile cancer. See Morris Shoulson, "Circumcision—A Covenant for the Preservation of the Jewish Family," in *Marriage and Family Life: A Jewish View* (ed. Abraham B. Shoulson; New York: Twayne Publishers, 1959), 113–14.

19. Gottlieb, *A Jewish Child Is Born,* 96–97. Gottlieb wrote in an era when many circumcisions were performed in the hospital as opposed to in a synagogue or at home, where the choice of a mohel as opposed to a doctor might be more likely. As a result, he advised readers to consult with the hospital about regulations and requirements for conducting the *brit milah* there, while adding that "It is optional and just as effective to perform the *brit* at home, as in the hospital" (21). See also Chanover, *Blessed Event,* 16–17. On the shift toward American Jewish circumcisions taking place in the hospital, see Leonard B. Glick, *Marked in Your Flesh: Circumcision from Ancient Judea to Modern America* (New York: Oxford University Press, 2005), 215–16.

20. Shoulson, "Circumcision," 110, 113.

21. Ibid., 113–14.

22. See, for example, Levi and Kaplan, *Across the Threshold,* 33–34; Chanover, *Blessed Event,* 15–17; Shoulson, "Circumcision," 109–16.

23. See Rabbi Levi Olan's sermon "Ceremonies Surrounding the Birth of a Child," dated January 23, 1947, Box 23, Folder 3, MS-181, Levi A. Olan Papers, American Jewish Archives. See also Rabbi Floyd Fierman's sermon "What Should Reform Jews Believe? Birth, Marriage, Death," n.d., in *Sermons, 1949–1958,* Box 3, Folder 1, MS-649, Floyd S. Fierman Papers, American Jewish Archives.

24. Norma Levitt and Esther Kaufman, *Covenants with the Lord* (New York: National Federation of Temple Sisterhoods, 1951), 1–8, in Box K-5, Folder 1, MS-73, Women of Reform Judaism Records, American Jewish Archives. The portrayal of the grandmothers in this play as arbiters between religious tradition and contemporary sensibilities echoes arguments made elsewhere about the role of women in both modernizing and maintaining Jewishness. See Marion A. Kaplan, *The Making of the Jewish Middle Class: Women, Family, and Identity in Imperial Germany* (New York: Oxford University Press, 1991); Melissa R. Klapper, *Jewish Girls Coming of Age in America, 1860–1920* (New York: New York University Press, 2005).

25. Chanover, *Blessed Event,* 11–14. For other brief explanations of the naming ceremony for girls, see Levi and Kaplan, *Across the Threshold,* 33; Gottlieb, *A Jewish Child Is Born,* 112–15.

26. A number of scholars have also noted how defenses of the *mikvah* [ritual bath] in interwar American Jewish culture similarly appealed to its health benefits as claimed by scientific research. See Beth S. Wenger, "Mitzvah and Medicine: Gender, Assimilation, and the Scientific Defense of 'Family Purity,'" in *Women and American Judaism: Historical Perspectives* (ed. Pamela S. Nadell and Jonathan D. Sarna; Hanover: University Press of New England/Brandeis University Press, 2001), 201–22; Jenna Weissman Joselit, *New York's Jewish Jews: The Orthodox Community in the Interwar Years* (Bloomington: Indiana University Press, 1990), 115–22.

27. Alfred J. Kolatch, *These Are the Names* (New York: Jonathan David, 1948), 20–24; Gottlieb, *A Jewish Child Is Born,* 109–11. For a brief overview of the distinctions between Ashkenazi and Sephardi Jews, see Raymond P. Scheindlin, *A Short History of the Jewish People* (New York: Macmillan, 1998), 121–47. On Sephardi and Mizrahi Jews, see *Sephardic and Mizrahi Jewry: From the Golden Age of Spain to Modern Times* (ed. Zion Zohar; New York: New York University Press, 2009).

28. Benzion C. Kaganoff, "Jewish First Names through the Ages," *Commentary* (November 1955): 447.

29. Ibid., 447–52. See also Chanover, *Blessed Event,* 9–10.

30. Very few other works for American Jewish audiences prior to Kolatch's volume dealt with Hebrew names and their origin and meaning. See David Bernard Swiren, *What's in Our Names? A Study* (Wilmington: Star Publishing, 1920); Lee M. Friedman, *American Jewish Names,* private reprint from *Historia Judaica* 4:2 (October 1944): 147–62.

31. Weequahic High School, a public school in Newark, New Jersey, has several famous Jewish alumni, including author Philip Roth. On this Jewish neighborhood in Newark, see Linda B. Forgosh, *Images of America: Jews of Weequahic* (Charleston: Arcadia Publishing, 2008).

32. Simon Chasen, "Now These Were the Names," *Women's League Outlook* (March 1954): 15, 30.

33. Levi and Kaplan, *Across the Treshold,* 32. See also Kolatch, *These Are the Names,* 25–26.

34. Albert I. Gordon, *Jews in Suburbia* (1959; reprint, Westport: Greenwood, 1973), 141–42.

35. Deborah M. Melamed, *The Three Pillars: Thought, Worship, and Practice for the Jewish Woman* (1927, reprint; New York: National Women's League of the United Synagogue of America, 1954), 30–31.

36. On the evolution of the notion that Jewish values shaped American political ideals, see Beth S. Wenger, *History Lessons: The Creation of American Jewish Heritage* (Princeton: Princeton University Press, 2010), 1–11, 37–41; Jonathan D. Sarna, "The Cult of Synthesis in American Jewish Culture," *Jewish Social Studies* 5:1–2 (Fall 1998–Winter 1999): 52–79.

37. "The Synagogue and the Jewish Home of Tomorrow" (New York: Synagogue Council of America, 1950), Box E-11, Folder 3, MS-73, Women of Reform Judaism Records, American Jewish Archives. On National Family Week, see "Jewish Groups Observe National Family Week throughout Nation, Sponsored by Synagogue Council of America," *Jewish Telegraphic Agency* (May 8, 1945), http://www.jta.org/1945/05/08/archive/jewish-groups-observe-national-family-week-throughout-nation-sponsored-by-synagogue-council (accessed July 25, 2013).

38. Evelyn Garfiel, "The Sabbath and Jewish Family Living," *Women's League Outlook* (September 1953): 5, 13. For a similar argument made to an Orthodox audience about the value of Sabbath rituals for improving family relations and instilling a sense of self-worth, see Irma Horowitz, "Education Begins at Home," *Jewish Life* (May–June 1952): 54–59.

39. Overwhelmingly, this genre focused on Passover and Hanukkah in particular, for two primary reasons. Their proximity to Easter and Christmas on the calendar and their abundance of rituals concentrated in the home rather than in the synagogue contributed to their relative popularity and observance among American Jews as compared to other holidays. Jenna Weissman Joselit has explained the enduring popularity of Passover observance among American Jews, even as many other Jewish holiday traditions have declined, as a result of the seder, Passover's home-centered "ritualized exercise in collective memory," with its special foods and time-honored customs. See Joselit, *The Wonders of America,* 225.

40. Albert I. Gordon, *How to Celebrate Purim at Home* (New York: United Synagogue of America, n.d. [1947?]), 1, Box 7, Folder 5, P-86, Rabbi Albert I. Gordon Papers, American Jewish Historical Society Archives, Boston.

41. Albert I. Gordon, *How to Celebrate Hanukah at Home* (New York: United Synagogue of America, 1947), and *How to Celebrate Passover at Home* (New York: United Synagogue of America, 1947). See also Lillian T. Leiderman and Lillian S. Abramson, *Jewish Holiday Party Book: A Practical Guide for Mother and Teacher Planned for Children Ages 5 to 12* (New York: Bloch Publishing, 1954); Alex J. Goldman, *A Handbook for the Jewish Famlly: Understanding and Enjoying the Sabbath and Holidays* (New York: Bloch Publishing, 1958).

42. Simon Glustrom, *When Your Child Asks: A Handbook for Jewish Parents* (New York: Bloch Publishing, 1956), 100–102, 106–11.

43. Kurt Lewin, "Bringing Up the Jewish Child," in *Resolving Social Conflicts: Selected Papers on Group Dynamics* (ed. Gertrud Weiss Lewin; New York: Harper & Row, 1948), 183. See also Kurt Lewin, "Psychological Problems in Jewish Education," *Jewish Social Service Quarterly* 23:3 (March 1947): 291–94; Margaret B. Mark and Bernard J. Starkoff, *The Jewish Family in the World Today* (Cincinnati: National Federation of Temple Sisterhoods, 1946); Samuel Markowitz, *Adjusting the Jewish Child to His World* (rev. ed.; New York: National Federation of Temple Sisterhoods, 1961), 3–5.

44. On how American Jews dealt with Christmas observances in the public school during the post–World War II period, see Deborah Dash Moore, *To the Golden Cities: Pursuing the American Jewish Dream in Miami and L.A.* (New York: Free Press, 1994), 178–87. For a historical overview of American Jews' relationship with Christmas, see Joshua Eli Plaut, *A Kosher Christmas: 'Tis the Season to Be Jewish* (New Brunswick: Rutgers University Press, 2012), 1–40.

45. Abraham J. Karp, "Our December Dilemma," in *Your Child and You: A Pamphlet Series for Jewish Parents,* Vol. 8 (New York: United Synagogue Commission on Jewish Education, 1958), 3–8.

46. Morris A. Landes, "Pro and Con: The Christmas Tree," *Jewish Advocate* [Boston] (December 22, 1949): 7. On the argument that Christians are offended when Jews decorate a Christmas tree, see also Glustrom, *When Your Child Asks,* 128; Rabbi Samuel Glasner, "A Jewish Attitude toward Christmas: A Letter to Parents," *Jewish Teacher* 23:1 (November 1954): 2–3.

47. Landes, "Pro and Con." For a parent's perspective on the issue, see Laura Pienkny Zakin, "A View of the 'Christmas Problem,'" *Congress Weekly* (December 12, 1955): 9–10; Grace Goldin, "Christmas-Chanukah: December Is the Cruelest Month," *Commentary* (November 1950): 417.

48. Karp, "Our December Dilemma," 4.

49. Ibid., 4–8; Glasner, "A Jewish Attitude," 3; Rabbi Floyd Fierman's sermon, "Christmas Observance," in *Sermons, 1949–1958,* Box 2, Folder 2, MS-649, Floyd S. Fierman Papers, American Jewish Archives. Unlike Karp, Fierman, a Reform rabbi, allowed parents to take their children to visit Santa Claus in public but insisted that they must not bring any Christmas traditions into their homes.

50. Mrs. David A. [Rose] Goldstein, "More on Hanukah in the Home," *Women's League Outlook* (December 1951): 16–17, 30. See also Gordon, *How to Celebrate Hanukah at Home,* 6–16.

51. Gordon, *How to Celebrate Hanukah at Home,* 7.

52. For more on the Americanization of Hanukkah in response to Christmas, see Plaut, *A Kosher Christmas,* 41–64; Joselit, *The Wonders of America,* 229–43; Dianne Ashton, *Hanukkah in America: A History* (New York: New York University Press, 2013).

53. Lillian Friedberg lecture notes, "Preparing Our Children for Living in Today's World," May 10, 1961, 4, Box 9, Folder 2, MS-283, Lillian A. Friedberg Papers, American Jewish Archives.

54. Ibid., 5.

Modern Families: Multifaceted Identities in the Jewish Adoptive Family

Jennifer Sartori

When the ABC sitcom *Modern Family* debuted in 2009, it was an instant hit. The show's funny but sympathetic portrayal of the diversity—in both structure and composition—that characterizes "modern families" clearly struck a chord with the American public. Among the branches of the extended family at the heart of the show are two multiracial families, a blended family, a gay family, and only one "traditional" nuclear family. Today's families, the show suggests, come in many colors, shapes, and sizes, mixing races, ethnicities, nationalities, ages, and sexualities, yet they are all still fundamentally families.

What would a Jewish "modern family" look like? As in the familiar joke about the Jewish community, like its non-Jewish counterpart, only more so. American Jewish families, like the Pritchett clan, are becoming increasingly variegated. Although communal discussions of the changes in the Jewish family often focus on the "problem" of intermarriage, American Jewish families are becoming increasingly "multi" in other ways as well: multiracial, multicultural, multiethnic, multinational. Identity for these families can be a complex and dynamic dance, bringing together influences that may be complementary or contradictory, that may blend seamlessly or be difficult to reconcile.

Adoptive families have been at the forefront of these trends. Because very few children adopted into the American Jewish community in recent decades were born to Jewish birth parents, the vast majority of adoptees—whether adopted transnationally and/or transracially or from white American parents of non-Jewish background—inherently bring with them identities that differ from those of their new parents. How do Jewish adoptive families respond to the issues that arise from these complexities? In particular, how do adoptees raised in Jewish families navigate the complicated waters of identity in relation to both their adoptive and their birth heritages? How do these two facets of their identities interact?

To learn more about this growing population, my colleague Jayne Guberman and I are engaged in a multipronged research study, the Adoption & Jewish Identity Project.

We began by conducting an in-depth online survey of Jewish adoptive parents to which close to 1,000 people responded, yielding 781 usable surveys.

Because the survey was conducted online and spread virally, the results are not necessarily representative of all Jewish adoptive parents. In particular, the respondents were younger than average, yielding more accurate information about more recent trends in adoption; whiter than average; and may be more strongly identified Jewishly than the norm.[1] However, the sample in many ways resembles the broader American Jewish population, and we believe that the data can yield valuable information regarding Jewish adoptive families.[2] We are also conducting an ongoing effort to gather the voices of young adult adoptees raised in Jewish families through a questionnaire, oral histories, and other submissions. This essay is drawn largely from these two sources.

Our research has created a portrait of the dramatic changes in Jewish adoptive families that have occurred over the past several decades, particularly the striking increase in the number of adoptions across racial, national, and religious lines. The majority of Jewish adoptees, we have found, regularly find themselves navigating multiple identities. Although for some one aspect of their identity is clearly primary and others more actively juggle the various elements, virtually all find that different aspects of their sense of self come to the fore in different contexts. This multifaceted sense of self is continually evolving, moreover, with identities developing long past the classic adolescent identity crisis.

MAJOR TRENDS IN ADOPTION

In order to comprehend the contemporary Jewish adoptive experience, it is necessary first to understand the major trends in adoption over the past several decades. Adoption today exists in significant contrast to fifty years ago, in both the profile of children being adopted and ideas about adoption, adoptive identity, and adoptive parenting.[3] For much of the mid-twentieth century, the reigning paradigm in adoption was "matching": matching children with prospective adoptive parents so as to create families that would seem to be biological or "natural."[4] Adoption experts believed strongly that adoptive families would be more "authentic," and thus more successful, if they resembled biological ones. Attempts were made to match in a wide variety of ways, not only by race and appearance but also by less visible criteria, such as personality, intellectual ability, and religion. Indeed, religion was one of the most deep-seated elements of matching, enshrined in law more often than any other aspect.[5] During this period, most formal adoptions were of white newborns adopted by white, middle-class, heterosexual couples; children of color and older children were often seen as "unadoptable" and shut out of the system, while parents of color, working-class families, and single parents, seen as unsuitable, could not meet agencies' strict criteria for adoptive parents.

The matching paradigm and the assumptions that underlay it fostered a culture of secrecy, stigma, and shame in adoption. If "matching" was successful, adoptive families could "pass" as biological families. That very effort to "pass," however, implied that adoptive families were inferior and that adoption was something to be ashamed of and to be shrouded in secrecy, both within the family and in the community. All members of the adoption triad (adoptive parents, adoptees, and birth parents) were encouraged to act essentially as if adoption had never happened. Adoptive parents were counseled to raise their children as if they had been born to them, and ties between children and their birth families and birth heritages were generally cut completely.[6]

By the end of the twentieth century, this paradigm had largely broken apart. The easy availability of birth control, the legalization of abortion with *Roe v. Wade* in 1973, and the growing acceptance of single motherhood caused the number of healthy white American newborns available for adoption to plummet, while demand from prospective adoptive parents continued to increase. In response, the definition of "adoptable children" expanded to include children from other countries, children of color, children with special needs, and older children in foster care.

Transnational adoption, begun as a humanitarian effort in the aftermath of World War II, emerged in earnest during the Korean War. The most prominent sending countries have varied over time but are generally poorer nations, mostly nonwhite, and often experiencing economic or political dislocation or natural disasters. Transnational adoption reached its peak in 2004, when 22,884 children were adopted into the United States; since then, the number has declined precipitously, to 5,647 in 2015.[7]

From the beginning, many transnational adoptions were also transracial. Domestic transracial adoption emerged later, beginning slowly in the 1960s and alternately expanding and contracting, shaped by changing racial attitudes, legal developments, and the evolution of ideas about what makes a good adoptive family.[8] In 1996, with the goal of increasing the number of adoptions from foster care by encouraging transracial adoption, the Interethnic Placement Provisions of the Multiethnic Placement Act (MEPA-IEP) prohibited agencies receiving federal funds from taking race into account in foster and adoptive placements.[9] Today, approximately 40 percent of American adoptions are transracial, including the vast majority of international adoptions and smaller but still substantial percentages of foster care and domestic infant adoptions.[10] The number of public adoptions from foster care—very often of older children, many of whom are children of color—also increased considerably, as policies shifted from encouraging reunification with birth families toward promoting adoption as a route to permanency.[11]

Accompanying these transformations have been sea changes in ideas about adoption and in understanding of adoptive identity. Three interrelated trends stand out: (1) an increasing openness both about and within adoption; (2) a growing recognition of the role of grief and loss, both personal and cultural, in adoption; and (3) an encouragement of active engagement with birth heritages and communities.

The secrecy that used to characterize adoption has been on the wane for several decades. Not only is secrecy generally impossible to maintain in cases of transracial and older child adoption, but the assault by a variety of nontraditional families on the idea of the inherent superiority of the traditional two-parent, heterosexual, biological nuclear family has also lessened the incentive to "pass" as a biological family. Adoptive parents are now encouraged to talk openly and regularly about adoption with their children from a young age and are far less likely to hide the fact of their adoptions from their children and their communities. Adoptees themselves have pushed, with varying levels of success, for access to their original birth certificates, the sealing of which often kept their backgrounds and origin shrouded in secrecy.[12]

Greater openness *within* adoption has paralleled greater openness *about* adoption. In private domestic adoptions, the vast majority of expectant parents now select their child's adoptive parents, and some level of contact between birth and adoptive families is increasingly the norm, ranging from occasional mediated contact (for example, a yearly exchange of letters and photos through the adoption agency) to regular direct contact (for example, phone calls, Skype chats, and in-person visits). Adoption experts now believe that such contact, when circumstances allow, is healthier for all members of the adoption triad.[13]

Adoption has also shifted from being seeing as a win-win situation for all concerned (in which a needy child receives a comfortable home, adoptive parents—often assumed to be infertile—receive a child, and a pregnant woman resolves a crisis and moves on with her life) to one that, while often filled with joy and love, is also characterized by loss and grief. While adoptees indeed gain new families, they also lose birth parents, extended family and community, cultural heritage, access to medical history, and often their place in the racial and/or ethnic group of their birth.[14] Adoption experts now argue that grieving such losses is natural and that recognition of them can be a healthier response than repressing them.

Connected to both of these trends has been a shift in emphasis toward the importance of knowledge of personal roots, whether biological, ethnic, or historical. The previous attitude that an adoptee who craved information about or contact with his or her birth family and heritage was maladjusted has largely given way to a sense that such a need is natural and deeply ingrained in humans.[15] In contrast to previous generations of adoptive parents, who were often counseled to raise their children as if they had been born to them, "best practices" in adoption now encourage parents to foster connections to their children's heritages and communities of origin. Such recommendations are often aimed especially at those who have adopted transracially and/or transnationally, as cultural competency and relationships with individuals of the child's race are seen as crucial to healthy racial and ethnic identity formation.[16] These developments have brought questions of multiple and blended identities (which previously often simmered under the surface) to the fore for many adoptive families.

MAJOR TRENDS IN JEWISH ADOPTION

How do Jews fit into these trends? Overall, American Jews appear to adopt at approximately twice the rate of non-Jews. In 2000, about 5 percent of Jewish households with children had an adopted child in the home, compared to 2.5 percent of American households overall; with that 5 percent having risen from only 3 percent in 1990, the percentage may well be even higher today.[17]

Not only have the numbers of Jewish adoptive families risen, but the characteristics of those families have also changed substantially. Perhaps the most striking demographic finding of our parent survey is the pronounced increase in adoptions across boundaries of identity, far greater than the already considerable increase in such adoptions among the American population as a whole. Survey respondents had adopted from the 1950s through the 2000s, allowing us to track change over time. In keeping with the "matching" paradigm, from the 1950s through the 1970s white Jewish families generally adopted white American newborns. All the children adopted in the 1950s and 1960s and 74 percent of those adopted in the 1970s were white; 94 percent of children adopted during these three decades were adopted domestically (65 percent through private adoptions, 29 percent through the public foster care system). These white American newborns, moreover, not infrequently had at least one Jewish birth parent: of children adopted in the 1950s, 1960s, and 1970s, 36 percent had a Jewish birth mother, and 15 percent had a Jewish birth father.[18]

By the early twenty-first century, the numbers had changed dramatically.[19] Only a tiny percentage of adoptees were born to Jewish parents (4 percent had a Jewish birth mother, 3 percent had a Jewish birth father), and the numbers of transracial and transnational adoptions had skyrocketed. A full 66 percent of respondents who adopted between 2000 and 2009 did so transnationally; by striking contrast, only approximately 15 percent of American adoptions overall in the same period were transnational.[20] Similarly, the percentage of nonwhite children adopted into Jewish families increased steadily each decade, to 65 percent in the decade 2000–2009 and a full 76 percent between 2010 and 2012.[21] Of the children adopted by survey respondents between 2000 and 2012, 34 percent were white, 32 percent were Asian or Asian-mixed, 17 percent were Latino or Latino-mixed, and 15 percent were black or black-mixed.[22]

IDENTITY FOR JEWISH ADOPTEES

American Jewish adoptive families, then, increasingly cross lines of race, culture, ethnicity, religion, and nationality. How, if at all, does Jewish identity make the experiences of these adoptees distinct from those of adoptees raised in non-Jewish families? How do their racial and/or ethnic identities and their affiliation with or knowledge of their communities and cultures of origin impact their Jewish identities? In short, how do these adoptees negotiate the often complex relationships between their birth and adoptive heritages?

Although these issues of identity are by no means absent for domestic same-race adoptees, they are generally most overt for transracial and/or transnational adoptees and their families. The complexities begin in childhood, when parents play a key role in shaping their children's experiences of adoption and must make important decisions about their Jewish upbringing and birth heritage socialization. Our survey indicates that the vast majority of Jewish parents who adopt transracially and/or transnationally have taken adoption professionals' advice to heart and believe that it is important to include elements of their children's birth heritages in their lives.[23] Indeed, given a list of fifteen possible birth heritage socialization practices, most who adopted in recent decades reported doing so in multiple ways, ranging from reading books to eating in ethnic restaurants to studying languages and developing relationships with people from the child's community of origin.[24]

Parents, however, do not exist in a vacuum. Asked about the responses of members of their immediate Jewish communities to their efforts to foster identification with their children's birth heritages and communities of origin, the majority of survey respondents reported positive or neutral reactions. Yet a substantial minority described disapproving or hostile responses from rabbis, synagogue communities, or their own families, and even those who described positive reactions sometimes hinted at considerable communal ambivalence. These childhood experiences may have a significant influence on adoptees' later sense of identity.

Much of the pushback described by parents appears to stem from familial and communal concerns that exposure to a child's culture of origin will foster an identification that will compete with or confuse the child's Jewish identity. Several parents commented specifically that their rabbis and communities communicated the distinct message that Jewish education should be primary, to the exclusion of any instruction related to their birth heritage. As one survey respondent reported, "[Our] rabbi, who is otherwise welcoming to my children, has discouraged pursuit of Chinese learning, as he would rather see them identify primarily as Jews. I don't see why they can't pursue both." "The Jewish community is very supportive . . . but somewhat from a distance," remarked another. "They still project . . . that Jewish education takes precedence over other choices (i.e., Hebrew over Vietnamese), which is a difficult choice, and VERY hard to do both!!"

More commonly, parents remarked not on a specific incident or episode but rather on a more general sense of communal disapproval of or ambivalence about their efforts to bring their children's birth heritages into their lives, or simply on a lack of awareness. "I get the feeling that others don't see birth heritage as being as important as Jewish heritage. Born of ignorance, I think," wrote one respondent. Some of the many additional comments were "They are wary"; "They are clueless"; "They seem . . . puzzled and mildly interested" [ellipses in original]; "Not a positive response in this particular suburban community"; "They do not seem to think of it as their issue"; "They're interested but often at arms' length, especially if they are uncomfortable with other cultures"; "With interest but not necessarily enthusiasm or approval"; and "Very poorly. It's either Ashkenazi or the highway. I've had to leave my synagogue because of it." Some parents remarked on family concerns about "identity confusion" or "conflicted identities," or grandparents wanting the children to be exposed as little as possible to their birth heritages.[25] "Some family members think it is a waste of time," wrote one parent, "since she is a Jewish kid being raised in a Jewish home."

Two comments in particular—both from parents who in fact described their communities as supportive—highlight the ambivalence that often characterizes the Jewish community's attitudes toward incorporation of another aspect of a child's identity. One woman with two adopted children of color wrote that "I tried to incorporate all I could from my children's birth heritage as long as it did not contradict Judaism. It is well accepted." In a similar vein, a woman who had adopted from China wrote that her community had responded "positively—everyone loved the Chinese vegan food at the bat mitzvah." These parents had clearly tried their best to incorporate their children's birth heritages into their lives in ways that felt fully compatible with their families' Jewish identity, and their communities had embraced their efforts. Their comments indicate, however, that adoptive families may find that such efforts are accepted only up to a certain point—as long as they do not explicitly "contradict" Judaism by, for example, including nonvegan (presumably *treif,* or nonkosher) Chinese food.

For some adoptees and their families, such limitations may be unproblematic. Others, however, craving connection with their birth heritage as well as their adoptive heritage, may find vegan Chinese food a superficial basis for a strong Chinese identity and may chafe under the sense that other elements of their birth heritage would be seen as unwelcome. When attachment to birth heritage goes beyond vegan Chinese food, whether simply to eating more authentic Chinese food or to wishing to explore the Catholic background of an adoptee from Latin America, for example, communal responses are likely to be far less enthusiastic.

Given Jewish communal concerns about continuity, such hesitation about alternative forms of identity is perhaps not surprising. Worried about the future of American Jewry, communal leaders—and adoptive parents themselves—may emphasize the importance of a strong and exclusive Jewish identity in the belief that it is most likely to strengthen American Jewry in the long run. Such concerns may lead some adoptive parents to shy away from serious engagement with birth heritage or community. Although the survey data cannot prove causality, many of the most common birth heritage socialization practices reported by parents were relatively low-commitment activities of the type less likely to foster deep attachment to a form of identity potentially "competing with" Jewishness, such as reading books (cited by 78 percent of parents of children of color and 73 percent of parents of children born abroad), buying arts and crafts (72 percent and 75 percent), and eating in ethnic restaurants (68 percent and 70 percent). Significantly fewer parents reported many of the higher-commitment activities that would have a higher likelihood of cultivating strong birth heritage identification, such as attending culture camps or classes (cited by 30 percent of parents of children of color and 31 percent of parents of children born abroad), studying languages (cited by 38 percent of parents of children born abroad), and visiting the child's birth country (cited by 31 percent of parents of children born abroad).[26]

Regardless of their own and their families' relationships to their birth heritage, transracially adopted children not infrequently experience considerable questioning of their Jewish identity. Like all Jews of color, Jewish adoptees of color are profoundly impacted by the deep-seated presumption—common to American Jews and non-Jews alike—that Jews are white. This presumption can be traced not simply to the East European origin of the majority of American Jews but also to the pervasive "whitening" of American Jews noted by so many scholars, a process that eventually placed Jews securely on the white side of the black-white binary historically characteristic of American race relations.[27] Because of the now widespread assumption that Jewish = white and despite the well-documented racial and ethnic diversity within the Jewish community, Jews of color very often find the authenticity of their Jewish identities questioned by both Jews and non-Jews, and children of color with white parents are by no means immune. When this questioning comes from within their own communities, it can be especially devastating. The following are a few of the countless examples that emerge from our research:

- A young woman adopted from China writes that "When I was eight years old, a fellow Hebrew school student asked if it was even legal to be Asian and Jewish. This hurt deeply, though he meant no harm. Eventually, I dropped out of Hebrew school for a number of years."[28]
- A Korean adoptee writes about a childhood experience in her own temple, where her family attended services regularly: "There was a family in front of us—a mom, dad, and three daughters. . . . The three girls kept turning around and staring at us. They would whisper to each other and kept talking about the 'Asians.' It definitely hurt my feelings . . . even more so because I felt like this was 'my temple' and I belonged here, and if anyone didn't belong there, it was those girls and that family."[29]
- A white mother of a multiracial son comments that "The sentiment, 'If you're Black, you can't be Jewish,' came up several times, including at [Jewish camp] and at Sunday School. Our son was treated, at

> times, as an exotic animal, when he desperately wanted to be one of the kids. He went from being proud of being Jewish to distancing himself from it."[30]

While such questioning of their Jewish identity can itself be harmful to a child's emerging sense of self, even more pernicious is the outright racism and discrimination that many experience within their Jewish communities. One young adult Korean adoptee wrote poignantly about her experience with racism as a child: "Most of the racism I have experienced was from within the Jewish community. My mom pulled me from Jewish pre-school before the second day was over, because the other kids refused to play with me. At JCC camp, other campers would make snide comments about me being a karate or kung-fu master, I never fit in at Hebrew school, and was an outcast in my class for most of my middle and high school years."[31]

In our parent survey, we asked parents of children of color if their children had experienced discrimination in the Jewish community. Perhaps not surprisingly, the responses differed by race: parents of black children were by far the most likely to say yes (28 percent), followed by parents of Latino children (15 percent) and of Asian children (11 percent). Given that research shows that transracially adopted children very often do not tell their parents about the discrimination they experience, the real rates of discrimination are likely considerably higher. And even without any explicit encounters with racism, many adoptees of color report having felt different, exoticized, marginalized, and even outcast within their largely white synagogues, day schools, Jewish camps, and other institutions, at a stage of life when children want nothing more than to feel like everyone else.[32]

Despite these sometimes ambivalent responses from families and communities, many of the transracially adopted young adults we have interviewed recall their Jewish identity as having been relatively uncomplicated as children. Like many transracial adoptees, they experienced a form of "honorary white privilege" as children; with their white, generally Ashkenazi parents serving as a kind of protective shell, they felt comfortable as Jews within their own communities where they were known and nurtured, especially in cases in which their parents had searched very deliberately for welcoming and inclusive congregations and institutions.

The issues of identity often become more complicated for transracial adoptees in the teen years and into young adulthood, as they begin to experience the world outside the partial cocoon of their immediate families and communities. As they go out into the world on their own, they lose the honorary white privilege they experienced as children and are seen for the first time fully as individuals of color, rather than as members of a white Jewish family. In doing so, they often find aspects of their identity questioned by both the Jewish community and members of their community of origin.

If transracial adoptees often find their Jewish identity questioned as children, such questioning becomes far more frequent when they experience the Jewish community as individuals, not as their parents' children. Going to Hillel, for example, many adoptees of color are met with incredulity and are sometimes told that the Korean, African American, or Latin American student group meets down the hall. As the white mother of a daughter adopted from Korea reflected, "It is always assumed that she is not Jewish, and after a while she seemed to feel that they must know something she didn't. It just wears her down when people always give her that 'WOW! You're Jewish?' look." Under these circumstances, many adoptees of color find themselves having to "prove" their Jewish identity over and over again, whether by providing detailed information about whether and how they were converted or demonstrating their cultural competency as Jews. As a woman adopted from Colombia commented, "I guess you could say I'm not your typical 'Jew,' whatever that means. As an adult I felt I always had to give an explanation as to how I could be Jewish. Or people would need to find a reason for how I am Jewish which pushes me away a little from the Jewish community. . . . People tend to not see ME when they find out I'm Jewish; all they see are my differences." Dating and marriage in particular can be challenging. As a Korean adoptee remarked, "As I've gotten older, especially with dating, I've found it more difficult. People have tried to 'test' me to see how Jewish I really am, which is actually quite racist and offensive."[33]

Conversely, many adult adoptees of color also find their identities questioned by their communities of origin. Echoing the assumption that Jews are white, black, Asian, and Latino communities may question the adoptee's Jewishness, presupposing another religious identity because he or she is of color. Often even more powerfully, they may also challenge the adoptee's cultural competency vis-à-vis black, Asian, or Latino identity, which indeed often *is* limited because of their upbringing. It is thus not uncommon for Jewish adoptees of color to report feeling out of place among people of their own racial or national background. As a Latino adoptee who began working with Latino youth writes, "I became aware of how little I shared in common with Latino students and my own Latino identity. It was one thing to identify as Mexican in the small town in Connecticut where I grew up, but here in New York, not speaking Spanish and not being aware of Mexican or Mexican-American culture, my Latino identity has begun to feel hollow." Under these circumstances, many adoptees feel that they do not fully fit into either their adoptive community or their birth community.

Transracial adoptees' identities continue to evolve throughout adulthood, with many feeling that they live at the nexus of multiple identities. Some say that they feel very comfortable with their Jewishness, especially within their own carefully chosen community or the community in which they grew up and feel known. Indeed, some feel *most* comfortable within a Jewish context, which feels more familiar than their communities of origin, where they continue to feel marginal or even rejected. As a young woman adopted from China wrote, "I've identified primarily as Jewish as it is the culture in which I was raised. Most of my role models are Jewish—not Asian." However, many continue to talk about feeling that they need to "prove" their Jewish identity repeatedly, especially when they step outside their own community and have to demonstrate that they are "really" Jewish.

Many parents who choose a same-race domestic adoption do so assuming that they will not have to face these complicated questions of multiple identities. Indeed, among our survey respondents, parents of same-race adoptees were far less likely to see their children as having a birth heritage different from their own (only 45 percent said their child had a different birth heritage, with another 10 percent saying they were unsure, in contrast to 91 percent of parents of transracial adoptees believing that their children had a different birth heritage). Even those who do identify their children as having a different birth heritage overwhelmingly do not see it as important to bring that heritage into their lives; a full 97 percent responded that it was either not at all important or not particularly important to do so. "Our son is the same race as us," wrote one respondent, "so other than different religions, there really wasn't anything to expose him to"; the implication was that this mother would have considered exposing her son to other elements of a birth heritage but not religious ones, given potential conflicts with Judaism. "[We] have absolutely nothing to do with her 'birth heritage,'" wrote another. "As she is white, there is little to celebrate in the way of her heritage; she is an American, apple pie and baseball kind of child."

Yet for many white adoptees raised in Jewish families, identity is not so simple. In part, their struggles stem from an often unacknowledged tendency in the Jewish community to conceive of Jewish identity in biological terms.

Indeed, this emphasis on "blood logic" in defining and maintaining Jewish identity appears to have increased in recent years; as many Jews cease to "do" much Jewishly, they fall back on genes, blood, and appearance to articulate their sense of their own Jewishness.[34] Despite valid conversions and Jewish upbringings, many adoptees—white as well as of color—report having their Jewish identity questioned because they were not "born Jewish." "For years my cousins all told me I wasn't 'really' Jewish because I'm not ethnically [read: biologically or racially] Jewish," writes a white domestically adopted woman. A white Orthodox woman writes that "It's looked down [on] by the community because even though I lived my whole life as a Jew, I'm still considered a 'convert.'"[35] And another white domestic Jewish adoptee remembers that "When I was older, questions at camp as to whether I was a *real Jew* since I was converted became more common and made me uncomfortable."[36] "Real Jew," "outcast," "not Jewish enough"—the words come up over and over again in our research and demonstrate how deep an impact thinking about Jewish blood has on adoptees not "born into" the Jewish community.

For many white adoptees not born to Jewish birth parents, the painful sense of biological difference from their family and the Jewish community is expressed through a concern about not "looking Jewish." Virtually every transracial Jewish adoptee at some point hears the "light-hearted" comment "Funny, you don't look Jewish" or is told that it "looks wrong" for them to be practicing Judaism.[37] Same-race adoptees, however, are by no means strangers to such remarks. Hair, eye color, and noses come up repeatedly in white adoptees' discussions of their experiences in the Jewish community. As a white domestically adopted man comments, "Being a blond haired, blue eyed kid at Solomon Schechter is not an easy thing for a young kid to do. I [was] plopped into the most homogeneous soup one could imagine, and expected to thrive. I was asked why I looked different—I wasn't really sure." Similarly, a white domestically adopted woman writes, "I have a very round 'button' nose. And I have been asked if my nose was a Bat Mitzvah gift. . . . I personally always wanted to appear and look more Jewish just to fit in." And from the white adopted daughter of a rabbi: "Community was hard. I didn't look Jewish. How did this Rabbi get a little blonde girl with a Shiksa nose?"[38]

Because of the American Jewish community's emphasis on academic achievement, learning disabilities too can be cause for a sense of biological alienation from Jewishness. As a white domestically adopted woman remembers poignantly:

> "Jews don't have learning disabilities," I mistakenly thought. One day I decided that I was not Jewish. I had been adopted by Jewish parents and it was their identity, not mine. I felt alienated and disconnected and left the community for many years. I was tired of hearing, "well, you don't look Jewish," too (what does that even mean?!). Today I can proudly say that I may not have been born Jewish and I may not have chosen to be Jewish, but Judaism chose me and I proudly identify as a Jewish American.

If we understand Jewishness to be a culture as well as a religion (which, as indicated by the 2013 Pew Research Center study "A Portrait of Jewish Americans," a majority of American Jews do[39]), then even domestic same-race adoptions into Jewish families are transcultural. As such, it should not be surprising that, like transracial or transnational adoptees, some of these adoptees feel conscious of bringing another identity into their families and are interested in connecting with their birth heritages. Coming from white, typically Christian birth families, however, they may struggle to find aspects of a birth culture with which to identify that do not seem threatening to their Jewish families and communities. For example, unlike Chinese adoptees, who may study the Chinese language or immerse themselves in the Chinese or Chinese American communities, white domestic adoptees may gravitate to Christmas trees, Easter bunnies, or a cross, lacking other obvious symbols.

The rabbi's daughter with the "Shiksa nose" quoted above grew up deeply embedded in the Jewish community, yet she writes that "I always 'missed' Christmas. An odd part of me thought that I should be celebrating Christmas. A small part of me buried somewhere inside thinks I should be Christian. I push that away. Have always thought that way since I was a kid."[40] Another white domestically adopted woman traces her alienation from Jewishness directly to her identity as an adoptee: "In terms of being Jewish, to me it just never fit, it never felt right. Like I could have been raised in any religion. I remember being young and thinking religion was like a part of your DNA, and that since I didn't share any with my family, maybe I wasn't Jewish. . . . As wonderful as it was to be raised Jewish, I wish I had felt a connection . . . Ever."

For the small number of today's adoptees with at least one Jewish birth parent, Jewish identity is, perhaps not surprisingly, generally uncomplicated—or at least no more complicated than it is for nonadoptees. The relationship between their birth and adoptive heritages is by and large a nonissue. Yet the way in which these adoptees discuss the relationship between their Jewish birth parentage and their sense of their place in the Jewish community highlights the complexities that often arise for those *not* born to Jewish birth parents.

Some adoptees know from the beginning that their birth mothers were Jewish and comment that it was this knowledge that allowed them to feel fully Jewish. As a white domestically adopted man reflects, "I always identified as a 'real' Jew because the adoption agency my parents used only . . . put children up for adoption [for] whom at least the birth mother is Jewish. . . . My birth mother was Jewish so I always felt that I was really a genuine part of the Jewish community and felt that I fit in. That helped me when I attended Jewish day school to not feel like an outcast."[41] The implication, of course, is that this young man believes that he likely *would* have felt like an outcast had he not had a Jewish birth mother. Similarly, a white Orthodox man writes that "I was born Jewish so I didn't have questions and possible . . . cultural differences that other adoptees [have,] converts and non-converts alike. Also no one looked at me different because I looked the same as everyone else." And a white domestically adopted woman comments that "Knowing my maternal grandma was Jewish also helps affirm that I am part of the tribe. I don't feel as much as an imposter because of this. My feelings of not being worthy of this aspect of my identity shift day to day. . . . I just know that 'legally' I am Jewish. This has been important to me as I have gotten older and felt the need to validate my experience of being a Jew. No one else has ever tested me or made me feel I had to prove myself, it comes from within."[42]

Other adoptees discover later that they were indeed "born Jewish," and the intense relief they often feel highlights the discomfort felt by many white adoptees who were not born to Jewish birth parents. "Two years ago, I took a DNA test to determine my haplogroup," writes a thirty-five-year-old white woman adopted by Jewish parents. "I did discover some pretty interesting things, including the fact that I am biologically Jewish. That was always a big question for me!"[43] When Jewish adoptees search for their birth parents, it is not uncommon for one of their first questions to be "Am I really Jewish?" (i.e., were my birth parents Jewish?).[44] If we take seriously current understandings of the importance of biological roots to adoptees, such questions should perhaps not be unexpected, but they also point to hesitancies about Jewish identity based on upbringing rather than birth.

CONCLUSION

Despite the complexities of the Jewish adoptive experience, it is important to acknowledge that many, if not most, Jewish adoptive families succeed in crafting personal, familial, and communal identities that work for them, even in cases where it may be impossible to fully reconcile various aspects of identity. Here the heterogeneity of American Jewry is an asset; with so many ways of being Jewish, adoptees and their families can search out communities and approaches to Jewishness that feel comfortable and welcoming to them. For transracial adoptive families, this often involves actively seeking out communities of Jews of color where the adoptee of color will not feel himself or herself outside the norm. The Jewish people have always been more racially and ethnically diverse than Americans commonly recognize, and this diversity has only increased as growing numbers of individuals of color have joined the Jewish community through conversion and/or marriage. Many multiracial Jewish adoptive families report how important it is to them to connect with other Jews of color, often through organizations such as the Jewish Multiracial Network and Be'chol Lashon or by specifically seeking out congregations, schools, camps, and youth groups with a critical mass of nonwhite members.

Challenges and complexities, moreover, can also be tremendous opportunities for growth and development, and the multifaceted nature of identity within the Jewish adoptive family is often a source of great enrichment. Many adoptive parents, especially of children of color, comment on how their experiences have broadened and deepened their own sense of Jewish identity. And many adoptees draw strength and inspiration from their diverse identities. The young adult Chinese adoptee cited above who was asked as a child if it was "legal" to be both Chinese and Jewish has grown up to be the president of her college Hillel and is strongly committed to issues of social and racial justice. "Being an adopted Asian American Jew has shaped my personal and career aspirations," she writes. "I am a sociology major focused on race and ethnic relations, and have always been interested in advocating for marginalized populations. I am hoping to write a senior thesis on transracial, transnational adoption and critical race theory."[45] And the family of a Korean adoptee whose mother pulled her from Jewish preschool because of racism invested considerable resources in raising her with strong identities as both Korean and Jewish; she writes that despite the racism she experienced in the Jewish community, "I really do cherish my Jewish heritage and feel that, without my

Jewish upbringing, I would be a very different and possibly less-well adjusted adopted person."

If the results of the recent Pew survey tell us anything, it is that questions of multiple and blended identities will only become more common and more pressing in the future as Jewish families increasingly cross a variety of racial, religious, and cultural boundaries. As they work to understand and respond to the Jewish "Modern Family," academic and communal observers can learn much from the experiences of adoptive families and work hard to become more welcoming to those who bring with them other forms of identity, rather than seeing those identities as "competing" with Jewishness. In the next phase of our research with the Adoption & Jewish Identity Project, we will continue to probe these complex issues by gathering the voices of young adult adoptees through oral histories and narrative and video testimonies, enabling us to create a much fuller picture of the Jewish adoptive experience and the evolving meaning of Jewish identity in America.

ACKNOWLEDGMENTS

I would like to thank my dear friend and colleague, Jayne Guberman, for our close collaboration on every step of this project.

NOTES

1. Ninety-five percent of respondents self-identified as white. Of the 3 percent who identified as "multiracial or other," almost half would traditionally be considered white (having identified themselves as "Jewish," "Ashkenazi Jew," or "Israeli-American") or identified themselves as "other" because their families were multiracial, not because they themselves were nonwhite. Fewer than 1 percent identified as black, Latino/a, or Asian. Although estimates of the number of Jews of color in the United States vary considerably, the percentage is surely more than 1 percent. See Dianne Tobin et al., *In Every Tongue: The Racial and Ethnic Diversity of the Jewish People* (San Francisco: Institute for Jewish & Community Research, 2005), and the websites of Be'chol Lashon (http://www.bechol lashon.org), the Jewish Multiracial Network (http://www.jewishmultiracialnetwork.org), and Jews in All Hues (http://www.jewsinallhues.org/).

2. For example, geographic distribution of survey respondents largely paralleled that of the American Jewish community, as did synagogue affiliation and involvement.

3. For the history of adoption in the United States, see, among many others, Adam Pertman, *Adoption Nation: How the Adoption Revolution Is Transforming America—and Our Families* (Boston: Harvard Common Press, 2011); Ellen Herman, *Kinship by Design:*

A History of Adoption in the United States (Chicago: University of Chicago Press, 2008); Ellen Herman, "The Adoption History Project," http://pages.uoregon.edu/adoption/; Barbara Melosh, *Strangers and Kin: The American Way of Adoption* (Cambridge: Harvard University Press, 2002); E. Wayne Carp, *Family Matters: Secrecy and Disclosure in the History of Adoption* (Cambridge: Harvard University Press, 1998); E. Wayne Carp, ed., *Adoption in America: Historical Perspectives* (Ann Arbor: University of Michigan Press, 2004).

4. See especially Brian Paul Gill, "Adoption Agencies and the Search for the Ideal Family, 1918–1965," in Carp, *Adoption in America,* 161–80.

5. Melosh, *Strangers and Kin,* 76–88.

6. On the development of the practices of severing ties between birth and adoptive families, sealing original birth certificates, and hiding adoption, see especially Carp, *Family Matters.*

7. For statistics regarding transnational adoption, see "Statistics," Bureau of Consular Affairs, U.S. Department of State, http://travel.state.gov/content/adoptionsabroad/en/about-us/statistics.html.

8. The ethics of both transnational and transracial adoption have been the subject of much debate. Some people view transnational adoption as cultural imperialism, exploitative of poor, generally nonwhite countries; inherently robbing children of their cultures and communities; and diverting attention and resources away from the true systemic problems. Others argue that it provides desperately needy children with families, rescuing them from lives of poverty and neglect in the streets, poor institutional care, or discrimination on the basis of race, ethnicity, illegitimacy, or disability. Debates about transracial adoption have generally focused largely on domestic adoption. Some have argued that the practice itself is racist, as it deprives communities of color (in particular, African American communities) of their children and children of color of their identities; others argue that opposition to transracial adoption is racist because it deprives children of potential families. For more discussion of these issues, see Jane Jeong Trenka et al., eds., *Outsiders Within: Writings on Transnational Adoption* (Brooklyn: South End Press, 2006); Laura Briggs, *Somebody's Children: The Politics of Transracial and Transnational Adoption* (Durham: Duke University Press, 2012); Herman, "The Difference Difference Makes," in *Kinship by Design.*

9. Many adoption experts take issue with MEPA-IEP, believing that "color blindness" in adoption is naive and often counter to the best interests of the child. See "Finding Families for African American Children: The Role of Race and Law in Adoption from Foster Care," Evan B. Donaldson Adoption Institute, 2008, http://adoptioninstitute.org/old/publications/MEPApaper20080527.pdf.

10. Cardell K. Jacobson, Leila Nielsen, and Andrea Hardeman, "Family Trends and Transracial Adoption in the United States," *Adoption Quarterly* 15 (2012): 73–74; "Adoption USA: A Chartbook Based on the 2007 National Survey of Adoptive Parents," U.S. Department of Health and Human Services, http://aspe.hhs.gov/hsp/09/nsap/chartbook/chartbook.cfm?id=15.

11. In particular, the Adoption and Safe Families Act of 1997 was intended to counter "foster care drift" by faster termination of parental rights and encouragement of adoption, although results have been mixed. See Cris Beam, *To the End of June: The Intimate Life of American Foster Care* (Boston: Houghton Mifflin, 2013), 43–45.

12. For an overview of debates about granting adoptees access to their original birth certificates, see "For the Records II: An Examination of the History and Impact of Adult Adoptee Access to Original Birth Certificates," Evan B. Donaldson Adoption Institute, http://adoptioninstitute.org/old/publications/7_14_2010_ForTheRecordsII.pdf. See also the website of Bastard Nation: The Adoptee Rights Organization, http://www.bastards.org/.

13. Considerable ongoing research focuses on the impact of open adoption on members of the adoption triad and the best ways of shaping contact between birth and adoptive families. Of particular concern is the lack of enforceability of open adoption agreements and how to manage disagreements about desired levels of contact. In general, however, some degree of openness is considered desirable. See Deborah H. Siegel and Susan Livingston Smith, "Openness in Adoption: From Secrecy and Stigma to Knowledge and Connections," Evan B. Donaldson Adoption Institute, http://adoptioninstitute.org/old/publications/2012_03_OpennessInAdoption.pdf; Ruth B. McRoy et al., "Open Adoptions: Longitudinal Outcomes for the Adoption Triad," in *Handbook of Adoption: Implications for Researchers, Practitioners, and Families* (ed. Rafael A. Javier et al.; Thousand Oaks: Sage Publications, 2006), 175–89.

14. On the seven core issues in adoption, see the foundational work of Deborah N. Silverstein and Sharon Kaplan, "Lifelong Issues in Adoption," FAIR Families, http://www.fairfamilies.org/2012/1999/99LifelongIssues.htm. Silverstein and Kaplan identified the seven core issues as loss, rejection, guilt/shame, grief, identity, intimacy and relationships, and control/gains.

15. See, for example, the many works of Betty Jean Lifton, including *Journey of the Adopted Self: A Quest for Wholeness* (New York City: Basic Books, 1994), *Twice Born: Memoirs of an Adopted Daughter* (New York City: McGraw Hill, 1975), and *Lost and Found: The Adoption Experience* (New York City: Harper Perennial, 1988). See also contemporary works written for adoptive parents, including, among many others, Sherrie Eldridge, *Twenty Things Adopted Kids Wish Their Adoptive Parents Knew* (New York: Dell, 1999); Susan TeBos and Carissa Woodwyk, *Before You Were Mine: Discovering Your Adopted Child's Lifestory* (Lima: FaithWalk Publishing, 2007); Jean MacLeod and Sheena Macrae, eds., *Adoption Parenting: Creating a Toolbox, Building Connections* (Warren: EMK Press, 2006).

16. For a useful overview of research, see "Beyond Culture Camp: Promoting Healthy Identity Formation in Adoption," Evan B. Donaldson Adoption Institute, 2009, http://adoptioninstitute.org/old/publications/2009_11_BeyondCultureCamp.pdf.

17. NJPS 2000–2001 Report, 4–5, Jewish DataBank, http://www.jewishdatabank.org/studies/downloadFile.cfm?FileID=1490 ; *Adopted Children and Stepchildren: 2000; Census 2000 Special Reports,* http://www.census.gov/prod/2003pubs/censr-6.pdf; Highlights

of the CJF National Jewish Population Survey, 16, Jewish DataBank, http://www.jewishdatabank.org/studies/downloadFile.cfm?FileID=3129. See also Moshe Aharon Bleich, "Attitudes of Jewish Clergy toward Adoption Issues," (Ph.D. Diss., Yeshiva University, 2003), 5.

18. Because the number of respondents who had adopted in the 1950s, 1960s, and 1970s was relatively small, the three decades were collapsed to increase the reliability of the statistical analysis. All of the children adopted in the 1950s and 1960s were born in the United States; in the 1970s, 8 percent of the adopted children were born abroad, reflecting the rise of transnational adoption over the period.

19. The survey was conducted between 2010 and 2012. Data were analyzed by decade of adoption. Unless otherwise noted, results for the years 2010–2012 have been included with results from 2000–2009 to generate statistics for the early twenty-first century.

20. "How Many Children Were Adopted in 2007 and 2008?," Child Welfare Information Gateway, September 2011, https://www.childwelfare.gov/pubs/adopted0708/. Given the rapid decrease in transnational adoption after 2004, it is not surprising that the percentage of transnational adoptions dropped to 32 percent for the years 2010–2012, and the numbers have likely dropped even further in the past few years. Even this percentage, however, remains considerably higher than in the American population as a whole.

21. Recall that only approximately 40 percent of American adoptions overall today are transracial.

22. Two percent of children were listed as "other."

23. Well over 80 percent of parents of both transracially and transnationally adopted children reported that it was either "very important" or "somewhat important" to bring their children's birth heritage into their lives. Seventy-five percent of parents of children of color and 74 percent of parents of children born abroad reported that at the time of adoption, they were interested in bringing their child's birth heritage into their lives and had a good sense of possible things to do; another 16 percent of parents of children of color and 17 percent of parents of children born abroad reported that they were interested but were not knowledgeable enough about their child's birth culture.

24. Those who had adopted in the 1990s or later reported a mean of 7.53 birth heritage socialization practices.

25. Perhaps not surprisingly, given the dramatic changes in understanding of adoptive identity in recent decades, older family members in particular were likely to disapprove of—or simply to be confused by—efforts to engage with birth heritage.

26. It is important to acknowledge that for some of the parents who had adopted most recently, their children might simply have been too young to have engaged in some of these practices yet. The main exception to this trend is developing relationships with people from the child's community of origin, cited by 61 percent of parents of children of color and 59 percent of parents of children born abroad. Developing such relationships requires considerable investment and is seen by adoption professionals and adult adoptees

as especially important to healthy racial and ethnic identity formation among transracial adoptees. From the survey, it is unfortunately impossible to know how substantive these relationships really were and if parents of children who were young at the time of the survey would continue to devote the time necessary to cultivate them as their children grew up.

27. This process has now been well explored by historians, anthropologists, and critical race theorists. To mention only a few, see especially Eric Goldstein, *The Price of Whiteness: Jews, Race, and American Identity* (Princeton: Princeton University Press, 2006); Karen Brodkin, *How Jews Became White Folks & What That Says about Race in America* (New Brunswick: Rutgers University Press, 1998); Matthew Jacobson, *Whiteness of a Different Color: European Immigrants and the Alchemy of Race* (Cambridge: Harvard University Press, 1998).

28. Adoptee Questionnaire, online questionnaire conducted by the Adoption and Jewish Identity Project and available to people eligible to participate.

29. Aura Lichtenberg, Oral History Pre-Interview Questionnaire, April 2015.

30. Adoption and Jewish Identity Project Adoptive Parents and Jewish Identity Survey.

31. Adoptee Questionnaire, online questionnaire conducted by the Adoption and Jewish Identity Project.

32. See, for example, the experiences of Avery Klein-Cloud, as portrayed in Nicole Opper's documentary *Off and Running.*

33. Lichtenberg, Oral History Pre-Interview Questionnaire.

34. See Goldstein, *The Price of Whiteness;* Susan Glenn, "'Funny, You Don't Look Jewish': Visual Stereotypes and the Making of Modern Jewish Identity," in *Boundaries of Jewish Identity* (ed. Susan A. Glenn and Naomi B. Sokoloff; Seattle: University of Washington Press, 2010); Lynn Davidman and Shelly Tenenbaum, "'It's in My Genes': Biological Discourse and Essentialist Views of Identity among Contemporary American Jews," *Sociological Quarterly* 48 (2007): 435–50; Susan Martha Kahn, "Are Genes Jewish? Conceptual Ambiguities in the New Genetic Age," in Glenn and Sokoloff, *Boundaries of Jewish Identity.*

35. Adoptee Questionnaire, online questionnaire conducted by the Adoption and Jewish Identity Project.

36. Ibid. (my emphasis).

37. A white adoptive mother of a daughter adopted from China remembers that "My old boss told me privately of witnessing a bat mitzvah of a Korean child adopted his family—he joked about feeling 'Something doesn't look right.' I wasn't amused." Adoption and Jewish Identity Project, Adoptive Parents and Jewish Identity survey.

38. Adoptee Questionnaire, online questionnaire conducted by the Adoption and Jewish Identity Project.

39. See Pew Research Center, "A Portrait of Jewish Americans," http://www.pewforum.org/files/2013/10/jewish-american-full-report-for-web.pdf.

40. Adoptee Questionnaire, online questionnaire conducted by the Adoption and Jewish Identity Project.

41. Ibid.

42. Ibid.

43. Ibid.

44. Shelley Kapnek Rosenberg, quoted in "Jewish Adoptees," http://jewish.adoption.com/faith-based/jewish-adoptees.html (accessed January 2, 2008).

45. Adoptee Questionnaire, online questionnaire conducted by the Adoption and Jewish Identity Project.

III. THE FUTURE

The Jewish Perspective in Creating Human Embryos Using Cloning Technologies

John D. Loike

INTRODUCTION

Molecular genetics and genetic engineering are some of the most exciting areas of modern-day biology. Since James Watson and Francis Crick deciphered the structure of DNA, scientists have made great progress in understanding human genetics and its role in disease processes. DNA is the universal code of life that provides the information for all cells and organisms to function. The human genome contains about twenty thousand genes that provide the instructions to synthesize and produce almost one hundred thousand different kinds of proteins that human beings need to function properly.

One of the most challenging areas of science is applying genetic technology in the hope of preventing genetic mistakes from affecting an embryo or an individual.[1] In recent years genetic technology is also being applied to other areas of reproductive medicine, such as human fertility.

Cloning technology received international publicity in 1997 when it was used to clone Dolly the sheep.[2] The cloning of Dolly was initially hailed as the great hope for a biomedical revolution because it offered an innovative method to genetically alter sheep and cows to produce expensive biological proteins in their milk.[3] In addition, there was hope that cloning techniques could create perfectly matched tissues that would someday cure ailments ranging from diabetes to Parkinson's disease.[4]

However, applying cloning technologies to human beings for either reproductive purposes or to generate embryonic stem cells spurred intense ethical debates. As this method requires the destruction of fertilized eggs, many cultures view this process as unethical. The Catholic Church, for example, believes that reproductive human cloning, as in vitro fertilization (IVF), is unethical for two reasons.[5] First, the destruction of human fertilized eggs is considered akin to murder because fertilized eggs have attained the status of personhood.[6] Second, children must be conceived within a marital context by engaging in marital relations. These cultural objections to cloning technologies have impacted the rate at which research in human cloning has progressed. For much of the last decade, federal funding did not support research in human reproductive cloning and even limited the generation of embryonic stem cells using this method.

In this essay, I review the latest technological advances of cloning and its potential applications to human disease and in particular to human reproduction. Then, I discuss, from a Jewish perspective, some challenging bioethical issues that emerge from this technology. Finally, I present potential ways to resolve some of these contentious issues.

WHAT IS CLONING TECHNOLOGY?

Reproductive cloning can be defined in broad terms as the identical reproduction of fragments of DNA, genes, cells, or whole organisms from a single ancestor. The term "clone" was coined by H. J. Webber and stems from the ancient Greek *klon,* which is a twig, and probably refers to the fact that a twig can give rise to another tree identical to its parent tree. Looking for a word to describe small sections of an organism that can be cut off and transplanted to form a whole entity, Webber chose the word "clone" for its uniqueness and easy pronunciation.

To clone Dolly, Ian Wilmut and his colleagues used a technology called somatic cell nuclear transfer (SCNT).[7] In SCNT, the genetic material contained in the nucleus from any cell is transferred or injected into an enucleated egg (i.e., an egg whose nuclear DNA has been physically removed) to initiate the creation of an embryo (see Figure 1). This reconstituted "fertilized egg" is then allowed to develop into a blastocyst in the laboratory and is subsequently implanted into a host animal for embryological development, similar to the protocol used in IVF. SCNT can also be used to generate a blastocyst from which embryonic stem cells can be obtained and maintained in the laboratory.

The clinical application of cloning (specifically SCNT) may have great potential to enhance the welfare and health of human beings. SCNT technologies may be used to enhance our knowledge of:

- *Human organ regeneration from stem cells.* Each person completely regenerates his or her own skin every seven days by triggering skin stem cells to replicate. Everyone has witnessed that any cut can heal itself and disappear within two weeks. The skeletal system can also utilize its own stem cells to replenish itself every seven years. One important future area of medicine lies in understanding how organs and tissues of the body creates themselves out of a single stem cell and the mechanisms by which specific organ systems are renewed throughout life. The use of patient-derived stem cells obtained via SCNT or

Figure 1- SCNT

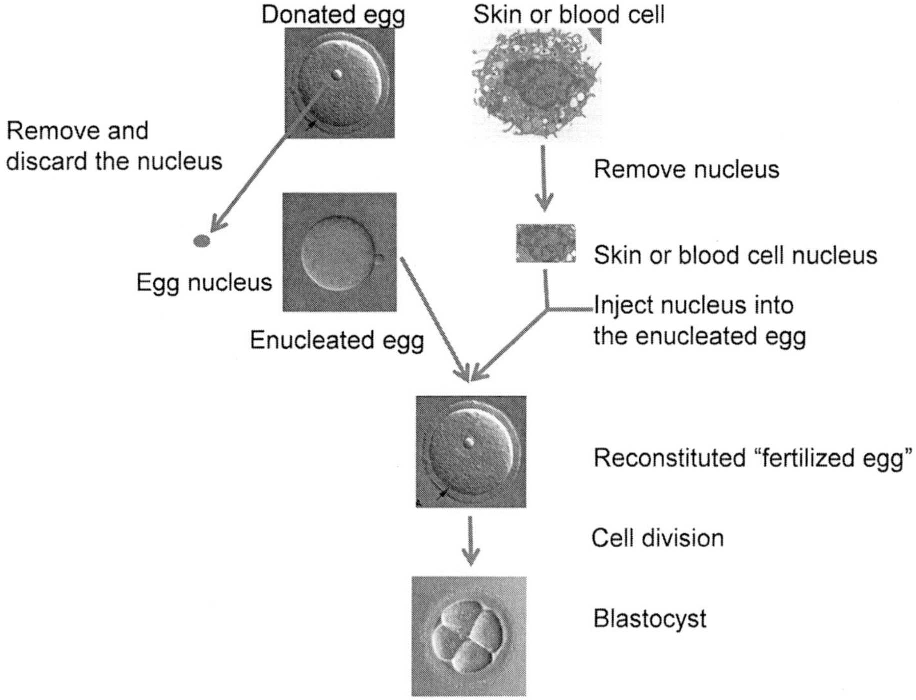

cloning technology offers the possibility to replace or repair damaged organs without the need of donor organ transplants.

- *Infertility and the design of new medical solutions for infertility.* Cloning technology offers the possibility for infertile men or women to use nonsperm or nonegg cells in creating a healthy embryo. According to the Centers for Disease Control and Prevention, about 6 percent of married women fifteen to forty-four years of age in the United States and 18 percent of men are infertile. In many of cases of male infertility, the nuclear genetic content obtained from skin or blood cells can be injected into an egg to trigger fertilization and the creation of an embryo.
- *Helping women with mitochondrial diseases to have healthy offspring.* In almost all cells of the body, 99.9 percent of the DNA is found in a cellular organelle called the nucleus, and less than 0.1 percent of the DNA is found in another organelle called the mitochondria. Mitochondria serve many functions but is best known as providing the cell with the chemical energy necessary to carry out all of its cellular activities. In a sense, they are the battery of the cell. Mistakes or

mutations in mitochondrial DNA can result in profound disease states that include muscular dystrophy, liver disease, lung disease, and, in rare instances, even death at an early stage. Only a few women have those types of mitochondria mutations that lead to serious clinical symptoms. In the United States, about 12,000 women are candidates for intervention to allow them to have healthy children free from mutations in their mitochondria. In Great Britain, there are about 6,500 women. Cloning technology can be utilized to transfer healthy mitochondria from a woman donor into the egg of another woman who has mitochondrial mutations to produce a healthy child.

NEW INNOVATIONS IN SCNT TECHNOLOGY

However, the development of SCNT using human cells has proven to be an exceedingly difficult task.[8] Many unsuccessful attempts were made at trying to generate a viable human preimplanted embryo or blastocyst via SCNT. In fact, it took sixteen years after the report of Dolly appeared in the press for Dr. Shoukhrat Mitalipov from the Oregon Health and Science University to lead an international team to modify SCNT technology to generate human blastocysts and patient-specific embryonic stem cell lines.[9] This was the first report that successfully applied SCNT to human cells and was an extension of their previous studies using SCNT to generate embryonic stem cell lines from nonhuman primates. Incorporating innovative technical modifications, Mitalipov and his colleagues successfully fused the nucleus obtained from a baby's skin cell with an enucleated egg and applied SCNT technology to generate a human blastocyst from which they could isolate and maintain human embryonic stem cells in the laboratory.

One innovation involved obtaining the eggs from women who did not receive high doses of hormones. Normally, IVF technology requires the physician to first hyperstimulate a woman with hormones in order to retrieve between ten to twenty eggs. Mitalipov discovered that milder hormonal stimulation allowed the retrieval of fewer eggs (only about five eggs), but their quality was much better than those eggs obtained from traditional hyperhormonal stimulation. The second innovation involved the use of gentler methods to fuse the donor cell with the enucleated egg.

Mitalipov's motivation to apply SCNT to human beings was not to clone a human being. Rather, it was to obtain patient-derived embryonic stem cell lines that can be used to study and potentially treat various human diseases. In fact, his group applied their technology to successfully generate embryonic stem cells from a patient with a genetic defect called Leigh syndrome. Leigh syndrome is a severe neurological genetic disorder that typically arises in the first year of life. This condition is characterized by progressive loss of mental and movement abilities (psychomotor regression) and typically results in respiratory failure that leads to death within a couple of years. The stem cells from this Leigh syndrome patient that were generated using SCNT will enable scientists to understand how mutations can lead to Leigh syndrome and then to use these cells to screen thousands of drugs in the search for a potential therapy.

Using SCNT to generate embryonic stem cells has broad applications for studying a wide variety of other genetic diseases. Patient-derived stem cells, generated via SCNT, can be obtained from individuals with Parkinson's disease, Huntington's disease, Lou Gehrig's disease, Alzheimer's disease, heart disease, and liver disease. These laboratory cultured stem cells would be a valuable scientific asset in designing and testing treatments to manage or cure these devastating diseases.

While Mitalipov and his colleagues claim that their technology is not designed to clone human beings, SCNT technology does in fact have the potential to be used to implant a human blastocyst into a woman to create a human embryo. What is significant here, from a scientific and Jewish legal (halachic) perspective, is that SCNT allows scientists to use a variety of cell sources aside from sperm and eggs to fuse with an egg to create a human embryo. From a medical perspective, this technology may create an effective method for infertile men who do not produce viable sperm to produce genetically related healthy children. In addition, genetic defects in SCNT-generated stem cells from patients could be corrected using gene editing technologies. In specific situations, these genetically corrected stem cells could be an effective method of cell replacement therapy. For example, if people have a genetic defect that limits their blood's capacity to clot, SCNT could be used to generate their own stem cells. These stems cells could be reengineered to correct this mutation and then reintroduced into these patients to reconstitute their blood-clotting capacity.[10]

JEWISH ETHICAL ISSUES ASSOCIATED WITH CLONING TECHNOLOGIES

Ethical considerations of any new technology usually focus on four fundamental principles of bioethics.[11] The first is autonomy/respect for persons—a person's right to choose and control his or her own life and destiny and the acceptance of individual responsibility for his or her medical choices. The second is beneficence—the moral and contractual calling to benefit a person who seeks help. The third is nonmaleficence—avoiding intentionally created, needless harm or injury to a person through acts of either commission or omission. The fourth is justice—allocating medical resources fairly.

While many secular bioethicists raise several of the above ethical considerations of cloning, other arguments for why cloning is unethical have been raised. Some critics argue that it is unethical for scientists to "play God" by engaging in technologies that alter the nature of human reproduction.[12] It is surprising how many papers written by scientists, many of whom are atheists or not religious, use this argument to declare cloning unethical. Other scientists declare that human cloning technology is unethical because of the "yuck factor." Dr. Leon Kass in 1997 explained that the "yuck factor" in bioethics is defined as an unethical technology based on an intuitive negative response or its evil characteristic.[13] In other words, one cannot argue that cloning violates any one of the basic principles of bioethics. Rather, for unspecified and simply intuitive reasons, this technology is deemed unethical.

In contrast, the Jewish perspective is quite different from those arguing against human cloning. Regarding the idea that scientists should not play God, the Jewish perspective states that God created an incomplete world where human beings are encouraged to partner with God to improve and perfect the world.[14] This directive is the basis of the commandment of circumcision. The newborn baby boy is physically and spiritually incomplete, and God directs the parents to complete the act of creation by having the baby boy circumcised on the eighth day.[15] The famous biblical commentator Rabbi Moshe ben Nachmonides states that "God gave man power and control on earth to do as he wishes with the animals and insects and everything which crawls on the earth, and to build, to uproot what is planted, to quarry copper from the mountains, etc."[16] In other words, human beings are commanded to serve as partners in God's creation in order to improve the human condition. Thus, Judaism values activities that "play God" as a positive challenge when applied to improve the human condition or when used to design a new therapy.

One must also consider that reproductive cloning has biological precedents. Many plant species and single-celled organisms such as bacteria reproduce via cloning. Higher-level species such as worms, fish, lizards, and frogs undergo a process called parthenogenesis whereby a female can produce genetically identical offspring without engaging a male partner. *Leiolepis ngovantrii,* for example, is a reptile commonly found in Vietnam that is an all-female species that reproduces via cloning. The female Amazonian ant *Mycocepurus smithi* is an example of an insect species that reproduces via cloning. These ants have reproduced via cloning for thousands of years, resulting in the virtual disappearance of their sexual organs. Finally, identical twins represent natural cloning occurring in human beings. Since cloning is part of the natural process of God's creation, Judaism would allow its therapeutic application to human reproduction.

With regard to the "yuck factor," there is no Jewish legal principle that incorporates a similar concept. In fact, Judaism believes that Jewish law is often based on logical and sound reasons. When there are medical benefits that justify a new technology, then there is no enforceable prohibition. Thus, there are no prohibitions against using SCNT to improve the health of an individual.

Another ethical challenge in SCNT technology is related to the status of personhood of a preimplanted embryo. As mentioned above, cloning technology requires the destruction of many fertilized eggs. How does Jewish law, or halachah, view the destruction of fertilized eggs? The general consensus in Orthodox Jewish law was expressed by the Union of Orthodox Jewish Congregations and the Rabbinical Council of America in 2004: personhood does not begin at conception but rather at some point during gestation.[17] While Jewish law does not encourage unnecessary destruction of a fertilized egg, it recognizes that fertilized eggs may be used in biomedical research in order to develop new therapies.

A fourth ethical challenge related to cloning is how Jewish law views the possibility of creating human embryos from more than two genetic parents. The preferred method of human reproduction in Jewish law is that conception should occur during marital relations. Moreover, the Talmud (*Niddah* 30) claims that the preferred method to produce children involves three partners: woman, man, and God. However, in situations of infertility and disease, Jewish law permits other technologies such as IVF to allow infertile parents to have healthy children. This is based in part on the biblical account in which Rachel declared to our forefather, Jacob, that she would rather die than remain infertile.[18] Several biblical commentaries, such as Rashi, use this episode to prove that Judaism views infertility as a serious medical condition.[19]

How does Judaism view the donation of genetic materials in creating a child? The normal procedure to create a child is to fertilize a woman's egg with sperm. Using SCNT and cloning technology, it is possible to use nonsperm cells to "fertilize" an egg. In cases where the husband cannot produce sperm, Jewish law would permit physicians to use nonsperm cells to obtain the nuclear material to fertilize an egg. Here is an excellent example where Jewish law recognizes the hardships of infertility and permits any safe medical intervention to allow a couple to fulfill the commandment of human reproduction.

What is uniquely innovative in this Jewish law is that scientific consensus can serve as the basis of halachic decisions and can serve as a precedent in addressing halachic issues, including those emerging from new reproductive biotechnologies. The basis of this law is derived from situations where halachah must establish whether a patient is seriously or terminally ill or has a sickness that is not serious. The halachic status of such patients is established by expert physicians and not by rabbis. Similarly, many Jewish legal scholars ascribe the intimate relationship of parenthood to genetics,[20] because scientists in our times view the genetic donors of the child as the legal parents of the child.

It is important to point out, however, that there are several situations where the Jewish definition of family relationships differs from a traditional genetic definition.

1. A child fathered by a non-Jew with a Jewish woman has a genetic father and is considered Jewish by virtue of the fact that the mother is Jewish. However, halachah does not grant the non-Jewish genetic father parenthood status, and no familial halachic relationship exists between the genetic non-Jewish father and the Jewish child. The child must give the genetic father parental respect, but other laws such as inheritance do not apply.
2. A Jewish man who fathers a child with a non-Jewish woman is not granted familial status with respect to the child. Although he remains the genetic father, the child is not Jewish according to Jewish law.
3. Any child who converts to Judaism severs most familial relationships with respect to parenthood, fatherhood, and even sibling status.

However, in situations where the genetic materials are obtained from a Jewish man and used to reconstitute a fertilized egg obtained from a Jewish woman, the child would be the legal child of both parties and would be fully Jewish.

A fifth ethical concern in Jewish law is whether a child produce via cloning technologies is viewed as a *mamzer*.[21] The Hebrew term *mamzer* [from the root meaning "corrupt"] functions as a euphemism for an illicit union in the person's lineage—a bastard or illegitimate child. In Judaism, a *mamzer* cannot marry another Jew because their children would also be considered illegitimate.

This Jewish law is based on a verse in the Bible (Deut 23:2), which states that "A bastard shall not enter into the congregation of the LORD; even to his tenth generation shall he not enter into the congregation of the LORD." The potential status of a child *mamzer* in reproductive medicine has been discussed: specifically, whether a married Jewish woman can use sperm from a nonspousal Jewish man for artificial insemination.[22]

In response to this issue, there are three different rabbinical opinions:

1. According to Jewish law, the child is considered a real *mamzer* (minority view).
2. The child is a *safek* [doubtful] *mamzer,* and all stringencies of *mamzer* apply (minority view).
3. The child is not illegitimate at all (the most accepted view in Jewish law).[23]

Several leading halachic scholars, including Rabbi Dr. Moshe Tendler, propose that regarding SCNT and cloning, the child conceived is not illegitimate, because unlike the classical case of *mamzer,* no forbidden marital act took place.[24]

In halachah, the Jewish status of a child is maternally transmitted. If the mother is Jewish, then the child is Jewish, regardless of the religion of the father. Cloning technologies can create complex legal issues regarding the Jewish status of the child. For example, suppose a human embryo is created from genetic material from one non-Jewish female and transferred into an egg obtained from another Jewish woman. Would the child be deemed Jewish in this situation, where two women contribute the genetic information to generate an embryo?

Interestingly, there is no clear Jewish legal precedent to this case. However, Jewish law has legal processes in resolving situations where there is no halachic precedent. This is well documented in the following case. Suppose a Jewish couple donates their fertilized egg to a gestational surrogate to allow the surrogate to gestate the embryo. The religious status of the child is controversial. Some rabbis believe that the religious status of the child should follow the religion of the woman who carries and delivers the child. Others argue that the genetic mother should establish the religious status of the child.

Despite the fact that there is no precedent in Jewish law regarding gestational surrogacy, Jewish law provides a tenable solution. Jewish law would recommend that the child undergo ritual conversion to ensure the he or she has full Jewish status. Converting such a child would thus avoid a plethora of complicated Jewish questions.

A final alleged ethical concern regarding human cloning is that it violates the divine gift of free will or divine providence by creating an individual who is a genetic copy of someone else. Judaism values the unique individuality of each and every person. No two people are alike. Will cloning violate the Jewish principle of individuality? This ethical concern is not valid within Jewish law for one major reason. Identical twins provide a biological situation whereby two individuals have the same genetic makeup. Despite the fact that identical twins possess an identical genetic code, they exhibit different behaviors, physical traits, and health issues due to the varied environmental experiences each twin experiences. Thus Judaism, like science, recognizes that personality is shaped by both genetics and environment and acknowledges the individuality of identical twins or cloned individuals.

FUTURE ETHICAL CHALLENGES

As with any new biotechnology, Judaism supports its clinical application to improve fertility or health. Thus, using mitochondrial replacement therapy to produce a healthy child from a woman affected with mitochondrial mutations would be encouraged, provided that it is a safe procedure.[25] In this cloning situation, the nucleus of a fertilized egg is obtained from a wife who expresses mutations in her mitochondrial DNA, and this is transferred into an enucleated egg that is obtained from a healthy woman donor. This donor egg would contain "healthy" mitochondria, allowing the fertilized egg to develop into a healthy child.

There remain other situations in cloning that will require rabbinical deliberation in the future. For example, if two men donate their genetic materials to be transplanted into an enucleated egg, will the child be viewed as Jewish even though there is no genetic female involved in the creation of this child? At first glace one could speculate that the woman who gestates this embryo may be considered the legal mother of the child; therefore, if the gestational woman is Jewish, then the child would be considered Jewish. However, not all rabbis would agree with this view. As mentioned above, there is a debate in gestational surrogacy as to whether the gestation woman or the woman who donates her egg is considered the legal mother of the child. A final undecided issue relates to the Jewish perspective on cloning a single woman using her own blood cells and eggs. Are there conditions in which rabbis would deem such cloning as permissible? These are complex issues beyond the scope of this essay, and we await rabbinical scholars to adjudicate these situations.

CONCLUSION

In this essay I have outlined some of the ethical challenges and resolutions regarding human cloning. Good decisions in Jewish law are predicated on obtaining valid scientific facts. In addition, Judaism recognizes that any medical intervention can have serious side effects and provides the patient with some autonomy to choose whether to engage in such potentially risky procedures. On the other hand, Judaism does not support unlimited autonomy.[26] A patient who is suffering from an end-of-life illness is not allowed to engage in euthanasia. Regarding the autonomous right of a woman to clone herself, Jewish law would not support such a procedure without medical justification. Finally, Judaism supports the principle that in research and medicine, your actions should be guided not by what you can do but rather by what you should do.

NOTES

1. B. C. J. M. Fauser, K. Diedrich, et al., "Contemporary Genetic Technologies and Female Reproduction," *Human Reproduction Update* 17:6 (2011): 829–47.

2. Ian Wilmut et al., "Viable Offspring Derived from Fetal and Adult Mammalian Cells," *Nature* 385 (1997): 810–13.

3. Elizabeth Pennisi, "After Dolly, a Pharming Frenzy," *Science* 279:5351 (1998): 646–48.

4. Philippe Taupin, "Derivation of Embryonic Stem Cells for Cellular Therapy: Challenges and New Strategies," *Medical Science and Technology* 12:4 (2006): RA75–RA78.

5. N. Ohara, "Ethical Consideration of Experimentation Using Living Human Embryos: The Catholic Church's Position on Human Embryonic Stem Cell Research and Human Cloning," *Clinical and Experimental Obstetrics & Gynecology* 30:2–3 (2002): 77–81.

6. For a review about cloning, see Mohammed Ali Al-Bar and Hassan Chamsi-Pasha, "Ethical Issues in Genetics (Premarital Counseling, Genetic Testing, Genetic Engineering, Cloning and Stem Cell Therapy, DNA Fingerprinting)," in *Contemporary Bioethics: Islamic Perspective* (Cham, Switzerland: Springer International, 2015), 187–207.

7. Wilmut et al., "Viable Offspring."

8. Henrik Semb, "Human Embryonic Stem Cells: Origin, Properties and Applications," *Apmis* 113:11–12 (2005): 743–50.

9. M. Tachibana, P. Amato, et al., "Human Embryonic Stem Cells Derived by Somatic Cell Nuclear Transfer," *Cell* 153:6 (2013): 1228–38.

10. Jennifer L. Gori, Patrick D. Hsu, et al., "Delivery and Specificity of CRISPR-Cas9 Genome Editing Technologies for Human Gene Therapy," *Human Gene Therapy* 26:7 (2015): 443–51.

11. Tom L. Beauchamp and James F. Childress, *Principles of Biomedical Ethics* (Oxford: Oxford University Press, 2001).

12. Ted Peters, *Playing God? Genetic Determinism and Human Freedom* (Abingdon: Routledge, 2014).

13. Charles W. Schmidt, "The Yuck Factor: When Disgust Meets Discovery," *Environmental Health Perspectives* 116:12 (2008): A524–A527.

14. John D. Loike and Avram Steinberg, "Human Cloning and Halakhic Perspectives," *Tradition* (1998): 31–46.

15. Abraham Steinberg and Mordechai Halperin, "A Jewish View," *Prospects* 32:2 (2002): 225–36.

16. See Ramban, *Bereishis by Nahmanides* (New York: Mesorah, 2005), and Genesis 1:26 and 1:28.

17. "Statement on Stem Cell Research: RCA Reissues 2001 Statement of RCA/OU on the Important Topic of Stem Cell Research, as Formulated as a Letter to President Bush," Rabbinical Council of America (October 22, 2014), http://www.rabbis.org/news/article.cfm?id=100553.

18. Genesis 30:1.

19. For a discussion on this topic, see Rav Amnon Bazak, "Parashat Hashavua, Parashat Vayishlach: Rachel," Etzion, http://etzion.org.il/vbm/english/parsha.59/08vayish.htm.

20. Yehezkel Margalit, Orrie Levy, and John D. Loike, "Advanced Reproductive Technologies: Reevaluating Modern Parentage," *Harvard Journal of Law and Gender* 37 (2104): 107–41; J. D. Loike and M. D. Tendler, "Creating Human Embryos Using Reproductive Cloning Technologies," *Journal of Halacha and Contemporary Society* 367 (2014): 37–60.

21. Loike and Steinberg, "Human Cloning and Halakhic Perspectives," 14.

22. J. D. Loike and M. D. Tendler, "Halachic Perspectives of Gestational Surrogacy," *Hakirah* 16 (2013): 115–32.

23. Avraham Steinberg and Fred Rosner, *Encyclopedia of Jewish Medical Ethics: A Compilation of Jewish Medical Law on All Topics of Medical Interest* (New York: Feldheim, 2003).

24. J. Loike and R. L. Fischbach, "New Ethical Horizons in Gestational Surrogacy," *Journal of Fertilization: In Vitro-IVF-Worldwide, Reproductive Medicine, Genetics & Stem Cell Biology* 1 (2013): 109; Loike and Tendler, "Creating Human Embryos."

25. J. D. Loike, M. Hirano, M., and H. Margalit, "Three-Way Parenthood: Dealing with the Logistics of Embryos Created by Three-Parent IVF Technologies That Avoid the Transmission of Mitochondrial Disease," *The Scientist* (October 1, 2013); Ruth L. Fischbach, Shawna Benston, and John D. Loike, "Creating a Three-Parent Child: An Educational Paradigm for the Responsible Conduct of Research," *Journal of Microbiology & Biology Education* 15 (2014): 186.

26. J. D. Loike and M. D. Tendler, "Halacha and Bioethics," *Journal of Halacha in Contemporary Society* 16 (2011): 92–118.

Multiplying Motherhood: Gestational Surrogate Motherhood and Jewish Law

Pamela Laufer-Ukeles

RELATIONSHIP BETWEEN JEWISH LAW AND THE JEWISH FAMILY IN A TRANSITIONAL ERA

The relationship between the Jewish family and Jewish family law is more complex that it would seem at first blush. The Jewish family is a cultural, traditional notion defined more by culture and history than by legal guidelines. Yet, Jewish family law is a complex and detailed system of laws and guidelines that structure marriage, divorce, parenthood, and parent-child relationships. Jewish family law is a practical legal system ordering the definition of Jewish families and governing marriage and divorce. In Israel, Jewish law governs marriage and divorce and also has exclusive jurisdiction over issues of personal status and Jewish identity.[1] However, in the diaspora Jewish persons abide by the state's civil laws of marriage and divorce, which may seem to dampen the impact of Jewish family law. Still, given the importance of the laws of personal status and their significance in preserving Jewish continuity, Jewish family law remains relevant and is exercised by rabbinical courts [*beit din*]. For instance, a Jewish woman needs a *get* in order to remarry according to Jewish law even if she has a civil divorce. And, it is the *beit din* that will ordinarily attempt to resolve disputes about the *get.*

Assisted reproductive technologies (ART) have posed many challenges to traditional Jewish family law and challenged accepted norms. On the one hand, using ART has garnered much support from the religious Jewish community for helping to solve problems of infertility that can pose severe problems for the Jewish family. Having progeny is extremely important under Jewish law. The commandment to be fruitful and multiply is a positive commandment upon men, fulfilled by producing at least two offspring.[2] Adopting a child does not fulfill this commandment. However, reproducing through ART—through surrogacy, in vitro fertilization (IVF), or egg donations—will fulfill the commandment for a man as long as the male sperm is used in reproducing the offspring. Indeed, rabbis have supported such options, certainly as a better prospect than being compelled to divorce a woman who is unable to produce offspring or fails to fulfill the commandment.[3]

On the other hand, certain concrete legal and ethical dilemmas arise when traditional Jewish law is faced with the modern reality of ART.[4] Defining parenthood when genetics is divorced from intent and gestation, putting into place appropriate regulations in order to maximize safety and preserve health, and, when using gamete donors, avoiding incest and providing health information to children are universal issues and concerns for any legal system. Under Jewish law there are added concerns of ensuring that the child is not considered illegitimate [*mamzerut*], which can have serious religious ramifications for children. Legal authorities, whether religious or civil, must determine who and when ART can be used and when it will be funded by the state. These dilemmas have resulted in much discussion and debate. Jewish law does not have concrete resolutions for all the quandaries that arise, but Jewish law can provide inspiration and insight in resolving these dilemmas.

When faced with these new legal and ethical dilemmas, traditional Jewish law struggles because the law was determined through ancient Scriptures and decisions, and it can be difficult to use these laws to solve these modern, technological dilemmas.[5] Yet, when constructing normative frameworks for resolving these dilemmas, it is helpful to look to Jewish law for inspiration. Still, particularly when exact solutions are not forthcoming from Scripture, there is also a need to keep a critical eye on the ramifications of Jewish law solutions that may be too narrow and could result in unfair and inappropriate consequences. Ultimately, using Jewish law to resolve legal dilemmas can allow us to gain from the wisdom of Jewish tradition, but we should take heed to avoid harsh and impractical applications in the context of new dilemmas not foreseen by Talmudic law.

In this essay, I will focus on the dilemmas surrounding gestational surrogate motherhood. Gestational surrogate motherhood is a process whereby an intended father and mother enlist, usually for payment, another women to carry an embryo that is not genetically related to the surrogate and is usually genetically related to both the intended parents, although not necessarily. However, for the purpose of this essay, I will assume that the intended parents are the genetic parents, as is almost always the case under Israeli law—by law for the intended father and in practice for the intended mother as well (egg donations in Israel are extremely rare). Determining motherhood and the legal permissibility of gestational surrogacy is clearly a new dilemma for Jewish law, as the idea of a woman carrying a child who is not genetically related to her on behalf of intended parents is not something considered in the Jewish Talmudic tradition. However, modern-day halachic authorities and those who study Jewish law have found that determining motherhood and opining on the permissibility of gestational surrogacy are important for a number of reasons.[6]

First, Judaism is passed to a child through the mother, and thus identifying the mother has important practical ramifications in terms of the religious identity of the child. Second, the status of motherhood imposes legal rights and obligations in Jewish family law in terms of custody and support and thus must be identified. Third, surrogate motherhood raises broader ethical questions about the permissibility of selling gestational services or babies and the potential for exploitation of women who act as surrogates. Jewish law, with its broad ethical precepts, can weigh in on these important ethical conversations.

In this essay I will consider three questions regarding surrogate motherhood that demand resolution: (1) Should gestational surrogacy be permitted at all? (2) In a case where gestational surrogacy is permitted, who is the legal mother? (3) What is the status of the woman who is not defined as the legal mother, given her role in the complex surrogacy process? I will first describe these three questions in depth, explaining their legal and ethical ramifications and the dilemmas they pose. I will then consider what Jewish law principles and decisions offer in resolving these dilemmas. I will focus on Jewish law's emphasis on procreation, discussions surrounding defining motherhood in gestational surrogacy, and Jewish law's precepts regarding the importance of human dignity. I will consider practical Jewish law responses by prominent rabbis to gestational surrogate motherhood, which often involve recognition of multiple motherhood. I will then critique these responses, because multiple motherhood is only recognized for purposes of stringency in conversion and avoiding illegitimacy as opposed to affirmative recognition of the role of the surrogate, who instead has been ignored. I argue that these stringencies can make surrogacy difficult for intended parents without affirmatively protecting and acknowledging the status of the surrogate mother. I will then suggest how Jewish law's raising of the possibility of multiple motherhood can be used to provide an ethical solution to the dilemmas that this essay addresses by embracing multiple motherhood in a more holistic fashion.

In this essay, I offer a unique Jewish law perspective for resolving the three dilemmas I present as central to gestational surrogate motherhood. I argue that Jewish law perspectives on surrogate motherhood result in the naming of two mothers: the surrogate and the egg donor/intended mother. This is either a result of rabbincial authorities affirmatively recognizing two mothers, in practice, due to doubt as to which of the two is the legal mother or because there is a significant mix of opinion as to who is the legal mother, and therefore both women are considered mothers for Jewish law purposes. Recognition of two mothers under Jewish law principles can be seen as giving dignity to multiple women who are engaged in the process of procreation. Recognizing multiple mothers is progressive in nature and also conforms to traditional Jewish family law. When both the surrogate and the intended mother are recognized and dignified with status, the entire process of surrogacy is more in line with ethical standards and makes commercialization of surrogacy less problematic. And Jewish law can still condone contractual or court-ordered assignments of the duties of parenthood. Therefore, recognizing the status of two women does not foreclose the use of gestational surrogacy. Thereby, traditional Jewish family law can help resolve the dilemmas of families in transition, both facilitating new family forms and instilling these families with ethical recognition of all participants in a manner that promotes human dignity.

A. THE THREE DILEMMAS OF SURROGATE MOTHERHOOD

1. SHOULD COMMERCIAL SURROGACY BE PERMITTED?

The first dilemma is whether to allow surrogacy at all, in particular commercial surrogacy, which involves the payment of money to the surrogate mother as consideration for the effort of gestating the baby. While noncommercial altruistic surrogacy is practiced, such as between family members and close friends, it is much more widely practiced as a form of commerce, because purely altruistic surrogates are hard to locate and usually involve family members.[7] Moreover, in some countries such as Israel, commercial surrogacy is preferred for the professional and less familial nature of the surrogacy relationship.[8]

There has been ongoing global tension surrounding the permissibility of commercial surrogate motherhood.[9] While it is permissible in many states, there are others that oppose it. Surrogacy promises to fulfill the procreative desires of couples or individuals who struggle with infertility or are in need of a female womb to procreate. And worldwide there is a plethora of women who are willing to act as surrogates, carrying children for money. Gestational surrogacy has been practiced for many years, and there are low levels of litigation and high levels of satisfaction with the process.[10] Despite these benefits, there are a number of ethical reasons for which some countries oppose surrogate motherhood. Indeed, these ethical concerns have been extremely influential despite the practical benefits of surrogacy.

The first concern is that of commodification. The argument is that due to the alleged unsuitability of financial transactions in the intimate services of creating a baby, surrogacy should be banned or severely regulated.[11]

Creating a baby involves deeply personal and intimate processes that, some argue, should not be sold in the market. The nature of the intimacy in surrogate motherhood can be described on a number of interrelated levels. First, surrogate agreements involve a long-lasting and intense involvement in the bodily integrity of the surrogate. Surrogate contracts assert control over the lives of surrogates while they gestate; a surrogate's body is literally being used for someone else's purposes in a constant and inseparable manner.[12] Once a pregnancy is initiated, surrogates are literally trapped, physically, into their agreements and into their entangled relationship with intentional parents. Second, from a biological perspective, gestation involves a real biological interdependency over the course of forty weeks that affects both the fetus and the surrogate and should not be ignored.[13] The surrogate is affected on a constant basis by the fetus growing inside her and vice versa. Finally, this physical involvement and interrelatedness are coupled with long-lasting emotional connections.[14] Such emotional connectedness and the humanity involved in these commercial transactions can create high-level disputes and suffering. Surrogate mothers have reported feeling devastated when their involvement in the process is minimized. Gestating a fetus may not lead to motherhood, but it is also not like building a cabinet. Commercializing the singular, long-term nature of the gestational process is complex. When human life is changing hands, the nature of these transactions should be considered to ensure that the interests of the children and the parties involved are being protected.

Due to the intimacy involved in surrogacy, a major critique of commercializing surrogacy is that such a market inappropriately commodifies the human body as a form of baby selling or as a form of selling gestational services.[15] As one scholar puts it, by commercializing the womb, "we potentially do harm to ourselves and to human flourishing if we treat something integral to ourselves as a commodity, i.e., as separate and fungible."[16] Allowing ourselves and our body parts to be traded for money forces us to perceive ourselves in terms of our own monetary worth. Surrogates thus might view themselves and their bodies merely in terms of their saleable worth and not for their essential value as part of humanity. Thus, commercializing intimacy is critiqued as problematic, because selling intimacy compromises the personal and emotional nature of that intimacy and treats female body parts not as an end in themselves but as a means to an end. Moreover, it is argued that the intimate nature of the surrogacy relationship warrants consideration to protect vulnerable parties from the emotional harm that such intimate contracts can cause. As one scholar noted, the commissioning couple does not just enter into a contract with the surrogate: they embark on a relationship with her.[17] Human emotions, pain and suffering as well as joy, often revolve around commercial surrogate transactions and can be devastating to participants whose expectations are not met.

Another commonly voiced concern about surrogate motherhood is that it exploits poor women who do not have other means of earning money.[18] Commentators previously predicted that these contracts would employ poor women as an underclass for the privileged. Concerns are also expressed that brokers take advantage of surrogates and make too much money from the use of the surrogate's body.[19] Images of Brave New World scenarios in which the rich hire the poor to incubate their children with much sacrifice and little profit abound in reaction to surrogacy.[20]

An additional ethical objection raised is that of patriarchy. Some feminists argue that using a woman's body in order to produce children on behalf of a biologically related father subsumes a woman's body for patriarchal purposes. Radical feminists argue that the consent to carry children for intended parents is compromised by the patriarchal system in which surrogates live.[21] This critique is highly intertwined with the concerns about commodification of surrogates and their exploitation.

2. WHO IS THE LEGAL MOTHER IN SURROGACY?

Because gestational surrogate motherhood separates the two primary indicators of motherhood—birth (gestation) and genetic connection—much scholarly effort has been invested in identifying the legal mother when a child is born of gestational surrogacy.[22] Moreover, as engaging in a surrogacy contract involves intentional contracting to create a baby for specific parents, the issue of intent and contractual enforcement are also serious considerations.

Genetic connection is perhaps the most obvious choice for determining motherhood. It is how fatherhood is determined in modern times and therefore provides a gender-neutral indicator of parenthood.[23] Moreover, genetic connection has always been considered an essential indicator of parenthood, as creation of the child comes about by the mixing of sperm and egg. Therefore, it is many people's instinct to argue that it is genetic connection that determines parenthood. However, if genetics determines motherhood, then women who receive egg donations would not legally be considered mothers of the children they birth. Despite the woman giving birth and gestating the fetus for the entire pregnancy, the fact that the egg was not produced from her own body would negate her legal motherhood. In order to differentiate surrogacy from egg donations, legal standards must then rely on intent to determine motherhood. Moreover, focusing on intent as the indicator of motherhood would facilitate the use of traditional surrogacy in which the surrogate is also the genetic mother. Alternately, babies born from traditional surrogacy could be adopted by intended parents. Of course, if categorized as a full adoptive process, the surrogate would have the ability to retract her consent to relinquishing parental rights until after the birth of the child.[24]

Moreover, choosing genetics over gestation as the marker of parenthood ignores a uniquely feminine aspect of parenting: gestation.[25] Essentially, as fatherhood is defined by genetic affiliation, a focus on genetics assumes that motherhood originates from genetics as well, despite the more complex manner in which a mother-child relationship is traditionally formed. Ignoring gestation, a forty-week continuous process of physical nurturing and complex interdependence, fails to recognize an involved and biologically significant process that is uniquely feminine. This focus on gestation is not, as some critiques have argued, due to a belief that women should gestate their own children[26] but rather recognition of the unique and valuable contribution of gestation when it is provided.[27]

Attempts to point to intent as creating a legally identifiable motherhood relationship are difficult to distinguish from simply enforcing contractual agreements. And enforcing contractual agreements regarding motherhood seems to belie notions that such relationships should not be bought or sold in the marketplace.[28] For instance, in the seminal case of *Johnson v. Calvert,* the court determined that in the context of gestational surrogacy, natural motherhood should be based on intent and not as a matter of contract.[29] But there is no real logical distinction between determining motherhood based on preconception intent and determining motherhood based on a contract prepared to detail and certify such intent. The contract may not be enforceable per se according to the court, but if parenthood is based on intent, then it is the contract that will determine parenthood. The discomfort with contracting for parenthood in adoption and surrogacy cannot be hidden by the language of intent. Adoption and surrogacy are often distinguished, because while an adoptive baby would have been born regardless of the legal transfer of the baby, a baby born of surrogacy is conceived due to the contract. However, a baby conceived through sexual relations for the purpose of adoption would still be subject to adoption regulations. Thus, intent alone cannot distinguish adoption from surrogacy.

Intentional arguments for parenthood are also undermined in contexts in which, despite agreements, biological donors or surrogate mothers function as parental figures. For instance, in the case of *K. M. v. E. G.*, the egg donor, who was also the partner of the intended mother, agreed not to lay parental claims to the child in a clear and explicit agreement.[30] Yet, she raised the child with the intended mother after the children were born. Courts in such circumstances legitimately do not want to deny the genetic mother her attachment to the child. Ultimately, when intentions break down or when practices do not track contractual intentions, we are still left with the biological indicators of genetics and gestation, and such affinities persist. Although in *K. M.* the court attempts to differentiate between the contractual waiver of parental rights, which is invalidated, and intent to raise the children in a joint home, which is adopted as a crucial indicator of parenthood, this distinction is hard to decipher. And ultimately, it is the genetic relationship added to the joint parenthood that ensued that seems to persuade the court. Indeed, had E. G. waived parental rights and not raised the child with K. M., it is highly doubtful that she would have succeeded in her parental claim. Intent alone by contract is then rejected when other elements such as actual parenting and genetics are present. Surrogacy thus creates a puzzle without an easier answer. The bottom line is that intent, genetics, gestation, and functional care all matter in determining parental ties, and it is difficult and perhaps artificial to separate one out as the exclusive indicator of legal parenthood.[31]

However, while intellectually interesting, such puzzles do not make families. What creates families are emotional ties that are often based on genetics or gestation but are also based on intent and functioning as a parent. Usually it is only the intended parents who want to raise the child, and no one else claims any rights or is tagged with obligations. But other persons may be involved as well. Surrogate mothers, gamete donors, extended kin, grandparents, and third parties who function as parents because they believe they are or because they have taken upon themselves the responsibility to do so may all be involved in raising and providing for children in a variety of ways. The more important question is how to treat these more complex familial ties that do not conform to traditional notions of the nuclear family and two clear, biological, exclusive parental figures.

3. WHAT SHOULD THE STATUS OF THE SURROGATE BE IF SHE IS NOT CONSIDERED THE MOTHER?

The third dilemma in the context of surrogate motherhood is—even presuming that the intended parents are those who will raise the child, as they almost always do absent horror stories of intended parents who abandon handicapped children[32]—what is the status of the surrogate, how should she be treated, and what rights does she retain?

To truly consider this final dilemma, the history of surrogacy in countries that have allowed it and the social science data need to be analyzed to determine how surrogates manage the surrogacy process. Empirical studies, which have sought to track the realities, concerns, and overall experiences of surrogate mothers and intended parents, have coalesced around a number of basic and important findings.[33] While empirical studies have not been as numerous as one might have predicted given the onslaught of controversy and discussion surrounding surrogacy, a reasonable stockpile of empirical data has been compiled since 1983, when surrogacy emerged as a fertility option.[34] What is particularly striking about these empirical findings is their consistency.

On the one hand, according to empirical studies, overall levels of litigation have been low and levels of satisfaction with surrogacy high, attesting to the overall success of surrogates in detaching themselves from the babies they carry. The vast majority of surrogate mothers do not attest to bonding with the babies they gestate to the extent that many predicted.[35] While most surrogates assert that parting with the baby is a difficult separation, it does not appear to be as traumatic as expected. Indeed, given the thousands of surrogacy contracts that are entered into each year, the lack of litigation is remarkable.[36] When asked, surrogate mothers do not generally indicate that the babies belong to them; rather, they feel that they are providing a meaningful and valuable service for the intended parents. While this appears to be true for both gestational and traditional surrogates (who are also genetically related to the baby whom they care on behalf of intended parents), it seems especially true for gestational surrogates who do not have a genetic connection to the fetus, as they consider the baby in the womb to be someone else's based on genetic affiliation.[37]

On the other hand, the surrogates do not feel like legal strangers vis-à-vis the intended families either. Instead of the close bond that researchers expected surrogates to develop with the baby, the predicted emotional connection seems to be forming between the surrogate mother and the commissioning couple.[38]

Studies indicate that because pregnancy lasts nine months and prenatal care can be intensive and involved, it is the long-term engagement between surrogate and intended parents that creates emotional bonds, reflecting the very intimate nature of the agreement.[39] Surrogates and intended parents tend to experience the pregnancy and labor together and become emotionally and intimately involved in each other's daily lives and relationships. Moreover, many describe postbirth relationships that continue between the adults, which involve but are not necessarily focused on the baby.[40]

Indeed, it is this bond between the surrogate and the intended parents that appears difficult to erase after the birth of the baby and that may cause emotional heartache as well as logistical and legal complications.[41] When relationships are good, many surrogates express a high level of contentment with the process postbirth. They are most satisfied with the process when they develop a connection with intended parents whom they feel appreciate their important contribution in helping them to create a family.[42] The more such feelings are reciprocated and the better the relations between surrogate and intended parents, the better the surrogate tends to feel about her experience and the lower the level of distress or exploitations she reports. Empirical studies demonstrate that when surrogates feel that the intended parents are distant and that the level of relationship did not meet their expectations, the surrogates are likely to express dissatisfaction and frustration with the process, testifying to exploitation and low sense of self-worth. In the short term, many surrogates contend that it is important to see the child born of the agreement and to be acknowledged by the new family during and after the birth. But overall, surrogates' expectations appear to be that the relationship will last well past the birth, perhaps in perpetuity.

Many surrogates express that they want to feel appreciated and thanked for their investment in time and effort beyond receiving payment. While they work for money, many surrogates express altruistic motives as well, and no amount of money could fully compensate women for the level of commitment they must make. In describing their work, surrogate narratives use concepts of gift giving and mission to accentuate the more altruistic side of their endeavors and to de-emphasize the commercial contractual nature of their work. Evidence suggests that surrogates want to be acknowledged for the altruistic aspects of their actions as well as paid for the commercial aspects.[43]

In sum, commercial surrogates work for money but also create deep emotional attachments with intended families. How should the law or ethics treat these complex relationships? What protections exist for surrogates who form these attachments? Some legal systems try to separate the attachment from the work to the greatest extent possible by not allowing surrogates to interact with intended parents or the babies once they are involved. Others allow only altruistic surrogacy and expect that surrogates and intended families have ongoing familial or friend-based relationships. But can commercial surrogates be recognized for both the commercial service they provide and the intimate relationships that are involved?

B. JEWISH LAW PERSPECTIVES ON SURROGATE MOTHERHOOD

Jewish law has unique insights to contribute to these three dilemmas. First, Jewish law has a distinctly strong focus on procreation in relation to other interests. Second, unlike under secular legal systems, Jewish law cannot use intent or contract as an indicator of parenthood, which is a natural status with religious significance. Finally, Jewish law puts high emphasis on the human dignity of each man or woman.

1. BALANCING INTERESTS: THE STRONG RIGHT TO PROCREATE UNDER JEWISH LAW

As compared to other legal systems, Jewish law puts a very high value on procreation.[44] The Jewish law commandment to be fruitful and multiply found in the book of Genesis has been a major source of procreative energy for the Jewish people.[45] This commandment, which applies only to men because childbearing is considered to be a danger to women's health and thus cannot be commanded upon her, is usually understood to be fulfilled if a man fathers two children.[46] This commandment has been particularly influential in Jewish legal decisions. Indeed, the commandment has been used to stretch Jewish law to embrace the use of ART.[47] Since the inability to bear children is adequate grounds to divorce one's wife and failure to fulfill the commandment can be considered a serious infraction of Jewish law, using ART, including surrogacy, to reproduce the male seed has been accepted in many Jewish religious communities.[48] Israel's surrogate motherhood agreements law was one of the first and most progressive of its kind to officially sanction and enforce surrogate motherhood agreements.[49] The commandment upon men to reproduce led noted rabbinic leaders, such as Rabbi Nechemia Goldberg, to allow Orthodox couples to use surrogate mothers in Israel under the Surrogate Motherhood

Law, despite numerous important rabbinical authorities' expressed belief that it is the gestational, surrogate mother who is the legal mother under Jewish law.[50]

Thus, while other systems create a certain balance between the fear of commodification and exploitation and the value of procreation, under Jewish law it is logical that the balance be weighted toward procreation and allowing surrogacy. Family life and reproduction are essential, and a judgment can be made that the risks of exploitation and commodification can be borne and limited through regulation for the benefit of fulfilling religious commandments and sustaining religious life.

2. SPLIT OF OPINION OVER THE LEGAL DEFINITION OF MOTHERHOOD

The leniency in allowing surrogate motherhood in order to fulfill the commandment to procreate does not cancel the need to determine legal parentage under Jewish law. Under Jewish law, the establishment of parenthood relates to the fulfillment of halachic obligations, issues of personal status, and civil law. With regard to religious obligations, the issue of parentage is relevant for matters of the father's obligation to "be fruitful and multiply" and the obligation of the child to honor his or her parents. The personal status of the child is relevant for determining the permissibility of certain marriages (e.g., there are laws against incest). Parental status is also relevant for determining Jewish status, parental obligations to children in regard to custody and support, and issues of inheritance.[51]

Jewish law sources are divided on the issue of who is the legal mother: the woman whose egg produces the baby or the woman who gestates the baby. Some authorities consider the egg donor or genetic mother to be the legal mother. Rabbi Shlomo Goren bases his determination on an argument in the Talmud in which two voices argue as to the time when souls are given.[52] He concludes that the soul is given from the time of counting or numbering the intended persons and not from the time of their creation. Therefore, at the earliest stage possible, the time of insemination, the identity of the child is already determined by its genetic makeup. He also argues that fatherhood and motherhood are defined in the same manner, from the first drop of seed from both male and female upon fertilization. Rabbi Itamar Warhaftig also asserts that logically it is the egg donor and not the surrogate mother who should be considered the mother.[53] His logical basis for this conclusion is that it is the genes of the genetic mother and father that will determine the characteristics of the child and that the womb of the surrogate is nothing more than the place of growth. Furthermore, he argues that conceptually, if not practically as of yet, gestation could even be done in a laboratory. In his opinion, genes are the only essential human contribution.

Other authorities consider the gestational surrogate to be the legal mother of the child. Rabbi Zalman Nechemia Goldberg and Rabbi Eliezer Yehudah Calev are two significant authorities who have determined that the woman who gestates the fetus is the legal mother. Rabbi Goldberg looks to Talmudic sources to identify motherhood with birth.[54] The Talmud explains that twin brothers, who are non-Jews and subsequently convert, have no obligations in *chalizah* or *yibum* [levirate marriage] and are not obligated to refrain from marrying each other's wives because upon conversion to Judaism, all prior familial relationships are legally severed according to Jewish law. However, twins who were conceived when their parents were non-Jews and were born to a Jewish woman (she converts while she is pregnant) are not obligated in *chalizah* and *yibum* but are obligated not to marry each other's wives. Since motherhood is established upon birth, Rabbi Goldberg argues, the obligations that are derived from lineage to their mother still hold. If motherhood were determined by genetic input or upon conception, the conversion of the mother would have severed her ties to her children and their ties to each other. However, after the twins' birth they are still considered brothers from their maternal lineage in that they are prohibited from marrying each other's wives.

Alternately, Rabbi Calev and others point to an aggadic interpretation [homiletic tale] of the biblical story of Rachel and Leah.[55] The allegorical source refers to an intrauterine transfer of Dinah from the womb of Rachel to the womb of Leah and an intrauterine transfer of Joseph from the womb of Leah to the womb of Rachel. Subsequent references in Scripture refer to Dinah as the daughter of Leah and to Joseph as the son of Rachel, despite the supposed switch. Ostensibly, this tale indicates that each child has a single mother and that the mother is the birth mother, not the genetic mother. This analogy marks parturition rather than gestation or egg donation as the establishing variable of motherhood. While some authorities will not use allegory in matters of determining Jewish law, many other authorities have held that if the allegorical interpretation does not conflict with other legal sources, it is acceptable to learn from these sources. In addition, Rabbi Ezra Bick offers a conceptual orientation to the issue from a broad overview of Jewish law.[56] He posits that Jewish law should give special consideration to the legal status of the surrogate as the birth mother due to the law's sensitivity to and emphasis on the differences between men and women. This understanding provides a broader philosophical background to the more legalistic determinations that have been made.

Although establishing parenthood based on intent or contract is foreign to Jewish law,[57] contracts can be used to transfer obligations or appoint guardians.[58] However, even so, for issues of conversion and inheritance motherhood is inalienable.

Due to the conflict of opinions, both of which are based on insights by well-regarded rabbis and differing sources, ultimately both genetic and gestational mothers are considered to be legal mothers due to doubt and uncertainty. In practice, conversion is required both for children who are born of non-Jewish surrogates and for children who are born of non-Jewish egg donors.[59] In order to be sure that a child is Jewish and not of compromised personal status [*mamzerut*],[60] both women are deemed to be "mothers" for purposes of personal status (preventing incest) and religious identity.

Indeed, Rabbi Mosh Shternbach, a prominent jurist and halachic authority in the Ultra-Orthodox community in Jerusalem, has decreed that in the case of gestational surrogacy, both women must be considered legal mothers of the child.[61] His argument is not just due to uncertainty whereby both woman are considered mothers due to lack of clarity as to which of the two women is the legal mother; it is also due to an affirmative need to recognize both women as legal mothers. He argues that women have two parts in producing a child, providing the egg and birthing the child, and both create the motherhood status. He says that since both women create the child, both have the legal status of mother. Multiplying motherhood, according to Shternbach, is not a logical impossibility.

In American law, on the other hand, the idea of multiple motherhood is frowned upon because it potentially threatens and violates the exclusive parenthood rights of the intended mother in surrogacy.[62] In the United States, the right to conceive and to raise one's own children has been deemed essential by the U.S. Supreme Court. Raising one's own child is a matter of rights to the child, even if custody is ultimately decided according to a "best interests" standard.[63] Both parents have standing to assert their rights to custody of the child and have rights to visitation.

But under Jewish law, parenthood is less a right than an obligation, and thus violating parenthood rights is not a cause for concern.[64] Indeed, Michael Broyde writes that although rabbinic discussions on surrogate motherhood have centered on the definition of the legal mother for various ritual obligations, he argues that these ritual issues tend not to be the crucial ones to the couple or the surrogate mother seeking such children.[65]

Broyde argues that when maternal identity is legally in doubt or in dispute and paternal identity is established, maternal custody should be granted to the wife of the father regardless of who is determined to be the legal mother under Jewish law. He offers two basic rationales for this determination. First, the obligation to financially support children is assigned primarily to men. Second, he explains that basic custody law holds that child custody should be determined according to the best interests of the child. Given the reality in surrogate motherhood that the intended parents are those of greater means and have initiated the conception of the child, Broyde argues that it would almost always be in the child's best interest for the intended parents to have custody.

However, while the basic principles stated by Broyde above may be substantial enough to usually lead rabbinical figures to give custody of the child to the father, it should be pointed out that the presumptions of the Talmud are that under certain situations the legal mother would have sole custody of the child.[66] The Talmud embraces three rules that generally govern child custody, which are adjusted according to factual findings of best interests of the child. First, custody of all children under the age of six is to be given to the mother; second, custody of boys over the age of six is to be given to the father; and third, custody of girls over the age of six is to be given to the mother. Moreover, financial means are not the only factor in considering what custody arrangement is in a child's best interest.[67]

These three guidelines have been widely interpreted to be simply presumptions. Rather, the overarching standard for determining custody should be the best interests of the child as determined by the *beit din.*[68] And under a best interests analysis that does not have to bend to parental rights, Jewish law authorities can be creative in custodial provisions that ensure what is best for the child.[69] Broyde's claim that the best interests of the child will always be with the legal father and intended mother is controversial even if usually accurate. It may be best for a child to have connections with all three biological parents, even if the primary duty of support rests with the father. Empirical studies do support that as long as tension levels are not high, multiple caregivers can be good for children's interests.[70] Most studies refer to mothers and fathers, but if other potential caregivers are available to give care and such care is helpful and not causing strife, there is support indicating that multiple caregivers beyond parents are good for children.[71] Not all parents are able to care for children, and many other kind family members or third parties take up significant portions of the obligations of custodial care. Here, we are dealing only with the possibility of two mother figures with potential obligations. Given that the obligation to parent and support a child can be divided or upheld by one of two parents and that multiplying parenthood is not a violation of exclusive rights, Jewish law seems well placed for engaging multiple parental figures. According to Rabbi Shternbach, because both women are legal parents, both could have the obligations of motherhood, and the child would have rights and obligations to both mothers.

Recognizing gestation as relevant to creating motherhood as opposed to intent or genetics is a contribution from Jewish law that is relatively rare. For the most part, gestational surrogates are treated by legal systems as incubators and wombs for hire.[72] Recognizing the biological, involved, and significant contribution that gestation plays in creating a child provides valuable insight from Jewish law. The emphasis on the unique contribution of gestation in Jewish law could serve as a solid platform for recognizing the role of surrogate mothers and giving credence to the importance of pregnancy and childbearing, the biological domain of women.

3. THE IMPORTANCE OF HUMAN DIGNITY IN JEWISH LAW

Human dignity is a central tenet of Jewish law. In the beginning of the book of Genesis we learn that man is created in God's image.[73] This is expressed in various more specific laws, including the obligation to respect the dead, to respect the human body, and to treasure every human life even if commandments need to be broken. Even prisoners and slaves must be treated with dignity under Jewish law.[74] Man is created in God's image, and thus each man must be treated with dignity and sanctity. Moreover, each man has a separate identity and significance in and of himself.[75] The Mishnah tells us that if one man is lost, it is as if the whole world is lost, and for every man who is saved, it is as if the whole world is saved.[76] It is as if the whole world was created for each individual man. This idea of the individual worth of each man has also been used to derive the principle of equality between men in Jewish law.

Moreover, respecting human dignity is not just a right belonging to the individual; it is a duty upon each individual to preserve one's own health as well as the lives of others.[77] It is even a duty upon the individual who would otherwise prefer to denigrate himself for money or other ends. Thus, a man is not allowed to harm himself or his own body. In Jewish law a man cannot actively cause his own death even if he is suffering and on his deathbed.[78]

Accordingly, it is important that the surrogate, as a human, be treated with dignity and be protected from shame, vulnerability, and heartbreak due to the surrogacy arrangement. It is not worthy for humans to be treated as wombs for rent or as commodities—each man must be treated as an end in himself, not just a means of production. Just as people cannot sell themselves into permanent servitude under Jewish law, a surrogate cannot sell her self-worth and dignity.

However, in Jewish law the idea of human dignity is not essentially tied to commodification. Human dignity can be preserved despite commercialization. For instance, in Jewish law, baby selling is less problematic than in other legal systems. Prohibitions against the selling of a person in Jewish law relate to the selling of a person into servitude.[79] In surrogacy arrangements, the child is not sold into slavery, and neither is the surrogate. Ostensibly, the prohibition against receiving money for the sale of persons is based on a fear of control over another human being in slavery and is not a blanket prohibition against transferring a child for consideration, and renting out a womb is not impermissible.[80]

Still, human dignity can be protected through regulations that recognize status and limitations on commodification so as to prevent the woman from being sold into servitude. She must retain sufficient autonomy over herself and be treated with dignity. This can be accomplished through regulations that limit the nature of surrogacy arrangements and how much control of herself she can agree to forfeit—human dignity is a duty and a right, and even if willing, no one can forfeit the right in a contract to refuse to live with dignity—as well as to refuse medical treatment if unwanted, to eat and sleep in a manner that is comfortable, or to give birth naturally instead of through medical intervention. Surrogacy arrangements have confined a woman's ability to travel and have demanded that she live in hostels, eat prescribed foods, and take prescribed medications.[81] Surrogacy arrangements preclude natural birth childbirth and even medical treatment that prioritizes the life of the fetus over the life of the surrogate.[82] Such contractual provisions or surrogacy arrangements should be regulated in order to preserve the dignity of the surrogate.

C. CRITIQUE OF THE JEWISH LAW PERSPECTIVE

The religious Jewish community, even the Ultra-Orthodox community, has, under certain circumstances, permitted surrogacy in order to allow infertile couples to procreate and fulfill their religious obligations. The Israel Surrogate

Agreements Law contains many provisions that attempt to incorporate aspects of Jewish law in order to avoid problems that might arise within the religious communities in Israel.[83] In Israel, surrogate motherhood has been expressly permitted by some of the most respected rabbinic authorities. Both the Sephardic chief rabbi, Rabbi Bakshi Doron, and Rabbi Zalman Nechemia Goldberg, a rabbinical court judge and highly regarded halachic *posek,* have given their approval to the law.[84] Rabbi Borshtein, director of the Puah Institute of Halachah and Reproductive Technology in Jerusalem, has stated that under his guidance a number of women have received private permission from various Orthodox halachic authorities, permitting the procedure and contract as it is designated in Israeli law.[85] In fact, the first couple to use the Israeli Surrogate Contracts law was a religious couple. However, others have voiced objections to the surrogate motherhood process due to misgivings about alienating child rearing from the sanctity of marriage and the marital bed and out of concern about the technology that facilitates it.[86]

In a private meeting with the Surrogate Agreements Approvals Committee appointed by the law, Rabbi Zalman Nechemia Goldberg explicitly condoned the law and made no mention of the surrogate mother's rights or claims to the child.[87] When asked by the committee who is the mother in a case of gestational surrogacy where the intended mother has donated her ovum, Rabbi Goldberg responded that this is a new issue and must be determined on the basis of analogies to related sources of halachah but cannot be determined with full certainty.[88] Therefore, he insisted that both mothers need to be treated as mothers for the sake of lineage to avoid any determination of *mamzerut.*[89] When asked whether he would permit a woman who sought his approval to use a surrogate mother, he answered that he would allow it if the woman could not have a child otherwise.[90] While Rabbi Zalman Nechemia Goldberg's conversation with the committee is the only written acceptance of the Israeli law by a renowned authority on Jewish law, there is an understanding among the religious communities that such procedures may be permissible, depending on a couple's specific circumstances and with direct approval of a rabbinic authority.

Although Jewish law authorities have recognized the surrogate mother as a legal mother, they have been willing to allow surrogacy despite the surrogate's potential status. The obligations and concerns of lineage can be managed and dealt with in order to allow fulfillment of the command to procreate. Motherhood status is natural and inalienable but can still be managed in the context of potential complications. Although halachic authorities could have insisted on recognizing the surrogate as the legal mother and perhaps having a formal adoption or guardianship process set up to transfer obligations, such formalities have been overlooked in accepting the Israeli law.[91]

Indeed, while allowing surrogacy, Jewish law authorities have not given much thought to what would become of these second mothers. Even if their motherhood is somehow recognized for purposes of conversion or the ability to marry and the status of *mamzerut*,[92] no positive position has been taken in order to recognize and protect these women from potential commodification or exploitation. According to significant Jewish authority, these women are mothers of the children they bear, yet rabbis seem more concerned about lineage, marital status, and whether or not the child is Jewish than in considering how to protect the woman who is a legal mother of the child, even if the intended mother is also a mother. Could she have rights to custody or visitation? Does she have a right to see the child? Could she be obliged to care for or support the child? Must contracts ensure that her dignity and humanity are preserved? What specifically does the need to protect the surrogates' dignity mean under Jewish law? These more human aspects of surrogacy are not spoken of by Jewish law authorities despite the surrogate's status as legal mother. While part of Jewish law concerns must contend with legal status and Jewish identity, it is disappointing that the recognition of multiple motherhood in this context has not been used to also explore the emotional impact of surrogacy on the surrogate mother and to protect her dignity in the process.

D. GUIDELINES FOR RESOLUTION BASED ON JEWISH LAW PRINCIPLES

As described above, Jewish law provides certain solutions for the three dilemmas of gestational surrogacy that I have posed. Jewish law would lead to the conclusions that commercial surrogacy should be allowed but only to resolve infertility in particular cases and only if the surrogate is property recognized and protected. The legal mother according to Jewish law is perhaps surprisingly best understood as being both women, and multiplying motherhood is not particularly problematic under Jewish law. Complications of having multiple natural mothers must be dealt with in any event, and any support and custodial obligations can in theory be divided and multiplied as well. Finally, as all persons must be treated with dignity, the surrogate, who is also a legal mother, should be protected and given recognition for her status and emotional attachments with the intended family.

However, Jewish authorities have been more concerned with preserving a child's status and Jewish identity than with recognizing the legal status and dignity of the surrogate. Jewish sources, however, provide good reason to recognize and protect the surrogate and can be relied upon to create a humane and regulated surrogacy system.

Under Jewish law, there are essentially two categories of ramifications for legal parenthood, the first technical and the second human. The first category concerns the status of the child and his or her Jewish identity and ability to marry under Jewish law—*mamzerut.* These are basically technical concerns due to the status of the surrogate as a mother that need to be dealt with to preserve the Jewish identity and personal status of the child. The second category concerns more human issues regarding the relationship of the surrogate to the child and intended family as well as her human dignity as a legal mother.

Jewish law already has recognized two mothers for the sake of personal status and Jewish identity. Jewish families who use non-Jewish surrogates or non-Jewish egg donors must convert their children to Judaism, according to most halachic authorities. Converting a baby to Judaism, at least in accordance with Orthodox restrictions that monopolize conversions in Israel, is not a simple procedure.[93] Generally, the parents must promise to raise the child in an observant Jewish environment, providing Jewish education and exposure to Jewish practice. For secular Jews, getting through this process of conversion can prove difficult.[94] And without conversion, these babies will not be able to marry in Israel. Even if heterosexual couples can succeed in navigating this process, homosexual couples, frequent users of international surrogacy, may experience more difficulties. Moreover, in order to avoid the status of *mamzer,* which would also make the child unable to marry under Jewish law, both women are considered mothers and thus cannot be related to the other (i.e., kin cannot act as surrogates for their kin). This first category of ramifications of multiplying motherhood creates hardship and confusion for those using surrogacy to procreate and puts burdens on parents to protect the personal status of the child born of surrogacy.

The second category of ramifications of the surrogate as legal mother should also be considered under Jewish law. This second category of ramifications regards the duty and rights of the legal mother and the dignity of the surrogate as a legal mother. As a legal mother, the surrogate may have duties imposed upon her for the care of the child. As there are two mothers and presumably also a father, such duties would be divided among the legal parents. As discussed above, the legal father has the primary financial duty toward his young children, but mothers also have duties of financial support and of care.[95] These duties can be contracted away to a willing person but not before the child is born, because that child would not yet be in existence. Under Jewish law a contract cannot be made for a thing that is not yet in existence.[96] Moreover, if the child becomes needy, such contracts would not be enforceable, as the child must be financially supported by his or her legal parents.[97]

With regard to custody, under Jewish law the principle of best interests governs, although for younger children a mother is presumed to be the best caregiver.[98] Even if a surrogate is recognized as a second mother, a surrogate would not be the sole or even primary custodial parent. Presumably, as per the contract, the intended parents would support and raise the child as primary custodians. If a dispute arose, the intended parents would likely win primary custody under a best interests analysis.[99] This may not always be the case, depending on the circumstances.

However, what of the possibility in Jewish law for multiple custodians? Even if one parent receives the primary custodial obligation, contact or visitation with other parents or kin can be relevant in making custodial arrangements under a best interests standard.[100] A surrogate could be given visitation or allowed contact with a child or even be appointed as a guardian of the child. A surrogate has a potential duty to the child and so may be recognized as a secondary guardian or secondary custodian.

A guardian under Jewish law is usually a legal parent but can be another kin appointed to care for and support the child.[101] And a guardian need not be the primary custodian of the child but can be another kin relation who manages the child's affairs.[102] Often a guardian is a kin of the child in times of crisis who has the ability to manage the assets of the child. Jewish courts prefer kin to act as guardians as opposed to strangers.[103] While authorities used to prohibit appointing a woman, even a mother, as guardian, modern authorities recognize women's and mothers' authority as guardians of their children.[104] Such guardianship or custody can also be based on emotional attachments that serve the best interests of the child.[105] While such possibilities for legal status unrelated to financial duties have not been fully developed under Jewish law by halachic authorities, the potential exists within the Jewish law framework for multiple guardians and custodians in complex situations, and kin relations are given priority over legal strangers.[106] Indeed, it has been said that a person who takes upon himself to care for a child may obtain the benefit of being a guardian to that child.[107] Accordingly, a surrogate who takes upon herself the task of gestating that child and thereby becoming a legal mother may claim a benefit of being a guardian to that child. Because the best interests standard has been increasingly relevant under Jewish law and because Jewish law courts have discretion to appoint guardians in children's best interests, such a possibility exists.[108]

There is also little discussion of visitation rights under Jewish law, as custody is considered an obligation and not a right. However, Jewish courts applying Jewish law regularly award visitation to a noncustodial parent under a best interests standard. Custodial decisions are based on best interests and not rights. However, if contact with multiple caregivers is deemed to be best for children, visitation arrangements can be ordered by Jewish law courts. And contact with multiple caring maternal figures may be good for children depending on the situation, particularly if the parties can work in a cooperative manner. If the surrogate had already developed connections with the child through consent of the intended parents, a court could consider awarding visitation rights to this second mother in the best interests of the child.

However, the possibility that the surrogate could be a legal guardian or have legal visitation rights imposed upon unwilling intended parents is unlikely under a best interests standard, given current social norms about the importance of two parents and the nuclear family. Most likely, as with an aunt or other relative, the surrogate would be dependent on the consent of primary custodians to have access to the child if she wanted it. Even without her legal rights of custody, being explicit about her status as a secondary legal mother can affect the nature of her relationship to the intended family and the child. According to the empirical studies cited above, the mere recognition that surrogates are more than a disposable womb for hire and have made a serious contribution to the creation of the baby and thus are worthy of respect and acknowledgement would likely be sufficient to cure the sense of abandonment, frustration, and exploitation that surrogates feel. Surrogates indicate that they expect a continued relationship with the intended family as a natural consequence of strong relationships that developed during the surrogacy process. As a secondary kin figure to the baby, recognized according to the law as much more than a mere incubator but as a second mother, such a relationship becomes more acceptable and reasonable. Following the lead of Jewish law and recognizing the significant contribution of the surrogate in a regulated and limited way can be used to resolve the dilemma of the emotional attachments formed during surrogacy. Unlike Western values that perceive such recognition as a violation of parental rights, the duties involved to bring children into the world and raise them should not involve excluding other important figures in a child's life.

Of course, best interests with regard to custody governs. And if the surrogate and the intended parents are in tension regarding the surrogate's role, then involving the surrogate in a continued manner in the child's life against the objections of the father and his wife could be problematic. However, affirmative recognition of the status of the surrogate as secondary mother or kin under Jewish law can enable recognition and encourage good relations between the parties.

Although her status as a second legal mother can feel threatening to the procreating intended parents, almost like a concubine or second wife must have been threatening to a primary wife in biblical times or perhaps in polygamous relationships even in modern times, the duties involved under Jewish law are to procreate and to raise the child appropriately. And as discussed above, she is unlikely to have legal rights that she could impose on the custodial father and mother. Still, the presence of a third party in the process is due to infertility, and the presence of the third party cannot be erased even if it would be emotionally easier. The surrogate needs to be acknowledged, protected, and included in the process as a partner and not treated as a disposable incubator. This is a complex family system, no doubt, but so is the surrogacy process itself. And pretending that the surrogate does not exist as a human partner and does not continue to exist after the child's birth may simplify the process for intended parents but does not give sufficient heed to the relevance of the gestating surrogate and her dignity.

Moreover, the Jewish law principle of human dignity demands the surrogate's recognition, protection, and inclusion. Recognition, protection, and inclusion humanize the surrogate and make her relevant not just for personal status and conversion issues but also as a human involved in the process of procreation. Human dignity is not respected if a person is used as a mere womb and then discarded. Jewish law authorities should not be concerned only with possible religious infractions and assuring personal status of the child but should also be concerned with protecting and recognizing the surrogate and her status as secondary mother in the process of gestational surrogacy. Contractual provisions should ensure her dignity and humanity under Jewish law. Contractual provisions that excessively constrain her freedom, demean her, or fail to sufficiently account for her role in the procreation by not allowing her to even see the baby should not be tolerated.

E. CONCLUSION

Jewish family law, like any system of family law, must recognize complex family networks in the modern era. Based on tradition, Jewish law can be used to widen its scope to enlighten families in transition.

In this essay, I rely on Jewish law for inspiration and seek creative resolution to complex problems. I pose dilemmas that exist in modern, secular thinking about surrogacy and then look to Jewish law principles to seek resolutions. I am not descriptively seeking to answer concrete problems in the manner of religious *poskim* or to describe their positions based on their religious authority. However, I rely on the principled decisions of such authorities to ask questions and resolve ethical tensions and dilemmas. I suggest solutions based on Jewish law principles that can enlighten and enrich our thinking about these dilemmas. Thereby, I look at Jewish law principles broadly and suggest resolutions for modern families that I believe can be derived from Jewish law. And I also criticize current narrow thinking about the relevance of Jewish law and suggest that the inquiries and resolutions be carried further.

I acknowledge that I am attempting to bridge modern intellectual inquiries and empirical studies with traditional halachic decision making that is made on a case-by-case basis and that such a bridge may seem irrelevant or ephemeral. Such inquiries, however, can provide powerful insight for resolution of modern dilemmas. The line between law and ethics, as well as principle and legal decision, is not necessarily black and white. Beyond providing concrete solutions in divorce and marriage law, Jewish law and ethics can be a guiding force for the resolution of modern dilemmas in Jewish family law. Jewish law can preserve its traditional precepts while still inspiring the modern family in transition.

NOTES

1. See Rabbinical Court Jurisdiction (marriage and divorce) Law 7 L.S.I.139 clause 1–3 (1953) (Isr.). Rabbinic courts have exclusive jurisdiction over matters of personal status; see the Rabbinical Court Jurisdiction (Marriage and Divorce) Law 7 L.S.I.139 (1953), clause 2, 3. Rabbinical courts also have concurrent jurisdiction on the request of the wife in maintenance claims that are not part of a divorce settlement. Questions of paternity, however, have been held not to be under concurrent jurisdiction; see *HCJ 283/72 Buaron v. The Rabbinical Tribunal,* 26(2) P.D. 727 (1972) (Isr.); for interesting discussions of the interaction between Jewish law and Israeli law, see generally Brayahy Lifshitz, "Israeli Law and Jewish Law—Interaction and Independence," *Israel Law Review* 24 (1990): 507;

Itzchak Englard, "The Place of Religious Law in the Israel Legal System," *Mishpatim* 2 (1970): 291 [in Hebrew] (translated by the author); Pinchas Shifman, "Family Law in Israel: The Struggle between Religious and Secular Law," *Hebrew University of Israel Legal Research Paper* (1995): 36–52 [in Hebrew] (translated by the author).

2. Mishnah *Yevamot* VI: 6 or B; Talmud *Yevamot* 61b; *Sefer Hachinuch,* Commandment 1, based on Genesis 1:28: "And God blessed them and said to them be fruitful and multiply." The details of this commandment, how many children and of what sex, are discussed in the Talmud, Tractate *Yevamot,* chap. 6: 61, p. 2, and in *Berachot* 15:1; Pinhas Shifman, "A Perspective on Surrogate Motherhood in Jewish Law," in *Frontiers of Family Law* (1993), chap. 5 [in Hebrew] (translated by author); Pinhas Shifman, "New Reproductive Technologies and Jewish Law," *Jewish Law Annual* 12 (1994): 133. According to most sources, a man must have one male and female child to fulfill the commandment. See Turei Zahav, Eben Ezra A:7; Questions and Answers by Peri Yitzcah 41 [Hebrew]. Daniel Sperling, "Commanding the 'Be Fruitful and Multiply' Directive: Reproductive Ethics, Law and Policy in Israel," *Cambridge Quarterly Healthcare Ethics* 19 (2010): 363–71.

3. See, e.g., Zalman Nechemia Goldberg, "On Donating Eggs, Surrogacy, Frozen Sperm of a Single Man, and Using Sperm of the Dead," *Asia A-B* 17 (Spring 1999): 45.

4. Menachem Elon, *The Principles of Jewish Law* (New York: Keter, 1975), 435; Noam Zohar, "Artificial Insemination and Surrogate Motherhood," *S'vara* 2:13 (1991) [in Hebrew]; "When the Child Falls through a Loophole in Jewish Law," *Haaretz* (June 17, 2002) [in Hebrew]; Rebecca L. Reichman, "The Rabbinic Conception of Conception: An Exercise in Fertility," in *Jewish Law and the New Reproductive Technologies* (ed. Emanuel Feldman and Joel Wolowelsky; New York: Keter, 1997), 1; Avraham Steinberg, *Encyclopedia of Jewish Medical Ethics* (New York: Feldheim, 1991), 118, 157a.

5. Ezra Bick, "Ovum Donations: A Rabbinic Conceptual Model," in *Jewish Law and the New Reproductive Technologies* (ed. Emanuel Feldman and Joel Wolowelsky; New York: Keter, 1997), 83–85. He argues that traditional sources cannot definitely solve all modern legal dilemmas of ART.

6. Susan Martha Kahn, *Reproducing Jews: A Cultural Account of Assisted Conception in Israel* (Durham: Duke University Press, 2000), 140–59.

7. In England, only noncommercial is permitted; see Surrogacy Arrangements Act 1985 and Human Fertilization and Embryology Act 1990. Karen Busby and Delaney Vun, "Revisiting the Handmaid's Tale: Feminist Theory Meets Empirical Research on Surrogate Mothers," *Canadian Journal of Family Law* 26 (2010): 82, describe how Canadians look abroad to find commercial surrogates.

8. *Liat Moshe v. the Approvals Committee for Embryo Carrying Agreements,* Bagatz 5771/12 (2013) (Hebrew). This describes the surrogacy process in Israel as one intended to create a professional distance between surrogate and intended parents.

9. Erin Nelson, "Global Trade and Assisted Reproduction Technologies: Regulatory Challenges in International Surrogacy," *Journal of Law and Medical Ethics* 41 (2013):

248; April Cherry, "The Rise of the Reproductive Brothel in the Global Economy: Some Thoughts on Reproductive Tourism, Autonomy and Justice," *University of Pennsylvania Journal of Law & Social Change* 17 (2014): 283–85.

10. J. Herbie DiFonzo and Ruth C. Stern, "The Children of Baby M.," *Capital University Law Review* 39 (2011): 357.

11. Sonia M. Suter, "Giving In to Baby Markets: Regulation without Prohibition," *Michigan Journal of Law and Gender* 16 (2009): 222; Margaret Jane Radin, "Market-Inalienability," *Harvard Law Review* 100 (1987): 1930–36.

12. Morgan Holcomb and Mary Patricia Byrn, "When Your Body Is Your Business," *Washington Law Review* 85 (2010): 657. "Provisions such as the specifics of the IVF treatment, prenatal care, and whether the intended parents can attend medical appointments are incorporated into the contract to reinforce that, while the surrogate may be the one carrying the child, it is not her pregnancy. From the parties' perspectives, the pregnancy belongs to the intended parents and the surrogate is hired to provide a valuable service."

13. *Gleitman v. Cosgrove,* 227 A.2d 689 (N.J. 1967), which discusses effects of rubella on the fetus; Cori S. Annapolen, "Maternal Smoking during Pregnancy: Legal Responses to the Public Health Crisis," *Virginia Journal of Social Policy and Law* 12 (2005): 744; Michelle Oberman, "Sex, Drugs, Pregnancy, and the Law: Rethinking the Problems of Pregnant Women Who Use Drugs," *Hastings Law Journal* 43 (1992): 505; Robert Martone, "Scientists Discover Children's Cells Living in Mothers' Brains," *Science America* (December 4, 2012), http://www.scientificamerican.com/article.cfm?id=scientists-discover-childrens-cells-living-in-mothers-brain; Nancy Shute, "Beyond Birth: A Child's Cells May Help or Harm the Mother Long after Delivery," *Science America* (April 30, 2010), http://www.scientificamerican.com/article.cfm?id=fetal-cells-microchimerism (this describes a process of cellular exchange between gestating mother and fetus known as microchimerism). See also Catherine Arcabascio, "Chimeras: Double the DNA—Double the Fun for Crime Scene Investigators, Prosecutors, and Defense Attorneys?," *Akron Law Review* 40 (2007): 435, 439.

14. Elly Teman, *Birthing a Mother: The Surrogate Body and the Pregnant Self* (Berkeley: University of California Press, 2010), 31–68, describes in great detail her in-depth interviews with more than twenty-six gestational surrogates and over forty-three intended families over a period of eight years. See also Hal B. Levine, "Gestational Surrogacy: Nature and Culture in Kinship," *Ethnology* (Summer 2003): 173–75; Olga B. A. van den Akker, "A Longitudinal Pre-Pregnancy to Post-Delivery Comparison of Genetic and Gestational Surrogate and Intended Mothers: Confidence and Genealogy," *Journal of Psychosomatic Obstetrics & Gynecology* 26 (2005): 281. Hazel Baslington, "The Social Organization of Surrogacy: Relinquishing a Baby and the Role of Payment in the Psychological Detachment Process," *Journal of Health Psychology* 7 (2002): 58, 64–67, describes the thesis of maternal-fetal detachment during commercial surrogacy, noting the strong relationships developed with infertile couples using the concept of deflection. See also Melinda M. Hohman and Christina B. Hagan, "Satisfaction with Surrogate Mothering: A Relational

Model," *Journal of Human Behavior and Social Environment* 4 (2001): 67–69, 81–82; Helena Ragoné, "Chasing the Blood Tie: Surrogate Mothers, Adoptive Mothers and Fathers," *American Ethnologist* 23 (1996): 359–62.

15. Margaret Jane Radin, *Contested Commodities* (Cambridge: Harvard University Press, 1996), 137–38. See also Michael J. Sandel, "What Money Can't Buy: The Moral Limits of Markets," in *The Tanner Lectures on Human Values,* Vol. 21 (ed. Grethe B. Peterson; Salt Lake City: University of Utah Press, 2000), 94–95; Glenn I. Cohen, "The Price of Everything, the Value of Nothing: Reframing the Commodification Debate," *Harvard Law Review* 117 (2003): 693; Jill Elaine Hasday, "Intimacy and Economic Exchange," *Harvard Law Review* 119 (2005): 493–96.

16. Suter, "Giving In to Baby Markets," 222; Radin, "Market-Inalienability," 1930–36.

17. See Jennifer A. Parks, "Care Ethics and the Global Practice of Commercial Surrogacy," *Bioethics* 24 (2010): 335.

18. Ruth Macklin, "Is There Anything Wrong with Surrogate Motherhood: An Ethical Analysis," in *Surrogate Motherhood: Politics and Privacy* (ed. Lawrence O. Gostin: Bloomington: Indiana University Press 1990), 136, 141–42; Christine Overall, *Ethics and Human Reproduction: A Feminist Analysis* (Crows Nest, Australia: Allen & Unwin, 1987): 118, 124–26; Janice G. Raymond, "Reproductive Gifts and Gift Giving: The Altruistic Woman," *Hastings Center Report* (November–December 1990): 7, 11.

19. Anne Donchin, "Reproductive Tourism and the Quest for Global Gender Justice," *Bioethics* 24 (2010): 328.

20. Aldous Huxley, *Brave New World* (New York: HarperCollins, 1932).

21. Andrea Dworkin, *Right-Wing Women* (New York: Perigee, 1983), 176–85.

22. A large number of articles have considered this dilemma, advocating one definition over another. Martha Field, *Surrogate Motherhood: The Legal and Human Issues* (Cambridge: Harvard University Press, 1988), argues for a best interests test with a presumption of maternal custody in traditional surrogacy. Scott B. Rae, *The Ethics of Commercial Surrogate Motherhood: Brave New Families?* (New York: Praeger, 1993), argues that the woman who gives birth to the child should be considered the legal mother of the child. Barbara Katz Rothman, *Recreating Motherhood* (New Brunswick: Rutgers University Press 1989), argues that the essential maternal tie is based on carrying the child in pregnancy.

23. Marjorie Maguire Shultz, "Reproductive Technology and Intent-Based Parenthood: An Opportunity for Gender Neutrality," *Wisconsin Law Review* (1990): 309.

24. ARIZ. REV. STAT. ANN. § 8–107(B) (1989) (West): consent valid only seventy-two hours after birth; *In re Timothy W.,* 223 Cal. App. 3d 437, 445 (Cal. Ct. App. 1990), which holds that when a birth mother has formally refused to give her consent, the court shall order the adoptive parents to relinquish the child; Carol Sanger, "Separating from Children," *Columbia Law Review* 96 (1996): 444.

25. See *Soos v. Superior Court,* 897 P.2d 1356, 1358–59 (Ariz. Ct. App. 1994), which holds that viewing gestation as opposed to genetics as the indicator of parenthood is not a violation of equal protection due to the differences between sexes in procreation. Field (*Surrogate Motherhood,* 123–25) discusses differences between gestation and artificial insemination by donor and the legal and practical differences between mothers and fathers at the moment when a child is born. See also Rothman, *Recreating Motherhood.*

26. Noa Ben-Asher, "The Curing Law: The Evolution of Baby-Making Markets," *Cardozo Law Review* 30 (2009): 1914.

27. Susan Frelich Appleton, "Presuming Women: Revisiting the Presumption of Legitimacy in the Same-Sex Couples Era," *Boston University Law Review* 86 (2006): 275–76; Jennifer S. Hendricks, "Essentially a Mother," *William and Mary Journal of Women and the Law* 13 (2007): 430–31, 474–78.

28. For a discussion of what is wrong with baby selling, see Radin, *Contested Commodities,* 137–38. "If we permit babies to be sold, we commodify not only the mother's (and father's) babymaking capacities—which might be analogous to commodifying sexuality—but also the baby herself. . . . Commodifying babies leads us to conceive of potentially all personal attributes in market rhetoric, not merely those of sexuality. Moreover, to conceive of infants in market rhetoric is likewise to conceive of the people they will become in market rhetoric, and this might well create in those people a commodified self-conception." See also Margaret Jane Radin, *What, If Anything, Is Wrong with Baby Selling?;* 26 PAC. L.J. 135, 144–45 (1995); and Margaret Jane Radin, *Reinterpreting Property* (Chicago: University of Chicago Press, 1993), 163–69.

29. *Johnson v. Calvert,* 851 P.2d 776 (Cal. 1993), cert. denied, 114 S. Ct. 206 (1993); *In re Marriage of Buzzanca,* 72 Cal. Rptr. 2d 280, 288–91 (Cal. Ct. App. 1998), which declared that when a child is conceived by implanting anonymously donated sperm and egg, the intended mother as expressed in the surrogacy contract—not the surrogate or the unknown egg donor—is the lawful mother.

30. *K. M. v. E. G.,* 117 P.3d 673, 675–76 (Cal. 2005).

31. See Pamela Laufer-Ukeles, "Mothering for Money: Regulating Commercial Intimacy," *Indiana Law Journal* 88 (2014): 1255–59.

32. Eric Blyth, "Baby Gammy: The Responsibilities of ART Professionals in International Surrogacy," *BioNews* 767 (August 18, 2014), http://www.bionews.org.uk/page_446406.asp.

33. Laufer-Ukeles, "Mothering for Money," 1230–35.

34. See Janice C. Ciccarelli and Linda J. Beckman, "Navigating Rough Waters: An Overview of Psychological Aspects of Surrogacy," *Journal of Social Issues* (2005): 22–24, reporting twenty-seven empirical studies from January 1983 to December 2003.

35. Teman, *Birthing a Mother,* 31–68, describes in great detail her in-depth interviews with more than twenty-six gestational surrogates and over forty-three intended families over a period of eight years. See also Hal B. Levine, "Gestational Surrogacy: Nature and Culture in Kinship," *Ethnology* (Summer 2003): 173, 175; van den Akker, "A Longitudinal

Pre-Pregnancy to Post-Delivery Comparison," 281; Baslington, "The Social Organization of Surrogacy," 64–67; Hohman and Hagan, "Satisfaction with Surrogate Mothering," 81–82; Ragoné, "Chasing the Blood Tie," 359–62.

36. See, for example, J. Herbie DiFonzo and Ruth C. Stern, "The Children of Baby M.," *Capital University Law Review* 39 (2011): 357.

37. See Olga van den Akker, "Genetic and Gestational Surrogate Mothers' Experience of Surrogacy," *Journal Reproduction and Infant Psychology* 21 (2003): 147.

38. See, for example, Teman, *Birthing a Mother,* 42–47, 205–29; Baslington, "The Social Organization of Surrogacy," 58, 64–67; Hohman and Hagan, "Satisfaction with Surrogate Mothering," 67–69, 81–82; Ragoné, "Chasing the Blood Tie," 359–62.

39. Teman, *Birthing a Mother,* 142–47, 205–9; Baslington, "The Social Organization of Surrogacy," 66–67; Hohman and Hagan, "Satisfaction with Surrogate Mothering," 67–82; Ragoné, "Chasing the Blood Tie," 359–62; *A. H. W. v. G. H. B.,* 339 N.J. Super. 495, 504 (2000). "A bond is created between a gestational mother and the baby she carries in her womb for nine months. During the pregnancy, the fetus relies on the gestational mother for a myriad of contributions. A gestational mother's endocrine system determines the timing, amount and components of hormones that affect the fetus. The absence of any component at its appropriate time will irreversibly alter the life, mental capacity, appearance, susceptibility to disease and structure of the fetus forever. The gestational mother contributes an endocrine cascade that determines how the child will grow, when its cells will divide and differentiate in the womb, and how the child will appear and function for the rest of its life." R. Bryan Oxman, "Maternal Fetal Relationships and Nongenetic Surrogates," *Jurimetrics* 3 (1993): 387.

40. See Teman, *Birthing a Mother,* 209, where she describes the case of a surrogate who refused payment for second surrogacy to express her love for the couple. Ibid., 221–25: the focus of relationship is with intended mother. See also Baslington, "The Social Organization of Surrogacy," 66, where the focus of relationship is with the couple; R. J. Edelmann, "Surrogacy: The Psychological Issues," *Journal of Reproductive and Infant Psychology* 22 (2004): 125–29; Hohman and Hagan, "Satisfaction with Surrogate Mothering," 69–70.

41. Teman, *Birthing a Mother,* 205–21.

42. Ibid., 225–29; Ciccarelli and Beckman, "Navigating Rough Waters," 32.

43. Liza Mundy, *Everything Conceivable: How Assisted Reproduction Is Changing Men, Women, and the World* (New York Anchor, 2008), 136; Teman, *Birthing a Mother,* 205–35.

44. See Pamela Laufer-Ukeles, "The Lost Children: When the Rights to Children Conflict with the Rights of Children," *Law and Ethics of Human Rights* 8 (2014): 233–37.

45. See sources cited in note 2.

46. Ibid.

47. Ibid.

48. See Pinhas Shifman, "A Perspective on Surrogate Motherhood in Jewish Law," in *Frontiers of Family Law* (ed. Andrew Bainham and David S. Pearl; London: Chancery Law Publishing, 1993). See also Pinhas Shifman, "New Reproductive Technologies and Jewish Law," *Jewish Law Annual* 12 (1997): 133.

49. Embryo Carrying Agreements Law 1996, S.H. 1577 (Isr.).

50. Goldberg, "On Donating Eggs," 45–46.

51. Yehoshua Ben-Meir, "Legal Parenthood and Genetic Parenthood in Jewish Law," *Jewish Law Annual* 12 (1993): 153.

52. See Rabbi Shlomo Goren, *Ha-Tzofeh,* 7 Adar I (1984).

53. Itamar Warhaftig, "Determining Motherhood: Notes on the Margins," *Tanchumin* 5 (1984): 269.

54. Zalman Nechemiah Goldberg, "Lineage of Mothers in Transferring a Fetus to the Womb of Another," *Tanchumin* 5 (1984): 248.

55. See Avraham Yitchak Halevi Calev, "Who is the Mother of the Child; the Parent or She Who Gives Birth?," *Tanchumin* 5 (1984): 260.

56. Bick, "Ovum Donations," 83.

57. Chaim Povarsky, "Regulating Advanced Reproductive Technologies: A Comparative Analysis of Jewish and American Law," *University of Toledo Law Review* 29 (1998): 461.

58. See B. Talmud, *Sanhedrin* 13(b), 19(b).

59. Rav Moshe Shternbach, *Answers and Directives,* 5:318 (Jerusalem Publishers, 1996–1997); "Babies Born to Surrogate Mothers in Nepal Face Religious Obstacles Once They Arrive Here," *Jerusalem Post* (29 April 2015).

60. See Memanchem Elon, *The Principles of Jewish Law* (Piscataway: Transaction Publishers 2007), 435; Noam Zohar, *Alternatives in Jewish Bioethics* (Albany: State University of New York Press, 1997), 78–80; "When the Child Falls through a Loophole in Jewish Law," *Haaretz* (June 17, 2002) [in Hebrew].

61. Shternbach, *Answers and Directives.* See also David J. Bleich, "In Vitro Fertilization: Questions of Maternal Identity and Conversion," in *Jewish Law and the New Reproductive Technologies* (ed. Emanuel Feldman and Joel Wolowelsky; New York: Keter, 1997), 47.

62. Melanie B. Jacobs, "Why Just Two? Disaggregating Traditional Parental Rights and Responsibilities to Recognize Multiple Parents," *Journal of Law and Family Studies* 9 (2007): 314–32; Matthew M. Kavanagh, "Rewriting the Legal Family: Beyond Exclusivity to a Care-Based Standard," *Yale Journal of Law and Feminism* 16 (2004): 85.

63. *Wisconsin v. Yoder,* 406 U.S. 205 (1972); *Troxel v. Granville,* 530 U.S. 57, 60 (2000); *Meyer v. Nebraska,* 262 U.S. 390, 400 (1923); *Skinner v. Oklahoma,* 316 U.S. 535, 541 (1942), holding that the right to conceive and raise one's own children is among the "basic civil rights of man."

64. Moshe Silberg, "Law and Morals in Jewish Jurisprudence," *Harvard Law Review* 75 (1961): 306. This is the English translation of a paper given at the Third J. L. Magnes Memorial Lecture at the Hebrew University in Jerusalem, 1951.

65. Michael J. Broyde, "Child Custody and Jewish Law: A Pure Law Analysis," *Jewish Law Association Studies* 7 (1988): 18–19n69. Silberg stresses the emphasis on duty as opposed to rights and the indelible place that the concept of duty has in Jewish law.

66. B. Talmud, *Eruvin* 82(a); B. Talmud *Ketubot* 65(b), 122(b)–23(a). For a detailed discussion of these sources, see Basil Herring, "Child Custody," in *Jewish Ethics and Halakhah for Our Times,* Vol. 2 (New York: Jewish Theological Seminary, 1989), 177.

67. See, for example, Bonnie Steinbock, "Surrogate Motherhood as Prenatal Adoption," *Law, Medicine and Health Care* 16 (1988): 44–46. Steinbock argues that the assessment of a surrogate mother's ability to be a good mother is biased by middle-class prejudices. See also Rothman, *Recreating Motherhood,* 242–45, who argues that pregnancy and interpersonal relationships determine fitness to parent and not genetic ties or intent.

68. Michael J. Broyde, "Child Custody in Jewish Law: A Conceptual Analysis," *Journal of Halakhah and Contemporary Society* 37 (1999): 26–27, 36–37.

69. Ibid.

70. Sara S. McLanahan and Irwin Garfinkel, "Fragile Families: Debates, Facts and Solutions," in *Marriage at the Crossroads* (ed. Marsha Garrison and Elizabeth S. Scott; Cambridge: Cambridge University Press, 2012), 142–44, who argue that single parent families result in poorer outcomes for children than multiple caregivers; Anne C. Dailey, "Children's Transitional Rights," *Law Culture and the Humanities* 10 (2014): 13–14, who discusses children's needs for multiple care relationships.

71. See, for example, Pamela Laufer-Ukeles and Ayelet Blecher-Prigat, "Between Function and Form: Towards a Differentiated Model of Functional Parenthood," *George Mason Law Review* 20 (2013): 421–23; Melissa Murray, "The Networked Family: Reframing the Legal Understanding of Caregiving and Caregivers," *Virginia Law Review* 94 (2008): 455.

72. *Soos v. Soos,* 897 P.2d 1356, 1361 (Ariz. Ct. App. 1994). This case holds that treating a gestational surrogate as a legal mother violates the equal protection clause of the U.S. Constitution. See also *Buzzanca v. Buzzanca,* 72 Cal. Rptr. 2d 280 (Cal. Ct. App. 1998); *Johnson v. Calvert,* 851 P.2d 776 (Cal. 1993); *Perry-Rogers v. Fasano,* 715 N.Y.S. 2d 19 (N.Y. App. Div. 2000); *Smith v. Jones,* No. 85-53201402 (Mich. Cir. Ct. Mar. 14, 1986), holding that the intended mother who donated the egg was the legal mother due to her genetic donation and proclaiming the gestational surrogate "a human incubator"; *Belsito v. Clark,* 644 N.E.2d 760 (Ohio C.P. 1994); *J. F. v. D. B.,* 897 A.2d 1261, 1280 (Pa. Super. Ct. 2006), in which a gestational surrogate is deemed an unrelated third-party without standing to seek custody of the child she carried.

73. Genesis 1:28; Menachem Elon, "In God's Image Man Was Created: Human Dignity and Freedom," in *Human Dignity and Freedom in the Methods of Enforcement of Judgments: The Values of a Jewish and Democratic State* (Jerusalem: Magnes, 1999).

74. Aviad Hacohen, "Human Dignity and Freedom in Genesis," in *Weekly Torah Portion* (ed. Aviad Hacohen and Michael Wigoda; Jerusalem: Ministry of Justice 2004) [in Hebrew], http://www.daat.ac.il/mishpat-ivri/skirot/150-2.htm.

75. *Sanhedrin* 31(a): "Man was born as an individual, because each man must say that for me the world was created."

76. Mishna, *Sanhedrin* 4, 5. Babylonian Talmud, *Sanhedrin* 37a, translated in J. David Bleich, "Life as an Intrinsic Rather Than Instrumental Good: The 'Spiritual' Case against Euthanasia," *Issues in Law & Medicine* 9 (1993): 139, 140: "Only a single human being was created in the world [at first], to teach that if any person has caused a single soul to perish, Scripture regards him as if he had caused an entire world to perish; and if any human being saves a single soul, Scripture regards him as if he had saved an entire world."

77. *Shulhan Arukh,* "Hoshen Mishpat," 427:9–10; Maimonides, *Mishneh Torah,* "Hilkhot De'ot," 4:1; Babylonian Talmud, *Berakhot* 32b.

78. Steven H. Resnicoff, "Jewish Law Perspectives on Suicide and Physician Assisted Dying," *Journal of Law and Religion* 13 (1998–1999): 289.

79. See Leviticus 25:39–42: "If thy brother who dwells by thee be grown poor, and be sold to thee, thou shalt not compel him to serve as a bondservant. . . . [H]e . . . shall serve thee until the year of the Jubilee, and then shall . . . he return to his own family. For they are my servants, whom I brought out of the land of Egypt; they shall not be sold as bondsmen."

80. David Bleich, "Surrogate Motherhood," in *Jerusalem City of Law and Justice* (ed. Nahum Rakover; Jerusalem: Library of Jewish Law, 1996), 406, 407, citing Rabbi Sefer Hasidim No. 245 (Jerusalem, 5720) (1960); Chaim Povarsky, "Regulating Advanced Reproductive Technologies: A Comparative Analysis of Jewish and American Law," *University of Toledo Law Review* 29 (1998): 461.

81. Kimberly R. Willoughby and Alisa A. Campbell, "Having My Baby: Surrogacy in Colorado," *Colorado Law Review* 31 (2002): 105–6, itemizing the kind of restrictions found in surrogacy contracts.

82. Alison Bailey, "Reconceiving Surrogacy: Toward a Reproductive Justice Account of Indian Surrogacy," *Hypath* 26 (2011): 721; Amrita Pande, "Commercial Surrogacy in India: Manufacturing a Perfect Mother-Worker," *Signs* 35 (2010): 972. See also Scott Carney, "Cash on Delivery," *Mother Jones* (March–April 2010): 68, who explains that although C-sections are often considered riskier for the baby and dramatically increase the woman's risk of death during childbirth, they are generally used for international surrogacy, perhaps because they are faster and less personal than vaginal deliveries. Carney's article is available electronically under an alternative title, "Inside India's Rent-a-Womb Business," available at http://www.motherjones.com/politics/2010/02/surrogacy-tourism-india-nayna-patel.

83. Ruth Halperin-Kaddari, "Redefining Parenthood," *California Western International Law Journal* 29 (1999): 334–45.

84. Telephone interview with Dr. Avraham Shteinberg, author of *The Encyclopedia of Jewish Medical Ethics* (trans. Fred Rosner; New York: Feldheim, 2006 [originally published 1988–1998]) and Israel Prize Winner (June 15, 2000). There is no official recording of the approval by Rabbi Bakshi Doron, but the law passed with the consent of the chief rabbinate of Israel. See also Goldberg, "On Donating Eggs," 45.

85. Telephone interview with Rabbi Borshtein, director of the Puah Institute of Halakhah and Reproductive Technology (June 16, 2000).

86. See, e.g., Moshe Tendler, "Infertility Management: Cure or Ill," *Sh'ma* 17 (1987): 109–10; Avraham Sofer Avraham, *Nishmat Avraham Eben Ha'ezer* [The Laws of Procreation] § 5, (1982): 184 (citing Rav Shalom Elyashiv and Rav Shlomo Zalman Auerbach as condemning in vitro fertilization and surrogate motherhood).

87. Goldberg, "On Donating Eggs," 45–46.

88. Ibid.

89. Ibid., 46–47.

90. Ibid.

91. Pamela Laufer-Ukeles, "Gestation: Work for Hire or the Essence of Motherhood?," *Duke Journal of Gender Law and Policy* 9 (2001): 127–30.

92. Zohar, *Alternatives in Jewish Bioethics,* 78–80.

93. See, e.g., "Religious Council Act as a Law unto Themselves," *Jersualem Post* (February 28, 2013), http://www.jpost.com/JewishWorld/JewishFeatures/Article.aspx?id=304814; "Rishon Rabbi Must Explain Referrals to Private Firm," *Jerusalem Post* (February 1, 2013), http://www.jpost.com/NationalNews/Article.aspx?id=301753: "Many people, especially immigrants; people whose parents married abroad; and converts, encounter serious obstacles in this process from local rabbinates." See also "Shas's Cynical Use of Conversion Shows Why Israel Needs to Divorce Politics and Religion," *Ha'aretz* (January 14, 2013), http://www.haaretz.com/opinion/shas-cynical-use-of-conversion-shows-why-israel-needs-to-divorce-politics-and-religion.premium-1.493917; "Criteria for Conversion Authority Chief to Narrow," *Jerusalem Post* (December 30, 2012), http://www.jpost.com/JewishWorld/JewishNews/Article.aspx?id=297744.

94. See sources cited in note 59.

95. Ayelet Blecher-Prigat, "The Cost of Raising Children," *Theoretical Inquiries in Law* 13 (2014): 197n55: "Under Jewish law, the primary duty of child support is placed on the father, who must provide his children with their basic needs. Beyond these needs, both the father and the mother are obligated to provide the children with a standard of living to which the children were accustomed, and in accordance with the parents' financial abilities."

96. See, e.g., B. Talmud, *Bava Metzia* 33(b); Moses Maimonides, *Mishneh Torah,* "Sefer Kinyan" [The Book of Acquisition], 22:1; "Choshen Mishpat," Shulchan Aruch, 209:4, relating to civil law and business ethics. See also Elon, *The Principles of Jewish Law,*

248–49; Mordechai Halperin, "Surrogate Mother," *Refuah U'Mishpat* [Medicine and Law] 7 (1997): 47.

97. See Ayelet Blecher-Prigat, "The Cost of Raising Children."

98. See Yehezkel Kaplan, "Child Custody in Jewish Law: From Authority of the Father to Best Interests of the Child," *Journal of Law and Religion* 24 (2008–2009): 99–119. Kaplan discusses the relevance of best interests and tender years presumption in Jewish law.

99. In the case of Baby M, when the contract was not enforced, the intended parents still won primary custody under a best interests analysis.

100. See Broyde, "Child Custody in Jewish Law," 32–33.

101. Yehezkel Kaplan, "The Power of Interpretation: Religious Scholars Elevate the Status of Female Guardians in Jewish Law," *Cardozo Journal of Law and Gender* 14 (2008): 536: a guardian need not be the primary custodian of a child. Elon, *The Principles of Jewish Law,* 18, 440–45: a guardian acts as a trustee of an estate.

102. Elon, *The Principles of Jewish Law,* 536.

103. Ibid., 442.

104. See Kaplan, "Child Custody in Jewish Law."

105. Elon, *The Principles of Jewish Law,* 544.

106. Broyde, "Child Custody in Jewish Law," 36–42.

107. See generally BT *Gittin* 52a, which discusses a guardian's role in caring for orphans; Elon, *The Principles of Jewish Law,* 442.

108. Elon, *The Principles of Jewish Law,* 442.